## DATE DUE

BRODART, CO.                    Cat. No. 23-221

NOT IN OUR NAME

NOT IN OUR NAME

## AMERICAN ANTIWAR SPEECHES, 1846 TO THE PRESENT

### EDITED BY JESSE STELLATO

THE PENNSYLVANIA STATE UNIVERSITY PRESS
UNIVERSITY PARK, PENNSYLVANIA

Library of Congress Cataloging-in-Publication Data

Not in our name : American antiwar speeches,
1846 to the present / edited by Jesse Stellato.
    p.   cm.
Includes bibliographical references and index.
Summary: "A collection of American antiwar speeches from
every major conflict starting with the Mexican-American
War. Includes critical analyses, biographical and
bibliographical information, and an appendix describing
common rhetorical devices used by antiwar
speakers"—Provided by publisher.
ISBN 978-0-271-04868-0 (cloth : alk. paper)
1.  Peace movements—United States—
History—Sources.
2.  Pacifism—United States—History—Sources.
3.  Pacifists—United States—History—Sources.
4.  Speeches, addresses, etc., American.
I. Stellato, Jesse, 1981–   .

JZ5584.U6N67 2012
303.6'60973—dc23
2012007181

The Pennsylvania State University Press is a member of the
Association of American University Presses.

It is the policy of The Pennsylvania State University Press
to use acid-free paper. Publications on uncoated stock
satisfy the minimum requirements of American National
Standard for Information Sciences—Permanence of
Paper for Printed Library Material, ANSI Z39.48-1992.

This book is printed on Nature's Natural,
which contains 50% post-consumer waste.

FOR *Peter, Roberta, and Rebecca*

Experience proves that the man who obstructs a war in which his nation is engaged, no matter whether right or wrong, occupies no enviable place in life or history. Better for him, individually, to advocate "war, pestilence, and famine" than to act as obstructionist to a war already begun. The history of the defeated rebel will be honorable hereafter, compared with that of the Northern man who aided him by conspiring against his government while protected by it. The most favorable posthumous history the stay-at-home traitor can hope for is—oblivion.

—Ulysses S. Grant, *Personal Memoirs of Ulysses S. Grant,* vol. 1 (New York: Charles L. Webster), 68

[T]he voice of protest, of warning, of appeal is never more needed than when the clamor of fife and drum, echoed by the press and too often by the pulpit, is bidding all men fall in and keep step and obey in silence the tyrannous word of command. Then, more than ever, it is the duty of the good citizen not to be silent, and spite of obloquy, misrepresentation and abuse, to insist on being heard.

—Charles Eliot Norton, "Professor Norton's View," *Boston Evening Transcript,* June 8, 1898, 12

# CONTENTS

## ACKNOWLEDGMENTS

While all errors of fact and judgment are exclusively my own, I would like to offer my most sincere thanks to all those who helped me prepare *Not in Our Name*.

When I began this project as an undergraduate in 2003, Professor James Engell at Harvard University kindly offered thoughtful and much-needed criticism of my outlines and drafts. In 2005, Sandy Thatcher at Penn State University Press began to provide me with editorial guidance, and I am deeply indebted to him for his longstanding, sensible advice. To this day I remain inspired by Sandy's consummate professionalism and dedication to the practice of publishing. Also at Penn State, I am grateful for the help of Laura Reed-Morrisson, who offered insightful and practical solutions to a host of difficult production issues, and John Morris, whose suggestions during the copyediting phase led me to make a number of important improvements to the text.

Because I am not a professional historian and also because this is my first book, I am particularly appreciative of the support offered to me by my friends and colleagues. Ivy Leung, Milan Dalal, and David Bartholomew were always willing to lend me their ears, and to offer feedback and criticism. I shall remain forever grateful to them for their encouragement, and consider myself lucky to count them as friends. I am also particularly thankful for the help and advice generously given to me by Danielle Spratt, Diana Gallon, Michele Latimer, Marin Blitzer, Austin Evers, Adam Brenner, Kara Shamy, Joe Fleming, David Carter, Francis Carter, Nancy Wolff, Matt Kaplan, Alexandria Nguyen, Eun Chang, Barry Turner, and Ji Hun Kim.

Over the course of my research, I had the privilege of working with many wonderful libraries and research centers, including the Widener and Houghton libraries at Harvard, the New York Public Library, the Boston Public Library, the Boston College Law School law library, Richter Library at the University of Miami, the libraries at Florida International University, the National Archives, the Andersen Library at the University of Minnesota, the Moorland-Spingarn Research Center at Howard University, Yale University Library, and the W. E. B. Du Bois Library at the University of Massachusetts Amherst. The support these libraries offer to researchers every day is a gift to our society and culture.

I owe the greatest debt of all to my parents, Peter and Roberta. Without their unflinching support, love, and encouragement, the entirety of which I will never be able to adequately acknowledge, this book would never have been written.

Most of the speeches in this book are excerpted rather than given in in full; omissions are indicated by ellipses. Citations to available full-text versions of each speech are given in appendix A.

The text used here is usually, but not always, the first published version, as noted in appendix A; capitalization, paragraphing, punctuation, and spelling have been adjusted only when it seemed necessary to make the meaning clear. In some cases I made a transcription myself from a sound recording. But it is worth remembering that written conventions are secondary to the fact that all of these speeches were originally *spoken*.

Almost all of the speeches in this anthology have appeared previously in print, and some of them in audio form as well. When possible, I drew on the audio recording to insert significant audience reactions within the text of the speech (e.g., [*Shouts and applause*]). With the exception of the speeches of William Jennings Bryan, Eugene V. Debs, Martin Luther King Jr., and John Kerry, in which the original stenographer included the audience's reactions, all such insertions are my own.

There is no way to be certain, when no audio recording exists, how faithful any printed version is to the speech as it was spoken. Members of Congress, for instance, are granted leave to extend and amend their remarks on the floor, and no doubt many of those whose speeches are printed here availed themselves of the opportunity.

Speakers who had newspaper reporters cover their speeches may have had similar opportunities for post hoc revision. Reporters did not necessarily take shorthand transcriptions of every word that speakers uttered; they may have taken note of the major passages and simply asked the speaker to forward a copy of the speech to the reporter's office the next day.

Nevertheless, it is worth considering that a speech may have been first heard by an audience that was quite small, but subsequently *read* by an audience that was quite large. The printed version in that case is the one that has come to be associated with the speaker, and thus the one that, at least arguably, most deserves to be anthologized. Thus a paradox can arise: the historical significance of a speech may derive from something in it that the speaker did not in fact say—or from something that he did say but that was not recorded.

I have attempted to resolve this paradox through compromise. While I have tried, as far as possible, to print the speeches as they were spoken, I have noted where there exist significant subsequently printed deviations from the original. In this way, I hope to be faithful both to history and those who (mis)record it.

# Introduction

## I

Why anthologize American antiwar speeches? Above all, the speeches contained in this anthology are important historical artifacts. They contribute to a unique understanding of the rhetorical history of America's wars and foreign policies. To be sure, much has been written on the rhetoric of war[1] and on antiwar movements,[2] but a survey of the literature reveals a startling imbalance between the attention given to prowar and antiwar speeches. Throughout the nineteenth and the twentieth centuries, few antiwar speeches were anthologized.[3] Even fewer antiwar speech anthologies have been published, and these have been starkly partisan or limited to particular military involvements. Their lack of objectivity and scope doubtless contributed to a limited viewership, and they have long been out of print.[4]

In contrast, speech anthologists have embraced "rallying-cry" speeches—the more incendiary, the better. Calls to arms by Patrick Henry ("Give me liberty or give me death"), Woodrow Wilson ("The world must be made safe for democracy"), Franklin D. Roosevelt ("December 7, 1941—a date that will live in infamy")—to say nothing of the militaristic exhortations of international leaders such as Hitler, Mussolini, and Churchill—are firmly entrenched in contemporary speech anthologies.[5] In *Lend Me Your Ears,* for example, William Safire includes a "War and Revolution Speeches" section that contains only one antiwar speech. The choices of other anthologists are often similarly skewed,[6] at the risk of distorting America's rhetorical history and obscuring the country's vibrant culture of dissent.

Conversely, while anthologies and critical studies of American antiwar essays,[7] novels,[8] poetry,[9] theater,[10] art,[11] motion pictures,[12] music,[13] pamphlets,[14] oral histories,[15] propaganda,[16] and literature generally[17] abound, speeches have received little attention. The only possible exception is material related to the Vietnam conflict, and even there speeches almost always play a peripheral role.[18] This lack of attention to antiwar speeches may be the product of the assumption that speeches themselves are comparatively uninteresting or unimportant. I believe that the material in this anthology proves quite the opposite. The speeches are interesting because they provide a glimpse into a liturgy between speaker and audience. Each speech is a type of ritual calculated, at times, to produce ecstasy or sorrow. The speaker becomes a priest leading his congregation to exorcise the demons of war. At the same time, the speeches are important because they are deliberate political acts with clearly defined, nontransitory, and historically significant effects. The ideas are profound, the words and phrases are stylized, the context is dramatic. These speeches, which lie squarely within our public sphere, thus fall within a genre of what I call *literary politics*—politics carried out through and reflected in literature.

In addition to attempting to redress the relative lack of attention given to speeches in American antiwar literature, this anthology helps illustrate the history of the extent to which Americans can—and cannot—oppose a wartime government and the majoritarian impulse that often accompanies and sustains it. Though it is well established that the First Amendment right to free speech contracts during wartime, the legal line between permissible and impermissible speech is not always bright.[19] In addition, extralegal sanctions available to prowar majorities represent real limits on free speech. The outspoken individuals included in this anthology were uniformly threatened with—and sometimes subjected to—social stigma, pecuniary loss, physical violence or imprisonment.

Finally, in a larger sense, these antiwar speeches represent a culture of dissent. On the intellectual battleground, the speakers rarely limit their scope to the issue of war and peace. The speeches often implicate much broader arguments concerning the distributions of political, social, and economic power within society, and the capacity of human beings to defend cruelty, champion arrogance, and justify avarice. Read in this way, the speeches offer commentaries on human nature, and the speakers offer critiques, hopefully constructive, of our American democracy itself.

In this anthology, for example, Robert Kennedy begins his antiwar speech at Kansas State University by reminding students that the presidential campaign of 1968 would be one in which "we choose not simply who will lead us, but where we wish to be led."[20] One might engage Kennedy's interpretive clue and read all of the speeches collected here as visions of America, that is, as attempts to answer such quintessentially American questions as Who should govern us? How should we be governed? Which values are fundamentally American? and What does it mean to be an American citizen? Thus, the subject of the speeches may be war, but their object is a more perfect union. As Paul Potter stated at a 1965 protest march in Washington, D.C.: "What is exciting about the participants in this march is that so many of us view ourselves consciously as participants . . . in a movement to build a more decent society."[21]


## II

Classical rhetoric provides a useful framework for understanding how great antiwar speeches are made, and why those speeches endure throughout history. The study of classical rhetoric is divided, mainly for pedagogical reasons, into five parts: *inventio* (creation or discovery of arguments), *dispositio* (arrangement), *elocutio* (style), *memoria* (memory), and *pronuntiatio* (delivery).[22] Some scholars consider these "canons of rhetoric" a paradigm for all communication theory.[23] Since invention and style play a particularly important role in antiwar speeches, I consider them in detail here.[24]

*Inventio*

First to the Greeks and then to the Romans, *inventio* encompassed both the invention of a new argument and the discovery of an old one.[25] A speaker would "create or discover" arguments by applying three *modes of persuasion* to certain *topoi,* or topics.[26]

The three modes of persuasion were analyzed by Aristotle in his *Rhetoric,* a book that Edward P. J. Corbett calls "the fountainhead of all later rhetorical theory."[27] The *Rhetoric* lays out an analytical framework with which to understand the modes, theorizing that the strength of a speaker's *logos* (logic), *ethos* (credibility and relationship with the audience), and *pathos* (emotional appeal) collectively constitute the speaker's persuasive effect.[28]

As profound as it is ancient, the *Rhetoric*'s analytical framework has found champions (and critics) throughout its twenty-three-hundred-year history. As Lane Cooper remarks, "the Rhetoric not only of Cicero and Quintilian, but of the Middle Ages, of the Renaissance, and of modern times, is, in its best elements, essentially Aristotelian."[29] A direct application of Aristotelian rhetorical theory appeared during the 2000 presidential election, when Gary Orren, a professor at Harvard University, applied the three modes of persuasion to the candidates themselves. In "It's All Greek to Me," Orren explained that the Democratic nominee, Al Gore, was "the most logos-oriented presidential candidate in memory," while the Republican nominee, George W. Bush, was "ethos incarnate," a man whose "rise in American politics is a triumph of personality over policy."[30]

The *topoi,* or topics, were once a widely taught method—to use the Greek term, heuristic—for helping speakers or writers who had "nothing to say."[31] The topics are not hard to understand conceptually; they are nothing more than a collection of generally accepted arguments.[32] It is not my purpose to survey them here, as Corbett discusses the "common topics" at length.[33] However, there are two special topics that students of antiwar speeches will find useful when dissecting a speech. The first is called, appropriately enough, "War and Peace."[34] Aristotle's treatment of this topic is brief and is worth quoting in full:

> As to Peace and War, he [i.e., the speaker] must know the extent of the military strength of his country, both actual and potential, and also the nature of that actual and potential strength; and further, what wars his country has waged, and how it has waged them. He must know these facts not only about his own country, but also about neighbouring countries; and also about countries with which war is likely, in order that peace may be maintained with those stronger than his own, and that his own may have power to make war or not against those that are weaker. He should know, too, whether the military power of another country is like or unlike that of his own; for this is a matter that may affect their relative strength.

With the same end in view he must, besides, have studied the wars of other countries as well as those of his own, and the way they ended; similar causes are likely
to have similar results.[35]

The second special topic is called "ceremonial topics," because it is a collection of
arguments unique to *ceremonial* discourse.[36] As this anthology demonstrates, antiwar
speeches are not solely deliberative. They contain ceremonial components as well.[37] Ceremonial topics come in two types: those that praise someone's *virtues,* and those that
denounce someone's *vices.*[38] Almost without exception, antiwar speakers focus on the
latter.

In the commentary that accompanies each speech in this anthology, I have highlighted
what I take to be the most interesting, idiosyncratic, and imaginative ways in which each
speaker assails an individual war. Implicit in this project is the notion that a norm does,
in fact, exist. Despite the different historical contexts and changing modes of communication over 150 years, recurrent modes of *logos, ethos,* and *pathos* can readily be found in
these speeches. The recurrent topic of *vice* is easily spotted as well.[39] Indeed, with respect
to these elements, the similarities between antiwar speeches in the last century and a half
are striking. Whereas other forms of antiwar dissent, such as poetry, have changed radi-
cally over the years, antiwar speeches appear remarkably consistent.[40] I will describe and
illustrate their likenesses briefly here, and more fully in the individual commentaries that
accompany each speech in this anthology.

LOGOS    The logic of antiwar speech is most broadly categorized as attacking either the
causes or the consequences of war. With respect to the former, little is more common
than indicting the war-maker's alleged motives. Thus, the Mexican-American War was
characterized by its detractors as a war to perpetuate slavery; the Civil War, to conquer
and command the Confederacy; the Spanish-American War, to create an empire; the
First World War, to protect capital investments in England; the Second World War, to
acquiesce to Jewish interests; the Korean War and Vietnam War, for economic coloniza-
tion; the war with Iraq, to control Middle Eastern oil production.

Subtlety is not a virtue in antiwar speeches, and most speakers appear to be indifferent,
if not downright hostile, to the possibility that the motive they assign to the president's
administration is neither the sole nor the determining factor in the decision to go to war.
The speaker's strategy is twofold: first, the speaker implies that a blameworthy, though
minor, intention can taint even the best justification for war. Secondly, as I have suggested above, the speaker assumes that the mere naming of the evils associated with a
particular war may, as the first stage in a type of exorcism, have some salutary effect by
itself.

A similarly ubiquitous antiwar argument concerns the consequences of war. At its
core, the argument is simply a cost-benefit analysis in which the cost of war is always too
high: the financial costs to the national treasury and to the individual taxpayer are too
much, the human cost of limbs and lives is too great, the psychological costs of fear and
anxiety are too severe, the cost of losing international repute is too high, and, perhaps

most common of all, the opportunity costs of war are too numerous. These propositions are commonly described and illustrated with statistics, anecdotes, or heartwrenching testimonials. When Robert Kennedy was campaigning for the presidency in 1968, for example, he often provided a vivid illustration of the opportunity costs of war: "When I see the numbers of all those boys killed in Vietnam, I wonder to myself: 'How many would have grown up to be poets, how many would have helped to cure cancer?'"[41]

ETHOS     The aim of every persuasive speaker is to establish himself as a trusted authority with his audience. Such a figure demands attention, and his opinions require respect. Aristotle referred to the general relationship between a speaker and his audience as that speaker's *ethos*. Ethical appeals are often of the "if you were there" variety. John Kerry's testimony before the Senate Foreign Relations Committee provides exactly this type of appeal. Kerry (who was wearing his military decorations) opens his speech by telling his audience that he is a veteran who had experienced firsthand the wrongs of the war. "I am not here as John Kerry," Kerry begins. "I am here as one member of the group of 1,000, which is a small representation of a very much larger group of veterans in this country, and were it possible for all of them to sit at this table they would be here and have the same kind of testimony."

Moorfield Storey used a common variation of this theme during the buildup to the Spanish-American War. Unlike Kerry, Storey was a practicing lawyer who had never been in the military, much less set foot on a battlefield. He had to find another way to assert ethos, and thereby lend credibility to his arguments. His solution? During an address to the Naval War College in Newport, Rhode Island in 1897, Storey discusses the courage of his *relatives:* "I sympathize with you and understand your hopes," Storey tells the war college, because "I could not spring from ancestors who for five successive generations died at sea, without some of a sailor's instincts, some comprehension of his feelings."

Barack Obama tried this same tactic, what I call *hereditary ethos,* in the run-up to the war in Iraq. Like Storey, Obama was a lawyer who had no military credentials whatsoever. Unlike Kerry, he could not speak while wearing a military uniform. Nevertheless, this did not stop Obama from tapping the wellspring of ethos to lend credibility to his antiwar cause. He thus invokes a warrior-relative, his soldier-grandfather: "My grandfather signed up for a war the day after Pearl Harbor was bombed, fought in Patton's army. He saw the dead and dying across the fields of Europe; he heard the stories of fellow troops who first entered Auschwitz and Treblinka. He fought in the name of a larger freedom, part of that arsenal of democracy that triumphed over evil, and he did not fight in vain." Why would Storey believe his dead relatives had anything to do with his opposition to the war? On what basis would Obama think that his grandfather's experience in World War II was relevant to the emerging conflict with Iraq? Storey and Obama were using their ancestors for persuasive effect. They summoned them not to draw *logical* parallels between wars, or to illustrate the *pathetic* futility of war in general; rather, they used their relatives to lend credibility to their own lackluster or even nonexistent experience in matters of war and peace. They were making an *ethical* appeal to their audience.

PATHOS    Cities scorched and razed, sons orphaned, mothers widowed, soldiers writhing in pain—antiwar speakers use this type of rending subject matter to represent the horrors of war. At best, the speakers' descriptions are graphic, but not gratuitous; at worst, their sentiments are stale and less illustrative than conclusory. In "Beyond Vietnam," Martin Luther King uses an emotional appeal to recount the effect of U.S. military involvement on the people of Vietnam:

> They move sadly and apathetically as we herd them off the land of their fathers into concentration camps where minimal social needs are rarely met. They know they must move on or be destroyed by our bombs.
>
> So they go, primarily women and children and the aged. They watch as we poison their water, as we kill a million acres of their crops. They must weep as the bulldozers roar through their areas preparing to destroy the precious trees. They wander into the hospitals with at least twenty casualties from American firepower for one Vietcong-inflicted injury. So far we may have killed a million of them, mostly children. They wander into the towns and see thousands of the children, homeless, without clothes, running in packs on the streets like animals. They see the children degraded by our soldiers as they beg for food. They see the children selling their sisters to our soldiers, soliciting for their mothers.

King's description is a fairly typical example of an emotional appeal. Even though the language is at times maudlin (the women and children and the aged move "sadly," as if they could move any other way under the circumstances) or tired (the children are "running in packs on the steet like animals"), the imagery works because the picture he paints is so pitiful.

Creating a successful image, or one that is both horrible and memorable, requires less scientific exactitude than imaginative artistry. The paradigmatic example of such art is Theodore Parker's 1846 "Sermon of War." Parker forgoes historical factuality in the middle of his speech and begins to recount a fictionalized battle of his own making. Imagining that Boston and Cambridge are at war, Parker tells his audience the wrenching story of a mother who travels to a battlefield on the banks of the Charles River to find her fallen son:

> Stealthily, by the pale moonlight, a mother of Boston treads the weary miles to reach that bloody spot; a widow she—seeking among the slain her only son. The arm of power drove him forth reluctant to the fight. A friendly soldier guides her way. Now she turns over this face, whose mouth is full of purple dust, bit out of the ground in his extremest agony—the last sacrament offered him by earth herself; now she raises that form, cold, stiff, stony, and ghastly as a dream of hell. But, lo! another comes—she too a woman—younger and fairer, yet not less bold, a maiden from the hostile town to seek her lover. They meet—two women among the corpses; two angels come to Golgotha, seeking to raise a man. There he lies before them; they look,—yes, 'tis he you seek; the same dress, form, features too;—'tis he,

the Son, the Lover. Maid and mother could tell *that* face in any light. The grass is wet with his blood. Yes, the ground is muddy with the life of men. The mother's innocent robe is drabbled in the blood her bosom bore. Their kisses, groans and tears recall the wounded man. He knows the mother's voice; that voice yet more beloved. His lips move only, for they cannot speak. He dies!

The switch from fact to fiction is not duplicitous—Parker tells his audience that the story is imaginative in order "to make the evils of war still clearer, to bring them home to your door." The mother's chance meeting with the "maiden from the hostile town," and their simultaneous discovery of the dying son-lover, are tragic. Parker thus produces nothing short of drama.

Does it matter that such an account is completely fictional? In a word, no. The true object of the emotional appeal is the heart, not the head. In other words, though Parker's account of war was perhaps less true than King's, in a sense it was no less real.

VICE   One of the most fascinating, and unusual, aspects of the material in this anthology is its incredibly hostile tone. Denigration, demonization, vilification—this is the stuff of which antiwar speeches are made.

In his first major speech as a congressman, Abraham Lincoln, of "with malice toward none" fame, criticizes President Polk for waging war on Mexico, calling him a "bewildered, confounded, and miserably-perplexed man." In the draft of Lincoln's speech, the future president was even more intemperate. Noting Polk's vacillating justifications for war, Lincoln wrote, "His mind, tasked beyond its power, is running hither and thither, like an ant on a hot stove, finding no position on which it can settle down, and be at ease."[42]

Even the Reverend Martin Luther King Jr. could not resist taking part in the ad hominem slugfest. Speaking of Ronald Reagan in 1967, King jabbed, "When a Hollywood performer, lacking distinction even as an actor, can become a leading war hawk candidate for the presidency only the irrationalities induced by a war psychosis can explain such a melancholy turn of events."[43]

Of all the antiwar voices, though, Eugene V. Debs's is the most unsettling. Debs argued that Wall Street's financial opportunism sparked the United States's entrance into World War I. In the process, he smeared the American "gentry" who, he claimed, traded their young daughters like the commodities in their portfolios:

To whom do the Wall Street junkers in our country—to whom do they marry their daughters? After they have wrung the countless hundreds of millions from your sweat, your agony, your life-blood, in a time of war as in a time of peace, they invest these billions and millions in the purchase of titles of broken-down aristocrats, and to buy counts of no-account (laughter). Are they satisfied to wed bad daughters to honest working men? (shouts from the crowd: "No.") to real Democrats? Oh, no. They scour the markets of Europe for fellows who have titles and nothing else (laughter). And they swap their millions for titles; so that matrimony, with them, becomes entirely a matter of money (laughter), literally so.

Why do so many of the great antiwar speeches exhibit such viciousness? One can understand the endemic ad hominem attacks contained in this anthology in various ways—as entertainment for an audience hungry for blood, as irresponsible intemperance on the part of the speaker, as a manifestation of political impotence, or, to use William Hazlitt's phrase, as calculated pandering to the "habitual prejudices of mankind."[44] Of all these critiques, the most compelling appear to be those that take into account the ceremonial function of the address. That is, antiwar speakers are at least partly concerned with pleasing, rather than merely exhorting, their audience. Understood in this way, these speeches serve the same function as Fourth of July speeches, funeral orations, and nominating speeches at political conventions.[45] But instead of paying tribute or lavishing praise, they offer blame and stern rebuke.

As previously stated, the classical rhetoricians developed a system of *topics,* or generally accepted arguments, that a speaker might use in crafting his speech. The ceremonial topics were generally accepted arguments used to praise virtues and vices. In books III and IV of his *Nicomachean Ethics,* Aristotle famously set forth the vices, which he defines as deformed or disproportionate virtues. Though presented outside the context of rhetoric, they serve as a perfect illustration of the ceremonial topics.

To illustrate how the these topics might be used in practice, consider the ways in which antiwar speakers often attack the president for his prosecution of a war. With respect to the virtue of courage, for example, one can find countless examples of antiwar speakers criticizing the president for acting with too much courage, that is, for acting rashly. With respect to the virtue of prudence, one can also find countless examples of antiwar speakers criticizing the president with acting with too little prudence, that is, for acting foolishly.

Of course, not all of these topics necessarily apply to the subject of a president and in the context of war. But many do. As one reads the speeches in this anthology, one might well remember these vices, and ask whether any given speech does not evidence a curious marriage between deliberative and ceremonial oratory.

*Elocutio*

*Elocutio,* or style, is a difficult concept to define. One of the most influential early definitions appears in the anonymous *Rhetorica ad Herennium* (ca. 80 BCE), where it is the "adaptation of suitable words and sentences to the matter devised."[46] Rhetoricians have struggled ever since to provide a more precise definition, and, failing that, have settled on the use of one metaphor or another.[47] Thus, style was defined as "clothing and ornament" by Cicero in the first century BCE.[48]

One ancient—and still relevant—debate over rhetorical style is whether it is merely decorative (the "dress of thought," as Cicero's metaphor suggests), or instead forms an essential part of one's argument or ideas (the "incarnation of thought").[49] These positions should be familiar to anyone who has heard the accusation that a speech is "mere rhetoric" or that a speaker "has style but lacks substance." The assumption in both cases is that a speaker is decorating his argument with pleasing phrases and memorable lines in order to dupe an unsuspecting audience. This is the modern-day connotation of the term "rhetoric"—that it is polish upon scuffed-up reasoning.

For example, take the charges leveled against Barack Obama, a figure whom I claim later in this anthology to be a "rhetorical leader." During his campaign for president, Obama was barraged by accusations that he had style but lacked substance. Thus, a reporter for the *New York Times* stated that "it remains unclear whether an Obama candidacy would present a slate of new ideas or just offer a fresh way of articulating familiar ideology."[50] Mario Cuomo, a former governor of New York, commented that Obama's campaign for president exemplified "pure, glorious rhetoric about hope and aspiration. Just lacking specifics."[51] New York's *Daily News* pointed out that "speechifying isn't leading,"[52] and the *Independent* in England asked baldly whether Obama had any "substance."[53] Again, these observations all assume that Obama's style of speaking can somehow be disentangled from the substance of his thought.

Despite the fact that the meaning of style has sparked considerable debate, there is a fundamental agreement as to many of its key features.[54] In the remainder of this section on style, and in appendix B, I describe and illustrate the *levels* of style as well as common *tropes* and *figures* or *schemes*.[55]

Classical rhetoric distinguished three levels of style: the *low* or *plain* style, the *middle* style, and the *high* or *grand* style. Each style has certain properties and purposes, and each is properly used in different forums. The low or plain style uses conversational words and makes little use of *tropes* or *figures* or *schemes* (rhetorical devices that I define below). It suits educational and instructional purposes, for example. The middle style is more refined than the low or plain style and often employs tropes and figures. It might be used, for example, in a ceremonial address.[56] The high or grand style often makes use of *hyperbole,* or exaggeration.[57] To use Quintilian's metaphor, if the middle style "flows gently like a clear stream overshadowed on both sides by banks of green wood," the high or grand style is "a great torrent that rolls down rocks" and "carves out banks for itself."[58] Epic poems and Shakespearian tragedies make use of the high or grand style.[59]

The styles used by antiwar speakers are diverse. The low or plain style appears in, for example, Noam Chomsky's lecture at Harvard University in 2002. Chomsky explains that one interpretation of the war in Iraq is the government's adherence to the "classic modern strategy of an endangered right-wing oligarchy, which is to divert mass discontent to nationalism." Related to this strategy, Chomsky explains, is the United States's attempt to dominate the world's oil resources:

> Well, that's one interpretation. One interpretation well within the mainstream establishment is what I just said: there's a long-term goal of regaining control over the second largest resources in the Middle East, and ensuring domination of one of the greatest material prizes in world history, and a stupendous source of strategic power. September 11 gave a pretext, as it gave a pretext around the world, for

an intensification of violence and disciplining of the populations, and domestic considerations in that very important security problem probably accounts for the timing. So it has to be *this* winter, not next winter. That'll be too late. By then we'll have been consumed by the mushroom cloud, which will avoid everyone else but hit us. And of course it's kind of like an accident that that will be right in the middle of the presidential campaign, just as it's an accident that the people of the region are afraid—but mostly of us, and joining most of the world in that. Well, that's one interpretation.

Chomsky is having a simple conversation with his audience. Though some rhetorical devices (e.g., irony) can be found in this excerpt, Chomsky is primarily speaking matter-of-factly. He uses conjunctions ("that's" and "that'll") and colloquialisms ("it's kind of like") that would be inappropriate in a more formal essay or in a book. Further, Chomsky's low or plain rhetoric is consistent with his academic forum: Chomsky was, after all, giving a lecture for educational purposes. For other examples of the low or plain style in the context of antiwar speeches, one might consider the Vietnam-era "teach-ins" held at universities across the United States.[60]

The high or grand style is best exemplified in this volume by speakers such as Theodore Parker and Clement Vallandigham. Arguing in the U.S. House of Representatives for peace during one of the bloodiest moments of the Civil War, Vallandigham said that the Union's war could not be won despite the massive resources at President Lincoln's disposal:

[W]ith twenty millions of people, and every element of strength and force at command—power, patronage, influence, unanimity, enthusiasm, confidence, credit, money, men, an Army and a Navy the largest and the noblest ever set in the field or afloat upon the sea; with the support, almost servile, of every State, county, and municipality in the North and West; with a Congress swift to do the bidding of the Executive; without opposition anywhere at home, and with an arbitrary power with which neither the Czar of Russia nor the Emperor of Austria dare exercise; yet after nearly two years of more vigorous prosecution of war than ever recorded in history; after more skirmishes, combats and battles than Alexander, Caesar, or the first Napoleon ever fought in any five years of their military career, you have utterly, signally, disastrously—I will not say ignominiously—failed to subdue ten millions of "rebels," whom you had taught the people of the North and West not only to hate but to despise. Rebels, did I say? Yes, your fathers were rebels, or your grandfathers. He who now before me on canvas looks down so sadly upon us, the false, degenerate, and imbecile guardians of the great Republic which he founded, was a rebel. And yet we, cradled ourselves in rebellion, and who have fostered and fraternized with every insurrection in the nineteenth century everywhere throughout the globe, would now, forsooth, make the word "rebel" a reproach. Rebels certainly they are; but all the persistent and stupendous efforts of the most gigantic warfare of modern times have, through your incompetency and folly, availed nothing to crush them out, cut off though they have been, by your blockade from all the world, and dependent only upon their own courage and resources. And yet they were to be utterly conquered and subdued in six weeks, or three months! Sir, my judgment was made up, and expressed from the first. I learned it from Chatham: "My lords, you cannot conquer America." And you have not conquered the South. You never will.

Here, Vallandigham makes ample use of hyperbole ("with an arbitrary power with which neither the Czar of Russia, nor the Emperor of Austria dare exercise" and "after more battles than Alexander, Caesar, or the first Napoleon ever fought"). Vallandigham also summons the words of England's Chatham ("You cannot conquer America"). This invocation is classic high style: Quintilian himself said that a defining mark of such a style could be the "the orator that will call the dead to life."[61]

Finally, different levels of styles can appear in one speech. As Wolfgang G. Müller points out, the high or grand style is well-suited for a speech's *peroration,* or closing. A good example here is Barack Obama's October 2, 2002, speech in Chicago's Federal Plaza. Most of Obama's speech could be described as either low or middle style. Some evidence of the low style appears with such plain phrases as "I'm opposed to dumb wars." Some evidence of the middle style appears with Obama's use of such rhetorical devices as alliteration, anaphora, and metaphor. But at the end of the speech, Obama elevates his language, bringing the full weight of his rhetorical power to bear on the audience: "The consequences of war are dire, the sacrifices immeasurable. We may have occasion in our lifetime to once again rise up in defense of our freedom, and pay the wages of war. But we ought not—we will not—travel down that hellish path blindly. Nor should we allow those who would march off and pay the ultimate sacrifice, who would prove the *full measure of devotion* with their blood, to make such an awful *sacrifice in vain.*" Obama is echoing Abraham Lincoln's November 19, 1863, speech at Gettysburg: "It is rather for us to be here dedicated to the great task remaining before us—that from these honored dead we take increased devotion to that cause for which they gave the last *full measure of devotion*—that we here highly resolve that these dead shall not have *died in vain.*" The style is high or grand not only because Obama is trying to move the audience through hyperbole but, again, because he is, in a way, summoning Lincoln and thereby "calling the dead to life."

In addition to distinguishing between the three levels of style, classical rhetoric was built on *tropes* and *figures* or *schemes.* Often referred to as *rhetorical devices* or *figures of speech,* these include such common devices as *metaphor, alliteration,* and *rhetorical questions.* They also include such uncommon devices such as *chiasmus, metonymy,* and *antimetabole.* A trope (from the Greek *tropein,* or "to turn") "involves a deviation from the ordinary and principal signification of a word."[62] A figure or scheme (from the Greek *schēma,* "form" or "shape") "involves a deviation from the ordinary pattern or arrangement of words."[63] As Corbett explains, "both types of figures involve a *transference* of some kind: a trope, a transference of meaning; a scheme, a transference of order."[64] See appendix B for definitions and discussions of the most important literary devices found in American antiwar speeches.


## III


At first glance, one may fault the speeches below for their manifest failure to avert war. This critique is misguided for a number of reasons. First, it ignores the value of dissent in a democratic society. As John Stuart Mill wrote in *On Liberty,* the incessant questioning of the status quo keeps opinions from becoming tired or stale: "if it is not fully, frequently, and fearlessly discussed, it will be held as a dead dogma, not a living truth."[65] Thus, at the very least, antiwar advocates may, paradoxically, function to reinforce the policies they oppose. Dissent also tends to purge lies and uncover truths. Readers may be familiar with those facts put forward by advocates of a given war. They may be less familiar with the facts put forward by the war's opponents. Listening or reading pro- and antiwar speeches together helps the listener or reader form a more nuanced understanding of each conflict.

Secondly, focusing on the purported "failure" of a particular speech to alter the course of an entire war can be unfairly shortsighted. Though antiwar speakers probably never had as great an impact on governmental decision making as they would have liked, they were often successful in galvanizing antiwar dissent and inspiring others to stand strong and keep the flame of peace alive. Fifty years after Eugene V. Debs uttered his "insubordinate" and "disloyal"[66] antiwar speech in Canton, Ohio, for example, Ray Ginger claimed that Debs's speech had become "a byword, a flaming document in the Socialist movement." "Thousands of Socialists," he wrote, "warmed themselves on bleak, cold days with the memory of Eugene Debs standing on the platform at Canton, speaking his mind."[67] Similarly, Clement Vallandigham, leader of the antiwar "Copperheads" during the Civil War, inspired pro-Lindbergh, noninterventionist students at the University of Southern California in the run-up to World War II some eighty years later to form a "Campus Copperheads" organization.[68] Thus, these speeches, shorn of their virtuous or vicious viewpoints (depending on one's point of view), can serve simply as examples of persuasive speech, as case studies of leadership through public speaking.

Thirdly, it is unclear how history might have looked without the contribution of antiwar speeches during a given war. To be sure, the United States would have continued its military involvement in, say, Vietnam whether any single antiwar speaker chose to speak out. But protest taken in the aggregate—John Kerry's speech to the Senate Foreign Relations committee in 1971, plus the speeches of the other members of Vietnam Veterans Against the War, plus the 1968 antiwar campaigns of Robert F. Kennedy and Eugene McCarthy, plus all the innumerable others who spoke out against American foreign policy in the 1960s and 1970s—makes the "no effect" argument less convincing. Some go so far as to say that certain individuals were critical in manufacturing dissent during wartime and changing history in important ways. Forty years after Eugene McCarthy broke with the Democratic Party and began campaigning against President Lyndon

Johnson on an antiwar platform, President Bill Clinton stated that McCarthy was instrumental in building opposition to the Vietnam War. "It all began with Gene McCarthy's willingness to stand alone and turn the tide of history," Clinton said.[69]

Fourthly, the government's reaction to many of the dissenters suggests that the speakers' antiwar dissent was far from nominal and, indeed, may have posed a serious threat to an administration's ability to stay in power. During the Civil War, for example, the Lincoln administration tried ex–United States Congressman Clement Vallandigham in a military tribunal for giving a "disloyal" speech to citizens of Ohio.[70] Vallandigham was convicted, imprisoned by the military, and banished from the North for the duration of the war. During World War I, the federal government convicted Socialist leader Eugene V. Debs for giving an antiwar speech in which he "obstructed and attempted to obstruct the recruiting and enlistment service of the United States."[71] Justice Oliver Wendell Holmes, writing for a unanimous Supreme Court, affirmed the trial court's ten-year prison sentence. Somewhat less dramatically, but still significantly, the Federal Bureau of Investigation (FBI) monitored the antiwar activities of many of the twentieth-century individuals in this anthology. This surveillance suggests that members of the executive branch believed that antiwar speakers were a potential threat to the war effort and perhaps even to the stability of the government itself.

Fifthly and finally, the speakers in this anthology can be appreciated in a biographical light outside the political arena. Even if these dissenters did not lessen the reach or intensity of war in any way, the personal consequences of their dissent make for compelling reading. Vallandigham and Debs are famous cases in point. Less well known, perhaps, is that of W. E. B. Du Bois, who ran for Congress on a peace platform in 1950, when he was eighty-two years old, and who soon after was indicted under the McCarran Act for failing to register with the government an antiwar organization he chaired.[72] Virtually unknown is the case of Kate Richards O'Hare, an antiwar Socialist in World War I whom her trial judged called "one of the most dangerous characters in the United States" before sentencing her to five years in prison.

Additionally, the biographies of antiwar leaders illustrate the fact that their antiwar dissent often took place within a much larger struggle to transform America into a place that, at least in each speaker's view, would be a better place to live. In this way, antiwar leaders function not merely as "antiwar activists," but also as reform-minded individuals whose ideas run far outside the ambit of war and peace. Fannie Lou Hamer, for example, was an outspoken critic of the Vietnam War, but also a staunch opponent of segregation and the racist voting policies of the South in the early 1960s. Forced into sharecropping by a jealous white neighbor, given a hysterectomy without her consent, arrested during the "Freedom Summer" of 1964 and beaten unconscious with a metal-studded blackjack in jail, Hamer is someone whose story few will read without admiring the strength and endurance she brought to bear in pursuit of a more free and more equal society.

In short, what remains of these speakers when the "effect on decision makers" dimension is stripped away is charisma reflected by and preserved in words. Such a perspective, as scholar James Darsey has explained, "reveals the falseness of the dilemma whereby we celebrate those rhetors who, in significant ways, failed to achieve their stated goals."

Darsey continues aptly, "It is because of their failure on behalf of noble principles that they continue to be celebrated and to rally those who must carry forward a principle against hopeless odds. They are less voices to us than ethical presences. It is in this continuing influence that they have achieved their greatest success."[73]

## IV

The specific conflicts examined in this anthology are the Mexican-American War, the Civil War, the Spanish-American War, World Wars I and II, the conflicts in Korea and Vietnam, and the so-called War on Terror in Iraq and Afghanistan.[74] Short introductions to each of the speeches examine how the speaker formulates his arguments, arranges his ideas, and stylizes his language. The introductions also consider the speech's place in its cultural, political, and historical context.

Ultimately, I hope this anthology will be neither pacifist nor partisan, but will instead provide compelling reading for a diversity of readers, including those interested in history, politics, rhetoric, literature, American studies, and the culture of dissent.

# Mexican-American War (1846-1848)

Before the Mexican-American War broke out in 1846, the United States encompassed approximately two million square miles, from Maine in the north to Florida in the south, and west far past the Mississippi River. At the end of the war in 1848, the size of the country had increased by 25 percent with territories obtained from Mexico, including present-day California, Nevada, Utah, most of New Mexico and Arizona, and parts of Colorado and Wyoming. From Mexico's perspective, during approximately the same amount of time its nominal territory was halved.[1]

The ultimate cause of the Mexican-American War is best attributed to the widespread sentiment for mid-nineteenth-century American expansionism. "To enlarge its limits is to extend the dominions of peace over additional territories and increasing millions," James K. Polk said of the United States during his 1845 inaugural.[2] "The world has nothing to fear from military ambition in our Government," he added.[3] John L. O'Sullivan, editor of the *United States Magazine and Democratic Review,* famously summed up the country's territorial ambition, writing that the United States meant to fulfill "our manifest destiny to overspread the continent allotted by Providence for the free development of our yearly multiplying millions."[4]

The proximate cause of the war was a boundary dispute between the United States and Mexico. The United States drew the line between itself and its southern neighbor along the Rio Grande. Mexico, for its part, believed the correct border to be the Nueces River, which ran some fifty to one hundred and fifty miles to the north. In fact, the disputed territory between the Rio Grande and the Nueces was settled almost entirely by Mexicans, and neither the United States nor Texas (which was annexed by the United States early in 1845 and admitted into the Union at the end of the year) had ever controlled it.[5] Nevertheless, President Polk ordered General Zachary Taylor and his troops to march past the Nueces and through the disputed region to the banks of the Rio Grande. Fighting ensued. President Polk asked Congress for a declaration of war on May 11, 1846, claiming that Mexico "has passed the boundary of the United States, has invaded our territory and shed American blood upon American soil."[6] Within two days, both the

House of Representatives (174–14)[7] and the Senate (40–2)[8] authorized Polk to make war on Mexico.

Over the course of the subsequent war nearly 80,000 Americans enlisted, over 13,000 of whom died.[9] While only 1,733 were killed in combat, disease overcame 11,550.[10] As for the Mexicans, it is commonly estimated that 25,000 died, but other estimates place the toll at twice that number.[11]

The Treaty of Guadalupe Hidalgo, which was signed on February 2, 1848, and ratified by the Senate on March 10, 1849, formally ended hostilities between the United States and Mexico. The terms established the Rio Grande as the southern boundary of Texas and provided for the acquisition of some 525,000 square miles of Mexican territory. In exchange, the United States would pay Mexico $15 million and assume up to $3.25 million in claims.[12] Adjusted for inflation, the total purchase price was just over $470 million. Of course, the agreement proved to be bountiful for the United States. California, for example, was a particularly valuable region: not only did it allow the United States to lay valid claim to lands stretching from the Atlantic to the Pacific, but gold was discovered at Sutter's Mill a few days before the treaty was signed. The discovery led to the California Gold Rush and the almost immediate industrialization of this new frontier.

Dissent during the Mexican-American War was animated, at different times, by political opportunism, concern that the war was being fought to perpetuate slavery in newly acquired territories, and the belief that the war was both morally and legally wrong. These threads, and others, are demonstrated in the speeches that follow. In "Sermon on War," delivered in Boston on June 7, 1846, Theodore Parker provides a wide-ranging antiwar critique with sustained metaphors. In "Withdrawal of American Troops from Mexico," delivered on February 4, 1847, Charles Sumner argues that the war in Mexico was a war of "offence" not of "defence" and appeals to the better angels of his audience's nature. Finally, in a speech to Congress on January 12, 1847, Congressman Abraham Lincoln speaks out against the war (and, in particular, against President Polk) by dissecting the president's earlier war message.

## Theodore Parker Delivers a "Sermon of War"

Teach your rulers that you are Americans, not slaves;
Christians, not Heathen; men, not murderers.

"The most forceful and eloquent of Unitarian dissenters" during the Mexican-American war, writes John H. Schroeder, "was the brilliant Theodore Parker."[13] Parker was indeed brilliant. After financial difficulties prevented him from completing his studies at Harvard College, the twenty-year-old Parker felt compelled to master the Harvard curriculum—by himself. In 1830 and 1831 he passed all the college's examinations, but as a nonresident, he received no degree. Harvard's Divinity School did not mind, though. It admitted Parker into its graduate program anyway. Graduating—this time with a degree—in 1836, Parker began his career as a Congregationalist minister. By twenty-seven, he was pastor of a church in West Roxbury, Massachusetts. Attending meetings of the Transcendental Club with Ralph Waldo Emerson and embarking on a reading program in twenty languages with William Ellery Channing, Parker quickly became a respected member of Boston's liberal elite.

As a minister, Parker focused on issues of practical significance to society. Far from restricting his sermons to dry moral theory, Parker used his pulpit to excoriate exploiters of the poor, to deride corruption in public office, and to criticize the national government for the mismanagement of Indian affairs. Indeed, as Robert C. Albrecht has noted, after Parker was offered the pulpit in Boston in 1845, he devoted fully half of his sermons to social reform.[14]

Parker's unconventional melding of traditional religious doctrine and sociopolitical issues attracted a new kind of parishioner, and his audiences—the largest in the Boston area—became noticeably different from those of other local churches: his congregation's dress was casual; members came and went freely; they sat where they wished to in the free pews; they even read newspapers before services.[15] Though most members of Boston's Unitarian clergy shunned Parker for these and other reasons,[16] Parker maintained resolutely that his social and political messages would help him bring about "absolute religion" in American society.[17]

After the Mexican-American War ended in 1848, this "moral agitator"[18] and "radical prophet"[19] began to channel much of his energy into the abolition of slavery. When Congress passed the Fugitive Slave Act of 1850, thereby allowing slave owners to capture runaway slaves in the free states of the North and return them to slavery in the South, Parker joined several anti–Fugitive Slave Act societies and protected escaped slaves in his own home.[20] He helped inspire and finance the "Kansas Crusade,"[21] and became a member of the secret committee of six that abetted John Brown in his armed insurrection at Harpers Ferry.[22]

In the last decade of his life, from 1850 until 1860, Parker lectured to a hundred thousand people every year through as many as a hundred annual lectures in every northern state east of the Mississippi River.[23] Parker's contemporary, New England intellectual Octavius Brooks Frothingham, wrote in 1874 that Parker was the greatest preacher of his generation.[24]

While Parker's name is now unknown to many, his words are actually unknown to few: one day in 1858, William Herndon, Abraham Lincoln's law partner in Illinois, brought to the office an antislavery speech Parker had delivered on Independence Day in Boston. "Democracy," Parker preached, is "Direct Self-government, over all the people, for all the people, by all the people."[25] Lincoln read the speech and marked the passage for further use.[26]

Parker presented a richly romantic and highly allegorical "Sermon of War," his first on the subject, at the Melodeon in Boston on June 7, 1846. The excerpt that follows preserves the most striking and most readable features of Parker's remarks: his imaginative virtuosity, his ability to inspire and rally supporters, and his capacity to understand the war as a symptom of a cultural disease. It omits the more pacifist features of his address, such as his conception of God as a "God of love" and not a "man of war," and also his economic analysis of the war's evils. In addition, the excerpt omits Parker's effort to distinguish "aggressive war" from "self-protecting war for freedom of mind, heart and soul." To Parker, the Mexican-American War was an aggressive war, while the American, English, and French revolutions were self-protecting wars, or wars of self-defense.

With respect to Parker's imaginative virtuosity, the introduction has explained how Parker's account of a fictionalized battle between the cities of Boston and Cambridge exemplifies the element of *pathos* included in most antiwar speeches.

With respect to Parker's ability to inspire and rally supporters, soon after Parker recounts this battle, he begins exhorting his audience with rhetorical questions: "But why talk forever? What shall we do?" Parker's battle plan is for citizens to attend public meetings, petition elected officials, and hold a national referendum on the question of war. These suggestions in themselves do not make Parker's speech great; it is the rhetorical techniques Parker employs that turn his plan of attack into an inspirational and memorable rallying cry. First, Parker constructs his exhortations around the virtuous qualities that his audience does, or at least should, possess: courage, generosity, selflessness, prudence, forethought, strength, filial piety, and religiosity. Sometimes, to make these qualities especially clear (and, incidentally, particularly quotable), Parker uses antithesis, or the juxtaposition of contrasting ideas, in parallel form. Thus, he urges his audience to "[t]each your rulers that you are Americans, not slaves; Christians, not Heathen; men, not murderers, to kill for hire!"

To understand why Parker's words work, it is crucial to realize that Parker's values are universal in their appeal, and hence available to *both* sides of the conflict. Put another way, the virtues Parker champions—courage, generosity, selflessness, and so on—support starkly partisan ends. But when viewed apart from the ends they serve, the qualities are much more palatable to even the most hostile critic. The universality of these virtues fuels the exhortation's inspirational qualities and, indeed, its greatness. Imagine, for a moment, the most notable *pro*war American exhortations. In these one finds the very same rhetoric that Parker employed, but applied to a diametrically opposed end. Abraham Lincoln's 1863 Gettysburg Address exhorts the living by extolling the dead. General George Patton's 1944 "That Sonofabitch Patton" speech and General Dwight D. Eisenhower's 1944 D-Day radio address all ready their audiences for battle by celebrating soldiers' strength and courage. More recently, President George W. Bush's September 20, 2001, address to Congress invokes America's secular ideals of "tolerance and freedom." In short, each of these speeches, like Parker's sermon, makes for great literary politics because each celebrates the timeless and universally admirable qualities—virtues—that inspire and excite members of the audience to live better lives.

Finally, Parker's remarks also represent his understanding of the war in Mexico as a symptom of a cultural disease much larger that the war itself. He reminds his audience that war "is the smallest part of our misfortune." The greatest part of the country's misfortune, Parker states, is "car[ing] more for the freedom of trade than the freedom of Men." Parker is directly referring to the "calamitous" possibility of expanding slavery into any newly acquired territories, a subject of hot debate between the North and the South at that time. Indirectly, Parker is also taking aim at a malady seemingly more pernicious than slavery itself. He is indicting a way of life that allows "the American sin" to be made possible in the first place. In this way, Parker looks at the Mexican-American War, but sees a culture that has lost "all reverence for Right, for Truth, all respect for Man and God."

At this point, one might note, as Schroeder does, that Parker is going beyond most antiwar clergymen and placing himself in a realm of dissent occupied by distinctively literary antiwar leaders.[27] Like Parker, the antiwar literati of the day were distressed that the current day's "pervasive materialism, grasping expansionism, and proslavery politics" were eclipsing the ideals on which the Union was originally based.[28] "America is not dead," wrote Margaret Fuller in 1847, "but in my time she sleepeth, and the spirit of our fathers flames no more, but lies hid beneath the ashes."[29] Ralph Waldo Emerson, Herman Melville, and Henry David Thoreau all expressed similar sentiments.[30] This editor agrees with Schroeder, and would reiterate that the capacity to understand war as "only one aspect of a pervasive disorder infecting American life,"[31] coupled with the ability to articulate that understanding in an eloquent way, lies at the center of literary politics and constitutes an essential element in any model antiwar address.

. . . NOW, to make the evils of war still clearer, and to bring them home to your door, let us suppose there was war between the counties of Suffolk, on the one side, and Middlesex on the other; this army at Boston, that at Cambridge. Suppose the subject in dispute was the boundary line between the two—Boston claiming a pitiful acre of flat land, which the ocean at low tide disdained to cover. To make sure of that Boston seizes whole miles of flat, unquestionably not its own. The rulers on one side are Fools, and Traitors on the other. The two commanders have issued their proclamations; the money is borrowed; the whiskey provided; the soldiers—Americans, Negroes, Irishman, all the able-bodied men—are enlisted. Prayers are offered in all the churches, and sermons preached, showing that God is a man of war, and Cain his first saint—an early Christian—a Christian before Christ. The Bostonians wish to seize Cambridge, burn the houses, churches, college-halls, and plunder the library. The men of Cambridge wish to seize Boston, burn its houses and ships, plundering its wares and its goods. Martial law is proclaimed on both sides. The men of Cambridge cut asunder the bridges, and make a huge breach in the mill-dam—planting cannon to enfilade all those avenues. Forts crown the hill-tops, else so green. Men, madder than lunatics, are crowded into the Asylum. The Bostonians re-build the old fortifications on the Neck, replace the forts on Beacon-hill, Fort-hill, Copps-hill, levelling houses to make room for redoubts and bastions. The batteries are planted, the mortars got ready; the furnaces and magazines are all prepared. The three hills are grim with war. From Copps-hill men look anxious to that memorable height the other side of the water. Provisions are cut off in Boston; no man may pass the lines; the aqueduct refuses its genial supply; children cry for their expected food. The soldiers parade—looking somewhat tremulous and pale; all the able-bodied have come, the vilest most willingly; some are brought by force of drink, some by force of arms. Some are in brilliant dresses—some in their working frocks. The banners are consecrated by solemn words.[32] Your church-towers are military posts of observation. There are Old Testament prayers to the "God of Hosts" in all the churches of Boston; prayers that God would curse the men of Cambridge, make their wives widows, their children fatherless, their houses a ruin, the men corpses, meat for the beast of the field and the bird of the air. Last night the Bostonians made a feint of attacking Charlestown, raining bombs and red hot cannon-balls from Copps-hill, till they have burnt a thousand houses, where the British burnt not half so many. Women and children fled screaming from the blazing rafters of their homes. The men of Middlesex crowd into Charlestown.

In the mean time the Bostonians hastily repair a bridge or two; some pass that way, some over the Neck—all stealthily by night—and while the foe expect them at Bunkers, amid the blazing town, they have stolen a march and rush upon Cambridge itself. The Cambridge men turn back. The battle is fiercely joined. You hear the cannon, the sharp report of musketry. You crowd the hills, the housetops; you line the Common, you cover the shore—yet you see but little in the sulfurous cloud. Now the Bostonians yield a little—a reinforcement goes over. All the men are gone; even the gray-headed who can shoulder a firelock. They plunge into battle, mad with rage, madder with rum. The chaplains loiter behind.

> "Pious men, whom duty brought,
> To dubious verge of battle fought,
> To shrive the dying, bless the dead."[33]

The battle hangs long in even scale. At length it turns. The Cambridge men retreat—they run—they fly. The houses burn. You see the churches and the colleges go up, a stream of fire. That library—founded 'mid want and war and sad sectarian strife, slowly gathered by the saving of two centuries, the hope of the poor scholar, the boast of the rich one—is scattered to the winds and burnt with fire, for the solid granite is blasted by powder, and the turrets fall. Victory is ours. Ten thousand men of Cambridge lie dead; eight thousand of Boston. There writhe the wounded; men who but few hours before were poured over the battle-field a lava-flood of fiery valor—fathers, brothers, husbands, sons. There they lie, torn and mangled; black with powder; red with blood; parched with thirst; cursing the load of life they now must bear with bruised frames and mutilated limbs. Gather them into hasty hospitals—let this man's daughter come to-morrow and sit by him, fanning away the flies; he shall linger out a life of wretched anguish unspoken and insupportable,[34] and when he dies his wife religiously will keep the shot which tore his limbs. There is the battle field! Here the horse charged; there the howitzers scattered their shells, pregnant with death; here the murderous canister and grape mowed down whole the crowded ranks; there the huge artillery, teeming with murder, was dragged o'er heaps of men—wounded friends who just now held its ropes, men yet curling with anguish, like worms in the fire. Hostile and friendly, head and trunk are crushed beneath those dreadful wheels. Here the infantry showered their murdering shot. That ghastly face was beautiful the day before—a sabre hewed its half away.

> "The earth is covered thick with other clay,
> Which her own clay must cover, heaped and pent,
> Rider and horse, friend, foe, in one red burial blent."[35]

Again 'tis night. Oh, what a night, and after what a day! Yet the pure tide of woman's love—which never ebbs since earth began—flows on in spite of war and battle. Stealthily, by the pale moonlight, a mother of Boston treads the weary miles to reach that bloody spot; a widow she—seeking among the slain her only son. The arm of power drove him forth reluctant to the fight. A friendly soldier guides her way. Now she turns over this face, whose mouth is full of purple dust, bit out of the ground in his extremest agony—the last sacrament offered him by earth herself; now she raises that form, cold, stiff, stony, and ghastly as a dream of hell. But, lo! another comes—she too a woman—younger and fairer, yet not less bold, a maiden from the hostile town to seek her lover. They meet—two women among the corpses; two angels come to Golgotha, seeking to raise a man. There he lies before them; they look,—yes, 'tis he you seek; the same dress, form, features too;—'tis he, the Son, the Lover. Maid and mother could tell *that* face in any light. The grass is wet with his blood. Yes, the ground is muddy with the life of men. The mother's innocent robe is drabbled in the blood her bosom bore. Their kisses, groans and tears recall the wounded man. He knows the mother's voice; that voice yet more beloved. His lips move only, for they cannot speak. He dies! The waxing moon moves high in heaven, walking in beauty 'mid the clouds, and murmurs soft her cradle song unto the slumbering earth. The broken sword reflects her placid beams. A star looks down and is imaged back in a pool of blood. The cool night wind plays in the branches of the trees shivered with shot. Nature is beautiful; that lovely grass underneath their feet; those pendulous branches of the leafy elm; the stars and that romantic moon lining the clouds with silver light! A groan of agony, hopeless and prolonged, wails out from that bloody ground. But in yonder farm the whippowil sings to her lover all night long; the rising tide ripples melodious against the shores. So wears the night away,—Nature, all sinless, round that field of wo.

> "The morn is up again, the dewy morn,
> With breath all incense and with cheek all bloom,
> Laughing the clouds away with playful scorn,
> And living as if earth contained no tomb,
> And glowing into day."[36]

What a scene that morning looks upon! I will not turn again.—Let the dead bury their dead. But their blood cries out of the ground against the rulers who shed it,—Cain! where are thy brothers? What shall the Fool answer; what the Traitor say?

Then comes thanksgiving in all the churches of Boston. The consecrated banners, stiff with blood and "glory," are hung over the altar. The minister preaches and the singer sings: "The Lord hath been on our side. He treadeth the people under me. He teacheth my hands to war, my fingers to fight. Yea, He giveth me the necks of mine enemies; for the Lord is His name;" and "'twas a famous victory!" Boston seizes miles square of land; but her houses are empty; her wives widows; her children fatherless. Rachel weeps for the murder of her innocents—yet dares not rebuke the rod. I know there is no fighting across Charles River, as in this poor fiction; but there was once, and instead of CHARLES say RIO GRANDE; for CAMBRIDGE read METAMORAS, and it is what your President recommended; what your Congress enacted; what your Governor issued his proclamation for; what your volunteers go to accomplish:—yes, what they fired cannon for on Boston Common t'other day. I wish *that* were a fiction of mine!

We are waging a most iniquitous war—so it seems to me. I know I may be wrong. But I am no partisan, and if I err, it is not wilfully, not rashly. I know the Mexicans are a wretched people—wretched in their origin, history and character. I know but two good things of them as a people—they abolished negro slavery, not long ago; they do not covet the lands of their neighbors. True, they have not paid all their debts; but it is scarcely decent in a nation with any repudiating States to throw the first stone at her for that!

I know the Mexicans cannot stand before this terrible Anglo-Saxon race, the most formidable and powerful the world ever saw; a race which has never turned back; which, though it number less than forty millions, yet holds the Indies, almost the whole of North America; which rules the commerce of the world; clutches at New Holland, China, New Zealand, Borneo, and seizes island after island in the farthest seas;—the race which invented steam as its awful type. The poor, wretched Mexicans can never stand before us. How they perished in battle! They must melt away as the Indians before the white man. Considering how we acquired Louisiana, Florida, Oregon, I cannot forbear thinking that this people will possess the whole of the continent before many years; perhaps before the century ends. But this may be had fairly; with no injustice to any one; by the steady advance of a superior race, with superior ideas and a better civilization; by commerce, trade, arts, by being better than Mexico, wiser, humaner, more free and manly. Is it not better to acquire it by the schoolmaster than the cannon; by peddling cloth, tin, any thing rather than bullets? It may not all belong to this Government—and yet to this race. It would be a gain to mankind if we could spread over that country the Idea of America—that all men are born free and equal in rights, and establish there political, social, and individual freedom. But to do that we must first make real these ideas at home.

In the general issue between this race and theirs, we are in the right. But in this special issue, and this particular war, it seems to me that we are wholly in the wrong; that our invasion of Mexico is as bad as the partition of Poland in the last century and in this. If I understand the matter—the whole movement, the settlement of Texas, the Texan revolution, the annexation of Texas, the invasion of Mexico has been a movement hostile to the American idea,—a movement to extend slavery. I do not say such was the design on the part of the people, but on the part of the politicians who pulled the strings. I think the papers of the Government and the debates of Congress prove that. The annexation has been declared unconstitutional in its mode,—a virtual dissolution of the Union—and that by very high and well known authority. It was expressly brought about for the purpose of extending Slavery. An attempt is now made to throw the shame of this on the Democrats. I think the Democrats deserve the shame; but I could never see that the Whigs, on the whole, deserved it any less; only they were not quite so open. Certainly, their leaders did not take ground against it,—never as against a modification of the tariff! When we annexed Texas we of course took her for better or worse, debts and all, and annexed her war along with her. I take it every body knew that; though now some seem to pretend a decent astonishment at the result. Now one party is ready to fight for it as the other! The North did not oppose the annexation of Texas. Why not? They knew they could make money by it. The eyes of the North are full of cotton; they see nothing else, for a *web* is before them; their ears are full of cotton, and they hear nothing but the buzz of their mills; their mouth is full of cotton, and they can speak audibly but two words—Tariff, Tariff, Dividends, Dividends. Yes, the talent of the North is blinded, deafened, gagged with its own cotton. The North clamored loudly when the nation's treasure was removed from the United States Bank;—it is almost silent at the annexation of a slave territory big as the kingdom of France, encumbered with debts—loaded with the entailment of war! Northern governors call for soldiers; our men volunteer to fight in a most infamous war for the extension of slavery! Tell it not in Boston, whisper it not in Faneuil Hall, lest you waken the slumbers of your fathers, and they curse you as cowards and traitors unto men! Not satisfied with annexing Texas and a war, we next invaded a territory which did not belong to Texas, and built a fort on the Rio Grande, where, I take it, we had no more right than the British, in 1841, had on the Penobscot or the Saco. Now the Government and its Congress would throw the blame on the innocent, and say war exists "by the act of Mexico!" If a lie was ever told, I think this is one. Then the "dear people" must be called on for money and men, for "the soil of this free republic is invaded," and the Governor of Massachusetts, one of the men who declared the annexation of Texas unconstitutional, recommends the war he just now told us to pray against, and appeals to our "patriotism," and "humanity," as arguments for butchering the Mexicans, when they are in the right and we in the wrong! The maxim is held up, "Our country, right or wrong;" "Our country howsoever bounded;" and it might as well be, "Our country, howsoever governed." It seems popularly and politically forgotten that there is such a thing as RIGHT. The nation's neck invites a Tyrant. I am not at all astonished that Northern Representatives voted for all this work of crime. They are no better than Southern Representatives; scarcely less in favour of slavery, and not half so open. They say: Let the North make money, and you may do what you please with the nation; and we will choose governors that dare not oppose you, for, though we are descended from the Puritans, we have but one article in our creed we never flinch from following, and that is—to make money; honestly, if we can; if not, as we can!

Look through the action of your Government, and your Congress. You see that no reference has been had in this affair to Christian ideas; none to Justice and the Eternal right. Nay, none at all! In the Churches, and among the people, how feeble has been the protest against this great wrong. How tamely the people yield their necks—and say: "Take our sons for the war—we care not, right or wrong." England butchers the Sikhs in India—her generals are elevated to the peerage, and the head of her church writes a form of thanksgiving for the victory—to be read in all the churches of that Christian land.[37] To make it still more abominable, the blasphemy is enacted on Easter Sunday, the great Holiday of men who serve the Prince of Peace. We have not had prayers in the churches, for we have no political Archbishop. But we fired cannon in joy that we had butchered a few wretched men—half starved, and forced into the ranks by fear of death! Your Peace-Societies, and your Churches, what can they do? What dare they? Verily, we are a faithless and perverse generation. God be merciful to us, sinners as we are!

But why *talk* forever? What shall we do? In regard to this present war, we can refuse to take any part in it; we can encourage others to do the same; we can aid men, if need be, who suffer because they refuse. Men will call us traitors, what then? That hurt nobody in '76! We are a rebellious nation; our whole history is treason; our blood was attainted before we were born; our Creeds are infidelity to the Mother-church; our Constitution treason to our father-land. What of that? Though all the Governors in the world bid us commit treason against Man, and set the example, let us never submit. Let God only be a Master to control our Conscience!

We can hold public meetings in favour of Peace, in which what is wrong shall be exposed and condemned. It is proof of our cowardice that this has not been done before now. We can show in what the infamy of a nation consists; in what its real glory. One of your own men, the last summer, startled the churches out of their sleep,[38] by his manly trumpet, talking with us and telling that the true grandeur of a nation was Justice not glory, Peace not war.

We can work now for future times, by taking pains to spread abroad the Sentiments of Peace, the Ideas of Peace, among the people in schools, churches—everywhere. At length we can diminish the power of the National Government, so that the people alone shall have the power to declare war, by a direct vote—the Congress only to recommend it. We can take from the Government the means of war by raising only revenue enough for the nation's actual wants, and raising that directly, so that each man knows what he pays, and when he pays it, and then he will take care that it is not paid to make him poor and keep him so. We can diffuse a real practical Christianity among the people, till the mass of men have courage enough to overcome evil with good, and look at war as the worst of treason and the foulest infidelity!

Now is the time to push and be active. War itself gives weight to words of peace. There will never be a better time, till we make the times better. It is not a day for cowardice, but for heroism. Fear not that the "honor of the nation" will suffer from Christian movements for Peace. What if your men of low degree are a vanity, and your men of high degree are a lie? That is no new thing. Let true men do their duty, and the lie and the vanity will pass each to its reward. Wait not for the Churches to move, or the State to become Christian. Let us bear our testimony like men, not fearing to be called Traitors, Infidels; fearing only to BE such.

I would call on Americans, by their love of our country, its great ideas, its real grandeur, its hopes, and the memory of its fathers—to come and help save that country from infamy and ruin. I would call on Christians, who believe that Christianity is a Truth, to lift up their voice, public and private, against the foulest violation of God's law, this blasphemy of the Holy Spirit of Christ, this worst form of infidelity to Man and God. I would call on all men, by the one nature that is in you, by the great human heart beating alike in all your bosoms, to protest manfully against this desecration of the earth, this high treason against both Man and God. Teach your rulers that you are Americans, not Slaves; Christians, not Heathen; men, not murderers, to kill for hire! You may effect little in this generation, for its head seems crazed and its heart rotten. But there will be a day after to-day. It is for you and me to make it better; a day of peace, when nation shall no longer lift up sword against nation; when all shall indeed be brothers, and all blest. Do this—you shall be worthy to dwell in this beautiful land; Christ will be near you; God work with you—and bless you forever!

This present trouble with Mexico may be very brief; surely it might be even now brought to an end with no unusual manhood in your rulers. Can we say we have not deserved it? Let it end, but let us remember that war, horrid as it is, is not the worst calamity which ever befalls a people. It is far worse for a people to lose all reverence for Right, for Truth, all respect for Man and God; to care more for the freedom of trade than the freedom of Men! more for a tariff than millions of souls. This calamity came upon us gradually, long before the present war, and will last long after that has died away. Like People like Ruler, is a true word. Look at your rulers, Representatives, and see our own likeness! We reverence FORCE, and have forgot there is any Right beyond the vote of Congress or a people; any good beside Dollars; any God but Majorities and Force. I think the present war, though it should cost 50,000 men and $50,000,000, the smallest part of our misfortune. Abroad we are looked on as a nation of swindlers and men-stealers! What can we say in our defence? Alas, the nation is a traitor to its great idea,—that all men are born equal, each with the same unalienable rights. We are infidels to Christianity. We have paid the price of our shame.

There have been dark days in this nation before now. It was gloomy when Washington with his little army fled through the Jerseys. It was a long dark day from '83 to '89. It was not so dark as now; the nation never so false. There was never a time when resistance to tyrants was so rare a virtue; when the people so tamely submitted to a wrong. Now you can feel the darkness. The sack of this city and the butchery of its people were a far less evil than the moral deadness of this nation. Men spring up again like the mown grass—but to raise up saints and heroes in a dead nation, corrupting beside its golden tomb, what shall do that for us? We must look not to the many for that, but to the few who are faithful unto God and Man.

I know the hardy vigor of our men, the stalwart intellect of this people. Would to God they could learn to love the Right and True. Then what a people should we be— spreading from the Madawaska to the Sacramento—diffusing our great Idea, and living our Religion, the Christianity of Christ! Oh, Lord! make the vision true; waken thy prophets and stir thy people till Righteousness exalt us! No wonders will be wrought for that. But the voice of Conscience speaks to you and me, and all of us: the Right shall prosper; the wicked States shall die; and History responds her long Amen.

What lessons come to us from the past! The Genius of the Old Civilization, solemn and sad, sits there on the Alps, his classic beard descending o'er his breast. Behind him arise the new nations, bustling with romantic life. He bends down over the midland sea, and counts up his children—Assyria, Egypt, Tyre, Carthage, Troy, Etruria, Corinth, Athens, Rome—once so renowned, now gathered with the dead, their giant ghosts still lingering pensive o'er the spot. He turns westward his face, too sad to weep, and raising from his palsied knee his trembling hand, looks on his brother Genius of the New Civilization. That young giant, strong and mocking, sits there on the Alleghanies. Before him lie the waters, covered with ships; behind him he hears the roar of the Mississippi and the far distant Oregon—rolling their riches to the sea. He bends down, and that far ocean murmurs pacific in his year. On his left, are the harbors, shops, and mills of the East, and a five-fold gleam of light goes up from Northern lakes. On his right, spread out the broad savannahs of the South, waiting to be blessed; and far off that Mexique bay bends round her tropic shores. A crown of stars is on that giant's head, some glorious with flashing, many-colored light; some bloody red; some pale and faint, of most uncertain hue. His right hand lies folded in his robe; the left rests on the Bible's opened page, and holds these sacred words—All men are equal, born with equal rights from God. The old man says to the young, "Brother, BEWARE!" and Alps and Rocky Mountains say "BEWARE!" That stripling giant, ill-bred and scoffing, shouts amain: "My feet are red with the Indian's blood; my hand has forged the negro's chain. I am strong; who dares assail me? I will drink his blood, for I have made my covenant of lies and leagued with hell for my support. There is no Right, no Truth; Christianity is false, and God a name." His left hand rends those sacred scrolls, casting his Bibles underneath his feet, and in his right he brandishes the negro-driver's whip—crying again—"Say, who is God, and what is Right." And all his mountains echo RIGHT. But the old Genius sadly says again: "Though hand join in hand, the wicked shall not prosper." The hollow tomb of Egypt, Athens, Rome, of every ancient State, with all their wandering ghosts, replies "AMEN."

## Charles Sumner Calls for the Withdrawal of American Troops from Mexico

With lying names, they call spoliation, murder, and rapine,
Empire; and when they have produced the desolation of
solitude, they call it *Peace*.

Charles Sumner's unyielding antislavery convictions came to a head, literally, in 1856 when South Carolina Congressman Preston Brooks attacked Sumner with his cane in retaliation for Sumner's Senate oration "The Crime Against Kansas."[39] Landing repeated blows to the head of his colleague, who was sitting at his desk in the Senate chamber, Brooks beat Sumner onto the floor, into bloody unconsciousness, and out of the Senate for three years. These were among "the first blows of the Civil War."[40] But before the events surrounding Sumner's famous antebellum advocacy, Sumner was an eloquent opponent of the Mexican-American War. Indeed, he began his public career as an antiwar activist.

Invited to present Boston's annual Fourth of July oration in 1845, Sumner used the occasion to attack militarism in United States, a country then on the verge of conflict with both Mexico and Great Britain. Inspired by Unitarian pacifist William Ellery Channing, Sumner explained in detail why war was "utterly and irreconcilably inconsistent with True Greatness." Sumner argued that the "true grandeur of nations" was, in fact, their capacity to preserve peace.[41] His first major public speech was a phenomenal success and catapulted the thirty-five-year-old into prominence. In 1846, Sumner gave another major address, "Slavery and the Mexican War," which was also well-received. In it, Sumner argued that Southern interests aimed to annex Texas and much of Mexico in order to perpetuate and expand slavery.[42]

I have chosen to anthologize a third address, "Withdrawal of American Troops from Mexico," which Sumner gave at a public meeting in Faneuil Hall in Boston on February 4, 1847.[43] Like "The True Grandeur of Nations" and "Slavery and the Mexican War," "Withdrawal of American Troops" is filled with Sumner's "usual eloquence."[44] Within two weeks it was reprinted on both sides of the Atlantic by the *Liberator,* whose editorial board wrote that it was "eloquent, timely and intrepid."[45] Sumner himself thought highly enough of the speech to include it alongside his other antiwar addresses in his *Works.*[46]

In the speech, Sumner departs from some of the radical views expressed in his other antiwar speeches. Almost wholly absent are the pacifism of "The True Grandeur of Nations" and the abolitionism of "Slavery and the Mexican War." Despite steering clear of his more radical arguments, though, the speech was not received quietly or without incident—Sumner notes in his *Works* that "there was interruption at times from lawless persons trying to drown the voice of the speaker,"[47] and the *Liberator* confirms that during Sumner's speech "a large number of the volunteers" prevented many from hearing Sumner distinctly by their "mobocratic turbulence."[48] Tensions were plainly high, and the *Boston Daily Whig* reported the next day that one volunteer who attended the meeting "drew a bayonet" in response to those asking him to be quiet.[49]

To understand the persuasive power of Charles Sumner's speech, it is useful to examine it in light of mid-nineteenth-century rhetorical theory, which held that a speaker's character as portrayed through his speech—his *ethos*—was central to the speech's persuasiveness. One characteristic central to constructing a positive ethos, and thus a persuasive address, was what Scottish New Rhetorician (and, only later, economist) Adam Smith identified as sympathy, or "fellow-feeling for the misery of others."[50] In his *Lectures on Rhetoric and Belles Lettres,* Smith was clear that when the speaker expressed sympathy for his subject, "then and then only then expression has all the force and beauty that language can give."[51]

One should read Sumner's speech as a quintessentially sympathetic address, the success or failure of which turns on Sumner's ability to make his audience share the feelings of the Mexicans whose land was currently occupied by U.S. forces. To this end, Sumner, speaking in Faneuil Hall to Bostonians, asks his audience to contemplate Boston's own history as an occupied city:

> Boston herself in former times suffered. The war-horse was stalled in one of her most venerable churches. Her streets echoed to the tread of hostile troops. Her

inhabitants were waked by the morning drum-beat of oppressors. On their own narrow peninsula they have seen the smoke of an enemy's camp. Though these things are beyond the memory of any in this multitude, yet faithful History has entered them on her record, so that they can never be forgotten. It is proper, then, that Boston, mindful of the past and of her own trials, mindful of her own pleadings for the withdrawal of the British troops, as the beginning of reconciliation, should now come forward and ask for *others* what she once so earnestly asked for *herself.*

In addition, Sumner, like Theodore Parker, galvanizes antiwar dissent by celebrating the virtuous qualities of his audience. In fact, Sumner appeals explicitly to the audience's "moral and intellectual character," thus buttressing his own ethos with that of his listeners:

Boston is the home of noble charities, the nurse of true learning, the city of churches. By all these tokens she stands conspicuous; and other parts of the country are not unwilling to follow her example. Athens was called "the eye of Greece." Boston may be called "the eye of America"; and the influence which she exerts proceeds not from size,—for there are other cities larger far,—but from moral and intellectual character. It is only just, then, that a town foremost in the struggles of the Revolution, foremost in all the humane and enlightened labors of our country, should take the lead now.

In the final analysis, then, Sumner's speech is significant in that it replaces ad hominem attacks with ennobling principles. Sumner appeals to the audience's virtue and capacity for sympathetic thought. There are some antiwar speeches—Abraham Lincoln's, to take just one example—that reek of bitterness; there are others, like Eugene V. Debs's, that descend to the depths of hatred. Unlike the vast majority of antiwar speakers, Sumner chooses neither strategy. Instead, he opts to appeal, as his famous compatriot later put it, to the better angels of our nature.

MR. CHAIRMAN AND FELLOW-CITIZENS,—

In the winter of 1775, five years after what was called the "massacre" in King Street, now State Street, a few months only before the Battles of Lexington and Bunker Hill, Boston was occupied by a British army under General Gage,—as Mexican Monterey, a town not far from the size of Boston in those days, is now occupied by American troops under General Taylor. The people of Boston felt keenly all the grievance of this garrison, holding the control of Massachusetts Bay with iron hand. With earnest voice they called for its withdrawal, as the beginning of reconciliation and peace. Their remonstrances found unexpected echo in the House of Lords, when Lord Chatham, on the 20th of January, brought forward his memorable motion for the withdrawal of the troops from Boston. Josiah Quincy, Jr., dear to Bostonians for his own services, and for the services of his descendants in two generations, was present on this occasion, and has preserved an interesting and authentic sketch of Lord Chatham's speech. From his report I take the following important words.

"There ought to be no delay in entering upon this matter. We ought to proceed to it immediately. We ought to seize the first moment to open the door of reconciliation. The Americans will never be in a temper or state to be reconciled,—they ought not to be,—till the troops are withdrawn. The troops are a perpetual irritation to these people; they are a bar to all confidence and all cordial reconcilement. I, therefore, my Lords, move, 'That an humble address be presented to His Majesty, most humbly to advise and beseech His Majesty, that, in order to open the way towards an happy settlement of the dangerous troubles in America, by beginning to allay ferments and soften animosities there, and above all for preventing in the mean time any sudden and fatal catastrophe at Boston, now suffering under the daily irritation of an army before their eyes, posted in their town, it may graciously please His Majesty *that immediate orders may be despatched to General Gage for removing His Majesty's forces from the town of Boston,* as soon as the rigor of the season, and other circumstances indispensable to the safety and accommodation of the said troops, may render the same practicable.'"[52]

It is to promote a similar measure of justice and reconciliation that we are now assembled. Adopting the language of Chatham, we ask the cessation of this unjust war, and the withdrawal of the American forces from Mexico, "as soon as the rigor of the season, and other circumstances indispensable to the safety and accommodation of the said troops, may render the same practicable."

It is hoped that this movement will extend throughout the country, but it is proper that it should begin here. Boston herself in former times suffered. The war-horse was stalled in one of her most venerable churches. Her streets echoed to the tread of hostile troops. Her inhabitants were waked by the morning drum-beat of oppressors. On their own narrow peninsula they have seen the smoke of an enemy's camp. Though these things are beyond the memory of any in this multitude, yet faithful History has entered them on her record, so that they can never be forgotten. It is proper, then, that Boston, mindful of the past and of her own trials, mindful of her own pleadings for the withdrawal of the British troops, as the beginning of reconciliation, should now come forward and ask for *others* what she once so earnestly asked for *herself.* It is proper that Boston should confess her obligations to the generous eloquence of Chatham, by vindicating his arguments of policy, humanity, and justice, in their application to the citizens of a sister Republic. Franklin, in dispensing a charity, said to the receiver, "When you are able, return this,—not to me but to some one in need, like yourself now." In the same spirit, Boston should now repay her debt by insisting on the withdrawal of the American troops from Mexico.

Other considerations call upon her to take the lead. Boston has always led the generous actions of our history. Boston led the cause of the Revolution. Here commenced that discussion, pregnant with independence, which, at first occupying a few warm, but true spirits only, finally absorbed all the best energies of the continent, the eloquence of Adams, the patriotism of Jefferson, the wisdom of Washington. Boston is the home of noble charities, the nurse of true learning, the city of churches. By all these tokens she stands conspicuous; and other parts of the country are not unwilling to follow her example. Athens was called "the eye of Greece." Boston may be called "the eye of America"; and the influence which she exerts proceeds not from size,—for there are other cities larger far,—but from moral and intellectual character. It is only just, then, that a town foremost in the struggles of the Revolution, foremost in all the humane and enlightened labors of our country, should take the lead now. . . .

We are told that the country is engaged in the war, and therefore it must be maintained, or, as it is sometimes expressed, vigorously prosecuted. In other words, the violation of the Constitution and the outrage upon justice sink out of sight, and we are urged to these same acts again. By what necromancy do these pass from wrong to right? In what book of morals is it written, that what is bad before it is undertaken becomes righteous merely from the circumstance that it is commenced? Who on earth is authorized to transmute wrong into right? Whoso admits the unconstitutionality and injustice of the war, and yet sanctions its prosecution, must approve the Heaven-defying sentiment, "Our country, right or wrong." Can this be the sentiment of Boston? If so, in vain are her children nurtured in the churches of the Pilgrims, in vain fed from the common table of knowledge bountifully supplied by our common schools. Who would profess allegiance to wrong? Who would deny allegiance to right? Right is one of the attributes of God, or rather it is part of his Divinity, immortal as himself. The mortal cannot be higher than the immortal. Had this sentiment been received by our English defenders in the war of the Revolution, no fiery tongue of Chatham, Burke, Fox, or Camden would have been heard in our behalf. Their great testimony would have failed. All would have been silenced, while crying that the country, right or wrong, must be carried through the war.

Here is a gross confusion of opposite duties in cases of *defence* and of *offence*. When a country is invaded, its soil pressed by hostile footsteps, its churches desecrated, its inhabitants despoiled of homes, its national life assailed, then the indignant spirit of a free people rises to repel the aggressor. Such an occasion challenges all the energies of *self-defence*. It has about it all that dismal glory which can be earned in scenes of human strife. But if it be right to persevere here in *defence,* it must be wrong to preserve in *offence.* If the Mexicans are right in defending their homes, we certainly are wrong in invading them.

The present war is *offensive* in essence. As such it loses all shadow of title to support. The acts of courage and hardihood which in a just cause might excite regard, when performed in an unrighteous cause, have no quality that can commend them to virtuous sympathy. The victories of aggression and injustice are a grief and shame. Blood wrongfully shed cries from the ground drenched with the fraternal tide.

The enormous expenditures lavished upon this war, now extending to fifty millions of dollars,—we have been told recently on the floor of the Senate that they were near one hundred millions,—are another reason for its cessation. The soul sickens at the contemplation of this incalculable sum diverted from purposes of usefulness and beneficence, from railroads, colleges, hospitals, schools, and churches, under whose genial influences the country would blossom as a rose, and desecrated to the wicked purposes of unjust war. In any righteous self-defence even these expenditures would be readily incurred. The saying of an early father of the Republic, which roused its enthusiasm to unwonted pitch, was, "Millions for Defence, not a cent for Tribute." Another sentiment more pertinent to our times would be, "Not a cent for OFFENCE."

And why is this war to be maintained? According to the jargon of the day, "to conquer a peace." But if we ask for peace in the spirit of peace, we must begin by doing justice to Mexico. We are the aggressors. We are now in the wrong. We must do all in our power to set ourselves right. This surely is not by brutal effort to conquer Mexico. Our military force is so far greater than hers, that even conquest must be without the wretched glory which men covet, while honor is impossible from successful adherence to original acts of wrong. "To conquer a peace" may have a sensible signification, when a nation is acting in *self-defence;* but it is base, unjust, and atrocious, when the war is of *offence.* Peace in such a war, if founded on conquest, must be the triumph of injustice, the consummation of wrong. It is unlike that true peace won by justice or forbearance. It cannot be sanctioned by the God of Christians. To the better divinities of heathenism it would be offensive. It is of such a peace that the Roman historian, who pen is as keen as a sword's sharp point, says, "*Auferre, trucidare, rapere, falsis nominibus,* IMPERIUM; *atque, ubi solitudinem faciunt,* PACEM *appellant*": With lying names, they call spoliation, murder, and rapine, Empire; and when they have produced the desolation of solitude, they call it *Peace. . . .*[53]

The struggle in Mexico against the United States, and that of our fathers against England, have their points of resemblance. Prominent among these is the aggressive character of the proceedings, in the hope of crushing a weaker people. But the parallel fails as yet in an important particular. The injustice of England roused her most distinguished sons, in her own Parliament, to call for the cessation of the war. It inspired the eloquence of Chatham to those strains of undying fame. In the Senate of the United States there is a favorite son of Massachusetts,[54] to whom has been accorded powers unsurpassed by those of any English orator. He has now before him the cause of Chatham. His country is engaged in unrighteous war. Join now in asking him to raise his eloquent voice in behalf of justice, and of peace founded on justice; and may the spirit of Chatham descend upon him!

Let us call upon the whole country to rally in this cause. And may a voice go forth from Faneuil Hall tonight, awakening fresh echoes throughout the valleys of New England,—swelling as it proceeds, and gathering new reverberations in its ample volume,—traversing the whole land, and still receiving other voices, till it reaches our rulers at Washington, and, in tones of thunder, demands the cessation of this unjust war!

## Abraham Lincoln Inveighs Against President Polk

[M]ilitary glory—that attractive rainbow that rises in showers
of blood—that serpent's eye that charms to destroy.

In January 1848, Whig politicians were confronted with mounting evidence that President Polk and the Democrats were winning the war in Mexico. By late 1847, General

Zachary Taylor had won battles at Palo Alto, Resaca de la Palma, Monterey, and Buena Vista. General Winfield Scott had captured Vera Cruz and Mexico City. Moreover, Polk and the Democrats had positioned the United States to acquire the large and valuable territories of California and New Mexico—territories that then represented an area half the size of Mexico, and one-third the size of the United States. The winds of "manifest destiny" at his back, Polk declared in December that the vast lands "should never be surrendered," but would be held as indemnity from the bankrupt Mexicans for their outstanding claims and the United States's war expenses.[55]

On the heels of a successful war prosecuted by Democrats, how were the Democrats' opponents, the Whigs, to capture the White House in the 1848 elections? One strategy the party developed was to attack not the administration's prosecution of the war, but Polk's "unnecessary and unconstitutional" origination of it in 1846.[56] Leading the charge in the 13th Congress was the freshman congressman from Illinois, Abraham Lincoln.

For his opening salvo, Lincoln addressed the annual message Polk had sent to Congress in December. In Polk's message, which was read to Congress by a presidential clerk, the president reasserted the Democratic party line: Mexico, not the United States, commenced hostilities by "invading the territory of the State of Texas, striking the first blow, and shedding the blood of our citizens on our own soil."[57] In response to the president's message, Lincoln submitted eight interrogatory-like resolutions to the House and demanded that the president establish "whether the particular spot of soil on which the blood of our *citizens* was so shed was, or was not, *our own soil*."[58] Lincoln's "Spot" resolutions, as they were soon dubbed, were intended to illustrate that Polk had unnecessarily commenced military action in Mexican territory.[59]

Three weeks later, Lincoln delivered his next volley, a bitter denunciation of the president. Lincoln worked quite hard on the viciously partisan address, which he delivered on January 12. He wrote to his law partner, William H. Herndon, a few days earlier, "I hope to succeed well enough to wish you to see it."[60] Following the Whig party line, Lincoln argued that the war in Mexico was "unnecessary and unconstitutional." Explaining that his speech was necessary to combat President Polk's repeated attempts to equate Congress's support for military supplies with an endorsement of the "justice and wisdom" of the president's conduct, Lincoln continued to hammer home his earlier critique that, as a legal matter, Polk did not present sufficient evidence that the United States *owned* the land on which American blood was first shed and, accordingly, had not sufficiently justified the commencement of hostilities. With a great rhetorical flourish, Lincoln concluded his speech by denouncing President Polk himself.

Most of the available evidence suggests that Lincoln's January speech in particular, and his antiwar stance generally, represented more political opportunism than the staunch reliance on principle for which he is better known.[61] For one, Lincoln said nothing opposing the war during the entirety of his congressional campaign. In fact, his only mention of the war in Mexico during his run for office was to deliver a "warm, thrilling and effective" speech at a public meeting in the Springfield statehouse *encouraging* enlistment.[62] Also, as Lincoln himself often pointed out, he supported the troops during the war by supporting Polk's supply bills and other appropriation measures.[63]

Finally, Lincoln may have cared little about at least one sentiment that fueled antiwar support—Mexican sovereignty. Early in his career, he once referred to Mexicans as "greasers."[64]

On the other hand, on January 12 Lincoln did offer a principled rationalization for his apparent change of position. Those who "could not conscientiously approve the conduct of the President," Lincoln explained, "because of knowing too *little,* or because of knowing too *much,*" should "as good citizens and patriots, remain silent on that point, at least till the war should be ended."[65] Is Lincoln's rationale persuasive? It appears to be a recipe for near-absolute presidential power in times of war—an anathematic proposition to the early Lincoln.[66] If one is to take seriously the future president's argument that the war with Mexico was "unnecessary and unconstitutional," one wonders why Lincoln would strike the sword from the hand of the legislature at the very moment when combating presidential power would have the most practical effect.[67]

In any event, Lincoln's speech failed to produce the praise he sought.[68] Except for a handful of scattered remarks, national reaction was nonexistent.[69] President Polk, who mentions countless other congressmen in his voluminous daily diary entries, does not once comment on Lincoln or respond publicly to his accusations. In the House, there were but three anti-Lincoln whispers: one from an obscure Democrat questioning Lincoln's patriotism,[70] another reproaching Lincoln for not informing his constituents of his antiwar position before his election,[71] and another stating that the burden lay on Lincoln to prove that the disputed lands initially belonged to the Mexicans.[72] Nothing Lincoln said on January 12 moved anyone to debate, much less adopt, the resolutions he had submitted a few weeks earlier.[73]

But the newspapers and voters of Illinois offered a very different response.[74] The *Belleville Advocate* summed up the state's anti-Lincoln sentiment, writing that "his course in denouncing his country, has called forth a stern rebuke from many of his constituents, and will be more signally condemned."[75] The Democratic *Illinois State Register* of Springfield led the pack in attacking the freshman congressman. "Out damned SPOT!"[76] blared one headline. The *State Register*'s editorials called the questions Lincoln raised "politically motivated," and predicted that he would "have a fearful account to settle" with the veterans when they came home.[77] The *Peoria Press,* unable to resist a pun, joked of Lincoln, "What an epitaph: 'Died of the *Spotted Fever.*'"[78]

Lincoln fared just as badly in public meetings throughout his district. A nonpartisan mass meeting held in Clark County declared that the "author of the 'spotty' resolutions," inflicted a "stain" on his constituents' "proud name of patriotism and glory."[79] On March 14, citizens in Morgan County passed a resolution stating, "Henceforth will the Benedict Arnold of our district be known here only as the Ranchero Spotty of one term."[80]

Lincoln was pestered by his early antiwar activities for the remainder of his life. Months after his speech, Democrats in Illinois were still trying to gain political capital at Lincoln's expense. The *Peoria Democratic Press* wrote in May 1848 that the "miserable man of 'Spots' will pass unnoticed save in the execration that his treason will bring upon his name." For the remainder of his life, the paper prophesied, Lincoln will be "dead whilst among the living."[81] In the Lincoln-Douglas debates in 1858, Stephen Douglas taunted his adversary on the subject with some success. In their first debate, for example, Douglas says of Lincoln, "Whilst in Congress, he distinguished himself by his opposition to the Mexican war, taking the side of the common enemy against his own country; ('*that's true*') and when he returned home he found that the indignation of the people followed him everywhere, and he was again submerged or obligated to retire into private life, forgotten by his former friends. ('*And will be again.*')" Though Lincoln repeatedly claimed the accusations were a malicious misreading of history, Douglas continued to hammer the point home in all but one of their famous debates.[82] That his adversary's criticism was to some extent working is evidenced by a campaign autobiography Lincoln drafted in 1860. This time, the presidential candidate took pains to explain the nature of his old antiwar position in decidedly nonincendiary language.[83]

The criticism dogged Lincoln in the few remaining years of his life as well. In 1863, after Lincoln had suspended the writ of habeas corpus, which dampened the ability of members of the public to vocalize any antiwar views, Congressman Clement L. Vallandigham noted the irony of the situation. In a speech to the House, Vallandigham posed the rhetorical question "Was Abraham Lincoln guilty [of treason], because he denounced [the Mexican-American] war while a Representative on the floor of this House?"[84] When Vallandigham was imprisoned for his own antiwar agitation during the Civil War, his supporters argued that their leader's allegedly traitorous speech was no worse to Lincoln's administration than Lincoln's own speech had been to Polk's fifteen years earlier.[85]

As a rhetorician, Lincoln stands out among presidents. William E. Gienapp goes so far as to say that Lincoln "is the one American president whose writings could be considered literature."[86] Lincoln's eloquence was not something that simply occurred; it came as a result of long and careful study. In *The Committed Word* James Engell points out that most Lincoln scholars have failed to appreciate the significance of the fact that the young Lincoln's library contained two standard textbooks of rhetoric, complete with commentary and examples.[87] One was William Scott's *Lessons in Elocution,* and the other was Lindley Murray's *English Reader.* In addition, Lincoln read, in excerpted form, volumes by James Beattie and Hugh Blair, two Scottish "New Rhetoricians." Lincoln studied his rhetoric books assiduously, going so far as to write out and memorize the passages of which he was most fond. And later Lincoln would not only quote from the anthologized speeches; he would also adopt the commentators' advice. In speaking, Lincoln was reported to have a "peculiar cadence" in his voice, caused by "laying emphasis upon the key-word of the sentence."[88] Lincoln's emphasis of key words—what Mark Twain later called "crash words"—can be traced back to Thomas Sheridan's *Elocution* (a precursor to Scott's *Lessons*), which advocated the stressing of one (and only one) word in each complete sentence.[89]

Engell also points out that Lincoln adopted much more than means of emphasis from his rhetoric textbooks and speech anthologies. Stressing the tone of *pietas* in his formal addresses, and his repeated use of the themes of "piety and virtue," Engell argues persuasively that Lincoln's rhetoric bears the defining marks of eighteenth century

English letters and criticism.[90] The following speech appears to be guided by such a principle.

Still, it is the exceptions to the rule that often prove most interesting, and Lincoln's antiwar speech is all the more remarkable for the localized, but often radical, departure from the measured tone that characterizes the other speeches of Lincoln's political career. In contrast to the House Divided speech, the Gettysburg Address, both of Lincoln's Inaugurals, and many other speeches, Lincoln's antiwar address evinces a rare venomousness. Poet and Lincoln historian Carl Sandburg has noted this discrepancy, writing that the January 12 speech was delivered "in a style Lincoln would in time abandon."[91] Historian William Lee Miller, commenting on Lincoln's "extravagant personal tone" and "insistent narrowness," puts it another way: "A large part of the mature Lincoln's genius will be the depth and care and courtesy with which he expresses the political moralities of the actual situation." On January 12, "he does not do that," but instead levels a "surprisingly personal" and even "nasty" attack on Polk in a way "not characteristic of Lincoln."[92] Of course, though not characteristic of Lincoln, the speech's bitter tone evidences an almost ubiquitous characteristic of antiwar addresses throughout American history.[93]

MR. CHAIRMAN:

Some, if not all, [of] the gentlemen on the other side of the House, who have addressed the committee within the last two days, have spoken rather complainingly, if I have rightly understood them, of the vote given a week or ten days ago, declaring that the war with Mexico was unnecessarily and unconstitutionally commenced by the President. I admit that such a vote should not be given in mere party wantonness, and that the one given is justly censurable, if it have no other or better foundation. I am one of those who joined in that vote; and I did so under my best impression of the *truth* of the case. How I got this impression, and how it may possibly be removed, I will now try to show. When the war began, it was my opinion that all those who, because of knowing too *little,* or because of knowing too *much,* could not conscientiously approve the conduct of the President, (in the beginning of it,) should, nevertheless, as good citizens and patriots, remain silent on that point, at least till the war should be ended. Some leading Democrats, including ex-President Van Buren, have taken this same view, as I understand them; and I adhered to it and acted upon it, until since I took my seat here; and I think I should still adhere to it, were it not that the President and his friends will not allow it to be so. Besides, the continual effort of the President to argue every silent vote given for supplies into an endorsement of the justice and wisdom of his conduct; besides that singularly candid paragraph in his late message, in which he tells us that Congress, with great unanimity, (only two in the Senate and fourteen in the House dissenting,) had declared that "by the act of the Republic of Mexico a state of war exists between that Government and the United States;" when the same journals that informed him of this, also informed him that, when that declaration stood disconnected from the question of supplies, sixty-seven in the House, and not fourteen, merely, voted against it; besides this open attempt to prove by telling the *truth,* what he could not prove by telling the *whole truth,* demanding of all who will not submit to be misrepresented, in justice to themselves, to speak out; besides all this, one of my colleagues, [Mr. RICHARDSON,] at a very early day in the session, brought in a set of resolutions, expressly endorsing the original justice of the war on the part of the President. Upon these resolutions, when they shall be put on their passage, I shall be *compelled* to vote; so that I cannot be silent if I would. Seeing this, I went about preparing myself to give the vote understandingly, when it should come. I carefully examined the President's messages, to ascertain what he himself had said and proved upon the point. The result of this examination was to make the impression, that, taking for true all the President states as facts, he falls far short of proving his justification; and that the President would have gone further with his proof, if it had not been for the small matter that the *truth* would not permit him. . . .

. . . My way of living leads me to be about the courts of justice; and there I have sometimes seen a good lawyer, struggling for his client's neck, in a desperate case, employing every artifice to work round, befog, and cover up with many words some position pressed upon him by the prosecution, which he *dared* not admit, and yet *could* not deny. Party bias may help to make it appear so; but, with all the allowance I can make for such bias, it still does appear to me that just such, and from just such necessity, is the President's struggles in this case.

Some time after my colleague [Mr. RICHARDSON] introduced the resolutions I have mentioned, I introduced a preamble, resolution, and interrogatories,[94] intended to draw the President out, if possible, on this hitherto untrodden ground. . . .

. . . [L]et the President answer the interrogatories I proposed. . . . Let him answer fully, fairly, and candidly. Let him answer with *facts,* and not with arguments. Let him remember he sits where Washington sat; and, so remembering, let him answer as Washington would answer. As a nation *should* not, and the Almighty *will* not, be evaded, so let him attempt no evasion, no equivocation. And if, so answering, he can show that the soil was ours where the first blood of the war was shed . . . then I am with him for his justification. In that case, I shall be most happy to reverse the vote I gave the other day. . . . But if he *cannot* or *will not* do this—if, on any pretence, or no pretence, he shall refuse or omit it—then I shall be fully convinced of what I more than suspect already, that he is deeply conscious of being in the wrong; that he feels the blood of this war, like the blood of Abel, is crying to Heaven against him; that he ordered General Taylor into the midst of a peaceful Mexican settlement, purposely to bring on a war; that originally having some strong motive—what I will not stop now to give my opinion concerning—to involve the two countries in a war, and trusting to escape scrutiny by fixing the public gaze upon the exceeding brightness of military glory—that attractive rainbow that rises in showers of blood—that serpent's eye that charms to destroy—he plunged into it, and has swept *on* and *on,* till, disappointed in his calculation of the ease with which Mexico might be subdued, he now finds himself he knows not where. How like the half insane mumbling of a fever dream is the whole war part of the late message! At one time telling us that Mexico has nothing whatever that we can get but territory; at another, showing us how we can support the war by levying contributions on Mexico. At one time urging the national honor, the security of the future, the prevention of foreign interference, and even the good of Mexico herself, as among the objects of the war; at another, telling us that, "to reject indemnity by refusing to accept a cession of territory, would be to abandon all our just demands, and to wage the war, bearing all its expenses, *without a purpose or definite object.*" So, then, the national honor, security of the future, and everything but territorial indemnity, may be considered the *no-purposes* and *indefinite* objects of the war! But, having it now settled that territorial indemnity is the only object, we are urged to seize, by legislation here, all that he was content to take a few months ago, and the whole province of Lower California to boot, and to still carry on the war—to take *all* we are fighting for, and *still* fight on. Again, the President is resolved, under all circumstances, to have full territorial indemnity for the expenses of the war; but he forgets to tell us how we are to get the *excess* after those expenses shall have surpassed the value of the *whole* of the Mexican territory. So, again, he insists that the separate national existence of Mexico shall be maintained; but he does not tell us *how* this can be done, after we shall have taken *all* her territory. Lest the questions I here suggest be considered speculative merely, let me be indulged a moment in trying to show they are not.

The war has gone on some twenty months; for the expenses of which, together with an inconsiderable old score, the President now claims about one-half of the Mexican territory, and that by far the better half, so far as concerns our ability to make anything out of it. *It* is comparatively uninhabited; so that we could establish land offices in it, and raise some money in that way. But the other half is already inhabited, as I understand it, tolerably densely for the nature of the country; and all its lands, or all that are valuable, already appropriated as private property. How, then, are we to make anything out of these lands with this encumbrance on them, or how remove the encumbrance? I suppose no one will say we should kill the people, or drive them out, or make slaves of them, or even confiscate their property? How, then, can we make much out of this part of the territory? If the prosecution of the war has, in expenses, already equalled the *better* half of the country, how long its future prosecution will be in equalling the less valuable half is not a *speculative,* but a *practical* question, pressing closely upon us; and yet it is a question which the President seems never to have thought of.

As to the mode of terminating the war and securing peace, the President is equally wandering and indefinite. First, it is to be done by a more vigorous prosecution of the war in the vital parts of the enemy's country; and, after apparently talking himself tired on this point, the President drops down into a half despairing tone, and tells us, that "with a people distracted and divided by contending factions, and a Government subject to constant changes, by successive revolutions, *the continued success of our arms may fail to obtain a satisfactory peace.*" Then he suggests the propriety of wheedling the Mexican people to desert the counsels of their own leaders, and, trusting in our protection, to set up a Government from which we can secure a satisfactory peace, telling us tha[t] "*this may become the only mode of obtaining such a peace.*" But soon he falls into doubt of this too, and then drops back on to the already half-abandoned ground of "more vigorous prosecution." All this shows that the President is in no wise satisfied with his own positions. First, he takes up one, and in attempting to argue us *into* it, he argues himself *out* of it; then seizes another and goes through the same process; and then, confused at being able to think of nothing new, he snatches up the old one again, which he has some time before cast off. His mind, tasked beyond its power, is running hither and thither, like some tortured creature on a burning surface, finding no position on which it can settle down, and be at ease.[95]

Again, it is a singular omission in this message, that it nowhere intimates *when* the President expects the war to terminate. At its beginning, General Scott was, by this same President, driven into disfavor, if not disgrace, for intimating that peace could not be conquered in less than three or four months. But now, at the end of about twenty months, during which time our arms have given us the most splendid successes—every department and every part, land and water, officers and privates, regulars and volunteers, doing all that men *could* do, and hundreds of things which it had ever before been thought men could *not* do; after all this, this same President gives a long message without showing us that, *as to the end,* he has himself even an imaginary conception. As I have before said, he knows not where he is. He is a bewildered, confounded, and miserably-perplexed man. God grant he may be able to show there is not something about his conscience more painful than all his mental perplexity!

## Civil War (1861–1865)

The single most important postrevolutionary event in American history, the Civil War ended the institution of slavery in the United States. The war began shortly after Abraham Lincoln was elected president in 1860, and lasted four years. Though Lincoln swept the Northern states, he did not receive a single electoral vote in the South. Starting in December, Southern states began to secede from the Union and formed a government led by former senator Jefferson Davis of Mississippi. The war itself was triggered by the Confederacy's attack on Fort Sumter in Charleston, South Carolina. Bloody battles throughout the country resulted in massive death tolls on both sides; more Americans lost their lives in the Civil War than any other war in American history. Of the approximately 3.2 million soldiers who fought,[1] 360,000 Union and 260,000 Confederate soldiers died.[2]

Antiwar speech-giving during the Civil War was severely muted. By suspending the writ of habeas corpus, Lincoln was able to imprison citizens without trial for as long as he saw fit, thereby establishing an effective deterrent against most anti-Union agitation. Government records peg the number of persons arrested by the federal government and confined indefinitely without trial in military prisons during the Civil War at 13,535.[3] This number may be incomplete,[4] however, and some estimates run as high as 38,000.[5] The preservation of wartime dissent simply was not a priority for Lincoln. "Must I shoot a simple-minded soldier boy who deserts, while I must not touch a hair of a wily agitator who induces him to desert?" Lincoln asked rhetorically in 1863.[6] "I think that in such a case, to silence the agitator, and save the boy, is not only constitutional, but, withal, a great mercy."[7]

Some antiwar speechifying nevertheless occurred. Major addresses were given by members of Congress, who enjoyed protection from arrest by virtue of the Speech and Debate clause of the Constitution.[8] Congressional antiwar dissenters were dubbed "Peace Democrats" or derisively called "Copperheads" for their supposed similarity to the poisonous snake.[9] In this anthology, I include representative speeches by Clement L. Vallandigham and Alexander Long, two members of the U.S. House of Representatives from Ohio who were both extremely critical of Lincoln and his policies. Vallandigham argued that the war could not be won, and Long went even further by questioning the war's legal basis and suggesting that the Confederacy's secession did not violate the Constitution. As one scholar put it, the representatives were saying things in the House for which they would have been arrested had they spoken in the street.[10]

## Clement Vallandigham Argues That the War Cannot Be Won

[Y]ou have not conquered the South. You never will.

In the early morning hours of May 5, 1863, sixty-seven militiamen surrounded the Dayton home of Clement L. Vallandigham, a recently ousted United States representative from Ohio. Vallandigham was the most visible leader of the Peace Democrats, or the so-called Copperheads, who opposed the president's prosecution of the Civil War. Major General Ambrose Burnside, a Lincoln appointee who presided over a newly organized military district that included Ohio, had instructed the militia to capture him in a predawn raid. Awakened by the gathering troops, Vallandigham rushed to the window to summon the Dayton police. But he was too late. As he opened the window, soldiers broke down the back door and stormed the house. Thirty minutes from the time that Vallandigham, a civilian, awoke in the middle of the night, he was being shuttled under military escort to Kemper Barracks, a military prison in Cincinnati.[11]

So began a controversy that would embroil the country in a debate over civil liberties in wartime and fascinate constitutional scholars and practitioners up to the present day.[12] Because the events surrounding Vallandigham's clandestine arrest (his "disloyal" antiwar speech days before, his imprisonment days after, and his ultimate banishment from the Union by President Lincoln[13]) are so dramatic, it is easy forget the eloquence with which Vallandigham spoke. Though some historians have noted Vallandigham's ability to create sound bites,[14] as well as his quirky megalomania (he once proclaimed himself in Congress "as good a Western fire-eater as the hottest salamander in this House"[15]), his speeches remain almost completely ignored.[16] Even the speech that landed Vallandigham in jail has been omitted from the historical record—it has still never been reprinted.[17] The story of Vallandigham is one in which victor's justice has prevailed: the history of his opposition to the Civil War is one clearly written by the winners.

In selecting one of Vallandigham's many antiwar speeches, I have chosen to portray Vallandigham at his best, for history has already documented his worst. In the lowest depth of his public career, Vallandigham was a committed obstructionist, a devout racist,[18] an often bitter and always self-important congressman, an uncompromising and prideful pest.[19] At his best, though, Vallandigham was a disciplined, self-made man who dedicated himself to public service, and resolved to end the war in a way that would leave the Union intact. In this very specific and limited way—and only in this way—despite his fiery rhetoric, Vallandigham was a moderate. Unlike fellow Peace Democrats James A. Bayard, William B. Reed, and Alexander Long, Vallandigham did not argue that the Confederacy ought to be recognized as a separate nation. Instead, he proposed that both sides withdraw their troops and declare a three-year interregnum during which "time [would] do his office—drying tears, dispelling sorrows, mellowing passions, and making herb and grass and tree grow again upon the hundred battle-fields of this terrible war."[20] At his best, Vallandigham was also a brilliant orator who captivated supporters and opponents alike with his grasp of history, his sense of humor, and the sheer beauty of his words.

Measured in terms of bipartisan acclaim, Vallandigham gave his best antiwar speech on January 14, 1863, to the United States House of Representatives. Upon completion of his speech—a well-prepared, formal bid to lead the antiwar movement, and, incidentally, one of the last speeches he gave in Congress—Democrats crowded around "their champion" and offered him congratulations with "faces wreathed in smiles."[21] "At a single step," the Washington correspondent for the *Cincinnati Gazette* observed, "the shunned and execrated Vallandigham has risen to the leadership of [his] party." "Deny it, as some of them still may" the *Gazette* continued, but "henceforth it is accomplished."[22] The *St. Louis Republican* noted that the House Republicans, for their part, received the speech "with remarkable and respectful attention." The speech was significant, the *Republican* added, as the first occasion in which Republicans "calmly listened to the semi-secession doctrines of Vallandigham, or any other peace man."[23]

Outside of Congress, the Democratic press hailed Vallandigham's address as "the crowning effort of his public life."[24] "No speech has been made in congress for years . . . that has been so universally admired," editorialized the *Cincinnati Enquirer*.[25] "It will be well if this nation ponders seriously and with judgment over the words of wisdom and burning eloquence," commented the *Columbus Crisis*.[26] Surprisingly, even the pro-Republican press offered Vallandigham qualified praise. The Congressman's "worst detractors" at the *Boston Globe* offered him grudging respect for uttering "words of brilliant and polished treason."[27]

Vallandigham never again won political office after his defeat in October 1862, although he did run for a variety of offices and was even nominated by the Democratic Party to run for governor of Ohio while in exile. Instead, in the closing months of the Civil War, Vallandigham returned to the United States to devote his energies to the practice of law. The bizarre circumstances of his death provide a fitting end to his unusual and remarkable life. In 1871, Vallandigham was defending a man accused of murder. In Vallandigham's hotel room during the evening before trial, Vallandigham attempted to demonstrate to opposing counsel how the decedent could have inadvertently killed himself. Eager to begin the demonstration, Vallandigham picked up the loaded pistol he had placed on his desk the day before, mistaking it for a similar, unloaded, one. Vallandigham won the case, but lost his life. He accidentally shot himself in the abdomen, and was dead before morning.

In the first part of the excerpt below, Vallandigham argues that his prewar prediction that "the South could never be conquered" had been vindicated by the Union Army's failure to win the war. In the second part, Vallandigham buttresses his argument by pointing to the massive resources at the Union's disposal: "Money and credit . . . you have had in prodigal profusion. And were men wanted? More than a million rushed to arms!" In the remainder of the excerpt, Vallandigham argues that the enormous number of Union fatalities serves as a painful reminder that "you have not conquered the South [and] never will."

Vallandigham's theme—the futility of war—is timeless, and his remarks on the topic are included in this anthology on that basis, but the excerpt below represents only a fraction of Vallandigham's breathless, fifteen-thousand-word speech. Vallandigham also was a fierce advocate of civil liberties (at least for white males), and believed that the war was emboldening President Lincoln's administration to exercise the "iron domination of arbitrary power." The history of the war so far, argued Vallandigham, was one in which "constitutional limitation was broken down; habeas corpus fell; liberty of the press, of speech, of the person, of the mails, of travel, of one's own house, and of religion; the right to bear arms, due process of law, judicial trial, trial by jury, trial at all." Vallandigham also endeavored to illustrate the North and South's economic interdependence and thereby establish that ending the war would be the self-interest of both sides. Finally, Vallandigham attempted to show that abolitionism's assumptions were unsound. For example, to Vallandigham, the Southern slave was not "panting for freedom," but "happy, contented, attached deeply to his master, and unwilling—at least not eager—to accept the precious boon of freedom." Thus, according to Vallandigham, one of the primary justifications for the war—the end of slavery—was not recognized by the very people for whose benefit the war was purportedly being fought.

Vallandigham delivered his antiwar speech on January 14, 1863, just a month after the Battle of Fredericksburg, where, from December 11 to December 15, 1862, Southern forces dealt the Union Army of one of its worst defeats and "brought home the horrors of war to northerners more vividly, perhaps, than any previous battle."[28] Nearly thirteen thousand Federals died at Fredericksburg, about the same number that had perished at Antietam in September. In contrast, the Confederates, fighting behind good cover, lost fewer than five thousand men. Such a defeat dealt a crushing blow to the Union's morale. The usually supportive *Harper's Weekly* wrote that the Union Army's supporters at home "cannot be expected to suffer that such massacres as this at Fredericksburg shall be repeated,"[29] and, as David Herbert Donald has pointed out, in the winter of 1862–63 volunteering in the Union Army almost stopped.[30] Thus, Vallandigham's bid to become an "apostle of peace" could hardly have been better timed, for he delivered it during one of the North's darkest moments in the Civil War.[31]

... [O]N THE 14TH OF APRIL,

I believed that coercion would bring on war, and war disunion. More than that, I believed, what you all in your hearts believe to-day, that the South could never be conquered—never. . . .

These were my convictions on the 14th of April. Had I changed them on the 15th, when I read the President's proclamation, and become convinced that I had been wrong all my life, and that all history was a fable, and all human nature false in its development from the beginning of time, I would have changed my public conduct also. But my convictions did not change. I thought that, if war was disunion on the 14th of April, it was equally disunion on the 15th, and at all times. Believing this, I could not, as an honest man, a Union man, and a patriot, lend an active support to the war; and I did not. I had rather my right arm were plucked from its socket, and cast into eternal burnings, than, with my convictions, to have thus defiled my soul with the guilt of moral perjury. Sir, I was not taught in that school which proclaims that "all is fair in politics." I loathe, abhor, and detest the execrable maxim. I stamp upon it. No State can endure a single generation whose public men practice it. Whoever teaches it is a corrupter of youth. What we most want in these times, and at all times, is honest and independent public men. That man who is dishonest in politics is not honest, at heart, in anything; and sometimes moral cowardice is dishonesty. Do right; and trust to God, and Truth, and the People. Perish office, perish honors, perish life itself; but do the thing that is right, and do it like a man. I did it. Certainly, sir, I could not doubt what he must suffer who dare defy the opinions and the passions, not to say the madness, of twenty millions of people. Had I not read history? Did I not know human nature? But I appealed to TIME, and right nobly hath the Avenger answered me. . . .

And now, sir, I recur to the state of the Union to-day. . . .

Money and credit . . . you have had in prodigal profusion. And were men wanted? More than a million rushed to arms! Seventy-five thousand first, (and the country stood aghast at the multitude), then eighty-three thousand more were demanded; and three hundred and ten thousand responded to the call. The President next asked for four hundred thousand, and Congress, in its generous confidence, gave him five hundred thousand; and, not to be outdone, he took six hundred and thirty-seven thousand. Half of these melted away in their first campaign; and the President demanded three hundred thousand more for the war, and then drafted yet another three hundred thousand for nine months. The fabled hosts of Xerxes have been outnumbered. And yet victory strangely follows the standards of the foe. From Great Bethel to Vicksburg, the battle has not been to the strong. Yet every disaster, except the last, has been followed by a call for more troops, and every time so far they have been promptly furnished. From the beginning the war has been conducted like a political campaign, and it has been the folly of the party in power that they have assumed that numbers alone would win the field in a contest not with ballots but with musket and sword. But numbers you have had almost without number—the largest, best appointed, best armed, fed, and clad host of brave men, well organized and well disciplined, ever marshaled. A Navy, too, not the most formidable perhaps, but the most numerous and gallant, and the costliest in the world, and against a foe almost without a navy at all. Thus with twenty millions of people, and every element of strength and force at command—power, patronage, influence, unanimity, enthusiasm, confidence, credit, money, men, an Army and a Navy the largest and the noblest ever set in the field or afloat upon the sea; with the support, almost servile, of every State, county, and municipality in the North and West; with a Congress swift to do the bidding of the Executive; without opposition anywhere at home, and with an arbitrary power with which neither the Czar of Russia nor the Emperor of Austria dare exercise; yet after nearly two years of more vigorous prosecution of war than ever recorded in history; after more skirmishes, combats and battles than Alexander,

Caesar, or the first Napoleon ever fought in any five years of their military career, you have utterly, signally, disastrously—I will not say ignominiously—failed to subdue ten millions of "rebels," whom you had taught the people of the North and West not only to hate but to despise. Rebels, did I say? Yes, your fathers were rebels, or your grandfathers. He who now before me on canvas looks down so sadly upon us, the false, degenerate, and imbecile guardians of the great Republic which he founded, was a rebel. And yet we, cradled ourselves in rebellion, and who have fostered and fraternized with every insurrection in the nineteenth century everywhere throughout the globe, would now, forsooth, make the word "rebel" a reproach. Rebels certainly they are; but all the persistent and stupendous efforts of the most gigantic warfare of modern times have, through your incompetency and folly, availed nothing to crush them out, cut off though they have been, by your blockade from all the world, and dependent only upon their own courage and resources. And yet they were to be utterly conquered and subdued in six weeks, or three months! Sir, my judgment was made up, and expressed from the first. I learned it from Chatham: "My lords, you cannot conquer America." And you have not conquered the South. You never will. It is not in the nature of things possible; much less under your auspices. But money you have expended without limit, and blood poured out like water. Defeat, debt, taxation, sepulchres, these are your trophies. In vain, the people gave you treasure, and the soldier yielded up his life. "Fight, tax, emancipate, let these," said the gentleman from Maine, [Mr. Pike,] at the last session, "be the trinity of our salvation." Sir, they have become the trinity of your deep damnation. The war for the Union is, in your hands, a most bloody and costly failure. The President confessed it on the 22d of September, solemnly, officially, and under the broad seal of the United States. And he has now repeated the confession. The priests and rabbis of abolition taught him that God would not prosper such a cause. War for the Union was abandoned; war for the negro openly begun, and with stronger battalions than before. With what success? Let the dead at Fredericksburg and Vicksburg answer.

And now, sir, can this war continue? Whence the money to carry it on? Where the men? Can you borrow? From whom? Can you tax more? Will the people bear it? Wait till you have collected what is already levied. How many millions more of "legal tender"—to-day forty-seven per cent. below the par of gold—can you float? Will men enlist now at any price? Ah, sir, it is easier to die at home. I beg pardon; but I trust I am not "discouraging enlistments." If I am, then first arrest Lincoln, Stanton, and Halleck, and some of your other generals; and I will retract; yes, I will recant. But can you draft again? Ask New England—New York. Ask Massachusetts. Where are the nine hundred thousand? Ask not Ohio—the Northwest. She thought you were in earnest, and gave you all, all—more than you demanded.

> "The wife whose babe first smiled that day,
>     The fair, fond bride of yester eve,
> And aged sire and matron gray,
> Saw the loved warriors haste away,
>     And deemed it sin to grieve."[32]

Sir, in blood she has atoned for her credulity; and now there is mourning in every house, and distress and sadness in every heart. Shall she give you any more?

## Alexander Long Proposes Peace at Any Price

It is the object of the sword to cut and cleave asunder, but
never to unite.

Antiwar speakers are usually animated by a feeling that their purpose is not merely to oppose war, but to help form a more perfect union. Paul Potter stated this idea explicitly at a 1965 protest march in Washington, D.C.: "What is exciting about the participants in this march is that so many of us view ourselves consciously as participants . . . in a movement to build a more decent society."[33] But though antiwar dissent during the Vietnam War provides ample evidence of this phenomenon, particularly when race-based, class-based, and postcolonial critiques championed by members of the civil rights movement bled into the burgeoning antiwar struggle (Muhammad Ali would famously say, for example, "No Vietcong ever called me Nigger"), antiwar dissent during the Civil War provides perhaps the best example of a way in which a national conversation about the war served merely as the stage upon which a more important conversation about the meaning of American democracy could take place.[34]

Thus, United States representative from Ohio Alexander Long argued in 1864 that the Civil War violated "the fundamental principles on which the federal Union was founded."[35] It is the exposition of these principles that make Long's speech so interesting and, at the same time, so dangerous. Long suggested that the fundamental principles upon which the federal Union was founded are both legal and supralegal. Legally, Long explained, Southern states had the power, if not the right, to secede from the Union. As precedent, Long quoted, among others, then-congressman Abraham Lincoln, who had said during his own antiwar speech on January 12, 1848, that "any people, anywhere, being inclined and having the power, have a right to rise up and *shake off the existing Government,* and form a *new one* that suits *them* better."[36]

Supralegally, Long argued that a principle of American democracy lay in its recognition that a commonality of interests is essential to American government and, conversely, that fundamentally opposed interests among the states would render that government "vain and nugatory."[37] Furthermore, these common interests seemed to precede the law; in other words, they animated the constitutional compact, giving it meaning and strength. As Long put it, quoting John Quincy Adams, "the indissoluble link of union between the people of several States of this confederated nation is, after all, not in the *right* but in the *heart.*"[38]

The excerpt of Long's speech that appears below should be understood in light of Long's supralegal principle of American democracy. Long perceived the South's interests to be fundamentally opposed to those of the North, and so believed that the antebellum union had *already* been lost and could never be restored. As a foreign entity, an "independent power de facto," the South had "cut asunder the ligaments" binding the two regions together. To recognize the South as a legally distinct political entity, then, would simply be to acknowledge the reality that the North and the South were vastly different. To refuse the legal recognition, however, would result in the destruction or, to use Long's term, the "conquest," of a people. Long wanted to avoid this type of cultural holocaust at all costs.

Despite the fact that the Civil War is the only *civil* war in this anthology, and that Long's assumptions regarding the merits of a slave society are predicated on antiquated and debunked concepts of racial inferiority, the terms that Long uses to oppose war are nevertheless remarkably similar to those used in different times and places. Like many antiwar speakers who came before and after him, Long states that the war is having the opposite of its intended effect. Instead of serving to help unite the country, he argues, the war is sowing seeds of disunion; instead of preserving free democracy, the war is instating an oppressive dictatorship; instead of serving the noble principle of self-determination, the war has manifested a national thirst for property, aggrandizement, and empire. The familiarity of these themes suggests that they play an important role in antiwar speeches throughout history, and that they are much more than "mere rhetoric."

The reaction to Long's speech in the House of Representatives was swift and severe. It started on the floor of the House. Another representative from Ohio, James A. Garfield, called Long a traitor and, invoking John Milton's epic 1667 poem *Paradise Lost*, compared Long to Satan. Theatrically asking the congressional sergeant-at-arms to plant a white flag in the aisle between himself and Long, the future president of the United States praised Long's bravery and honesty for speaking his mind. But Garfield's tone soon changed, and, continuing to speak to the sergeant and the House, he issued a scathing and poetic indictment:

> But now I ask you to take away the flag of truce; and I will go back inside the Union lines, and speak of what he has done. I am reminded by it of a distinguished character in Paradise Lost. When he had rebelled against the glory of God and "led away a third part of heaven's sons, conjured against the Highest," when after terrible battles in which mountains and hills were hurled by each contending host "with 'jaculations dire;" when at last the leader and his hosts were hurled down "nine times the space that measures day and night," and after the terrible fall lay stretched prone on the burning lake, Satan lifted up his shattered bulk, crossed the abyss, looked down into Paradise, and, soliloquizing, said:
>
> "Which way I fly is hell; myself am hell."
>
> It seems to me in that utterance he expressed the very sentiment to which you have just listened; uttered by one no less brave, maligned, and fallen. This man gathers up the meaning of this great contest, the philosophy of the moment, the prophecies of the hour, and, in sight of the paradise of victory and peace, utters them all in this wail of terrible despair, "Which way I fly is hell." He ought to add, "Myself am hell." . . .

But now, when hundreds of thousands of brave souls have gone up to God under the shadow of the flag, and when thousands more, maimed and shattered in the contest, are sadly awaiting the deliverance of death; now, when three years of terrific warfare have raged over us, when our armies have pushed the rebellion back over mountains and rivers and crowded it back into narrow limits, until a wall of fire girds it; now, when the uplifted hand of a majestic people is about to let fall the lightning of its conquering power upon the rebellion; now, in the quiet of this Hall, hatched in the lowest depths of a similar dark treason, there rises a Benedict Arnold and proposes to surrender us all up, body and spirit, the nation and the flag, its genius and its honor, now and forever, to the accursed traitors to our country. And that proposition comes—God forgive and pity my beloved State!—it comes from a citizen of the honored and loyal Commonwealth of Ohio.

I implore you, brethren in this House, not to believe that many such births ever gave pangs to my mother State such as she suffered when that traitor was born. [Suppressed applause and sensation.] I beg you not to believe that on the soil of that State another such growth has ever deformed the face of nature and darkened the light of God's day. [An audible whisper, "Vallandigham."][39]

"But ah," Garfield continued, after the accusation of treason had been hurled and much of the damage done, "I am reminded that there are other such." Continuing sarcastically, he offered, "My zeal and love for Ohio have carried me too far. I retract."[40]

Long had an equally biting reply, stating to the House that "the difference between him and me to-day is that while he would violate that oath which he took before that desk the first day of the session, and would overleap the barriers of the Constitution which he has sworn to support, I choose rather to stand on this floor and be denounced as a traitor for keeping my obligation to my country, to my own conscience, and to my God."[41] He continued in the same self-righteous vein:

I choose rather to consult my own conscience and judgment than to follow his lead in the ranks of a party that is always ready to take the oath to support the Constitution with a mental reservation. I have never so taken it, and so help me God, I never will. I will support the Constitution despite the threats which may be brought from any quarter, and with the fixed purpose and full determination to stand upon the principles which I have avowed here to-day if I stand solitary and alone, even if it were necessary to brave bayonets and prisons and all the tyranny which may be imposed by the whole power and force of the Administration. I have deliberately uttered my sentiments in that speech, and I will not retract one syllable of it.[42]

"Give me liberty," Long concluded, alluding to Patrick Henry's historic "give me liberty, or give me death" peroration in 1775, "even if confined to an island of Greece or a canton of Switzerland, rather than an empire and a despotism, as we have here to-day."[43]

Garfield's denunciations on April 8 were only the beginning of a much larger onslaught aimed at Long that ended, finally, with his defeat in the election of 1864. On the morning of April 9, for example, Schuyler Colfax, a Republican representative from Indiana and also the speaker of the House, immediately introduced an expulsion resolution: "*Resolved,* That Alexander Long, a representative from the second district of Ohio, having, on the 8th of April, 1864, declared himself in favor of recognizing the independence and nationality of the so-called confederacy now in arms against the Union, and thereby 'given aid, countenance and encouragement to persons engaged in armed hostility to the United States,' is hereby expelled."[44] Colfax explained that he owed the resolution to expel Long not only to Colfax's constituents in Indiana, but to his constituents on the battlefield and "to the many widowed and orphaned families in the district whose natural protectors have been stricken down by the bloodied hands of treason, and lost to them in this world forever."[45]

The Colfax resolution eventually failed for lack of support, but no sooner had the resolution been withdrawn than Republican representatives substituted a censure resolution in its place: "*Resolved,* That said ALEXANDER LONG, a Representative from the second district of Ohio, be, and is hereby, declared to be an unworthy member of the House of Representatives.[46] The censure resolution passed, eighty yeas to sixty-nine nays, on April 14, 1864.[47] By that time, as the *Cincinnati Daily Commercial* reported, the proceedings had captivated the House for nearly one week: fully twenty-six speeches had already been given in the debate over Long's address.[48]

Some Union soldiers sent Long hate mail and death threats. One soldier wrote to Long on April 12 that "500,000 Men of the Union Army would ten times *rather* shoot you and *all* of your traitorous crew than fight the nearest Rebel in Arms. They are infinitely more honorable than you."[49] Another soldier threatened Long's life.[50] Underneath the resentment, though, there is some evidence that Long's speech did, at the very least, make some Union soldiers think twice about the likelihood of a Union victory. Writing privately to his wife in Ohio on April 17, 1864, one distinguished Union officer, Rufus Robinson Dawes, wrote that "the manner in which the whole opposition party in Congress has shown sympathy for the traitorous sentiments of Representative Long, of Ohio, has created a profound impression in the army. It is asked how many reverses to our plans and our arms will bring the great political party these people represent to Mr. Long's conviction of the necessity of recognition. They have shown favor to Mr. Long's avowal upon the floor of Congress of his conviction of our defeat, and of the triumph of our enemy."[51] Indeed, as Dawes implies, Long did receive some support along party lines. A number of newspapers, friends, and congressmen came to Long's aid. The sympathetic *Cincinnati Enquirer* (apparently forgetting the praise it had heaped upon Vallandigham's speech in Congress in January of the previous year[52]) wrote on April 10 that Long's speech was "the first words of free speech spoken in the halls of Congress for three long years."[53] On April 12, it wrote that Long's speech "hit where it was intended to hit and hurt."[54] There were reports that one ward in Ohio held a meeting on April 19 and formally approved Long's proposal. However, as the *Cincinnati Daily Commercial* pointed out, fewer than 150 persons attended, and instead of demonstrating the vitality of peace sentiment, the meeting illustrated the party's feebleness.[55] Representative Benjamin G. Harris of Maryland aligned himself with Long, and was himself then targeted for expulsion by Elihu B. Washburne, a Republican congressman from Illinois.[56] When this latter measure failed, Representative Fernando Wood from New York told Congress that he too shared Long's sentiments, and desired to be included in the expulsion resolution as well.[57]

On July 9, 1864, Long received a hero's welcome upon returning to Ohio's Second District. With a banner inscribed with the words "Peace and State Rights" hanging in the background, a local lawyer and politician, William M. Corry, welcomed Long by stating that Long was his constituents' "true representative in all he so boldly spoke for peace in preference to the extermination of the southern people, and for the immediate termination of the war."[58] "We are here," Corry continued, "to share the censure with him by solemnly assuming the very same responsibility."[59]

Long spoke at the welcome rally as well, defiantly stating that subsequent events and reconsideration had further convinced him of the correctness of his April 8 speech[60] and the priority of states' rights: "The conclusion to which I arrive is, that the people of each State constitute substantially a sovereign nation, that each one, by the adoption of the Federal Constitution, and also of a State Constitution, created for itself two distinct governments or agents, upon each of which it conferred certain specified powers, and that the powers of one or both of these agents may be revoked by the people of any State themselves, whenever, in their sovereign will, such revocation may become desirable."[61] The winds of public opinion, according to Long, were at his back: "I believe the people," he stated, "the great mass of the people, who neither hold office nor are in any way benefited by government contracts, or government patronage, are for peace."[62] As for the majority of the democratically elected House that had officially censured him, Long argued that his prosecution only illustrated the "blindness of party rage and terrible vindictiveness of political passion."[63] Defying his detractors, he promised to continue working for peace despite the likelihood that he would be victimized again by "cowardly minions of power who fear open discussion, shut themselves up in Loyal Leagues and plot treason at midnight."[64] Despite an effigy with Long's name found hanging from a tree and that Long supporters promptly tore down, Long apparently received enthusiastic support from the rally's attendees. After the band played a patriotic march, they passed resolutions calling for the endorsement of Long's April 8 speech, the advocacy of immediate peace, the opposition to federal coercion of sovereign states, and even Long's candidacy for the presidency of the United States in the next election.[65]

All things considered, it appears that the real significance of Long's speech was not the enmity it spawned among some, or the respect it garnered among others. Rather, the speech seems to have "played havoc" within Long's Democratic Party and helped widen a growing gap between different factions of the antiwar contingent.[66] As the *Cincinnati Daily Times* observed, there now existed a rift between "war" and "peace" Democrats.[67] Because Long had advocated the extreme position of secession and disunion, Democrats were forced to "reconsider, redefine and possible to realign themselves within the party structure."[68] After Long spoke, the Democrats were unable to close ranks; the speech produced a schism among the Peace Democrats between the "ultraconservative" Long and the relatively moderate Vallandigham.[69]

In other words, the speech completely backfired. Far from being the lodestone of antiwar sentiment Long intended it to be, the speech counteracted the Democratic Party's more practicable antiwar policy of compromise, and, as the *New York Times* editorialized, evidenced Long's political impotence:

> The vast majority of the Northern people ever have been, and ever will be, firm as adamant in their determination to save this Republic undivided from the Lakes to the Gulf. The speeches of such men as ALEXANDER LONG have no more effect upon that determination than pop-guns upon Gibraltar. The open peace men who stand under their own white flag where they can be seen and known, are impotent. They who, with peace in their hearts, stand under the war flag, plotting all the while how to balk its true defenders and bring it to the dust, are the men to be feared. And we say that when an Anti-Administration Member of Congress plants himself boldly on peace ground and tells the dissemblers of his party that they are in a false position—that honor and consistency demand that they should either sustain the Administration or else move squarely over to his place—he has rendered a positive service to the Government and deserves thanks rather than expulsion.[70]

After Long's speech, the Peace Democrats seemed to lose their vitality. As Louise Heidish has observed, the Lincoln supporters and party operatives in the presidential election of 1864 tried to exploit Long's speech to their political advantage by using it as a piece of *Republican* propaganda: in fact, it was the Republicans, not the Democrats, who ordered large numbers of Long's speech to be distributed prior to the 1864 presidential election.

MR. CHAIRMAN,

I speak to-day for the preservation of the Government, and although for the first time within these walls, I propose to indulge in that freedom of speech and latitude of debate so freely exercised by other gentleman for the past four months, and which is admissible under the rules in the present condition of the House. But for what I may say and the position I shall occupy upon this floor and before the country I alone will be responsible, and in the independence of a Representative of the people I intend to proclaim the deliberate convictions of my judgment in this fearful hour of the country's peril. . . .

I regret as much, Mr. Chairman, as any gentleman upon this floor, that any of our sister States should have desired to cut asunder the ligaments that bound them to us. None would be more willing than myself to make any reasonable sacrifice to induce them to return to their partnership with us; but still recognizing the truth of the doctrine taught by the fathers of the Republic and so fairly expressed by Mr. John Quincy Adams, that our Government was, after all, in the *heart,* and that it would be better, severe as would be the pang of regret, to part in friendship rather than to hold sovereign States pinned to us by the bayonet, as Mr. Greeley expressed it in 1861. What advance have we made in the science and principles of government?

Mr. Chairman, if we cannot rise above the Austro-Russian principle of holding subject provinces by the power of force and coercion, what becomes of the Declaration of Independence, and of all our teachings for eighty years? After all, Mr. Chairman, it is not the extent of territory which should be the object of our desires. Better sacrifice even nine tenths of the territory than destroy our republican form of government. What our people desired in 1861, and which I honored, though I regarded as mistaken, was the preservation of the Government and the retention of our jurisdiction of the whole territory. They were rightly willing to sacrifice every material consideration for that purpose. Land is nothing, Mr. Chairman, compared to liberty. We existed as a Republic when the mouth of the Mississippi was held by a foreign Power, when we had nothing west of that river; when Florida was held against us; and we could exist again, if by the chastisement of Heaven we should be curtailed to our old territorial dimensions. For $15,000,000 we purchased the whole of that immense territory; and were it a hundred thousand times as valuable its preservation would not be worth our admirable form of government.

Pride of territorial ambition is a vulgar and low ambition of national greatness. Russia, and even China, can vie with us in that, but who would not rather reside in one of the cantons of Switzerland, or in Great Britain, than in those countries? It is not in the extent of territory we possess, but in the manner in which we govern it that renders us respectable. Many gentlemen seem rather to look at the quantity than the quality. All republics have been destroyed by the thirst of territorial aggrandizement and the lust of conquest. The great object of our Government should be to develop and cultivate the internal resources of those friendly to its jurisdiction, rather than to extend it over hostile and foreign peoples. It is in that character that true patriotism is to be cultivated and true national glory found. Especially should all republics cultivate the arts of peace, since it is by the war power that free Governments are commonly overturned.

The charge has been made that democracy is turbulent, warlike, and aggressive, but if so, it is a terrible misconception of its true interests, for upon the people fall the awful calamities of armed collisions. An eminent poet (Lord Byron) has said that war was a game which, if the people were wise, kings and princes would never play at. The venerable Dr. Franklin, at the close of his illustrious career, remarked that there never was a good war and a bad peace. We have made, Mr. Chairman, by this war, eight million bitter enemies upon the American continent. While time shall last the recollections of this bloody strife will never fade from the memories of the people, North and South, but will be handed down to the latest generation. The words Shiloh, Antietam, Gettysburg, Murfreesboro', Richmond, Vicksburg, and Fort Donelson, are words of division and disunion, and will serve to bring emotions of eternal hate. If it was true, as was suggested by a distinguished Senator from Ohio [Mr. WADE] in a speech in Portland in 1855, that he believed "that no two nations on earth hated each other as much as the North and South," how much more true is the remark now after they have been arrayed in such bloody conquests.

[Here the hammer fell.]

Mr. WASHBURNE, of Illinois. As the speech of the gentleman from Ohio is the keynote of the Democratic party in the coming election, I hope there will be no objection to his finishing his speech. [Cries of "Order!"] It means recognition of the confederacy by foreign Powers, and peace upon terms of disunion. [Renewed cries of "Order!"]

No objection being made,

Mr. LONG proceeded: It is the object of the sword to cut and cleave asunder, but never to unite. What union is there between Russia and Poland, between Austria and Hungary, between England and Catholic Ireland, where the sword and the bayonet for centuries have been employed? Instead of conferring national strength, they are sources of weakness to the countries that hold them in subjection; and which would this day be stronger without them than with them.

Mr. Chairman, these lessons of history are full of warning and example. Much better would it have been for us in the beginning, much better would it be for us now, to consent to a division of our magnificent empire and cultivate amicable relations with our estranged brethren, than to seek to hold them to us by the power of the sword. . . .

. . . As will be judged, perhaps, by the tenor of these remarks, I am reluctantly and despondingly forced to the conclusion that the Union is lost never to be restored. I regard all dreams of the restoration of the Union which was the pride of my life, and to restore which even now I would pour out my heart's blood, as worse than idle. I see, neither North nor South, any sentiment on which it is possible to build a Union. Those elements of Union which Mr. Adams described have, by the process of time, been destroyed. Worse, yea, worse than that, Mr. Chairman, I am reluctantly forced to the conclusion that in attempting to preserve our jurisdiction over the southern States we have lost our constitutional form of government over the northern. What has been predicted by our wisest and most eminent statesmen has come to pass; in grasping at the shadow we have lost the substance; in striving to retain the casket of liberty in which our jewels were confined we have lost those precious muniments of freedom. Our Government, as all know, is not anything resembling what it was three years ago; there is not one single vestige of the Constitution remaining; every clause and every letter of it has been violated, and I have no idea myself that it will ever again be respected; revolutions never go backward to the point at which they started. There has always been a large party in this country favorable to a strong or monarchical Government, and they have now all ele- ments upon which to establish one: they have a vast army, an immense public debt, and an irresponsible Executive. Ambitious to retain power, he is a candidate for reëlection. . . .

The very idea upon which this war is founded, coercion of States, leads to despotism. To preserve a republican form of government under any constitution, under the preva- lence of the doctrines now in vogue, is clearly impossible. These convictions of the complete overthrow of our Government are as unwelcome and unpleasant to me as they are to any member of this House. Would to God the facts were such that I could cherish other convictions. I may be denounced as disloyal and unpatriotic for entertaining them, but it will only be by shallow fools and arrant knaves, who do not know or will not admit the difference between recognizing a fact and creating its existence. A man may not desire to die, but nevertheless his belief will not alter the fact of his mortality.

I shall not, in these remarks, recur to the unpleasant and acrimonious controversy of who is responsible for the death and destruction of our Republic. I do not see that any such discussion now would be productive of good. I entertain clear and strong convictions upon that point, convictions that I have no doubt will be shared in by the impartial historian of the future; for the present I am willing to let the past with all its recollections rest, provided we can snatch from the common ruin some of our old relics of freedom.

I do not share in the belief entertained by many of my political friends on this floor and elsewhere, that any peace is attainable upon the basis of union and reconstruction. If the Democratic party were in power to-day I have no idea, and honesty compels me to declare it, that they could restore the Union of thirty-four States. My mind has undergone an entire change upon that subject; and I now believe that there are but two alternatives, and they are either an acknowledgment of the independence of the South as an independent nation, or their complete subjugation and extermination as a people; and of these alternatives I prefer the former.

Mr. Chairman, I take little or no interest in the discussion of the question which many of my political friends would make an issue, as to how this war shall be prosecuted, its manner and object. I regard that as worse than trifling with the great question. I do not believe there can be any prosecution of the war against a sovereign State under the Constitution, and I do not believe that a war so carried on can be prosecuted so as to render it proper, justifiable, or expedient. *An unconstitutional war can only be carried on in an unconstitutional manner,* and to prosecute it further under the idea of the gentleman from Pennsylvania, [Mr. STEVENS,] as a war waged against the confederates as an independent nation, for the purpose of conquest and subjugation, as he proposes, and the Administration is in truth and in fact doing, I am equally opposed.

I say further, Mr. Chairman, that if this war is to be still further prosecuted, I, for one, prefer that it shall be done under the auspices of those who now conduct its management, as I do not want the party with which I am connected to be in any degree responsible for its result, which cannot be otherwise than disastrous and suicidal; let the responsibility remain where it is, until we can have a change of policy instead of men, if such a thing is possible. Nothing could be more fatal for the Democratic party than to seek to come into power pledged to a continuance of the war policy. Such a policy would be a libel upon its creed in the past and the ideas that lay at the basis of all free government, and would lead to its complete demoralization and ruin. I believe the masses of the Democratic party are for peace, that they would be placed in a false position if they should nominate a war candidate for the Presidency and seek to make the issue upon the narrow basis of how the war should be prosecuted.

For my own part, as I have already indicated, I fear that our old Government cannot be preserved, even under the best auspices and with any policy that may be now adopted, yet I desire to see the Democratic party, with which I have always been connected, preserve its consistency and republican character unshaken.

# Spanish-American War (1898-1899) and Philippine Insurrection (1899-1902)

The Spanish-American War and the Philippine Insurrection, two successive turn-of-the-century conflicts, are among the smallest wars covered in this anthology in terms of American fatalities. Nevertheless, they occupy an important place in American history. More than ever before, the United States claimed to be fighting on behalf of oppressed people outside its borders. And more than ever before, antiwar leaders attacked the U.S. government for subjugating the very populations the United States purported to liberate.

The Spanish-American War and the Philippine Insurrection also gave birth to two war-related terms used extensively in the twenty-first century. The first, "concentration camp," or a place in which noncombatants are placed during war, is usually associated with Germany in World War II or Lord Herbert Kitchener's policy during Great Britain's Second Boer War (1899–1902) in South Africa. However, the term is better attributed to the late nineteenth-century Spanish commander Arsenio Martinez Campos. In 1895, Campos was fending off a never-ending series of local insurgencies in the Spanish colony of Cuba.[1] Looking for a permanent end to the Cuban independence struggle, the conflict that ultimately resulted in the Spanish-American War, Campos confidentially proposed to the Spanish government to "reconcentrate" the civilian inhabitants of the rural districts into camps.[2] Although Campos conceded that the policy might lead to "misery and famine," it would also, he explained, deprive the insurgents of food, shelter, and support, thereby bringing the war to a more rapid conclusion.[3] While Campos did not carry out his policy, his successor, General Valeriano "Butcher" Weyler, did.[4]

The second term, "quagmire," meaning a difficult, precarious, or entrapping position, was applied in the context of war by Mark Twain. Since then, it has come to be used frequently in that context.[5] Speaking of the Philippine Insurrection, Twain stated in 1900 that "we have got into a mess, a quagmire from which each fresh step renders the difficulty of extrication immensely greater."[6]

The United States declared war on Spain over Cuba on April 25, 1898. American involvement is usually attributed to the mysterious explosion of the U.S. battleship *Maine* in Havana Harbor on February 15, 1898, the sensationalist "yellow journalism" of newspapermen Joseph Pulitzer and William Randolph Hearst, and American sympathy for a burgeoning independence movement in Cuba and corresponding contempt for Spain's brutal tactics in putting down the rebellion. Other causes may have been the island's strategic position in the Caribbean and American financial interests in the island's agriculture industry.[7]

Particularly because of its strong navy, the United States had complete military superiority over Spain, and "this splendid little war" was over in less than a hundred days.[8] On August 12, 1898, Spain granted Cuba its independence and ceded Puerto Rico and Guam to the United States. Over the course of the war, the American military suffered fewer than four hundred combat-related deaths.[9] The greater cost came from environmental factors: there were approximately two thousand non-combat-related fatalities resulting from food poisoning, yellow fever, malaria, and other diseases.[10]

But even as the war with Spain ended, another war—this one far less "splendid" than the first—began. Under the Treaty of Paris, which formally ended the Spanish-American War, Spain ceded the Philippine Islands (as well as Puerto Rico and Guam) to the United States, and accepted $20 million in return. But by the time the United States and Spain signed the treaty on December 10, 1898, and the U.S. Senate ratified it on February 6, 1899, the Filipino nationalist Emilio Aguinaldo had proclaimed Philippine independence.

Of the hundred and twenty-five thousand American troops that fought in the Philippines between 1899 and 1903, four thousand were killed.[11] In addition, approximately twenty thousand Filipino insurgents died, and civilian casualties were heavy as well; John A. Larkin has written that the war cost the lives of "hundreds of thousands" of Filipinos from both injury and disease.[12] The war involved open battles and guerrilla campaigns by both sides, and reputed American atrocities were eventually investigated in the U.S. Senate.[13] The United States exerted less and less control over the Philippines over the following decades, and the country's independence was formally recognized by the United States on July 4, 1946.

Wartime dissent at the dawn of the twentieth century had two dominant catchwords: imperialism and patriotism. First, dissenters began to focus their criticism on a particular type of American imperialism—one that prioritized influence over a country's moral, religious, and cultural practices, rather than, for example, ownership of that country's land. Starting with the Spanish-American War, "anti-imperialist leagues" began to sprout up around the country. These associations, which were strongest in New England in general and Boston in particular, were the most visible and vocal antiwar groups in the United States. Second, dissenters questioned the assumptions of wartime patriotism. Opponents of the war argued that the sentiment was a peculiar and often false type of national pride, because it conflated loving one's country with loving the country's policies. These two themes, anti-imperialism and counterfeit patriotism, would resonate with antiwar protestors for many wars to come, and would play a particularly important role in opposition to the War on Terror.

In this chapter, Moorfield Storey delivers a prewar lecture, "A Civilian's View of the Navy," to the Naval War College in Newport, Rhode Island, on September 6, 1897. In his speech, Storey questions the U.S. naval buildup and argues that there is more glory in peace than in empire and war. Charles Eliot Norton speaks twice on the subject of patriotism. In "True Patriotism," presented on June 8, 1898, in Boston, during a frenzy of nationalist pride, Norton argues that dissent is most necessary during times of war. In "Counterfeit Patriotism," delivered on August 21, 1902, near Boston, he goes on the attack and makes the heretical argument that American soldiers were being held in exaggerated esteem for their participation in what Norton calls a "bad war." Finally, in "The Policy of Imperialism," delivered on October 17, 1899, in Chicago, Carl Schurz discusses the perils faced by the United States as an occupying force in the Philippines. Schurz also redefines and reappropriates American patriotism with a catchy phrase: "Our country—when right to be kept right; when wrong to be put right."

## Moorfield Storey Warns of a Dangerous and Growing Militarism

I can imagine no greater calamity to this country than a
successful war.

Lawyer, author, and champion of civil rights, Moorfield Storey was born on March 19, 1845, in Roxbury, Massachusetts. Raised by a family that moved in Boston Brahmin society, Storey attended both Harvard College and Harvard Law School. Upon graduation, he served as secretary to U.S. Senator Charles Sumner and helped to impeach Andrew Johnson. Later in his career, Storey worked to extend Radical Republican principles in American society—not only as a prominent advocate of rights for African Americans, but also as a champion of the causes of Native Americans and Filipinos.

A *New York Times* obituary in 1927 notes that Storey was "known in many lands for his defense of the weak and oppressed."[14] The leadership roles Storey played in an astonishingly numerous assortment of progressive organizations supports such a reputation. At different times in his career, Storey served as president of the Massachusetts Reform Club, vice president of the National Civil Service Reform League, president of the Massachusetts Civil Service Reform Association, president of the Anti-Imperialist League, and honorary president of the Indian Rights Association. Storey became the first president of the National Association for the Advancement of Colored People (NAACP) in 1910. His other roles—editor of the *American Law Review,* president of the American Bar Association, overseer at Harvard College, and senior member of the prominent law firm Storey, Thorndike, Palmer and Dodge—illustrate Storey's power and influence in professional society as well.

Storey delivered the following lecture on September 6, 1897, at the Naval War College in Newport, Rhode Island.[15] His address came three months after Theodore Roosevelt, then assistant secretary of the navy, presented a bellicose speech to the same audience justifying the United States's imperialistic and interventionist policies: "All great masterful races," the future president declared, "have been fighting races. . . . No triumph of peace is quite so great as the supreme triumphs of war."[16]

In a tone respectfully critical of the navy's role in world affairs, Storey did not address Roosevelt by name, but firmly decried the assistant secretary's views. Recognizing what he perceived as a dangerous and growing militarism in the United States, Storey urged the navy to practice restraint. The differences of opinion between these two great speakers, and the fact that both were provided a governmentally sanctioned stage on which to express their views, illustrate how wide the gulf was in American society with respect to interventionist foreign policies just one year before the outbreak of the Spanish-American War.

When Aristotle wrote the *Rhetoric,* arguably the single most influential treatise on persuasion, he paid special attention to *ethos,* or a speaker's ability to portray a personal character that makes the speech credible to the audience.[17] The most impressive aspect of Storey's speech at the Naval War College is the way in which he situates himself as a credible speaker. This is particularly important because he is an outsider addressing military personnel. As a civilian lawyer, Storey simply had no personal knowledge of military affairs, much less the affairs of the navy in particular. How, then, could he give himself credibility with his audience?

Storey begins his speech by celebrating the popular "romantic" notions of the sea and naval warfare. He surveys the great naval battles of history and glorifies their participants. The daring officers who orchestrated the battles, Story declares, are "heroes" who "inspire" us. Storey also extols the American navy in general, which is "especially glorious" for its "almost unbroken series of triumphs." In contrast to the remainder of the speech, nearly all of Storey's introduction is celebratory of the navy. Before beginning the critical portion of his speech, he showered the original audience with at least ten minutes of uninterrupted praise.

The intended effect of such an introduction of what quickly becomes a resolutely antiwar speech is to situate the speaker as a knowledgeable authority whose opinion matters. Storey's praise creates a friendly rapport with his audience. What he says subsequently is therefore less likely to be understood as malicious or ill-intentioned. In addition, Storey's celebration of the navy demonstrates that despite his doveish views, he does not subscribe to a peace-at-any-price mentality. Taken as a whole, Storey's introduction functions to preempt the stock of arguments that might be leveled against him—that he is an ill-informed outsider, a hostile agitator, or a naive pacifist.

The speaker's tone changes from high praise to reasoned criticism in the paragraph beginning "Believe me, gentlemen, I sympathize with you and understand your hopes." As discussed in the introduction, Storey attempts to establish *hereditary ethos* when he tells the audience that he himself "spring[s] from ancestors who for five successive generations died at sea." His credibility presumably established, Storey begins to censure the administration's foreign policy. Initially, Storey proposes that conflicts between nations be resolved by "international arbitration," not armed conflict. Next, Storey argues that the country's militarism is distracting its leaders from the country's central problems: problems relating to immigration, voting rights, poverty, and the rising tide of socialism. By the end of the speech, Storey's praise and politeness give way to more pointed criticism. The United States should not "win the confidence of our neighbors by constantly considering how we can most completely ruin them," he warns. In the most quotable line of the speech (which utilizes the rhetorical trope of paradox) Storey proclaims, "I can imagine no greater calamity to this country than a successful war."

FROM THE EARLIEST DAYS there has been always an atmosphere of romance about the sea, and if there ever was a man who failed to feel it, he certainty was not born of Anglo-Saxon stock. No one ever dwelt within sight of the waves who did not believe that sooner or later they would bring to his feet "something rich and strange," who did not smell in the sea breeze a faint aroma of spice borne from distant shores, who did not dream of finding beyond the horizon untold wonder, beauty, and wealth. Every boy at some time in his life has determined to be at least a sailor if not a buccaneer, and has turned with reluctance from his vision of the quarter deck to the humdrum pursuits of ordinary life. . . .

But if our common associations with the sea are romantic, how much more romantic is everything connected with naval war. All that is horrible in warfare, the beleaguered town with its starving inhabitants, the stricken field with its thousands of wounded suffering every extremity of torture from pain and thirst, the sack of great cities, the ruin and exhaustion of the peasants robbed alike by friend and foe, all the cruel facts which led Sidney Smith to say "In war God is forgotten," we associate with war on land. The waves which mercifully receive the dead and wash away the stains of conflict, the ocean air which blows away the smoke of battle, make us forget that in the sea fight also there are horrors and that the sailor knows hardship and suffering at least as great as the soldier's.

When we think of Themistocles breaking the whole power of the barbarians at Salamis, of Dandolo storming Constantinople, of Sir Richard Grenville in the *Revenge* fighting single-handed Spaniard after Spaniard, of Howard and Drake destroying the Armada, of Peterboro at Barcelona, of Nelson at Trafalgar, of Tromp sweeping the British channel with his broom at his masthead, of John Paul Jones fighting England in her own waters and making her shores ring with the echoes of his cannon, of Farragut at New Orleans, we never remember what it cost in wounds and death to win their fame. These great figures stand out on the canvas of history in singularly vivid colors, and the man does not live whose blood is not quickened by the story of their exploits. They are heroes whose examples are peculiarly inspiring. There is a gay and reckless daring about the sailor that must always fascinate us. The very children in our schools remember the naval battles of the Revolution and of 1812 better than anything else in history, and fight them over again in their play. As a result I am afraid they are too apt to carry through life the feeling of the actual combatants.

If such is the influence which the history of naval battles exerts upon us all, it is impossible that you whom I address should not feel it with peculiar strength. War upon the ocean is your profession. It is for this that you are educated, and to it you must inevitably look for the greatest success and the highest distinction that your profession offers. The traditions of our service are especially glorious, for however our fortune may have varied on land, our flag has witnessed an almost unbroken series of triumphs on the water, whether salt or fresh. Hull, the Porters, Perry, McDonough, Decatur, Preble, Dupont, Foote, Worden, Cushing,—how much does each of these names recall? The list might be lengthened indefinitely, but it is not necessary here, for the complete roll of our naval heroes is graven on the memory of every man before me. Their trophies will not let you sleep. There is not one of you to whom their example does not appeal, who has not in his daydreams stood by Decatur's side at Tripoli, or sunk with the *Cumberland* in Hampton Roads, or shared the Bay Fight with Farragut, or done some deed of desperate courage like Cushing. Unless you hoped some day to say with Perry "We've met the enemy and they are ours," or at least to die like Lawrence on the *Chesapeake,* or Smith on the *Congress,* or Craven at Mobile, you would not be fit to remain in your country's service, and to undertake the difficult task of keeping untarnished the glorious record of her navy.

Believe me, gentlemen, I sympathize with you and understand your hopes. I could not spring from ancestors who for five successive generations died at sea, without some of a sailor's instincts, some comprehension of his feelings. I appreciate therefore the difficulties of my position, perhaps my own audacity, in undertaking to speak as I propose to speak to-day. I hope you will bear with me while I try to make my meaning plain. We are all Americans, having, let us hope, the true interests of our country at heart, and it may be worth your while to hear what some of your fellow countrymen consider the real function of your chosen profession. . . .

Behind emperors and kings and ministers of state lie the people, on whom fall the burdens of war and who dread it. They cannot welcome the conscription which carries off their sons and postpones the marriage of their daughters, and which shortens the industrial and family life of each generation. Millions of men, who produce nothing and consume much, must strain the resources of any country and entail poverty and hardship on its inhabitants. It is these and not "peace and plenty" which are to-day the uncompromising facts of everyday life to the nations of Europe.

It is not surprising, therefore, that men should seek some escape from this situation, some method of laying aside the armaments which they cannot support and which they dare not use. Not merely the moral but the political and economical considerations demand permanent peace. How can it be secured? This is the great question of the day.

We may draw a lesson from experience. In early days men settled their disputes by private war, but as civilization advanced society found that the system was too expensive. Bullets aimed with the best intentions sometimes hit the wrong man, and a fight begun between two men may grow into a riot which would threaten a whole city. It became necessary to suppress family feuds and duels and to punish every breach of the peace, not to save the combatants but to protect their neighbors. If you will examine an indictment for any crime you will find it alleged as the gravamen of the offense that it was committed against the public peace. It is to preserve this that our whole system of police exists.

Nations are now so connected by ties of every kind that a war between any two injures all. To-day the powers combine to stop the war between Turkey and Greece. When they are more civilized and stronger, war between any two countries will be prevented by all others acting together, because such a war hurts all.

For private war men have substituted courts of justice. The State decides the quarrel of her citizens, and behind her judgments lies the whole force of the community. In like manner impartial tribunals must decide the quarrels of nations, and their decrees must be enforced by the whole power of the world. This is international arbitration, for which statesmen, teachers, and all enlightened men who have the welfare of the world at heart are now striving. This is the practical, indeed the only escape from the frightful dangers and burdens of constant preparation for war.

Our country stands at the parting of the ways. Shall we, with all its evils before us, deliberately assume the burden which Europe is so anxious to lay aside? Shall we enter the frightful competition in destruction, which crushes the populations of Europe and creates the "pauper labor" of which we hear so much? Or shall we throw our weight with the forces that make for a more perfect civilization? Shall we strive to establish peace, or seek to provoke war? This is to-day a very practical question in this country.

We are singularly favored in our situation. Separated by two great oceans from dangerous enemies, and unquestionably the most powerful nation in our own hemisphere, we have thus far felt the inspiration of Washington and the founders of our Government, and have pursued the policy of peace. Secure in our own strength, we have never had a standing army nor sought to vie with foreign powers by creating a powerful Navy. We have believed that, if we dealt with other nations justly, we need fear no attacks, and our experience has shown that we were right. For more than three-quarters of a century we have never known a foreign war, save that which we caused by attacking our helpless neighbor Mexico, and meanwhile we have grown rich and great. We have enjoyed the friendship of the world and have profited by it as a nation and as individuals. Our dangers and difficulties have come from within, and never in the history of the world was there a country with less to fear from foreign enemies and less to gain by war.

Yet many of our politicians, supported by some reckless newspapers and with a noisy following of unthinking or irresponsible men, have been doing their best to embroil us in some foreign war. This has always been the method by which rulers who feel their positions in peril have sought to divert attention from the consequences of their misrule, and to reëstablish their own power by an appeal to patriotic feeling. Our country has been embarked in the work of building ships and forts with a vigor which is new in our experience. Wars and rumors of wars are the daily food of our political warriors. The supposed wrongs of naturalized citizens, who recognize this country as their own only when they wish its protection from the consequences of their conspiracies against some friendly power, engross the attention which should be given to the interests of us all; and we never know what resolution breathing fire and sword may pass our Senate, what hostile message come from our Department of State.

We are in the throes of a "vigorous foreign policy," which seems to mean a general interference with the affairs of other nations, and a tone in the conduct of our diplomatic correspondence, which is only excused by the general concession that we are ignorant of the usages which prevail in the polite society of nations. This policy and the legislation which fetters our commercial intercourse with our greatest customers have helped to alienate all our friends in Europe, and it might be difficult for us now to specify a single powerful nation which has not some grievance against us, except perhaps Russia, whose despotic government can have no real sympathy with our own. . . .

I think it may be fairly said that our dangers to-day lie within and not without. . . .

To reconcile the conflict of interests, to educate the ignorant, to make the natives of other countries into true Americans, to give our colored fellow citizens their proper standing in the community, to secure labor its just rights while preventing its organizations from oppressing men who do not join them, to regulate the aggregations of capital, to control for good the socialistic movements, and to remove the causes of dangerous discontent—in short, to secure for our whole people the benefit of wise and honest government—these are things which may well tax all the ability and patriotism that our country can command, and they are things which must be done, if our institutions are to endure. . . .

We may overcome our difficulties in peace, but what must be the effect of a war? If our expenses are enormous now, what would they become? If our system of taxation is oppressive, war would multiply our burdens. Another generation would lose, perhaps, a large share of its best men, and a new crop of adventurers and "bummers" would spring up to curse our children with their clamor for office and their demands on the treasury. Worse than all this, the attention of men would be diverted from the evils which we are struggling to cure, and a new party spirit, a fresh legacy of hatred and unreasoning prejudice, would obstruct the progress of civilization in the nation. War is demoralizing, uncivilizing, corrupting, and its worst effects are not wounds and death, the loss of life and property, all that we usually term the horrors of war. Far worse are its less direct results. War turns the minds of men away from their domestic questions and surrounds them with an atmosphere of excitement. The patriotic citizen devotes his time and his thought, perhaps his property and his life to his country's service. But there are thousands of others who see in the confusion which war causes a chance to advance their own prospects at the expense of their fellows. There are fraudulent contractors, general waste, unnecessary increase of offices, fortunes rapidly made by individuals while the community grows poorer. War is the great opportunity of adventurers and charlatans. It is a debauch from which a nation recovers slowly.

The more successful the war, the worse the danger. Easy victory intoxicates a people, fills them with arrogance and the desire of public conquest, in short, with that pride which goes before destruction. The victories of Hannibal and Louis XIV and Napoleon paved the way for the gravest disaster to their countries. From the Second Punic War dates the decline of the Roman Republic. The seeds of Caesarism were sown at Zama. Were we to wage a successful war, our political leaders would preach the annexation of neighboring territory, and would declaim about our manifest destiny. The greater we grow, the more diverse our interests would become, the more difficult the problems of government, and the harder it would be to preserve our Union. . . .

. . . I can imagine no greater calamity to this country than a successful war, which should lead us to enlarge our boundaries, and to assume greater responsibilities.

It is easy to begin a war, and the prospect seems brilliantly attractive to men who have never known its horrors. We see the war of 1812 and the civil war already through a distance which lends the usual enchantment. Read the history of your country and you will see how anxiously during those wars men longed for peace, and how joyfully peace was hailed when it came. The generation that knew by personal experience what war meant would have given scant countenance to the jingoes of to-day. God grant that the present generation may learn from them, and not insist upon a bitter lesson from their own experience.

There are many of your fellow citizens, gentlemen, who share these views, and who watch the growth of our Navy with anxiety. They feel that a powerful fleet may be as dangerous in the hands of reckless politicians on shore or an indiscreet commander at sea as a new rifle is in the hands of a boy. The young proprietor of the rifle will find some way of testing its power, and the community is fortunate if his experiments are not fatal. Something of the boy's temper seems to show itself among our rulers, and occasionally, as at the time of the Chilian difficulty some years ago, it has been suggested that their spirit found supporters in the Navy. Let us hope that there was no foundation for such suspicions. Could we be assured that the influence of your profession would be thrown against hostilities, the growth of the Navy would be regarded with far less solicitude. We approve new rifles, but we want them in the hands of men who realize how far they carry a ball, and who will not fire recklessly. We want no new difficulties till we have conquered what we have, no new territory, till we govern well what we now own, no new war till we have recovered from the last.

When that time comes, the danger of war will be over. When wise and strong men control the government, it will not play with fire. That childish fancy of the hour, "a vigorous foreign policy," will be forgotten. It will have given place to a just foreign policy, under which our country, conscious of its power, will consider the rights of others while maintaining its own, and our statesmen will have learned that courtesy in the expression of an opinion or the assertion of a claim is a sign of strength, not weakness, as well in a nation as in a man. Under such a government a strong navy may never be employed in war, though it may help the progress of civilization or advance the cause of science in ways familiar to you all. Its great office is to make war impossible, and this is the function of the greatest navy that the world now knows. . . .

In a word, our action would invite attack, and so far from securing peace would insure war. There is no more Utopian dream than that two equally powerful fleets can exist together without conflict, or that England and America can proceed harmoniously with such missionary appliances to civilize and Christianize the world. The lion and the lamb will lie down together when two great Anglo-Saxon nations go hand in hand to conquer, and agree upon the division of the spoil. The lessons of Christian[i]ty are not taught by bayonets and cannon balls. In those communities where men go armed, quarrels are more frequent, and hence we have laws against carrying weapons. Human nature is the same in nations as in men. The best way to insure peace is not steadily to contemplate war, nor do we win the confidence of our neighbors by constantly considering how we can most completely ruin them.

Our interest, like England's, is to preserve the public peace for every reason. To the great police force of the world we must contribute our share, and we shall do so willingly, but we do not need a great Navy to protect our rights, to defend our shores, or to make good our claim to the respect of the world. If we are willing to be just, we are strong enough to fear not, and I have no doubt you will join with me in the sincere hope that our Navy, like the English, may always mean peace, and be needed only to make it sure that the decrees of international courts will be unquestioningly obeyed.

I can not close better than by repeating the words of Lord Russell at Saratoga, in his speech on international arbitration:

> What indeed is true civilization? By its fruit you shall know it. It is not dominion, wealth, material luxury; nay, not even a great literature and education widespread—good though these things be. Civilization is not a veneer; it must penetrate to the very heart and core of societies of men.
>
> Its true signs are thought for the poor and suffering, chivalrous regard and respect for woman, the frank recognition of human brotherhood, irrespective of race or color or nation or religion, the narrowing of the domain of mere force as a governing factor in the world, the love of ordered freedom, abhorrence of what is mean and cruel and vile, ceaseless devotion to the claims of justice. Civilization in that[,] its true, its highest sense, must make for peace. The abiding sentiment of the masses is for peace—for peace to live industrious lives and to be at rest with all mankind. With the prophet of old they feel, though the feeling may find no articulate utterance, "how beautiful upon the mountains are the feet of him that bringeth good tidings, that publisheth peace."[18]

## Charles Eliot Norton Defines "True Patriotism"

A declaration of war does not change the moral law.

Scholar, critic, and professor of the arts at Harvard University, Charles Eliot Norton was born on November 16, 1827, in Cambridge, Massachusetts.[19] Like Moorfield Storey, Norton was the product of an intellectually and materially privileged class of Boston Brahmins. Despite his life being full of learning and leisure, or perhaps because of it, Norton expressed a keen sense of cultural awareness and civic duty. He graduated from Harvard College in 1846, and, while writing articles and helping friends publish books, he founded a night school for Irish immigrants—possibly the first school of its kind in the United States.

After spending three years in India as a businessman and experiencing firsthand the intersection between Indian culture and British colonial rule, Norton traveled through Europe in the 1850s, cultivating his artistic predilections with miscellaneous publications and literary associations. His social status at home facilitated connections abroad, and in Europe Norton counted as friends the Brownings, Dante Gabriel Rossetti, Elizabeth Gaskell, and John Ruskin.

Back in the United States in the 1860s, the Civil War inaugurated Norton's increasingly active role in political affairs. Though he was no politician, his consistent efforts at liberal reform reflected a mindfulness of current affairs and a penchant for politics. During the war he promulgated pro-Union propaganda as editor of the New England

Loyal Publication Society. His interest in political publications continued throughout his long life, and in 1895 Norton and newspaperman Edwin L. Godkin founded the *Nation,* a weekly liberal magazine still published today.

In 1875, the president of Harvard University (and Norton's first cousin), Charles W. Eliot, invited Norton to join the Harvard faculty. Norton became the first professor of art history in the country, and by the late 1880s he was the country's most prominent social critic. Norton argued that art, architecture, and politics were all intertwined in the web of "culture." Norton was a snooty professor, fond of lamenting the effects of cultural degeneration in colorful language. In 1890, he wrote in *Harper's Magazine* that the demolition of every building Harvard erected in the last fifty years would be a "superb work of patriotism."[20]

In few places did Norton's cross-pollination of politics and art become more apparent than in a lecture Norton delivered at Harvard in late April 1898, immediately after the declaration of war with Spain. Norton's art lectures were always steeped with caustic comments on public affairs, and one student noted favorably that Norton had a practice of "call[ing] politicians by their right names."[21] Whether because Norton was more scathing than usual, or, more likely, because the United States was then at war, Norton's April lecture produced national condemnation.

In Norton's recollection of events, which may be self-serving, he devoted part of his art lecture to denouncing the war in Cuba and encouraging students to promote peace rather than enlist in the military. In the spirit of academic debate, Norton presented his captive audience with the opportunity to rebut him:

> I told them that in time of need every man should be ready to go to the defense of his country, but that this was not in any sense a national war, and as they owed it to the United States to give as good an account of themselves as possible, I advised them not to enlist, but to leave that for the present to men more in sympathy with the cause with which the war was concerned.
>
> My remarks would have attracted no attention if one of the older men present had not got up and asked permission to speak. Then he disappointed me by making a speech abusing Spain—rather jingoish in tone and accompanied by extravagant gesticulation. There were about 400 students present. They began to laugh at first, but I asked them to be quiet and after that they were as orderly as though they been in church.
>
> When the young man was through I simply said that the country of which he had been speaking was a strong illustration of the unhappy effects of belligerency. Spain had lived by war, and we could see to what condition it had brought her.[22]

Local outbursts of hostility followed. "Professor Charles E. Norton is an un-American ass," wrote one individual who identified himself only as a "Massachusetts Soldier." Thomas J. Gargan, a local orator and former state representative, went so far as to propose a lynching party for the seventy-one-year-old professor.[23] Newspapers as far away as San Francisco reported Norton's remarks.[24]

Faced with growing public condemnation, Norton decided to clarify the views he expressed in his Harvard lecture. On June 7, 1898, he addressed the Men's Club of the Prospect Street Congregational Church in Cambridge. Norton supplied the *Boston Evening Transcript,* a paper sympathetic to him, with a copy of his speech, and the *Transcript* printed it under Norton's title, "True Patriotism," the following day.[25]

Unfortunately for Norton, his public-relations gambit failed. The public's criticism of Norton's Prospect Street speech was quick, overwhelming, and more severe than before. On June 24, 1898, Norton wrote of the backlash to a friend: "My mail was loaded down with letters and post-cards full of abuse, mostly anonymous, some of them going so far as to bid me look out for a stray bullet!"[26] One anonymous writer urged Norton to "find a hollow log and crawl into it—and stay there. That would be a fitting place for a patriot of your kind."[27] Another said ominously,

> You had better pull out
> Yours with contempt
> A white man.[28]

U.S. Senator George Hoar, an old classmate and one-time friend of Norton's, summed up the national outcry in an address at the opening of Clark University's summer school session in July: "The trouble with Professor Norton, who thinks his countrymen are lacking in a sense of honour, is that there are two things he cannot in the least comprehend—he cannot comprehend his countrymen, and he cannot comprehend honour."[29]

Norton constructs his speech around a definition of patriotism. After describing the democratic values explicit and implicit in American life, Norton shows how the current war fails to uphold those basic values. Norton thus opposes the war while championing the core values of democratic republicanism. This stance forms the basis of his "enlightened patriotism."

Though strongly disfavoring war, Norton claims that he is no pacifist and notes that the historical record provides many examples of just wars. Norton's concern, he says, is that "the excitement of passion" brings nations to ignore alternatives to violent conflict. Under these circumstances, Norton's position is clear: "[I]f a war be undertaken for the most righteous end, before the resources of peace have been tried and proved vain to secure it, that war has no defence; it is a national crime."

The style of Norton's speech may at times sound labored to our modern, sound bite–accustomed ears. His sentences sometimes sprawl across the page, and it is easy to lose sight of their beginning and ending. At the same time, the many long sentences create opportunities for emphasis in shorter sentences. "A declaration of war does not change the moral law," Norton states in one of the shortest and most memorable lines in the speech.

Most troubling about Norton's address is his haughty, perhaps even contemptuous, attitude toward his critics. He holds that "no thoughtful American" can disagree with him. He states that "America has been compelled against the will of all her wisest and best to enter into a path of darkness and peril." Advertising one's intelligence is a dangerous gamble, for while it may impress some, it is easily interpreted as condescension in the minds of all but one's most enthusiastic supporters.

Overall, however, the speech is excellent because of Norton's eloquent indictment of the Spanish-American War, and his defiant reappropriation of the term "patriotism."

GENTLEMEN—

There are moments in every man's life, in the life of every nation, when, under the excitement of passion, the simple truths which in common times are the foundation upon which the right order and conduct of life depend are apt to be forgotten and disregarded. I shall venture tonight to recall to you some of these commonplace truths, which in these days of war need more than ever to be kept in mind.

There never was a land that better deserved the love of her people than America, for there was never a mother-country kinder to her children. She has given to them all that she could give. Her boundless resources have lain open to them, to use at their will. And the consequence has been that never in the history of man has there been so splendid a spectacle of widely diffused and steadily increasing material welfare as America has displayed during the last hundred years. Millions upon millions of men have lived here with more comfort, with less fear, than any such numbers elsewhere in any age have lived. Countless multitudes, whose forefathers from the beginning of human life on earth have spent weary lives in unrewarded toil, in anxiety, in helplessness, in ignorance, have risen here, in the course of even a single generation, to the full and secure enjoyment of the fruits of their labor, to confident hope, to intelligent possession of their own faculties. Is not the land to be dearly loved in which this has been possible, in which this has been achieved?

But there is a deeper source of love of country than the material advantages and benefits it may afford. It is in the character of its people, in their moral life, in the type of civilization which they exhibit. The elements of human nature are indeed so fixed that favorable or unfavorable circumstances have little effect upon its essential constitution, but prosperity or the reverse brings different traits into prominence. The conditions which have prevailed in America have, if broadly considered, tended steadily and strongly to certain good results in the national character; not, indeed, to unmixed good, but to a preponderance of good. The institutions established for self-government have been founded with intent to secure justice and independence for all. The social relations among the whole body of the people, are humane and simple. The general spirit of the people is liberal, is kindly, is considerate. The ideals for the realization of which in private and public conduct there is more or less steady and consistent effort, are as high and as worthy as any which men have pursued. Every genuine American holds to the ideal of justice for all men, of independence, including free speech and free action within the limits of law, of obedience to law, of universal education, of material well-being for all the well-behaving and industrious, of peace and good-will among men. These, however far short the nation may fall in expressing them in its actual life, are, no one will deny it, the ideals of our American democracy. And it is because America represents these ideals that the deepest love for his country glows in the heart of the American, and inspires him with that patriotism which counts no cost, which esteems no sacrifice too great to maintain and to increase the influence of these principles which embody themselves in the fair shape of his native land, and have their expressive symbol in her flag. The spirit of his patriotism is not an intermittent impulse; it is an abiding principle; it is the strongest motive of his life; it is his religion.

And because it is so, and just in proportion to his love of the ideals for which his country stands, is his hatred of whatever is opposed to them in private conduct or public policy. Against injustice, against dishonesty, against lawlessness, against whatever may make for war instead of peace, the good citizen is always in arms.

No thoughtful American can have watched the course of affairs among us during the last thirty years without grave anxiety from the apparent decline in power to control the direction of public and private conduct, of the principles upon regard for which the permanent and progressive welfare of America depends; and especially the course of events during the last few months and the actual condition of the country to-day, should bring home to every man the question whether or not the nation is true to one of the chief of the ideals to which it has professed allegiance. A generation has grown up that has known nothing of war. The blessings of peace have been poured out upon us. We have congratulated ourselves that we were free from the misery and the burdens that war and standing armies have brought upon the nations of the Old World. "Their fires"—I cite a fine phrase of Sir Philip Sidney in a letter to Queen Elizabeth—"Their fires have given us light to see our own quietness." And now of a sudden, without cool deliberation, without prudent preparation, the nation is hurried into war, and America, she who more than any other land was pledged to peace and goodwill on earth, unsheathes her sword, compels a weak and unwilling nation to a fight, rejecting without due consideration her earnest and repeated offers to meet every legitimate demand of the United States. It is a bitter disappointment to the lover of his country; it is a turning-back from the path of civilization to that of barbarism.

"There never was a good war," said Franklin. There have indeed been many wars in which a good man must take part, and take part with grave gladness to defend the cause of justice, to die for it if need be, a willing sacrifice, thankful to give life for what is dearer than life, and happy that even by death in war he is serving the cause of peace. But if a war be undertaken for the most righteous end, before the resources of peace have been tried and proved vain to secure it, that war has no defence; it is a national crime. And however right, however unavoidable a war may be, and those of us who are old enough to remember the war for the Union know that war may be right and unavoidable, yet, I repeat the words of Franklin, "There never was a good war." It is evil in itself, it is evil in its never-ending train of consequences. No man has known the nature of war better than General Sherman, and in his immortal phrase he has condensed its description— "War is hell." "From the earliest dawnings of policy to this day," said Edmund Burke, more than a hundred years ago, "the invention of men has been sharpening and improving the mystery of murder, from the first rude essays of clubs and stones to the present perfection of gunnery, cannoneering, bombarding, mining, and all these species of artificial, learned and refined cruelty, in which we are now so expert, and which make a principal part of what politicians have taught us to believe is our principal glory." And it is now, at the end of this century, the century in which beyond any other in history knowledge has increased and the arts of peace have advanced, that America has been brought by politicians and writers for the press, faithless to her noble ideals, against the will of every right-minded citizen, to resort to these cruel arts, these arts of violence, these arts which rouse the passions of the beast in man, before the resources of peace had been fairly tested and proved insufficient to secure the professed ends which, however humane and desirable, afford no sufficient justification for resorting to the dread arbitrament of arms.

There are, indeed, many among us who find justification of the present war in the plea that its motive is to give independence to the people of Cuba, long burdened by the oppressive and corrupt rule of Spain, and especially to relieve the suffering of multitudes deprived of their homes and of means of subsistence by the cruel policy of the general who exercised for a time a practical dictatorship over the island. The plea so far as it is genuine deserves the respect due to every humane sentiment. But independence secured for Cuba by forcible overthrow of the Spanish rule, means either practical anarchy or the substitution of the authority of the United States for that of Spain. Either alternative might well give us pause. And as for the relief of suffering, surely it is a strange procedure to begin by inflicting worse suffering still. It is fighting the devil with his own arms. That the end justifies the means is a dangerous doctrine, and no wise man will advise doing evil for the sake of an uncertain good. But the plea that the better government of Cuba and the relief of the reconcentrados could only be secured by war is the plea either of ignorance or of hypocrisy.

But the war is declared; and on all hands we hear the cry that he is no patriot who fails to shout for it, and to urge the youth of the country to enlist, and to rejoice that they are called to the service of their native land. The sober counsels that were appropriate before the war was entered upon must give way to blind enthusiasm, and the voice of condemnation must be silenced by the thunders of the guns and the hurrahs of the crowd. Stop! A declaration of war does not change the moral law. "The ten commandments will not budge" at a joint resolve of Congress. Was James Russell Lowell aught but a good patriot when during the Mexican war he sent the singing shafts of his matchless satire at the heart of the monstrous iniquity, or when, years afterward, he declared, that he thought at the time and that he still thought the Mexican war was a national crime? Did John Bright ever render greater service to his country than when, during the Crimean war, he denounced the Administration which had plunged England into it, and employed his magnificent power of earnest and incisive speech in the endeavor to repress the evil spirit which it evoked in the heart of the nation? No! the voice of protest, of warning, of appeal is never more needed than when the clamor of fife and drum, echoed by the press and too often by the pulpit, is bidding all men fall in and keep step and obey in silence the tyrannous word of command. Then, more than ever, it is the duty of the good citizen not to be silent, and spite of obloquy, misrepresentation and abuse, to insist on being heard, and with sober counsel to maintain the everlasting validity of the principles of the moral law.

So confused are men by false teaching in regard to national honor and the duty of the citizen that it is easy to fall into the error of holding a declaration of war, however brought about, as a sacred decision of the national will, and to fancy that a call to arms from the Administration has the force of a call from the lips of the country, of the America to whom all her sons are ready to pay the full measure of devotion. This is indeed a natural and for many a youth not a discreditable error. But if the nominal, though authorized, representatives of the country have brought us into a war that might and should have been avoided, and which consequently is an unrighteous war, then, so long as the safety of the State is not at risk, the duty of the good citizen is plain. He is to help to provide the Administration responsible for the conduct of the war with every means that may serve to bring it to the speediest end. He is to do this alike that the immediate evils of the war may be as brief and as few as possible, and also that its miserable train of after evils may be diminished and the vicious passions excited by it be the sooner allayed. Men, money, must be abundantly supplied. But must he himself enlist or quicken the ardent youth to enter service in such a cause? The need is not yet. The country is in no peril. There is always in a vast population like ours an immense, a sufficient supply of material of a fighting order, often of a heroic courage, ready and eager for the excitement of battle, filled with the old notion that patriotism is best expressed in readiness to fight for our country, be she right or wrong. Better the paying of bounties to such men to fill the ranks than that they should be filled by those whose higher duty is to fit themselves for the service of their country in the patriotic labors of peace. We mourn the deaths of our noble youth fallen in the cause of their country when she stands for the right; but we may mourn with a deeper sadness for those who have fallen in a cause which their generous hearts mistook for one worthy of the last sacrifice.

My friends, America has been compelled against the will of all her wisest and best to enter into a path of darkness and peril. Against their will she has been forced to turn back from the way of civilization to the way of barbarism, to renounce for the time her own ideals. With grief, with anxiety must the lover of his country regard the present aspect and the future prospect of the nation's life. With serious purpose, with utter self-devotion he should prepare himself for the untried and difficult service to which it is plain he is to be called in the quick-coming years.

Two months ago America stood at the parting of the ways. Her first step is irretrievable. It depends on the virtue, on the enlightened patriotism of her children whether her future steps shall be upward to the light or downward to the darkness.

Nil desperandum de republica.[30]

## Carl Schurz Discusses the Perils Faced by an Occupying Force

Our country—when right to be kept right; when wrong to be
put right.

"I didn't read what Schurz said; I don't care what that prattling foreigner shrieks or prattles in this crisis."[31] So wrote Secretary of War Theodore Roosevelt to Henry Cabot

Lodge days after Carl Schurz delivered his antiwar address "The Policy of Imperialism" at the Anti-Imperialist Conference in Chicago on October 17, 1899.[32] Former U.S. senator Schurz was a foreign-born naturalized citizen, not a foreigner per se, but the rough-riding future president was right about one thing: there was a foreign policy crisis. Seeking to articulate the Monroe Doctrine of regional dominance, and with the breath of "manifest destiny" still between the nation's lips, the United States was struggling to win control over the Philippines.

One of the problems for the U.S. military during the Philippine Insurrection was not "winning the war," but, as one might say today, "winning the peace." Despite its strength, it had little control over the civilian population. Emilio Aguinaldo, an exiled Filipino nationalist whom the United States recruited to help fight Spain in 1898, demanded independence for the Philippines and set up a revolutionary government after Spain ceded the territory to the United States. But few in the United States believed that Aguinaldo and the "insurgents" were ready to govern themselves. Another war thus ensued, and the Philippine Insurrection—mostly guerrilla warfare on the part of the largely disbanded but still spirited Filipinos—proved to be longer, bloodier, and infinitely more savage than the Spanish-American war itself.[33]

Responding to sobering conditions on the ground in the Philippines and the nation's perceived acquisitiveness, "anti-imperialist" groups sprouted up in America. Concentrated most heavily in New England and the Northeast, these grassroots organizations were the most visible part of the antiwar movement. Carl Schurz—German immigrant, lawyer, U.S. ambassador to Spain, Civil War commander, Lincoln biographer, reconstruction advocate, proponent of civil service reform—was one of their leaders.

In the excerpt below, Schurz argues that the purpose of the U.S. military involvement in the Philippines ("fitting a people for self-government") is flawed because "no people were ever made 'fit' for self-government by being kept in the leading-strings of a foreign Power." By describing the difficulties faced by an occupying force (or a "liberating" force, depending on one's perspective), Schurz makes a valuable contribution to the genre of antiwar speeches.

The excerpt below omits the portions of Schurz's lengthy (thirteen-thousand-word) speech that provide a history of U.S. military actions in the Philippines and respond to the various arguments used by the war's supporters, among them (1) that the Filipino soldiers were the original aggressors; (2) that the United States had authority to exercise jurisdiction over the Philippines pursuant to its December 10, 1898, peace treaty with Spain; (3) that the nationalist movement of Aguinaldo operated in only part of the Philippines and thus lacked authority to bind the country; (4) that U.S. involvement was essential to restoring order and preventing anarchy; and (5) that the United States would suffer a loss of international reputation by "surrendering" to the Philippine nationalists. The excerpt also omits the portion of Schurz's speech dealing with the constitutionality of President McKinley's action in the absence of an express congressional declaration of war, and the brief portion of the speech in which Schurz proposes that the United States sign an armistice with the Filipinos and appoint "not a small politician, nor a meddlesome martinet, but a statesmen of large mind and genuine sympathy who will not merely deal in sanctimonious cant and oily promises, but who will prove *by his acts* that he and we are honest" and who will "keep in mind that their government is not merely to suit us, but to suit them."

The most valuable part of Schurz's address, which is preserved in the short excerpt below, is his discussion of the presence of racism in wartime. As this anthology demonstrates, there is a clear and consistent line of antiwar dissent that finds racially oriented motivations behind war. The speeches of Paul Robeson and Martin Luther King Jr. are examples. A related line of antiwar dissent suggests that racism is not so much the cause of war as one of war's terrible effects. "It is of ominous significance," Schurz states, "that to so many of our soldiers the Filipinos were only 'niggers,' and that they likened their fights against them to the 'shooting of rabbits.'"[34] In shifting his critical eye away from the decision makers in Washington and toward those with boots on the ground—foot soldiers who had no practical say in how the war was being fought—Schurz suggests that war brings out pernicious racist beliefs in those who fight in it. Later, Schurz would remark that he opposed war in the Philippines because "one South was enough."[35]

Cary Edwards wrote of Carl Schurz's rhetoric in the *New York Times* in 1899, "The strength of Mr. Schurz in his public addresses lay in his clear and cogent reasoning, in his succinct and searching analysis, his simple and vigorous comparison, his swift and direct logic. There were few figures of rhetoric [in his speeches] and there was no appeal to prejudice or transient passion. Sentiment there was, deep and pervading, but it was the sentiment of deep conviction, of conscience, and of courage."[36] Edwards's description is a good one, but there is another literary quality of Schurz's address—intertextualism—worth noting. Towards the end of the speech, in what the Romans called the *refutatio,* or rebuttal section, Schurz says the following: "I know the imperialists will say that I have been pleading here for Aguinaldo and his Filipinos against our republic. No—not for the Filipinos merely, although as one of those who have grown gray in the struggle for free and honest government, I would never be ashamed to plead for the cause of freedom and independence, even when its banner is carried by dusky and feeble hands." Besides being a fine specimen of Schurz's ability to produce a dramatic refutation, the excerpt echoes another, more famous, speech in American history: "Gentlemen, you will permit me to put on my spectacles, for I have not only grown gray but almost blind in the service of my country."[37] So spoke General George Washington at the end of the Revolutionary War in dissuading his unpaid officers from insurrection. Thus, Schurz does not merely align himself with one of the most revered figures in American history; he also invokes a war hero who by 1783 was urging moderation, temperance, and peace.

. . . WE ALL KNOW that the popular mind is much disturbed by the Philippine war, and that, however highly we admire the bravery of our soldiers, nobody professes to be proud of the war itself. There are few Americans who do not frankly admit their regret that this war should ever have happened. I think I risk nothing when I say that it is not merely the bungling conduct of military operations, but a serious trouble of conscience, that disturbs the American heart about this war, and that this trouble of conscience will not be allayed by a more successful military campaign, just as fifty years ago the trouble of conscience about slavery could not be allayed by any compromise. . . .

. . . [W]hat do we represent there? At first, while the islanders confided in us as their liberators, we represented their hope for freedom and independence. Since we have betrayed that hope and have begun to slaughter them, we represent, as a brute force bent upon subjugating them, only their bitter hatred and detestation. We have managed to turn virtually that whole people who at first greeted us with childlike trust as their beloved deliverers, into deadly enemies. For it is a notorious fact that those we regard as *amigos* to-day will to-morrow stand in the ranks of our foes. We have not a true friend left among the islanders unless it be some speculators and the Sultan of Sulu with his harem and his slaves, whose support we have bought with a stipend like that which the Republic in its feeble infancy paid to the pirates of the Barbary States. And even his friendship will hardly last long. Yes, it is a terrible fact that in one year we have made them hate us more, perhaps, than they hated even their Spanish oppressors, who were at least less foreign to them, and that the manner in which we are treating them has caused many, if not most, of the Filipinos, to wish that they had patiently suffered Spanish tyranny rather than be "liberated" by us. . . .

Those who talk so much about "fitting a people for self-government" often forget that no people were ever made "fit" for self-government by being kept in the leading-strings of a foreign Power. You learn to walk by doing your own crawling and stumbling. Self-government is learned only by exercising it upon one's own responsibility. Of course there will be mistakes, and troubles and disorders. We have had and now have these, too—at the beginning our persecution of the Tories, our flounderings before the Constitution was formed, our Shays's rebellion, our whisky war, and various failures and disturbances—among them a civil war that cost us a loss of life and treasure horrible to think of, and the murder of two Presidents. But who will say that on account of these things some foreign Power should have kept the American people in leading-strings to teach them to govern themselves? . . .

It is useless to say that the subjugated Philippine Islanders will become our friends if we give them good government. However good that government may be, it will, to them, be foreign rule, and foreign rule especially hateful when begun by broken faith, cemented by streams of innocent blood and erected upon the ruins of devastated homes. The American will be and remain to them more a foreigner, an unsympathetic foreigner, than the Spaniard ever was. Let us indulge in no delusion about this. People of our race are but too much inclined to have little tenderness for the rights of what we regard as inferior races, especially those of darker skin. It is of ominous significance that to so many of our soldiers the Filipinos were only "niggers," and that they likened their fights against them to the "shooting of rabbits." . . .

Now, a last word to those of our fellow-citizens who feel and recognize as we do that the Philippine war of subjugation is wrong and cruel, and that we ought to recognize the independence of those people, but who insist that, having begun that war, we must continue it until the submission of the Filipinos is complete. I detest, but I can understand, the Jingo whose moral sense is obscured by intoxicating dreams of wild adventure and conquest, and to whom bloodshed and devastation have become a reckless sport. I detest even more, but still I can understand, the cruel logic of those to whom everything is a matter of dollars and cents and whose greed of gain will walk coolly over slaughtered populations. But I must confess I cannot understand the reasoning of those who have moral sense enough to recognize that this war is criminal aggression—who must say to themselves that every drop of blood shed in it by friend or foe is blood wantonly and wickedly shed, and that every act of devastation is barbarous cruelty inflicted upon an innocent people—but who still maintain that we must go on killing, and devastating, and driving our brave soldiers into a fight which they themselves are cursing, because we have once begun it. This I cannot understand. Do they not consider that in such a war, which they themselves condemn as wanton and iniquitous, the more complete our success, the greater will be our disgrace? . . .

I know the imperialists will say that I have been pleading here for Aguinaldo and his Filipinos against our republic. No—not for the Filipinos merely, although as one of those who have grown gray in the struggle for free and honest government, I would never be ashamed to plead for the cause of freedom and independence, even when its banner is carried by dusky and feeble hands. But I am pleading for more. I am pleading for the cause of American honor and self-respect, American interests, American democracy—aye, for the cause of the American people against an administration of our public affairs which has wantonly plunged this country into an iniquitous war; which has disgraced the Republic by a scandalous breach of faith to a people struggling for their freedom whom we had used as allies; which has been systematically seeking to deceive and mislead the public mind by the manufacture of false news; which has struck at the very foundation of our Constitutional government by an executive usurpation of the war-power; which makes sport of the great principles and high ideals that have been and should ever remain the guiding star of our course; and which, unless stopped in time, will transform this government of the people, for the people and by the people into an imperial government cynically calling itself republican—a government in which the noisy worship of arrogant might will drown the voice of right; which will impose upon the people a burdensome and demoralizing militarism, and which will be driven into a policy of wild and rapacious adventure by the unscrupulous greed of the exploiter—a policy always fatal to democracy.

I plead the cause of the American people against all this, and I here declare my profound conviction that if this administration of our affairs were submitted for judgment to a popular vote on a clear issue, it would be condemned by an overwhelming majority.

I confidently trust that the American people will prove themselves too clear-headed not to appreciate the vital difference between the expansion of the Republic and its free institutions over contiguous territory and kindred populations, which we all gladly welcome if accomplished peaceably and honorably—and imperialism which reaches out for distant lands to be ruled as subject provinces; too intelligent not to perceive that our very first step on the road of imperialism has been a betrayal of the fundamental principles of democracy, followed by disaster and disgrace; too enlightened not to understand that a monarchy may do such things and still remain a strong monarchy, while a democracy cannot do them and still remain a democracy; too wise not to detect the false pride or the dangerous ambitions or the selfish schemes which so often hide themselves under that deceptive cry of mock patriotism: "Our country, right or wrong!" They will not fail to recognize that our dignity, our free institutions and the peace and welfare of this and coming generations of Americans will be secure only as we cling to the watchword of *true* patriotism: "Our country—when right to be kept right; when wrong to be put right."

## Charles Eliot Norton Accuses America of "Counterfeit Patriotism"

It is a counterfeit patriotism which confuses service in a bad
war with service to country.

In early July 1865, the Norton family moved into a "good old-fashioned farm house" in Ashfield, a rustic town in central Massachusetts.[38] Norton's Ashfield retreat was a welcome alternative to the excitement of Boston. With its "homogeneous folk, its life rooted in the soil, its rough village equality, its prosperless but independent people, its artless literacy, its sturdy moralism," Ashfield was Norton's "ideal of republican existence."[39] The only quality this near-utopia did not possess, it seems, was culture. And so, in the spirit of his proudly paternalistic brand of civic republicanism, Norton resolved to improve the town by importing those refinements which, in his eyes, it so sorely needed. Despite being only a part-time resident there, he threw himself into community projects, founding, for example, the Ashfield Library Association in 1865. The locals cottoned to Norton's enthusiasm; in the words of one, he "entered with zest and wisdom into nearly every local activity."[40] Norton's stature in the town grew steadily, so that after thirty years his contributions to the town were famous. In 1898, the *Daily Hampshire Gazette* wrote that Norton lifted Ashfield "from the obscurity of a small 'hill town,' far removed from a railroad, to a place famed for its men of learning and for that quietness and refinement which are the delight of so many city people who seek in the country freedom from metropolitan troubles."[41]

One activity in particular that Norton organized in Ashfield was an annual fundraising dinner held at his home for the local Sanderson Academy. In 1880, Norton and long-time friend George William Curtis invited local luminaries to lend their oratorical talents to benefit the local school, and for over twenty years Norton presided over every dinner but one. But before long, what originated as a single apolitical fundraiser started to become, as one reporter put it, an "unfettered forum for the discussion of public questions."[42] So significant did the annual dinner become, in fact, that it was covered on the front pages of the New York dailies and even reached foreign shores.[43]

Such publicity had costs, of course, and "sneers and jeers" began to accompany the increasingly political events.[44] Eventually, the dinners developed a reputation for fanning the flames of their audiences' political discontent. By 1902, the *Boston Evening Transcript* wrote that the annual Ashfield dinners "have of late years called forth hearty disapproval from many inclined to accept conditions as they are, no matter whether right or wrong."[45]

After the dinner in 1901, tolerance for Norton's outspokenness bottomed out—some managing the event believed that Norton's agitation was ruining the affair. When word reached Norton, he offered to withdraw from his presiding role. But, as the sympathetic *Boston Evening Transcript* reported, "his critics from the management . . . were not ready for such heroic measures," and when the dinner began, Professor Norton "was in his accustomed place."[46]

To no one's surprise, Norton's 1902 "rebellious dinner at Ashfield" caused, as William James put it, more "bad blood and tribulation."[47] Norton did indeed bring "culture" to Ashfield—a culture, that is, of dissent.

In the following speech, subsequently published by the *Boston Evening Transcript*, Norton returns to the subjects of war, patriotism, and civilization. He begins by noting that war is at best a "deplorable necessity," and at worst a "national crime." Unsurprisingly, he then places the Spanish-American war in the latter category. Those who led the country into the Philippines were a "band of designing politicians" who exploited the nation's "unexampled prosperity" with their "commercial greed and militarism." Stepping beyond the pale of any but the most audacious antiwar dissenters, Norton concludes that the country's troops were being held in "exaggerated esteem." In the most memorable language of the speech, Norton adds that the honor bestowed upon those, like Theodore Roosevelt, who fought or endorsed the Spanish-American War is fictitious, the product of "counterfeit patriotism." In fact, Norton suggests that such praise does not merely misname, but actually conceals such vices as greed, oppression, hypocrisy, and even "evil" itself.

The boldness of Norton's accusations constitutes the speech's major weakness. Norton renders national events in broad strokes: "In three hundred years civilization has made slow progress"; "There has developed a materialistic temper, which finds its expression in commercial greed and militarism"; "The great forces of evil are in the ascendant." Such grandiose pronouncements, made with little or no supporting detail, run the risk of alienating those not predisposed to agree with Norton's sour assessments of the national character or the war. One wonders whether Norton could have actually intended to convert any of the war's supporters to his own antiwar ranks.

It is not entirely fair, however, to conclude that Norton's boldness makes his speech ineffective, for his sweeping generalizations also function to puncture the pressure chamber of national pride and galvanize his core supporters. In addition, by reducing a complicated set of events to a series of simple dichotomies of progress and backwardness, generosity and greed, right and wrong, good and evil, Norton provides concepts digestible to a wider population. The fact that the Ashfield dinners served as a national and international podium could not have been lost on Norton. As his audience became larger, he may have sought increasingly digestible messages. This would help explain this speech's decided lack of subtly and nuance, particularly in contrast to his "True Patriotism" address three years earlier.

Norton begins his speech by quoting the advice of Sir Philip Sidney to his younger brother Robert, then traveling on continental Europe, to the effect that if there were any good wars he should go to them. Unfortunately, the very beginning of Norton's speech was not reported.

. . . IT WAS WISE ADVICE, for in those days the national existence of England was in peril, and it was well that a youth of high station in life should get experience in arms, and learn the lessons which he might be called upon to put in practice in defence of his native land. In three hundred years civilization has made slow progress, and with this progress the convictions of enlightened men concerning war have changed, yet there may still be occasions when Sidney's advice might well be repeated to a high-spirited youth. It may still happen that a people may be compelled to defend itself against predatory attack, or to assist a weaker ally unjustly threatened; but save in cases of this sort war is rarely justifiable. War at the best is a most deplorable necessity, while a needless war, a war of ambition, arrogance and greed, or aggression and conquest, is the worst of crimes. It is a reversion toward barbarism, a confession that the baser passions have gotten the upper hand of reason and intelligence.

A few years ago such doctrine met general acceptance, but a new spirit now prevails. There has developed a materialistic temper, which finds its expression in commercial greed and militarism. The unexampled prosperity of the United States has stimulated to the highest degree the growth of this temper among our people. It has subtly undermined their regard for the principles on which our institutions are founded. Four years ago the nation rushed headlong into a needless and criminal war, led by a band of designing politicians. Pulpit and press lent themselves to the task of exalting war as a blessing, as a needful corrective of the evils of peace. Many a youth has been misled, taught that no matter what the war, when once the country has engaged in it he must maintain the cause. But the call to war is not always—nay, it is seldom—the call to duty. It is a counterfeit patriotism which confuses service in a bad war with service to country. Of all the illusions which hinder the progress of humanity there is none that is more deeply rooted than that which assigns exceptional credit to the soldier and gives special glory to war. The soldier is the representative of physical force, and with the organization and increasing strength of settled institutions, with law established as the rule of life, the relative importance of physical force has diminished. Yet its representative in the soldier is held in exaggerated esteem. From the days of Homer to Kipling the pomp, pride and circumstance of glorious war have been the theme of poets. The brutal savagery of war is overlooked in the excitement of victory and the satisfaction of conquest. But the glory of war is not the light of heaven, but the flames of hell. The soldier's profession is the last to which a man of high character would, in our country, desire to belong, for in adopting it he sacrifices his independence as a man. He is not likely to be called upon to defend his country; instead, he is far more likely to be called upon to take part in a war which his conscience does not approve. The letters of our New England boys, who were deluded into volunteering for the war with Spain, and who afterward found themselves engaged in the anti-American task of subjugating a people fighting for their liberties, bear witness to the disgust of some of these young soldiers, and to the rapid demoralization of others.

Among wars which, even in the warlike days of the seventeenth century Bacon ranked as unjustifiable, were "wars made by foreigners under pretence of justice or protection to deliver the subjects of others from tyranny and oppression." If under pretence of humanity it engage in a war of aggression for the sake of acquisition of territory or other gain, it adds hypocrisy to the crime of unjustifiable war. And what else but this is to be said of our war with Spain? What credit have we won by that war, save such as comes to a robust man when he knocks down a weakling who has begged for mercy? What credit do we get from our pitiless fightings but the credit of the bully and the ruffian? What service can President Roosevelt, with every good intention and with every good fortune attending him—what service can he render that will ever compensate for the evil which he renders by his exaltation of war? The lovers of peace and justice, of their country's honor, are powerless against the madness and folly of the rampant materialism and militarism of the day. The great forces of evil are in the ascendant. But, however dark the skies, the lover of peace and justice knows that the stars are with him.

# World War I (1914–1918)

The assassination of Archduke Franz Ferdinand, heir to the Austro-Hungarian throne, in Sarajevo on June 28, 1914, triggered a series of events culminating in the First World War. Austria declared war on Serbia in late July. Germany declared war against Russia and France in early August. At the same time, Britain declared war on Germany. Later that August, President Woodrow Wilson proclaimed that the United States would remain neutral and, until at least January 1917, argued for "peace without victory." But the resumption of unrestricted German submarine warfare against American shipping vessels in commerce with the Allies all but forced Wilson's hand. On April 2, 1917, Wilson asked a joint session of Congress for a declaration of war against Germany in order that the world "be made safe for democracy." Over the objection of six senators and fifty congressmen, the United States Congress declared war against Germany four days later. America's entrance proved decisive for the Allied powers, and on November 11, 1918, an armistice was signed.

At its height, World War I pitted Germany, Austria-Hungary, the Ottoman Empire, and Bulgaria against Serbia, Russia, France, Belgium, Luxembourg, the British Empire, Japan, Italy, Romania, Portugal, Greece, and the United States. New military technologies, including machine guns, poison gas, submarines, tanks, and airplanes, coupled with the innovation of trench warfare, made World War I the most deadly in history (until World War II). Approximately sixty-five million soldiers participated.[1] Of these, some twenty-one million were wounded, and nearly ten million died.[2] The United States employed almost five million service members worldwide.[3] Of these, two hundred thousand were wounded and over one hundred and fifteen thousand died.[4]

Antiwar dissent during World War I grew mostly out of a broader critique of American capitalism. George Norris was concerned that capitalism gave Wall Street a perverse incentive to support war, for only if the Allies won could they honor their debts to the United States. Robert La Follette was concerned that capitalism had left the poor with a disproportionately small voice in national politics, and Eugene Debs summarized World War I as another "rich man's war, poor man's fight."

Still, there were a number of other types of critiques as well. In this anthology, William Jennings Bryan spins a parable about the danger of an arms race, and Kate Richards O'Hare examines the war's devastating effect on women. On the whole, though, these criticisms were not as prominent as those stemming from a profound dissatisfaction with American capitalism.

## William Jennings Bryan Resigns as Secretary of State to Launch an Antiwar Crusade

If civilization is to advance, the day must come when a nation
will feel no more obligated to accept a challenge to war than
an American citizen now feels obligated to accept a challenge
to fight a duel.

William Jennings Bryan, a three-time democratic presidential contender, America's most prominent orator, and President Woodrow Wilson's first secretary of state, resigned from his post on June 7, 1915, in response to what he believed to be the president's mismanagement of foreign affairs. As Bryan put it to members of the president's cabinet, "I believe that I can do more on the outside to prevent war than I can do on the inside."[5]

In the end, of course, Bryan failed to convince the nation to maintain neutrality, and the United States entered the Great War on April 6, 1917. But in the twenty-two months between his resignation and the outbreak of war, Bryan spoke tirelessly against the U.S. policy of "preparedness."[6] That policy, Bryan preached, was "not only a menace to our peace and safety, but a challenge to the spirit of Christianity which teaches us to influence others by example rather than by exciting fear."[7]

The force that Bryan and his antipreparedness allies marshaled can scarcely be exaggerated. Historian Arthur S. Link has written that the preparedness debate was "one of the fiercest legislative controversies of the decade."[8] And as the leader of the antiwar faction, Bryan spoke to enormous crowds of cheering supporters throughout the country.[9] In fact, during the months immediately after his resignation, it appeared to many that Bryan and his allies had wrested control of the Democratic Party from President Wilson himself.[10] In February 1916, for example, the *New Republic* editorialized that Wilson's opponents, including Bryan, had started the president "on a slide down hill towards an abyss from which he would never emerge as an influential political leader."[11]

Bryan crystallized his antiwar views in a suspenseful moment on February 2, 1917, at Madison Square Garden.[12] In his speech, Bryan told an audience of five thousand at a rally organized by the American Neutral Conference Committee that "some nation must lift the world out of the black night of war into the light of that day when peace can be made enduring by being built on love and brotherhood."[13] Merle Eugene Curti, an early scholar of Bryan's crusade for world peace, called the speech one of his "best efforts,"[14] and the *New York Times* noted how the audience "cheered and rose to its feet several times when Mr. Bryan reached eloquent climaxes and laughed uproariously at the jocular passages, which were frequent."[15]

Despite Bryan's best efforts, however, events beyond his control eclipsed the power of his words. The day before he spoke, the press reported that Germany had informed Washington that they would disavow the *Sussex* pledge and begin unrestricted submarine warfare in a zone around the British Isles. Many Americans were dismayed; only one week earlier the president had reached out to both sides in his "Peace Without Victory" address. Now the Germans had spurned the U.S. overtures of mediation and threatened attack should U.S. vessels cross the blockade. "This means war," the president confided to his personal secretary.[16] Unfortunately for Bryan and his antiwar crusade, the president was right.

William Jennings Bryan needs little introduction as a speaker. One of the foremost orators in American history, and perhaps the single most well-known speaker in turn-of-the-century America, the "Great Commoner" first won countrywide acclaim through a speaking schedule that regularly involved hundreds of engagements a year. In his legendary campaign for president in 1896, for example, the thirty-six-year-old Bryan traveled eighteen thousand miles and delivered six hundred speeches to nearly 5 million people in twenty-seven states—all in a matter of months.[17] In his 1900 presidential campaign, Bryan gave more speeches than all previous candidates for president combined, excluding his own four years earlier, and at one point delivered thirty speeches in a single day.[18] Even in that pre-Internet, pretelevision, and preradio era, where a great deal of political discussion and debate was witnessed in person, this was a striking number. As one contemporary humorously put it, the "Boy Orator of the Platte" was like the Platte River for which he was named: "Six inches deep and six miles wide at the mouth."[19] Another joked simply, "When does he think?"[20]

Bryan possessed more than an indefatigable voice; he also had an uncanny ability to electrify audiences. Crowds at Chautauquas, the big-tent fair-style educational lecture tours popular at the time,[21] loved Bryan. "He was the best drawing card Chautauqua ever knew. He was the highest-paid lecturer and brought the most money into the box office," his manager reported, possibly with some bias, adding that Bryan was "good for 'forty acres of parked Fords, anywhere, at any time of the day or night.'"[22] In 1896, Bryan rallied the Democrats to a fever pitch at the Democratic National Convention with his "Cross of Gold" oration, and inaugurated an entirely new era of highly partisan convention speeches that endures to the present day. At the end of his life, Bryan again captivated the nation in his famous face-off with prominent defense attorney Clarence Darrow over the teaching of evolution in schools. Today, the "Scopes Monkey Trial" is settled comfortably in American memory through high school textbooks and the film *Inherit the Wind.*

What gave Bryan the ability to hold a crowd spellbound? He was no wordsmith; his success as a speaker did not arise out of a consistent ability to coin short, quotable phrases—sound bites—that audiences could easily swallow and digest. Instead, much of Bryan's persuasive force arose out of his ability to apply a very basic moral philosophy to complicated political problems. People believed Bryan because they could understand him.[23]

In the abridged version of the speech that follows, I have preserved Bryan's introduction, his conclusion, and two sections of the speech proper, each of which was subtitled in the original publication in pamphlet form. These two sections in particular have been preserved because both embody a striking feature of Bryan's address, and both exemplify Bryan's religions influence, his storytelling ability, and his manner of reasoning by analogy—three qualities that helped make Bryan an effective speaker throughout his career. In the remaining, unexcerpted portions of Bryan's speech, Bryan endorses President Wilson's "Speech Without Victory" address, observes that the current war is already the largest in history, measured by fatalities, cost, and soldiers, and proposes a constitutional amendment requiring a popular referendum on a declaration of war, except in cases of actual invasion.

The first excerpted section, "The False Philosophy of Force," portrays Bryan's ability to entertain and inform simultaneously. In a short, parable-like narrative, Bryan imagines the international arms race as a competition between two neighboring Christians dead-set on protecting their adjacent farms.[24] When one buys a gun, he puts a notice in the local newspaper warning his neighbor of the dangers of trespass, even while claiming he would love to live in peace. The neighbor responds by buying a bigger gun, and the cycle continues. Bryan then drops the punch line: "Now, what would happen? Every undertaker in the town would be going out to get personally acquainted with those two men, for business reasons." As the transcript of the speech shows, and as the *New York Times* confirmed, the crowd was delighted by Bryan's humor.[25] But beneath the comedy, serious issues were at stake, and Bryan makes this clear in the narration's conclusion that arms races spell death, not for individuals alone, but for nations.

In the second section, "Our Supreme Opportunity," Bryan turns to the topic of national honor in the prelude to war. In doing so, he addresses a question faced by many speakers in this anthology: Can a country with a strong moral character and a sense of dignity answer aggression with restraint? Can the United States, as Barbara Lee put it after September 11, 2001, respond to violence without becoming the evil it deplores? Bryan had little choice but to address the topic of national honor, because the political atmosphere in the run-up to the country's entrance into World War I was charged with moralism and concerns over the nation's dignity. In 1916, for example, President Wilson wrote publicly to Senator Stone, chairman of the Committee on Foreign Relations, that the "the honor and self respect of the nation are involved" in curtailing Americans' neutral rights on the high seas. "To forbid our people to exercise their rights for fear we might be called upon to vindicate them," the president continued, "would be a deep humiliation indeed."[26] Newspapers throughout the country expressed similar views.[27]

In "Our Supreme Opportunity," Bryan questions the assumptions in the president's and much of the nation's moral position. To Bryan, "honor" is not, as Wilson and his supporters would have it, the ability to travel freely in international waters. Instead, honor to Bryan means the courage to oppose conformity and defy outdated customs; honor means caring for one's family; honor means saving one's soul; honor means peace.

Bryan's treatment of honor highlights the speaker at his best—or worst—because, as I have suggested, Bryan was a master of simplifying moral philosophy. Bryan first redefines "honor" in a way that suits his own beliefs. Then, having laid this foundation, Bryan concludes that such a definition precludes the United States from entering the war. The critical reader, or attentive listener, recognizes that Bryan's argument is defective because, while he successfully redefines national "honor" and in so doing offers Americans a viable moral alternative, he fails to explain why his own values are necessarily superior to those of the president. Those who fail to notice Bryan's sleight of hand—or mouth, as it were—would more easily find themselves convinced.

MR. CHAIRMAN, LADIES AND GENTLEMEN:

I am very glad to take part in this meeting, and I confess to my surprise at the size of this audience. I expressed a very strong preference for Carnegie Hall, because I was afraid that, at such a time as this, with no campaign on, and no means of reaching the public except the notice that would go through the press, we could not interest enough people to justify the use of this hall. It certainly is evidence of the deep interest that you feel in the subject under consideration that you are here in such numbers to-night, and I feel justified in the trouble that I have taken to come, traveling from Atlanta, where I turned back from my trip down to the South, that I might join these friends of our own country and the friends of all the countries, in this expression of sentiment to-night. I am glad to speak in behalf of the resolutions that have been presented for your consideration, and upon which your vote will be asked at the conclusion of my address. . . .[28]

*The False Philosophy of Force*

. . . I call your attention to that wonderfully eloquent appeal of the President to the nations that are at war. He has asked them to build peace upon a foundation that is new to them. Why? Because they built their hope of peace on a false foundation over there. The only hope of peace they have had rested on force and the exciting of fear; they have piled up taxes on their people, trying to terrorize each other into the maintenance of peace. This is the false philosophy that has made a slaughter house out of the Old World. (*Applause.*)

And it is this philosophy that the President has asked them to abandon. If you want to know how false it is apply it to a neighborhood and see how miserably it will fail to preserve peace.

Go out into an agricultural community; you may select the best that you have. Pick out two men living side by side on farms, with nothing but an imaginary line between their land. Pick out two farmers, who are honest and well meaning, and, to make it as strong as you can, take two belonging to the same church and sitting in adjoining pews under the same interpretation of the Scripture. Suppose they try to preserve peace on the European plan, how will they go at it? One of them will go to town and get the best gun he can find, and then he will go to the newspaper office and put in a notice like this: "I love peace, and I have no thought of trespassing on my neighbor's rights, but I am determined to protect my own rights and defend my honor at any cost, and I now have the best gun that money will buy (*laughter*), and it is only fair that my neighbor should know that if he ever interferes with my rights I will blow his head off, in a neighborly way." (*Laughter and applause.*)

Then suppose the next day the other man goes to town and buys a bigger gun and with the same frankness goes to the same newspaper office and puts in a similar notice, and I may pause to say that that kind of a notice would always be accepted and would appear in a prominent place. (*Laughter and applause.*) He would say: "I love peace as much as my neighbor, and I have no more thought of trespassing on his rights than he says he has on mine, but I am just as determined as he is to protect my rights and defend my honor, and besides, I have a better gun then he has (*laughter*) and I want him distinctly to understand that if he ever puts his foot across my line I will shoot him full of holes, in a Christian spirit." (*Laughter and applause.*)

Then suppose the first man got two guns, and the second man two, and the first man three, and the second man three; and suppose they went on buying guns alternately, and every time one of them bought a new gun he put a new notice in the paper saying how much he loved peace and how ready he was for a fight. (*Laughter.*)

Now, what would happen? Every undertaker in the town would be going out to get personally acquainted with those two men, for business reasons. (*Laughter and applause.*) Have you any doubt that this is the way that philosophy would work in a neighborhood between individuals? How can you doubt that this is the way it would work between the nations living side by side, with nothing but an imaginary line between them? (*Applause.*)

And, my friends, if you had any doubt before, how can you have any doubt now since you have seen just how it has worked?

One nation would build a battleship and notify the world that it was ready to blow any other battleship out of the water, and a rival nation would build a dreadnaught, and advertise that a dreadnaught could sink any battleship afloat, and then the first one would build a superdreadnaught and then they would go to the dictionary and look up Greek and Latin terms, to use as prefixes for ships, as they built them bigger and bigger, and as they made guns bigger and bigger, and as they collected armies bigger and bigger, all the time talking about how much they loved peace and boasting how ready they were for war. (*Applause.*)

Now, my friends, that is exactly what has been done in the Old World; if any philosophy has ever been exploded it is the philosophy that you can keep the peace of the world by being armed to the teeth. (*Great applause.*) . . .

*Our Supreme Opportunity*

Yes, and more glorious than any page of history that has yet been written will be that page that will record our nation's claim to the promise made to the peacemaker. Our nation is less hampered by precedent than the nations of the Old World, and we are the greatest of the Christian nations, spending more money every year to carry the Bible to those who know it not than any other nation living or that has lived, and the world looks to us to lead the way from the bloodstained precedents of the past out into the larger and the brighter future. I believe that God, in His providence, has reserved for this nation the task of lifting the moral code that is now used between man and man up to the level of nations and making it prevail throughout the world. (*Applause.*) That is what we can do, but we cannot do it if we go into this war.

We used to have duelling in this country, and when it was supported by public senti-ment men had to fight duels because of public sentiment. They would be called cowards if they declined, and in that time a great man like Alexander Hamilton fought a duel and fell. The last thing he did before he went out to that the fatal field was to write out a protest against the entire system of duelling, and he left the protest to posterity, while he left his body upon the field. Why? Because he thought that, as for himself, it was neces-sary to conform to the custom in order to be useful in crises that he thought he saw approaching.

What was the duellist's standard of honor? It was at this: If a man had a wife and she needed him, he had no right to think of his wife; if he had children and they needed him, he had no right to think of his children, and no matter how much his country needed him, he had no right to think of his country. If a man received a challenge to fight a duel he could not reply: "I would be glad to accommodate you but my wife needs me," or "My children need me," or "My country needs me." No, he only had a right to think of one thing—that he must kill somebody or be killed by somebody. It took moral courage to lead the crusade that has resulted in the change, but we have it to-day, and in every State in the Union there is a law against duelling and it is supported by public sentiment.

Fifty years ago a great statesman of Georgia received a challenge from another great statesman of that State. Had a challenge passed between two such men a hundred years ago, instead of fifty, it is not likely that it would have been declined, but fifty years ago the sentiment was changing and so instead of accepting the challenge this man sent an answer that has found a place in history. He said: "No, I have a family to take care of and I have a soul to save, and as you have neither we would not fight on equal terms." (*Laughter.*)

No nation has challenged us and I do not think any nation will, but if in a moment of excitement one of these mad man in Europe should challenge us, I believe it would be the part of wisdom to answer in the spirit of the answer of the Georgia statesman and say: "No, we have the welfare of one hundred millions of people to guard and we have priceless ideals to preserve, and we will not get down and wallow with you in the mire of human blood to conform to a false standard of honor." (*Applause.*)

If civilization is to advance, the day must come when a nation will feel no more obligated to accept a challenge to war than an American citizen now feels obligated to accept a challenge to fight a duel, and if that time must come sometime, why not now? If some nation must lead the way, why not our nation? (*Applause.*)

*Our Duty in the Present Crisis*

. . . If any nation ever attacks this nation, I do not care what nation it is, I believe we ought to fight until the last man is dead, but I am not willing that one single mother's son shall be carried across an ocean three thousand miles wide to march under the banner of any European monarch, or die on European soil, in the settlement of European quarrels. (*Applause.*)

If anybody tells you that it may become necessary to go into this war to preserve our honor let me answer him that there is no honor that we can preserve or secure by going into this war that is comparable with the honor which we can achieve if we can but persuade those nations to turn like prodigal sons from the husks on which they have fed. If we can but lift them out of the bloody mire in which they fight and help them to build a permanent peace on a foundation that will endure. That, my friends, is it the greatest glory that this nation can achieve. If some say that we should now mingle our standards with the standards of Europe I answer that I would not exchange the moral prestige of this Republic for the martial glory of all the empires that have risen and fallen since time began. (*Great applause.*)

## George Norris Assails the Senate's War Resolution

I feel that we are about to put the dollar sign upon the
American flag.

On the floor of the United States Senate on April 4, 1917, watched by a throng of spectators in the galleries, six senators voiced their objections to the resolution that would soon plunge the people of the United States into the Great War. Few senators were denounced for doing so as bitterly as George W. Norris of Nebraska. "If that not be treason," said Senator James A. Reed of Norris's speech, "it grazes the edge of treason."[29]

In retrospect, such vituperativeness—by no means unique to Senator Reed—makes subsequent history's warm praise of this "insurgent" all the more remarkable. In 1936, President Franklin D. Roosevelt, a Democrat, broke party lines to support Republican Norris's reelection to the Senate. In 1956, then-Senator John F. Kennedy featured Norris in his book *Profiles in Courage,* praising his predecessor as "an idealist, an independent, a fighter—a man of deep conviction, fearless courage, sincere honesty."[30]

Norris was born in the Civil War era, the son of poor midwestern farmers. He went to law school, built a successful legal practice, worked in the local judicial system, and served in the U.S. House of Representatives. After being elected to the Senate, he helped to define what became known as Progressivism.

One of Norris's most significant biographical details with respect to this anthology, though, is his dedication to speech, debate, and literary societies during his formative years. In the nineteenth century, such organizations played an essential role in the education of public-minded and ambitious students. Unlike colleges today, nineteenth-century colleges commonly required instruction in speech, debate, rhetoric, and oratory.[31] Such emphasis, of course, made sense—in those pretelevision, preradio days, speeches served as a dominant form of political expression that vied only with the press. In his 1944 autobiography, Norris himself explains the critical role that these clubs played in American society: "Debating societies flourished widely throughout the country. They were the natural offspring of the old form of Town Hall meetings which gave such vigor to American colonial life, and which stimulated so much interest in public discussion. They were healthy and invaluable to the development of American citizenship and to American political progress. Their gradual decline has been a loss to the nation."[32]

Norris gained an immense amount of personal satisfaction and success from the clubs. An eager and able debater in secondary school,[33] Norris continued his speech and debate activities in college. While enrolled at what is now Valparaiso University, or as it was sometimes called then, "the poor man's Harvard," the future senator joined the Crescent Literary Society, an organization that offered Friday-night public programs of speeches, essays, and music.[34] Competition was fierce among members, and when Norris won a contest with an address entitled "The Traitor's Deathbed," his opponent sought revenge and defeated Norris by one vote for the presidency of the society. Not to be outdone, Norris and his followers formed a rival organization with Norris as chairman. The club—whose name was a tightly guarded secret at the time—was known only as "L.U.N.," for "Loyal United Nine"; to Norris's opponents, however, it was known as "Lunatics Under Norris."

Of the "little group of willful men" who voiced their objections to the war resolution on April 4, 1917, Norris produced the clearest and most memorable argument that commercialism had prompted the nation to disavow its pledge of neutrality.[35] Norris accomplished this by employing a simple, damning metaphor: "I feel that we are about to put the dollar sign upon the American flag." Not since Mark Twain, who wrote during the Philippine Insurrection fifteen years earlier that the American flag should have the "white strips painted black and the stars replaced by the skill and cross-bones," had an antiwar metaphor been so powerful.[36]

Norris's phrase is actually the culmination of his peroration (the conclusion of an oration), which invests heavily in images of gold and blood: "We are going into war upon the command of gold. We are going to run the risk of sacrificing millions of our countrymen's lives in order that other countrymen may coin their lifeblood into money. . . . I feel that we are committing a sin against humanity and against our countrymen. I would like to say to this war god, You shall not coin into gold the lifeblood of my brethren."

Norris's words evoke William Jennings Bryan's famous "Cross of Gold" peroration: "You shall not press down upon the brow of labor this crown of thorns, you shall not crucify mankind upon a cross of gold."[37] Both have religious overtones (Norris uses "sin," while Bryan evokes Christ's crucifixion), and the phrasing of the formal, final commandment "You shall not coin into gold the lifeblood of my brethren" matches Bryan's as well. This echo of defiance provides yet more evidene of the lasting power of the simplest rhetorical device—the metaphor.

MR. PRESIDENT, while I am most emphatically and sincerely opposed to taking any step that will force our country into the useless and senseless war now being waged in Europe, yet if this resolution passes I shall not permit my feeling of opposition to its passage to interfere in any way with my duty either as a Senator or as a citizen in bringing success and victory to American arms. I am bitterly opposed to my country entering the war, but if, notwithstanding my opposition, we do enter it, all of my energy and all of my power will be behind our flag in carrying it on to victory. . . .

There are a great many American citizens who feel that we owe it as a duty to humanity to take part in this war. . . . While many such people are moved by selfish motives and hopes of gain, I have no doubt but that in a great many instances, through what I believe to be a misunderstanding of the real condition, there are many honest, patriotic citizens who think we ought to engage in this war and who are behind the President in his demand that we should declare war against Germany. I think such people err in judgment and to a great extent have been misled as to the real history and the true facts by the almost unanimous demand of the great combination of wealth that has a direct financial interest in our participation in the war. We have loaned many hundreds of millions of dollars to the allies in this controversy. While such action was legal and countenanced by international law, there is no doubt in my mind but the enormous amount of money loaned to the allies in this country has been instrumental in bringing about a public sentiment in favor of our country taking a course that would make every bond worth a hundred cents on the dollar and making the payment of every debt certain and sure. Through this instrumentality and also through the instrumentality of others who have not only made millions out of the war in the manufacture of munitions, etc., and who would expect to make millions more if our country can be drawn into the catastrophe, a large number of the great newspapers and news agencies of the country have been controlled and enlisted in the greatest propaganda that the world has ever known, to manufacture sentiment in favor of war. It is now demanded that the American citizens shall be used as insurance policies to guarantee the safe delivery of munitions of war to belligerent nations. The enormous profits of munition manufacturers, stockbrokers, and bond dealers must be still further increased by our entrance into the war. This has brought us to the present moment, when Congress, urged by the President and backed by the artificial sentiment, is about to declare war and engulf our country in the greatest holocaust that the world has ever known.

In showing the position of the bondholder and the stockbroker I desire to read an extract from a letter written by a member of the New York Stock Exchange to his customers. This writer says:

> Regarding the war as inevitable, Wall Street believes that it would be preferable to this uncertainty about the actual date of its commencement. Canada and Japan are at war and are more prosperous than ever before. The popular view is that stocks would have a quick, clear, sharp reaction immediately upon outbreak of hostilities, and that then they would enjoy an old-fashioned bull market such as followed the outbreak of war with Spain in 1898. The advent of peace would force a readjustment of commodity prices and would probably mean a postponement of new enterprises. As peace negotiations would be long drawn out, the period of waiting and uncertainty for business would be long. If the United States does not go to

war it is nevertheless good opinion that the preparedness program will compensate in good measure for the loss of the stimulus of actual war. . . .

Their object in having war and in preparing for war is to make money. Human suffering and the sacrifice of human life are necessary, but Wall Street considers only the dollars and the cents. The men who do the fighting, the people who make the sacrifices, are the ones who will not be counted in the measure of this great prosperity that he depicts. The stock brokers would not, of course, go to war, because the very object they have in bringing on the war is profit, and therefore they must remain in their Wall Street offices in order to share in that great prosperity which they say war will bring. The volunteer officer, even the drafting officer, will not find them. They will be concealed in their palatial offices on Wall Street, sitting behind mahogany desks, covered up with clipped coupons—coupons soiled with the sweat of honest toil, coupons stained with mothers' tears, coupons dyed in the lifeblood of their fellow men.

We are taking a step to-day that is fraught with untold danger. We are going into war upon the command of gold. We are going to run the risk of sacrificing millions of our countrymen's lives in order that other countrymen may coin their lifeblood into money. . . .

I know that I am powerless to stop it. I know that this war madness has taken possession of the financial and political powers of our country. I know that nothing I can say will stay the blow that is soon to fall. I feel that we are committing a sin against humanity and against our countrymen. I would like to say to this war god, You shall not coin into gold the lifeblood of my brethren. I would like to prevent this terrible catastrophe from falling upon my people. I would be willing to surrender my own life if I could cause this awful cup to pass. I charge no man here with a wrong motive, but it seems to me that this war craze has robbed us of our judgment. I wish we might delay our action until reason could again be enthroned in the brain of man. I feel that we are about to put the dollar sign upon the American flag.

## Robert La Follette Argues That the War Lacks Popular Support

We should not seek to hide our blunder behind the smoke
of battle.

On April 4, 1917, Senator Robert M. La Follette of Wisconsin rose in the Senate to speak against the war declaration. Senators Vardaman, Stone, Norris, and Gronna had spoken first; La Follette was to have the last antiwar word. In opposing war, he stood against eighty-two others, most of whom were already incensed at the heresy of George Norris, who had just accused the Senate of "putting a dollar sign upon the American flag."[38]

At four o'clock, when La Follette began to speak, a stir of interest traveled across the Senate. Those who had been smoking hurried to their seats, and in the crowded galleries spectators leaned forward expectantly.[39] For over three hours, La Follette presented his case. As Congressman Lincoln had done to President Polk during the Mexican-American War, La Follette dissected President Wilson's April 2 "War Message," breaking it into parts and refuting the president sentence by sentence. In great detail, La Follette argued that Great Britain and Germany were violating a settled principle of international law that granted a neutral nation the right to trade with belligerents: Germany by way of its submarine warfare and Great Britain by way of its mines in the North Sea. By failing to exact from Great Britain what it was attempting to exact from Germany (i.e., the unfettered right to trade with each belligerent's enemy), "our people," La Follette stated, "had lost the protection that belongs to neutrals." The implication from La Follette's remarks was that Germany's sinking of American vessels, including the *Lusitania,* was excusable, and perhaps even justified, under the settled laws of war.

As an alternative to favoring Great Britain, La Follette urged the Senate to recommit to the principle of neutrality: enforce the right of the United States to transact commerce on the high seas against *both* belligerents, or stop trading with either. "The mere suggestion that food supplies would be withheld from both sides impartially would compel belligerents to observe the principle of freedom of the seas for neutral commerce," he predicted.

One of La Follette's argument stood above, and helped legitimate, the others: "Who has registered the knowledge or approval of the American people of the course this Congress is called upon to take in declaring war upon Germany? Submit the question to the people, you who support it. You who support it dare not do it, for you know that by a vote of more than ten to one the American people as a body would register their declaration against it."

La Follette's simple, *ad populum* appeal, which began the speech, helped him establish that his dissent was not merely a statement of conscience. Years before, in 1909, La Follette had acknowledged the problems inherent in war, writing that war and rumors of war are "a dreadful diversion for peoples demanding juster distribution of wealth" and that war "is the money-changer's opportunity, and the social reformer's doom."[40] In his April 4 speech, though, La Follette focused on one war in particular, rather than war in general. He established early on that he was opposing the United States's entry into the Great War because he took seriously his obligation as an elected official to reflect the opinions of his constituents. He also insulated himself from the recurrent charge of pacifism leveled against most antiwar dissenters. Thus, La Follette's *ad populum* appeal helped establish him more as a credible decision maker to be believed, and less as an outlying antiwar agitator to be dismissed.[41]

Despite his best efforts, La Follette's colleagues in the Senate were unreceptive to his pleas. Afterwards, Senator John Sharp Williams of Mississippi rose to suggest that La Follette was "a pusillanimous, degenerate coward,"[42] that his colleague's speech was fit more for the German Reichstag than the United States Senate,[43] and that La Follette was "not only our enemy but the enemy of the human race." Citizens throughout the country were similarly disdainful: La Follette received hate mail and was even spat upon in Washington.[44] But perhaps a scene from Washington, D.C., the next day best captures the violent animosity many felt toward the antiwar senator from Wisconsin. On Wednesday, April 5, a large crowd gathered at 10 p.m. near the corner of Fourteenth and H Streets, just four blocks from the White House. A five-foot-high effigy dangled from a light pole. It was made of white cloth, stuffed with newspaper, and had its eyes, nose, and mouth crudely marked with black paint. On the front side of the figure, members of the crowd had written the name "La Follette" and that of La Follette's colleague, "Stone." A yellow streak appeared across the back, and dangling from the figure's feet was a streamer bearing a simple inscription: "Traitors."[45]

The effigy swung from the lamppost for about an hour, and "Bicycle Policeman Adams" removed it, as a reporter from the *Washington Post* wrote, only "after other policemen had been indifferent about its presence." Policeman Adams may not have done so, though, out of respect for the senators. After cutting the figure down, Adams brought it to the First Precinct station, where the *Washington Post* noted in graphic detail what became of it: "It was placed in a big swivel chair, in the captain's office, the feet dangling, while the body was in the position of a crouching figure, with the head fallen over on the breast, as if the neck had been broken."[46]

La Follette's early years as a speaker shed some useful light on the techniques he later perfected as an adult. Dubbed "the Little Lion of the Northwest" by his college peers, and feted by notables at the state capitol for winning a six-state, ten-thousand-student oratory contest, La Follette was a rhetorical virtuoso. For his victory, the young orator received more press coverage in Madison, Wisconsin, than President Rutherford B. Hayes's visit to the state capitol at about the same time.[47]

According to biographer Nancy C. Unger, La Follette's lifelong renown as an orator was due to his ability to "gauge his audiences' desire to be entertained, educated, challenged, provoked, soothed, and/or inspired."[48] As a "four-pitcher man" (orators supposedly downed a pitcher of water an hour), La Follette must have said *something* the audience deemed important.[49]

Carl R. Burgchardt's "rhetorical biography" of La Follette offers another, perhaps more helpful, explanation of La Follette's ability to captivate a crowd. Burgchardt suggests that La Follette, springboarding off his prizewinning college oration on the role of Iago in Shakespeare's *Othello*, employed a "melodramatic scenario" to mesmerize audiences throughout his entire political career.[50] Though Burgchardt does not cover La Follette's antiwar speeches in his study, this analytical insight readily applies to the Senator's April 4 address.[51]

La Follette's introductory remarks, in which he refuses to "back the President," are a case in point: La Follette presents himself as the lone individual who, faced with the awesome power of a sitting president and beset on all sides by allegedly hysterical war hawks, must arm himself with the only weapon he possesses—the steadfast devotion to Right. A similarly melodramatic moment occurs later in the speech, in which La Follette waxes poetic about "the poor, sir, who are the ones called upon to rot in the trenches." La Follette again presents an instance of the weak clashing with the strong. In perhaps the only extemporaneous paragraph of his three-hour address, La Follette prophesizes how the poor will rise up and strike down those who have silenced them: "There will come an awakening; they will have their day and they will be heard. It will be as certain and as inevitable as the return of the tides, and as resistless, too."

These passages are "melodramatic scenarios" because they present clearly defined conflicts between plainly mismatched foes, with La Follette himself and the poor as sympathetically powerless underdogs who strive for victory against hopeless odds. La Follette and the poor are Davids, and the rich are Goliaths who, in spite of their strength, will ultimately fall to their smaller rivals. In short, La Follette's melodrama—his stereotyped characters, his exaggerated emotions, and his one-dimensional conflicts—lies at the center of his rhetorical technique and constitutes his primary achievement as a speaker. Of course, these strengths can also be interpreted as weaknesses. Perhaps this is what Senator Williams of Mississippi had in mind when he commented after La Follette's speech, "As a rule the Senator from Wisconsin does not speak until the curtain is about to fall upon the drama and until he can pose as the last, if not the chief, actor in the scene."[52]

La Follette's talents and techniques as a speaker might be said to vindicate Edward Corbett and Robert Connors's only half-joking quip that "all the great orators in history have been great 'hams.' "[53] Indeed, after college La Follette seriously contemplated acting as a career.[54] Perhaps this is less surprising, though, when one considers that La Follette had earlier been employed as an "elocutionist."[55] During the summer between his junior and senior years in college, La Follette actually supported himself by giving dialect readings and reciting Edgar Allan Poe's *The Raven*. As one of his fellow performers put it, "He put more in it than Poe ever did."[56]

In conclusion, one might say that even though La Follette's subsequent career did not involve acting, it was marked by nothing if not drama: after his April 4 address, a stranger reportedly handed La Follette not a bouquet of flowers, but a rope.[57]

MR. PRESIDENT, I had supposed until recently that it was the duty of Senators and Representatives in Congress to vote and act according to their convictions on all public matters that came before them for consideration and decision.

Quite another doctrine has recently been promulgated by certain newspapers, which unfortunately seems to have found considerable support elsewhere, and that is the doctrine of "standing back of the President," without inquiring whether the President is right or wrong. For myself I have never subscribed to that doctrine and never shall. I shall support the President in the measures he proposes when I believe them to be right. I shall oppose measures proposed by the President when I believe them to be wrong. The fact that the matter which the President submits for consideration is of the greatest importance is only an additional reason why we should be sure that we are right and not to be swerved from that conviction or intimidated in its expression by any influence of power whatsoever. . . .

Mr. President, many of my colleagues on both sides of this floor have from day to day offered for publication in the RECORD messages and letters received from their constituents. I have received some 15,000 letters and telegrams. They have come from 44 States in the Union. They have been assorted according to whether they speak in criticism or commendation of my course in opposing war.

Assorting the 15,000 letters and telegrams by States in that way, 9 out of 10 are an unqualified indorsement of my course in opposing war with Germany on the issue presented. I offer only a few selected hastily just before I came upon the floor which especially relate to public sentiment on the question of war. . . .

[Here Senator La Follette submitted letters and telegrams documenting various polls, elections, and referendums that he claimed evidenced widespread opposition to the proposed war.—ed.]

Do not these messages indicate on the part of the people a deep-seated conviction that the United States should not enter the European war? . . .

. . . There is always lodged, and always will be, thank the God above us, power in the people supreme. Sometimes it sleeps, sometimes it seems the sleep of death; but, sir, the sovereign power of the people never dies. It may be suppressed for a time, it may be misled, be fooled, silenced. I think, Mr. President, that it is being denied expression now. I think there will come a day when it will have expression.

The poor, sir, who are the ones called upon to rot in the trenches, have no organized power, have no press to voice their will upon this question of peace or war; but, oh, Mr. President, at some time they will be heard. I hope and I believe they will be heard in an orderly and a peaceful way. I think they may be heard from before long. I think, sir, if we take this step, when the people to-day who are staggering under the burden of supporting families at the present prices of the necessaries of life find those prices multiplied, when they are raised a hundred per cent, or 200 per cent, as they will be quickly, aye, sir, when beyond that those who pay taxes come to have their taxes doubled and again doubled to pay the interest on the nontaxable bonds held by Morgan and his combinations, which have been issued to meet this war, there will come an awakening; they will have their day and they will be heard. It will be as certain and as inevitable as the return of the tides, and as resistless, too. . . .

Who has registered the knowledge or approval of the American people of the course of this Congress is called upon to take in declaring war upon Germany? Submit the question to the people, you who support it. You who support it dare not do it, for you know that by a vote of more than ten to one the American people as a body would register their declaration against it. . . .

. . . The espionage bills, the conscription bills, and other forcible military measures which we understand are being ground out of the war machine in this country is the complete proof that those responsible for this war fear that it has no popular support and that armies sufficient to satisfy the demand of the entente allies can not be recruited by voluntary enlistments. . . .

Jefferson asserted that we could not permit one warring nation to curtail our neutral rights if we were not ready to allow her enemy the same privileges, and that any other course entailed the sacrifice of our neutrality. . . .

Had the plain principle of international law announced by Jefferson been followed by us, we would not be called on to-day to declare war upon any of the belligerents. The failure to treat the belligerent nations of Europe alike, the failure to reject the unlawful "war zones" of both Germany and Great Britain, is wholly accountable for our present dilemma. We should not seek to hide our blunder behind the smoke of battle, to inflame the mind of our people by half truths into the frenzy of war, in order that they may never appreciate the real cause of it until it is too late. I do not believe that our national honor is served by such a course. The right way is the honorable way. . . .

## Kate Richards O'Hare Discusses the War's Degradation of Women

When I picture the bearded face of a man, swollen and bloated
in the July heat, it is not only the man I see, but the women
he left behind.

Federal Judge Martin J. Wade of Davenport, Iowa, wrote in 1919, one year after sentencing Kate Richards O'Hare to five years in prison, that O'Hare was "one of the most dangerous characters in the United States." "She has no equal," he explained, "in the matter of poisoning the minds of the struggling masses unless it be Debs." In fact, he wrote, "I think she is more dangerous than Debs, because she is more subtle."[58]

Kate Richards O'Hare was a national Socialist leader, a trained agitator, a popular columnist, a brilliant orator, and a mother of four. When she married fellow Socialist Francis Patrick O'Hare in 1902, the couple spent their honeymoon barnstorming through Kansas and Missouri, giving speeches to all who would listen.[59] When World War I erupted in Europe in 1914, O'Hare crisscrossed the United States with Eugene Debs to rail against capitalism and the war. In 1916—four years before the Nineteenth Amendment gave women the right to vote—O'Hare became the first American woman to run for the U.S. Senate.[60] Dubbed "Red Kate" by her detractors and "Queen of the Lecture Platform" by her admirers, O'Hare may have been the most visible female Socialist during the "Golden Age" of the Socialist Party of America from 1901 to 1917. In overall popularity, she was second only to Eugene V. Debs himself.[61]

An antiwar speech O'Hare delivered on the evening of July 17, 1917, in Bowman, North Dakota, a town O'Hare described as a "little, sordid, wind-blown, sun-blistered, frost-scarred town on the plains of Western Dakota," precipitated her arrest and subsequent imprisonment for violating the newly enacted Espionage Act.[62] O'Hare's audience consisted of a mere 150 people,[63] most of whom were women and children.[64] Still, this modest number was significant, as it represented perhaps a quarter of a town whose population in 1910 was 481.[65] The local Cozy Theatre, where O'Hare spoke, was filled to capacity, and an undetermined number stood outside to hear the "First Lady of American Socialism" speak.[66]

O'Hare said little that day that she had not said many times before. In fact, she had presented the same lecture, "Socialism and the World War," seventy-five times previously.[67] Moreover, these previous occasions had not been overlooked or forgotten by the government; besides being publicized in advance by Socialist organizers, O'Hare also took the added precaution of inviting federal, state, and local law enforcement authorities to hear her. Though many government officials attended O'Hare's lectures and wrote detailed reports on them, none ever stated that O'Hare's remarks were disloyal, seditious, or treasonous.[68]

What, then, could explain O'Hare's sudden arrest and the government's change in policy? The most obvious cause would be Congress's passage of the Espionage Act in June and its declaration of war earlier in July. Bernard Brommel subscribes to this view, writing that by the summer of 1917, an "atmosphere of intolerance for antiwar speakers had been created in this country," and "the time was right for North Dakota's first trial for violation of the Espionage Law."[69] Other factors may have contributed to O'Hare's arrest as well. According to Sally Miller, O'Hare's arrest "was not so much due to the incendiary atmosphere caused by the war as a result of political infighting in Bowman unrelated to her."[70] Kathleen Kennedy suggests another explanation: "Although anti-socialism played a role in her conviction, the charges against O'Hare did not ultimately focus on her argument that the war served the interest of capitalism. Instead, the Justice Department indicted her for alleging that the war corrupted motherhood."[71] Judge Wade's remarks at sentencing clearly demonstrate an atmosphere of intolerance for antiwar views, but also suggest that O'Hare's motherhood played an important part in her conviction: "This is a nation of free speech; but this is a time of sacrifice, when mothers are sacrificing their sons, when all men and women who are not at heart traitors are sacrificing their time and their hard earned money in defense of the flag. Is it too much to ask that for the time being men shall suppress any desire which they may have to utter words which may tend to weaken the spirit, or destroy the faith or confidence of the people."[72]

What were O'Hare's controversial remarks? In this speech, she had remarked, "When the governments of Europe, and the clergy of Europe demanded of the women that they give themselves in marriage, or out, in order that men might 'breed before they die,' that was not the crime of maddened passion, it was the cold-blooded crime of brutal selfishness, and by that crime the women of Europe were reduced to the status of breeding animals on a stock farm." Later she said, "They tell you that we are opposing enlistment. This is not true. Please understand me now and do not misquote what I say. If any young man feels that it is his duty to enlist, then with all my heart I say—'Go and God bless you. Your blood may enrich the battlefields of France, but that may be for the best.'" Her concern about being misquoted was relevant, as it turned out, to the case against her. The charge in O'Hare's indictment (which she contested) alleged that O'Hare said the following: "That any person who enlisted in the Army of the United States for service in France would be used for fertilizer, and that is all that he was good for, and that the women of the United States were nothing more or less than brood sows to raise children to get into the Army and be made into fertilizer."[73] Other versions of the speech proliferated.[74] The many variations of O'Hare's text exist because no transcript of O'Hare's speech appears ever to have been made. Indeed, as Brommel has pointed out, no witness at O'Hare's trial had a verbatim copy of her remarks, and each could only report from memory what he thought he had heard.[75] The speech in this volume is the product of O'Hare's husband, Frank O'Hare, who, after unsuccessfully exhausting all judicial recourse, took his wife's case to the court of public opinion. One of the pamphlets he published and sold purported to present "now for the judgment of the American people the absolute and exact reproduction of [Kate's] lecture at Bowman."[76]

President Wilson commuted O'Hare's sentence in 1920, fourteen months into an exceedingly arduous incarceration.[77] President Calvin Coolidge later restored her civil rights in full. O'Hare spent much of her later life fighting for penal reform in America. She died in 1948 at the age of seventy-two.

Kate Richards O'Hare's speech is significant because of both its unique viewpoint and its careful attention to language. O'Hare's standard socialist argument that capitalism, not socialism, caused the war and that an international community would emerge upon the war's conclusion is not unique and is not excerpted here. O'Hare's self-consciously feminine lens through which to understand the First World War is, however, excerpted in substantial part. Though O'Hare's critique of "patriotic motherhood" is not the only speech of its kind, it is exceedingly rare.[78] Throughout history women have had to fight merely to be heard, regardless of their point of view. In the words of S. Michele Nix, "Speak softly and carry a big lipstick" was the prevailing doctrine.[79]

O'Hare's speech is notable not merely because it was *presented* by a woman, but because it is *about* women. "When I picture the bearded face of a man, swollen and bloated in the July heat," O'Hare declares, "it is not only the man I see, but the women he left behind." She continues in the same vein: "When I see the downy face of a boy upturned in death on the battlefield, I see not only the young life wasted, but I see back of that boy the mother who gave him life." Margaret Thatcher, deemed shrill by the press, took voice lessons to lower her pitch.[80] In a very literal way, she tried to "speak like a man." But Kate O'Hare, albeit more thematically than literally, refuses to speak like a man. In highlighting the war's effect on women, she occupies an altogether unique place within the genre of antiwar speech.

O'Hare's language reflects her own experience as a homesteader who lived and worked among dirt farmers, migratory share tenants, lumberjacks, and their hardworking families—all of whom were anchored to, and oriented around, the land. She uses words, images, and metaphors that would have been natural to her and doubtless would have resonated with her rural audiences. Thus, O'Hare suggests that the capitalist media "planted and cultivated" prejudice in the commoners' minds; she denies that Socialists are "breeders" of war; describing the scare tactics of Peter Collins and Davy Goldstein, two antisocialists who trailed socialist speakers around the region in order to rebut their views, O'Hare speaks of the "scarecrow which these gentlemen were wont to dangle from the string of their oratory"; to illustrate the Great War's devastation, she remarks that Europe is now a "howling wilderness" and that "the tenderly tilled fields are ruined wastes that never can be brought back to fertility"; civil liberties in wartime, she says, must be placed in "cold storage" until the war is done.

O'Hare also demonstrates a particularly masterful, and humorous, deployment of dialect when she offers the following message to antisocialist farmers (in a passage not included below):

Again, do remember, you perfectly respectable, smug, self-righteous gentlemen, you men who sit about on dry-goods boxes and grocery store counters, do you remember the dire threats you used to make of what an awful fate would befall "them durned Socialists." You were wont to get a stick and a jack-knife and a generous chew of tobacco and expound thusly:

"Ya, them durned Socialists, they think that our children ort to belong to the government, by Jimminey! They say that the government has got a right to take our children away from us and make 'em serve the state, if the state needs 'em and we ain't got a right to say a word. But, by cracky! if any low-down Socialist official ever tries to come inside my door and take one of my boys away from me, I'll fill his dirty hide so full of buckshot that it won't hold corn shucks."

O'Hare exploits her characters by amplifying their rustic background and silly unsophistication. Her homespun humor has teeth, demonstrating that even in the most serious antiwar speech, there is still room for a laugh.

IN THIS, the most trying hour of the life of not only this nation but of the human race, I am glad that I am to have the privilege of speaking to this audience of sober, thinking men and women. These are days that try men's souls;[81] and, if ever in all the history of the world the need for deep, clear and heart-seeking thought has been necessary, it is necessary today. I shall discuss with you the effect that I think that this world-war is having. . . .

. . . I had the wonderful privilege of visiting Europe just a few months before the war and of learning to know and love many of the men who have died on the battlefield, and many of the women whose lives have been utterly shattered. . . .

. . . [M]emories sweep over me, and then—I try to imagine what Europe must be like now. I know that beautiful cities, with their busy marts of trade, are either blackened ruins, or given over wholly to the grim and wasteful trade of making war. I know that the wonderful roads are scarred by cannon and exploding shell, and deeply rutted by the traffic of war. I know that the tenderly tilled fields are ruined wastes that never can be brought back to fertility. I know that the quaint cottages of the workers are shattered; that the castles have been turned into hospitals; that the churches are battered down and the priceless works of art destroyed. I know that the Europe that I loved is but a howling wilderness now, a blackened, war-scarred ruin, an inferno such as Dante never painted.

I know that, in this blood-stained hell which war has made, death has come in most frightful forms to men whom I knew and loved, and worse than death to the women they loved. I know that on the bloody fields of France and Belgium, Serbia and Poland, there is festering in the July heat the bodies of millions of men. I know that, scattered there, are the bodies of the boys with whom I worked in Dublin; there are the miners who sang for me in Wales; there are the Scottish Highlanders and the London newspaper men. I know also that it is not only the workers who have died, but the men of brains and learning and culture as well. I know that, side by side with the humblest peasant, or the most illiterate serf, there lies the artist and the musician; the doctor and the scientist;

the college professor and the inventor. Dead and decaying on these battlefields are the pick and flower of modern civilization. In the masses of corrupting human flesh there lies all that ten thousand years of civilization, of science, of knowledge, of culture, and all that two thousand years of Christianity could do for the human race.

I know also that it is not alone the achievements of the past that decay there, but the hopes of the future as well. When I picture the bearded face of a man, swollen and bloated in the July heat, it is not only the man I see, but the women he left behind. . . .

When I see the downy face of a boy upturned in death on the battlefield, I see not only the young life wasted, but I see back of that boy the mother who gave him life. . . .

I can sense the agony and hopelessness and despair of the mother whose boy lies dead on the battlefield, for I am a mother and I have sons. True, none of my sons are old enough to be drawn into this war, and I pray God that, long before they are old enough to be sent to the battlefield, the workers of the world shall have learned their bitter lesson. I hope that they will have thrown territory-mad kings and profit-mad capitalists into the scrapheap of discarded things, and established a social and economic system to which wars will never come. . . .

I wonder how many of you men in my audience ever went about saying that Socialism would degrade womanhood, debase motherhood, debauch childhood and people the world with illegitimate children? If any of you did say these things your words have come home to you with brutal, chilling force. For our souls sicken when we think of how these things have come to pass. Never in all the history of the human race, not even among our cave dwelling ancestors or the Indians who lived on these plains, has womanhood been so degraded, and motherhood so debased as in the most civilized and cultured countries of Europe. No language can tell the tale; no brain can grasp the horrors and no soul can sense the degradation that has come to the women of war scarred Europe. Lust and rapine and outrage ran riot. The women have not only been forced to endure the horrors of unleashed passion; of blood drunken lust; of the unholy embrace of enemies; they have not only been forced to pay the price of millions of men being forced to live unnatural lives; but they have had a greater degradation forced upon them by state and clergy.

**When the governments of Europe, and the clergy of Europe demanded of the women that they give themselves in marriage, or out, in order that men might "breed before they die," that was not the crime of maddened passion, it was the cold-blooded crime of brutal selfishness, and by that crime the women of Europe were reduced to the status of breeding animals on a stock farm.\***

You sneered at us and said that Socialism would people the world with illegitimate children. Socialism never came, but the war did, and our faces scorch with shame when we think of the illegitimate children of the war zone. In Europe there are thousands of babies, and thousands more will be. These are illegitimate children; they are ill-begotten children; they are children whose fathers they will never know; whose fathers' language they will never speak. These children are not the fruits of marriage; they are not the

---

*The bolded words in O'Hare's speech, both here and below, indicate O'Hare's controversial remarks.

flowers of love; they were not begotten in wedlock and decency. These are the children of invasion and rapine and outrage. They were conceived in lust, nurtured in hate, born to poverty and pestilence and famine. All of you know something of the laws governing the coming of a human life, and you know that children so conceived and so nurtured and so born cannot be normal human beings. I have talked with physicians who have been in the war zone, and they tell me that the very sight of these children is enough to turn the soul sick with horror. They are deaf, dumb, blind, idiot, imbecile and deformed monstrosities that can be nothing but a burden to themselves and a curse to the race. And remember, you dear old, rock-ribbed, hide-bound, moss-backed democrats, these are not Socialist babies—they are war babies. . . .

They tell you that we [Socialists] are attempting to hinder the draft. That is not true. Once again I say that it would not have been our method, but the draft is forcing on every human being, in the most striking manner, the fact that the State is superior to the individual. Of course, since the conscription of life had been demanded, we are going to demand the conscription of wealth. I am free to confess that we don't relish the idea of having a small group of men pass on the matter of life and death for millions of other men, particularly when the men who do the passing also pass up the fighting, because they are either too old, or too fat, or too busy to go to war.

**They tell you that we are opposing enlistment. This is not true. Please understand me now and do not misquote what I say. If any young man feels that it is his duty to enlist, then with all my heart I say—"Go and God bless you. Your blood may enrich the battlefields of France, but that may be for the best. . . ."**

I shall close now, Comrades, and I wish to leave this thought with you. Dark as are the days, heavy as are our hearts, sick as are our souls, we are not hopeless. We know that out of this war must come peace; let us hope it will be an everlasting peace. We know that out of this struggle will come strength; let us hope it will be righteous strength. We know that out of this clash of the capitalist struggle will come co-operation; let us hope it will reach around the earth until every land is welded into the great United States of the World.

I have finished now, Comrades, and the last message that I want to leave with you, the last prayer of my heart, is that you will think and reason and seek diligently for light that you may know that only through intelligence, and co-operation, and brotherhood, and faith, and loyalty to God, and country, and fellowman, can salvation come for this war-sick world.

## Eugene V. Debs Argues that the Working Class Will "Furnish the Corpses" of War

The master class has always declared the war; the subject class
has always fought the battles.

Eugene Victor Debs, the self-acknowledged father of the socialist movement, was a charismatic labor leader in the late nineteenth and early twentieth centuries. He rose to national prominence in an age when the Industrial Revolution was upending Americans' patterns of life and work and forcing millions of rank and file Americans into dangerous and poorly compensated jobs. The newly industrialized economy produced fortunes for a few, but Debs—who as a boy earned fifty cents a day scraping paint from locomotives—focused on the class resentment it fomented in the many. To his detractors, he was a rabble-rouser and a peripheral, albeit fiery, figure in national politics who never succeeded in transforming his angry rhetoric into practical reform. By his supporters, though, Debs was idolized, even deified, for his lifelong commitment to the working class. "There he is, there he is!" one woman shouted upon spotting Debs on stage in New York's Carnegie Hall in 1908. She exclaimed, "Gene Debs, not the missing link but the living link between God and man . . . Here is the God consciousness, come down to earth."[82]

In what has come to be known as the "Debs Legend" there are two central mythic events.[83] The first concerns Debs's six-month imprisonment for his leading role in the Pullman Strike of 1894, the so-called Debs Rebellion. When the American Railroad Union (ARU), founded by Debs the previous year, joined a wildcat strike by employees of the Pullman company, which manufactured railroad cars, President Grover Cleveland sent federal troops to Chicago for what quickly became a violent showdown. With the U.S. military literally encamped along the railroad tracks, the ARU and the strike crumbled quickly. But even though his union was crippled and would never recover, Debs managed to glean a message for socialism from the crushing defeat: "In the gleam of every bayonet and the flash of every rifle *the class struggle was revealed*."[84] Defeated by the railroad corporations, Debs entered federal prison in 1894. Six months later, he emerged as a hero. As Debs biographer Nick Salvatore writes, "adherents to almost every leftist tendency in twentieth-century America" came to see in that six-month sentence something akin to "the origins of a fundamental change in Debs's life, in the history of their society, and, for many, in their own lives as well."[85]

The second seminal event in the Debs Legend concerns Debs's remarks at Canton, Ohio. "The most famous protest speech of its time," Debs's antiwar address at Canton is central to this anthology.[86] By June 16, 1918, when Debs spoke at Nimisilla Park to some twelve hundred supporters, he was already an internationally known Socialist and had run for president of the United States four times. In his speech, Debs denounced the Wilson administration for waging a war "for conquest, for plunder." He argued that throughout history "the master class has always declared the war; the subject class has always fought the battles." And he criticized the United States's use of patriotism and religion for political purposes: "In every age it has been the tyrant, who has wrapped himself in the cloak of patriotism, or religion, or both."[87]

As Debs spoke, a stenographer sent by U.S. attorney E. S. Wertz took careful notes. By the end of the month, Debs was in jail for the first time since his release in 1895, charged with ten violations of the newly enacted Espionage Act. Tried in federal court in September, Debs instructed his lawyers to forgo their affirmative defenses and opted instead to address the jury in his own way: "I have been accused of obstructing the war. I admit it. Gentlemen, I abhor war. I would oppose the war if I stood alone."[88] Though the speech later earned Debs high marks in anthologies such as Senator Robert Torricelli's *In Our Own Words,* the jurors were less impressed.[89] One day after Debs spoke, the jury found Debs guilty of, among other things, intentionally obstructing the draft and inciting "insubordination, disloyalty, mutiny and refusal of duty in the military and naval forces of the United States." About to be sentenced, Debs began his statement to the court by uttering the words for which he is best known: "While there is a lower class, I am in it; while there is a criminal element, I am of it; while there is a soul in prison, I am not free."[90] The trial judge, even as he acknowledged Debs's sincerity and courage, implied that the Socialist leader would "strike the sword from the hand of this nation while she is engaged in defending herself against a foreign and brutal power."[91] On September 14, 1918, the judge sentenced the sixty-three-year-old Debs to ten years in federal prison.

On appeal, the Supreme Court rejected Debs's argument that his words were protected by the First Amendment. In a unanimous decision written by Justice Oliver Wendell Holmes in March 1919, the high court affirmed the trial court's conviction and sentence. In April, President Woodrow Wilson informed Attorney General A. Richard Palmer that he might be "willing to grant a respite in the case of Eugene V. Debs."[92] The war was over. The Germans had surrendered on November 11, and Wilson himself was cabling from the Paris Peace Conference, where he was negotiating the Fourteen Points and would soon sign the Treaty of Versailles. Unfortunately for Debs, however, Palmer successfully lobbied Wilson against clemency: Debs's "attitude of challenging and defying the administration of law," he wrote to Wilson, "makes it imperative that no respite of clemency be shown at the present time."[93]

All avenues of potential redress exhausted, Debs went to prison. Though federal convict 9,653 ran for president of the United States out of Atlanta Federal Penitentiary and received over nine hundred thousand votes in the 1920 election—nearly 3 1/2 percent of the popular vote—Debs's imprisonment marked the beginning of his end. In prison, the normally prolific Debs was allowed to write but one single-page letter per week, and then to only one of a preapproved list of family members.[94] The government denied Debs access to all socialist literature and forbade him from keeping the many letters that poured in from unapproved correspondents.[95] The socialist movement and the party he had championed for decades splintered while he was in prison; the Communist Party formed; America began a postwar economic boom. Debs himself was sick, emaciated, and depressed, and his importance in American society was beginning to track the downward trajectory of his health.[96]

In December 1921, President Warren G. Harding responded to growing public pressure by pardoning the ailing Debs and commuting Debs's sentence to time already served. Debs was released on a Christmas afternoon, after more than two and a half years of incarceration. As he walked away, an ovation escaped from the prison. Warden Fred Zerbst had opened each cell block and, in contravention of prison regulations, allowed the more than twenty-three hundred inmates to crowd into the front building and say goodbye. In one of the few motion pictures of Debs known to exist, one can see the gaunt Socialist, tears streaming down his cheeks, turn back to face the prison. Hands outstretched, his hat held high above his head, Debs pauses and bids his friends a final farewell.[97] Though he spoke many times after his release, Debs grew progressively weaker until his death in 1926.

Debs's rapid-fire invective and his ability to illustrate his basic thesis with vivid images are the most significant literary aspects of his speech. After a polite and good-humored introduction, Debs begins "a little history," first about Theodore Roosevelt and then about "Wall Street junkers." The diatribe is full of vitriol: Roosevelt, once "cheek by jowl" with the "Beast of Berlin," now wants "to murder his former friend and pal." Debs describes the American gentry as "red-handed robbers and murders" who trade their daughters as if they were commodities in their portfolios. And the *coup de grâce,* Debs suggests, is that "these autocrats, these conspirators" cloaked themselves in patriotism in order to (as it was later put) "deceive and overawe the people."[98] The only thing worse than hypocrisy, materialism, and greed, Debs suggests, is hypocrisy, materialism, and greed masquerading as virtue. Though such invective could only have infuriated his opponents, the tactic—judging by the frequent shouts and applause of the audience—delighted his supporters.

Debs uses the rhetorical trope of *metonymy,* or the substitution of some attributive or suggestive word for what is actually meant, to create many of the speech's unusual and memorable images. Thus, Roosevelt does not merely dine at the table of Kaiser Wilhelm II, but has his "feet under the [Kaiser's] mahogany." Upper-class Americans do not "dissemble" but instead "wrap" and "cloak" themselves in the "American flag." Working-class men do not "die," but "shed their blood" and "furnish the corpses" of war.

In the unexcerpted portion of the speech, Debs praises other prominent Socialists, such as Kate Richards O'Hare (who is also featured in this anthology), and presents the standard Socialist recruitment message that the party is ascendant and the "emancipation of the working class" is forthcoming.[99]

Though it is always difficult to capture the lasting importance of speech, Ray Ginger, a largely sympathetic Debs biographer, has tried to capture the impact of Debs's words among Debs's supporters. The Canton speech, Ginger writes, became "a byword, a flaming document in the Socialist movement, because this was war, and men did not say the things they might say in time of peace. Thousands of Socialists warmed themselves on bleak, cold days with the memory of Eugene Debs standing on the platform at Canton, speaking his mind."[100]

COMRADES, FRIENDS AND FELLOW-WORKERS, for this very cordial greeting, this very hearty reception, I thank you all with the fullest appreciation of your interest in, your devotion to, the cause for which I am to speak to you this afternoon. (Applause.)

To speak for labor; to plead the cause of the men and women and children who toil; to serve the working class, has always been to me a high privilege; (applause) a duty of love.

I have just returned from a visit over yonder (pointing to the workhouse) (laughter), where three of our most loyal comrades (applause) are paying the penalty for their devotion to the cause of the working class. (Applause.) They have come to realize, as many of us have, that it is extremely dangerous to exercise the constitutional right of free speech in a country fighting to make democracy safe in the world. (Applause)

I realize that, in speaking to you this afternoon, that there are certain limitations placed upon the right of free speech. I must be exceedingly careful, prudent, as to what I say, and even more careful and more prudent as to how I say it. (Laughter) I may not be able to say all I think (laughter and applause); but I am not going to say anything that I do not think (applause). But, I would rather a thousand times be a free soul in jail than to be a sycophant and coward on the streets (applause and shouts). They may put those boys in jail—and some of the rest of us in jail—but they can not put the Socialist movement in jail (applause and shouts). . . .

Are we opposed to Prussian militarism (laughter)? (Shouts from the crowd of "Yes, Yes.") Why, we have been fighting it since the day the Socialist movement was born (applause); and we are going to continue to fight it, day and night, until it is wiped from the face of the earth (thunderous applause and cheers). Between us there is no truce—no compromise.

But, before I proceed, along this line, let me recall a little history, in which I think we are all interested. . . .

. . . You remember that, at the close of Theodore Roosevelt's second term as President, he went over to Africa (laughter) to make war on some of his ancestors (laughter) (continued shouts, cheers, laughter and applause). You remember that, at the close of his expedition, he visited all of the capitals of Europe; and he was wined and dined, dignified and glorified by all the Kaisers and Czars and emperors of the old world (applause). He visited Potsdam while the Kaiser was there; and, according to the accounts published in the American newspapers, he and the Kaiser were soon on the most familiar terms (laughter.) They were hilariously intimate with each other, and slapped each other on the back (laughter). After Roosevelt had reviewed the Kaiser's troops, and according to the same accounts, he became enthusiastic over the Kaiser's troops, and said: "If I had that kind of an army, I would conquer the world" (laughter). He knew the Kaiser then just as well as he knows him now (laughter). He knew that he was the Kaiser, the Beast of Berlin. And yet, he permitted himself to be entertained by the Beast of Berlin (applause); had his feet under the mahogany of the Beast of Berlin; was cheek by jowl with the Beast of Berlin (applause). And, while Roosevelt was being entertained royally by the German Kaiser, that same Kaiser was putting the leaders of the Socialist party in jail for fighting the Kaiser and the junkers of Germany (applause). Roosevelt was the guest of honor in the whitehouse of the Kaiser, while the Socialists were in the jails of the Kaiser for fighting the Kaiser (applause). Who then was fighting for democracy? Roosevelt? (Shouts of "no.") Roosevelt, who was honored by the Kaiser, or the Socialists who were in jail by order of the Kaiser? (applause)

"Birds of a feather flock together" (laughter).

. . . Now, after being the guest of Emperor William, the Beast of Berlin, he came back to this country, and he wants you to send ten million men over there to kill the Kaiser (applause and laughter), to murder his former friend and pal (laughter). Rather queer, isn't it? And yet, he is the patriot, and we are the traitors (applause). And I challenge you to find a Socialist anywhere on the face of the earth who was ever the guest of the Beast of Berlin (applause), except as an inmate of his prison. . . .

. . . And still our plutocracy, our junkers—don't think for a moment that the junkers are confined to Germany (applause). It is precisely because we refuse to believe this [that] they brand us as disloyalists. They want our eyes focused on the junkers in Berlin, so that we will not see those within our own borders.

I hate; I loathe; I despise junkerdom. I have no earthly use for the junkers of Germany, and not one particle more use for the junkers in the United States (thunderous applause and cheers).

They tell us we live in a great Republic; our institutions are democratic; we are a free people (laughter). This is too much, even as a joke (laughter). It is not a subject for levity; it is an exceedingly serious matter.

To whom do the Wall Street junkers in our country—to whom do they marry their daughters? After they have wrung the countless hundreds of millions from your sweat, your agony, your life-blood, in a time of war as in a time of peace, they invest these billions and millions in the purchase of titles of broken-down aristocrats, and to buy counts of no-account (laughter). Are they satisfied to wed bad daughters to honest working men? (shouts from the crowd: "No.") to real Democrats? Oh, no. They scour the markets of Europe for fellows who have titles and nothing else (laughter). And they swap their millions for titles; so that matrimony, with them, becomes entirely a matter of money (laughter), literally so.

These very gentry, who are today wrapped up in the American flag, who make the claim that they are the only patriots, who have their magnifying glasses in hand, who are scanning the country for some evidence of disloyalty, so eager, so ready to apply the brand to the men who dare to even whisper their opposition to junker rule in the United States. No wonder Jackson [*sic*] said that "Patriotism is the last refuge of scoundrels." He had the Wall Street gentry in mind or their prototypes, at least; for in every age it has been the tyrant, who has wrapped himself in the cloak of patriotism, or religion, or both. . . .[101]

. . . Every solitary—every one of them claims to be an arch-patriot; every one insists through his newspapers that he is fighting make Democracy safe in the world. What humbug! What rot! What false pretense! These autocrats, these tyrants, these red-handed robbers and murderers, the patriots, while the men who have the courage to stand up face to face with them and fight them in the interest of their exploited victims—they are the disloyalists and traitors. If this be true, I want to take my place side by side with the traitors in this fight (great applause). . . .

. . . Wars have been waged for conquest, for plunder. In the middle ages the feudal lords, who inhabited the castles whose towers may still be seen along the Rhine—whenever one of these feudal lords wished to enrich himself, then he made war on the other. Why? They wanted to enlarge their domains. They wanted to increase their power, their wealth, and so they declared war upon each other. But they did not go to war any more than the Wall street junkers go to war (applause). The feudal lords, the barons, the economic predecessors of the modern capitalist, they declared all the wars. Who fought the battles? Their miserable serfs. And the serfs had been taught to believe that when their masters declared and waged war upon one another, it was their patriotic duty to fall upon one another, and to cut one another's throats, to murder one another for the profit and the glory of the plutocrats, the barons, the lords who held them in contempt. And that is war in a nut-shell. The master class has always declared the war; the subject class has always fought the battles; the master class has had all to gain, nothing to lose, and the subject class has had nothing to gain and all to lose including their lives (applause). They have always taught you that it is your patriotic duty to go to war and to have yourselves slaughtered at a command. But in all of the history of the world you, the people, never had a voice in declaring war. You have never yet had. And here let me state a fact—and it cannot be repeated too often: the working class who fight all the battles, the working class who make the sacrifices, the working class who shed the blood, the working class who furnish the corpses, the working class have never yet had a voice in declaring war. The working class have never yet had a voice in making peace. It is the ruling class that does both. They declare war; they make peace.

> "Yours not to ask the question why;
> Yours but to do and die."[102]

That is their motto, and we object on the part of the awakened workers.

If war is right, let it be declared by the people—you have your lives to lose; you certainly ought to have the right to declare war, if you consider a war necessary (applause). . . .[103]

. . . [D]on't worry over the charge of treason to your masters; but be concerned about the treason that involves yourselves (applause). Be true to yourselves, and you can not be a traitor to any good cause on earth. . . .

# World War II (1939-1945)

Two decades after the Treaty of Versailles, the world was once again ensnared in total war. At its height, World War II pitted the Allied powers, including the United States, Great Britain, France, and the Soviet Union against the Axis powers of Germany, Japan, and Italy. Battles were fought in Europe, North Africa, the Middle East, East Asia, and throughout the Pacific.

Massive troop mobilizations and newer, more deadly technologies helped make the Second World War far more destructive than the First. The United States employed over sixteen million service members from 1941 to 1945.[1] Nearly three hundred thousand of them died in battle.[2] Worldwide, an estimated 15 million military personnel and 35 million civilians lost their lives.[3] All told, 50 million people died as a result of World War II.[4]

World War II was the first war in which political leaders communicated to the masses through the relatively new media of film and radio. For the first time in history, people would hear the voices and sometimes even see the leaders of the world as those leaders attempted to enlist entire populations into the war effort. Franklin Delano Roosevelt, Winston Churchill, and Adolf Hitler all delivered iconic speeches that helped to galvanize the citizens of their respective countries. Of course, antiwar leaders were able to exploit the new media as well. Norman Thomas and Charles Lindbergh reached far more people via the radio than they ever did by speaking at rallies.

Before the Japanese attacked Pearl Harbor and the United States declared war on Japan, there were at least four strains of antiwar discourse. The first, represented here by Norman Thomas, expressed concern that war would lead to the erosion of civil liberties. The second, represented by Charles Lindbergh and the America First Committee, stemmed from the philosophy of isolationism and the belief the United States simply had no significant interest in the European war. The third, represented by Richard Wright, agitated for the civil rights of African Americans living in the United States. These protestors were infuriated at what they viewed as deep-seated racism and hypocrisy. How, they asked, could the United States fight for the freedom of Europeans abroad when African Americans were denied so many basic freedoms at home? The fourth, which is also implicitly represented by Richard Wright, stemmed from Communist sympathies, or even downright allegiance to the Soviet Union. So long as the Soviets pledged to stay neutral with respect to Germany, Communists in the United States would too. The willingness of American Communists to side with the Soviets is perhaps best illustrated by their reversal of views in 1941: when Hitler broke the Nazi-Soviet Pact by invading Russia in June 1941, the antiwar Communist Party in the United States turned prowar literally overnight.[5]

## Norman Thomas Discusses the War's Effect on Civil Liberties

Not war *for* democracy, but war *or* democracy is the choice
before the American people.

As the successor of Eugene V. Debs, Norman Thomas led the Socialist Party from 1926 to 1948, running as the party's presidential candidate in every election within that period. Also a lifelong champion of civil liberties, civil rights, and peace, Thomas helped found the National Civil Liberties Bureau, which later became the American Civil Liberties Union (ACLU), and the Committee for a Sane Nuclear Policy (SANE).

The years immediately preceding the Second World War are the most controversial period in Thomas's career. Though strong pacifist beliefs had been one of his chief reasons for originally entering the Socialist Party in 1918, Thomas supported the sending of arms to Spanish Loyalists in their fight against General Francisco Franco. Military victory over Franco, Thomas believed, was a prerequisite for the avoidance of a second war "far worse than the first."[6] This, coupled with Thomas's contempt for fascism, led Thomas to deride President Roosevelt for the president's decision not to intervene in Spain.[7]

Still, despite his interventionist stance in the context of Spain, Thomas was wholly unwilling to approve any foreign policy he deemed would make U.S. involvement in any war against Nazi Germany more likely.[8] Thomas explained, "We who insist that Americans must keep out of war do not do it because we condone fascism, but because American participation in war will bring new horrors and sure fascism to America without curing fascism abroad."[9]

In the speech that follows, which was broadcast nationwide from Los Angeles on September 21, 1940, Thomas crystallized his antiwar arguments in the provocative opening line: "Not war *for* democracy, but war *or* democracy is the choice before the American people." War, Thomas predicts, will be attended by a "reckless repudiation of our liberties." War would require "a morale of hate and fear," and could only be maintained by "ruthless propaganda, complete censorship, and total conscription." This sort of regime, in Thomas's view, constituted the essence of fascism. In other words, by acting to curb Nazi aggression, the United States would become the evil it deplored.

The *Army and Navy Register,* incensed by Thomas's broadcast, called for him to be jailed and deported.[10] The magazine deemed Thomas's anticonscription views in particular a "menace" to national security. Residents of Carbondale, Illinois, would probably have agreed. Responding to protests from the American Legion in the wake of Thomas's broadcast, the mayor of Carbondale attempted to ban Thomas from speaking in the city by forcing the owners of a local theater to cancel their existing contract with him.[11] This action lent support to Thomas's argument about the wartime repression of civil liberties, and served to galvanized his supporters. When the president of Carbondale's Southern Illinois Normal University offered Thomas the use of the university's auditorium to give his speech there instead, Thomas accepted, and an audience of fourteen hundred students and townspeople cheered as Thomas defied the "little Hitlers" who had tried to prevent his speaking.[12]

Pearl Harbor ended Thomas's hopes for nonintervention. In keeping with an earlier promise to do "the best I could, in the event of our involvement in war, to defeat my own worst prophecies,"[13] Thomas offered the country his "critical support."[14] As he reflected in 1944, "We had to choose between the circles of hell, but to escape the lowest circle of fascist victory was a choice worth making."[15]

NOT WAR *FOR* DEMOCRACY, but war *or* democracy is the choice before the American people. We cannot enter the insensate horror which now threatens to make the great cities of Europe "one with Nineveh and Tyre", or seek to parallel its destruction in the Far East or in South America without a complete loss of our democracy. It is possible that the English people, fighting with desperate courage to save their nation, may also preserve that spirit which at the end of the war will re-create democracy; but so great is modern war's destruction, so essential is virtual dictatorship to waging it, and probably to the task of rebuilding when at last the guns are stilled, that it may be doubted how soon any nation, caught in it, can establish democracy.

In our case we should be fighting an unpopular war, far from home, which a wise statesmanship would have avoided. To fight it would require a morale of hate and fear created and maintained by ruthless propaganda, complete censorship, and total conscription. We have not, alas, the genius for tolerance and the preservation of civil liberty which the English have shown within their own Island even during war. To this fact our mobs, our lynchings, our racial discrimination, bear melancholy witness. The panic fear which has obsessed both government and people since the blitzkreig [*sic*] began has been attended already by a reckless repudiation of our liberties in the name of saving liberty. The Smith Alien and Sedition Law can be used to end free discussion of foreign policy. The decision of the Supreme Court denying to the Witnesses for Jehovah constitutional protection of freedom of conscience has laid a basis for an American religion of the state. By such acts we have shown how completely we would surrender our liberties in war. Have we not already in peacetime accepted the principle of military conscription which is essential to the totalitarian state? Have we not already given to the President the power to send our sons to lands more distant than Europe, to fight and die without even the requirement that the Representatives of the people must first declare war?

No one who looks objectively at the situation can imagine that American participation in a new World war, a war all too likely to be fought on both great oceans, in Asia as well as in Europe, will bring to the world a small part of the liberty and democracy we should lose. It is time to face facts and to use words correctly. If all we want is a "good" dictatorship, or an American dictatorship, rather than a "bad" dictatorship or a foreign dictatorship, let us be men enough to say so. If we want war, let us say so. But let us not dare to talk about the possibility of throwing one hundred and thirty million Americans into the incalculable suffering and loss of distant war and still saving democracy. There would be no halfway war. Whatever might be the intention, real or professed, of the government which would enter war, it would mean for us and for mankind the loss, perhaps for generations, of the last great opportunity the world affords to make democracy work over any large area on the surface of this earth. The choice is war *or* democracy. . . .

. . . [T]he effective choice of democracy and peace requires something even more important than negative opposition to the death, destruction, and military fascism inherent in war. We must make democracy work so well that it will be an alternative to war. There is a terrible morale which both war and fascism create. We Americans shall not forever escape either war or fascism unless we can consciously create a nobler morale of dedication to winning and sharing the blessings of plenty, peace and freedom. . . .

Triumphant democracy requires that we produce what America can produce when her engineers will work for the well-being of all of us and not for the profits of private owners or the greatness of the military machine. It will create a morale of a people the least of whom will have reason for sacrificial devotion to a land in which he has so precious a share of abundance. Out of their abundance, and by ending the present military chaos, Americans can find the means to defend themselves. Surely the sons and daughters of the men of 1776 who dared to establish a democracy on the edge of wilderness in a world of despotisms must have the courage and intelligence to make their democracy a living and vital thing even though dictatorship is triumphant abroad. We cannot play God to the world but by making our own democracy work we can bring to mankind a hope and a confidence before which at last the power of the dictators will fall. . . .

It is for these ends, in a world of danger but not of hopeless despair, that we Socialists ask the support of our fellow citizens. If we Americans dare, and dare intelligently, we can escape war and fascism by the vigor of a dynamic democracy dedicated to the conquest of poverty and the brotherhood of men. . . .

## Richard Wright Justifies African American Opposition to World War II

Bitter and obstinate memories separate 15,000,000 Negroes
from this war.

In 1940, thirty-two-year-old Richard Wright published *Native Son* and instantly became the wealthiest and most respected black writer in America. The first best-selling novel by an African American, it sold two hundred and fifteen thousand copies in its first three weeks.[16] *Native Son* incriminates American society for the crimes committed by its "brute Negro" protagonist, Bigger Thomas.

On June 6, 1941, a little more than a year after the publication of his provocative novel, Richard Wright delivered a virulent antiwar speech, "Not My People's War," to the American Writers Congress in New York City.[17] Just as he had done in *Native Son,* Wright forced his audience to grapple with a guilt-of-the-nation thesis, but this time in the context of World War II. In his speech, which marks the fullest exposition of his antiwar views, Wright argues that the "dogged reluctance on the part of the Negro people to support this war" is "rooted deep in historical background" and "undeniably justified." Pointing to the indignities black soldiers and their families suffered at the hands of their white countrymen during and after World War I, Wright suggests that it is time for America to deal with its own unclean hands and the festering wounds it inflicted on its black citizens and soldiers thirty years before.[18]

Wright's antiwar activities attracted a wider audience than those at the Writers Congress. In fact, by the time Wright spoke on June 6, he was already an active antiwar leader. On the governing board of the American Peace Mobilization—a Communist Party organization that counted writer Theodore Dreiser and singer Paul Robeson among its board members—Wright, a card-carrying Communist, helped organize a month-long, twenty-four-hour-a-day "perpetual peace vigil" opposite the White House. He also published antiwar articles and statements in the Communist *Daily Worker,*[19] lectured at Columbia University[20] and the New York Public Library,[21] and participated in rallies as far away as Wisconsin.[22] The leftist magazine *New Masses* guaranteed Wright a relatively wide audience when it featured the following speech in its June 17, 1941, issue. The speech was also reprinted in *Magazine Abstracts*, a weekly publication "prepared for the use of government officials" by the United States Division of Intelligence.[23]

In the speech, Richard Wright refuses to relegate the debate over war to questions relating to war generally. Instead, he focuses his attention on his own country and the unjust treatment of African Americans in the United States, particularly in wartime. Thus, Wright simultaneously narrows and broadens the debate over war: narrowing it by considering its effects on a particular group of people (African Americans), and broadening it by identifying the role war plays in American civil society ("continu[ing] and deepen[ing] discriminatory tactics against the Negro people"). In making this analytical move, Wright is not alone. As indicated in the introduction, virtually all antiwar dissenters extend their scope beyond war and peace; they also endeavor to critique the status quo and, in their own way, to forge a more decent union.

Wright's speech also stands out as an antiwar speech because of the dramatic context in which it took place. The overt, legally sanctioned, and widely accepted practice of racial discrimination in the United States in 1941 allowed Wright to leverage the power of black America at the expense of a white ruling class extremely vulnerable to racially oriented critiques. One of President Roosevelt's chief criticisms of Nazi Germany, for example, was Hitler's attempt to produce a "superior" race. At the same time, Jim Crow laws throughout the southern United States illustrated the imposition of a racial caste system much closer to home. How could Roosevelt disparage Hitler's policy of Aryan supremacy when white supremacy in America was at that time—to use just one example—still separating the blood of blacks and whites in blood banks throughout the country?

Wright makes fine, cynical use of America's dilemma in the first section of his speech, where he states that "the Negro's experience with past wars, his attitude toward the present one . . . constitute the most incisive and graphic refutation of every idealistic statement made by the war leaders as to the alleged democratic goal and aim of this war." Wright then painstakingly details the government's alleged hypocrisy by listing ten excruciating instances of racial injustice. "Negro memory," he declares, is filled with a "bitter disillusionment," a deep "humiliation," and a level of physical and emotional brutality that "cannot be forgotten" or ignored. In light of blacks' disenchantment, Roosevelt's attempt to preserve the "majesty of [America's] human soul" seems like a cruelly ironic joke, or as Wright calls it, a "metaphysical obscenity."

If the first section of the speech represents Wright's "anti-imperialist pacifism," the second represents his "black militarism."[24] Indeed, by the end of the speech, one might conclude that Wright opposed World War II because Roosevelt was not willing to wage it widely enough. "If this is a war for democracy, for freedom, then we [shall] fight in it, for democracy, for freedom," Wright states. But echoing W. E. B. Du Bois's calls for a "Double Victory" in World War I, Wright qualifies: "We shall fight as determinedly against those who deny freedom at home as we shall fight against those who deny it to others abroad."

By the time Wright finishes his speech, his tone has changed from that of casual observer, to wary cynic, to angry prophet. What began as an antiwar speech ends as a call to arms. "A wave of terror impends, not only against us, but against you," he warns. Wright then offers a quick peroration: "A Hitler victory will not end this war. An English victory will not end this war. And America's entrance into this war will not decide its ultimate outcome. . . . When the voice sounds for peace, the Negro people will answer it." Wright's words are layered. In one sense, "this war" refers to the physical war then waging in Europe; in another, it refers to an ideological war over the good or evil of Communism (the discussion of which is not included in the excerpt below); in still another sense, "this war" refers to a parallel war, one for full citizenship and equal rights, one which Wright realizes that African Americans may soon be compelled to fight—perhaps were already fighting—not on the battlefields of Europe, but at home on American soil. One is left to wonder at the last line: exactly what sort of "peace" does Wright have in mind?

SOME OF YOU may wonder why a writer, at a congress of writers, should make the theme of war the main burden of a public talk. Some of you may be expecting to hear writers discuss and compare books and stories. Others of you may be expecting to hear what writers think of what has been recently written, or of what other writers are now in engaged in writing. Well, I, for one, find such an order impossible to fill. My eyes are drawn toward war. Frankly and unfortunately, there's not much else in this world tonight that means one-half as much as war. Every single human aspiration is dwarfed by the forces of war that grip and restrict the movement of men today. War overshadows and dominates all other meanings and activities. War is hourly changing the look of reality. War is creating a new and terrifying subject matter for writers. . . .

So the nature of my remarks here tonight is in the form of a report to you upon a new array of subject matter which the war is bringing into view in Negro life in the United States. The texture of what I have to say deals with the state of feeling that exists among the Negro people in this country toward the current war. That state of feeling is so clear and unmistakable that the war leaders in our nation recognize and fear it. It is the *one* thing on the war horizon in which they cannot "explain away." Indeed, the Negro's experience with past wars, his attitude toward the present one, his attitude of chronic distrust, constitute the most incisive and graphic refutation of every idealistic statement made by the war leaders as to the alleged democratic goal and aim of this war.

Against the background of Hitler's treatment of the Jews, the Negroes' plight in this country is what even labor-baiting Westbrook Pegler quaintly calls an "embarrassment" to the efforts of the war leaders! Throughout the high, ruling circles of the nation, the attitude toward the Negro is: Oh, why should we be bothered with this old Negro question? Or, The Negro issue is a dead issue. Or, Listen, all you do in bringing up the Negro issue is to make things worse for them. Or, Oh, the Negroes . . . Why, they're getting along all right. And so on. The Negro people are aware of this, and their attitude toward this war is conditioned by it.

The dogged reluctance on the part of the Negro people to support this war is undeniably justified and is rooted deep in historical background. Bitter and obstinate memories separate 15,000,000 Negroes from this war, memories of hypocrisy, of glib promises easily given and quickly betrayed, of cynical exploitation of hope, of double-dealing, memories which are impossible to forget or ignore.

My report shall deal with these memories, what they are, and how they have molded the feelings, stained the vision, and colored the attitudes of the Negroes in America toward war, and of how these memories have served as a basis for the Negroes' definition of this war.

Negro memory informs us with clarity that there are but ten points of difference between Wilson's Fourteen Points of Peace and Roosevelt's Four Freedoms, and that these ten points of difference mean precisely nothing insofar as the Negro is concerned.

Negro memory remembers with shame those honeyed words and phrases used by those leaders who persuaded him to hope for a betterment of his lot after the first world war, and Negro memory remembers the bitter disillusionment that followed in the wake of that war "to make the world safe for a democracy" which Negroes have never known.

Negro memory recalls the brazen official orders of the generals of the American Expeditionary Force which were issued on Aug. 7, 1918, to the French people and the French Army, urging them to segregate and insult the Negro troops, to refrain from honoring their gallantry; orders which declared:

> We must prevent the rise of any pronounced degree of intimacy between French officers and black officers. We may be courteous and amiable with these last, but we cannot deal with them on the same plane as with the white American officers

without deeply wounding the latter. We must not eat with them, must not shake hands with them or seek to talk with them outside of the regular requirements of military service.

We must not commend too highly the black American troops, particularly in the presence of (white) Americans. It is all right to recognize their good qualities and their services, but only in moderate terms, strictly in keeping with the truth. . . .

This same cynicism accompanies the present call to war;[25] this same falsehood walks side by side with Roosevelt's attempt to preserve what he calls the "majesty of the human soul"!

Negro memory still recollects the humiliations heaped upon the Gold Star Negro war mothers who were sent to France in cattle boats to see the graves of their dead in Flanders, while white war mothers sailed in first class on luxury liners.

Negro memory cannot forget the lynching of a young Negro soldier, Private Felix Hall, who was found only a few weeks ago in Fort Benning, Ga., still clad in the uniform of the United States Army, hanging from a tree; and Negro memory links this lynching to the memory of the many Negroes who were lynched in their United States Army uniforms during and after the first world war.

Negro memory knows that the same program of job discrimination which accompanied the First World War accompanies the second world war, but with a wider scope and in an intensified degree.

Negro memory has not forgotten that Congress has yet to pass an anti-lynching bill, and that the poll tax laws still disfranchise millions of poor blacks as well as poor whites in the South.

Negro memory tells us that Atlanta, Ga., was our Marne and Brownsville, Texas, was our Chateau-Thierry; what happened to us after we came back from the desperate struggles in Flanders will never be forgotten; it is written into the pages of our blood, into the ledger sheets of our bleeding bodies, into the balance statements in the lobes of our brains.

In short, Negro memory in the United States is forced to recognize that the character of the present war in no wise differs from the previous world war. . . .

The problems facing the Negro people in the United States lie squarely within the continental boundaries of the United States. We Negroes have no issues to settle in Mexico. We Negroes have no issues to settle in Brazil. We Negroes those have no issues to settle in Martinique. We Negroes have no issues to settle in the Argentine. We Negroes have no issues to settle the Azores or the Cape Verde Islands. And, above all, we Negroes have no issues to settle in Dakar.

Our primary problem is a domestic problem, a problem concerned with the processes of democracy at home. We need jobs. We need shelter. We urgently need an enormous increase in health, school, recreational, and other facilities. We need to see the Thirteenth and Fourteenth Amendments to the Constitution enforced. We need to see the Bill of Rights translated into living reality. We need to see anti-lynching bills and anti–poll tax bills passed by the Congress of the United States. . . .

We are being told to wait until the war is over to fight for these things; Negro memory recalls that those same words were used in the first world war. We are skeptical. We no longer trust promises. We prefer to fight now. We will not retreat. If this is a war for democracy, for freedom, then we [shall] fight in it, for democracy, for freedom. We shall fight as determinedly against those who deny freedom at home as we shall fight against those who deny it to others abroad. . . .

One of the main purposes of this report on the state of feeling among Negroes is to inform you emphatically that reaction and restrictions are hitting us now, that lynching is on the increase, that a wave of terror impends, not only against us, but against you. . . .

. . . A Hitler victory will not end this war. An English victory will not end this war. And America's entrance into this war will not decide its ultimate outcome. Those facts comprise the most optimistic aspect of this war; it is what separates this war from all other wars. And that is why the warring nations dare not mention their war aims, save in but the most general terms. They are afraid.

When the voice sounds for peace, the Negro people will answer it.

## Charles Lindbergh Asks, "Who Are the War Agitators?"

The three most important groups who have been pressing this
country toward war are the British, the Jewish, and the
Roosevelt administration.

Charles Lindbergh, America's famed aviator, was the most visible antiwar leader in the years immediately preceding the country's entrance into World War II. As the face of the America First Committee, a bipartisan pressure group formed in 1940 to keep the United States out of the European war, Lindbergh gave a total of thirteen speeches throughout the country. In addition, he gave radio addresses as early as September 15, 1939, and published isolationist essays in such magazines as *Reader's Digest* and the *Atlantic Monthly*.[26]

Occasionally infamous and always controversial, Lindberg's outspoken opposition to war, coupled with his preexisting fame, guaranteed him outpourings of both glowing praise and outright denunciation. Paul Palmer, a *Reader's Digest* editor, said in the summer of 1940 that more mail followed a Lindbergh radio address than that of any other person in America, including President Roosevelt.[27] Particularly noteworthy, Palmer continued, was "the amazing fact that over 94% of these thousands of letters and telegrams express ardent approval of the Colonel's anti-war position."[28] The architect Frank Lloyd Wright wrote to Lindbergh that "we all knew you could fly straight. Now we know you can think straight."[29] And shortly before Lindbergh's second radio address in the fall of 1939, Republican Senator William E. Borah of Idaho suggested that Lindbergh would make a good candidate for president.[30]

In contrast, the *Richmond News Leader* summed up the anti-Lindbergh sentiment in America when it editorialized, "Millions would vote today to hang LINDBERGH or to exile him—as enthusiastically as they cheered and extolled him."[31] Dorothy Thompson, a prominent journalist, wrote in her syndicated column that Lindbergh was a "somber cretin," a man "without human feeling," and a "pro-Nazi recipient of a German medal."[32] Walter Winchell, perhaps the nation's most powerful columnist and also a popular radio commentator, called the "Lone Eagle" the "Lone Ostrich."[33] Once in 1940, when Lindbergh went to a theater to watch footage of one of his recent speeches, many in the audience hissed as the famous pilot's image appeared on screen.[34] That same year, the Lindberghs received such a large amount of obscene letters—largely unsigned— that the Post Office took the precaution of inspecting their mail.[35]

As controversy swirled around Lindbergh in public, the Roosevelt administration worked intently to lessen his impact in private. Indeed, the extent to which the administration went to neutralize Lindbergh illustrates the incredible power this icon of isolationism wielded in prewar America. Hours before his first radio address, "America and European Wars," on September 15, 1939, the administration informed Lindbergh that it was "very much worried" that he intended to broadcast his views. If Lindbergh would refrain from speaking out, he was told, the administration would create for him the cabinet position secretary of air.[36]

In response to another broadcast, "The Air Defense of America," which Lindbergh gave on May 19, 1940, Roosevelt wrote to Secretary of War Henry L. Stimson that "this youngster has completely abandoned his belief in our form of government." Lindbergh's speech, the president added, "could not have been better put if it had been written by Goebbels himself."[37] At the same time, Roosevelt asked J. Edgar Hoover and the FBI to investigate hundreds of people who wired their support of Lindbergh's opposition to the president's preparedness program.[38] "I'll clip that young man's wings," the president later said.[39]

Though the administration's anti-Lindbergh activities took place behind the scenes, President Roosevelt's enmity occasionally bubbled to the surface in the form of good-humored, though still sharp, jabs. When asked at a press conference why Colonel Lindbergh had not been called into service, Roosevelt launched into what biographer A. Scott Berg aptly calls a "folksy history lesson" on the Civil War's "Vallandighams."

> If you go back to the roster of the Army in the Civil War—we called on people there from liberty-loving people on both sides—both the Confederates and the North . . . On the other hand, the Confederacy and the North let certain people go. In other words, in both armies there were—what shall I call them?—there were Vallandighams. . . .
>
> Well, Vallandigham, as you know, was an appeaser. [*Laughter.*] He wanted to make peace from 1863 on because the North "couldn't win." Once upon a time there was a place called Valley Forge and there were an awful lot of appeasers that pleaded with Washington to quit, because he "couldn't win."

A reporter piped in: "Were you still talking about Mr. Lindbergh?" "Yes," the president replied, drawing laughter and the next day's headlines.[40]

At no time was any reaction so intense, and any denunciation so severe, as that following Lindbergh's antiwar address on September 11, 1941, at the Des Moines Coliseum in Iowa. In this culmination of a series of speeches in which Lindbergh had hinted at mysterious groups that were selfishly and unnecessarily pushing the country towards war, Lindbergh named them publicly in Des Moines for the first time: "The three most important groups who have been pressing this country toward war are the British, the Jewish, and the Roosevelt administration." "If any one of these groups . . . stops agitating for war," Lindbergh explained to the crowd of eight thousand, "I believe there will be little danger of our involvement."

Despite the fact that support for U.S. entrance into the European war was below 15 percent in September 1941,[41] publishers of all stripes throughout the nation carried vituperative attacks on the speech.[42] The *Des Moines Register* called it the "the worst speech he has made so far."[43] The *New York Herald Tribune* excoriated the speech for its anti-Semitism and called it an appeal to "dark forces of prejudice and intolerance." To the *New York Times* Lindbergh's words were "completely un-American."[44] On September 27, the *Nation* summarized popular sentiment: "Reactions to Lindbergh's speech at Des Moines continue, two weeks after the event, to be vigorous and almost universally unfavorable. Scarcely a newspaper has failed to rebuke the ex-colonel."[45]

Politicians joined in the buffeting as well. Presidential secretary Stephen Early compared Lindbergh's words with the recent "outpouring from Berlin."[46] Wendell Wilkie called the Des Moines speech "the most un-American talk made in my time by any person of national reputation."[47] Even the lower house of the Texas Legislature went so far as to adopt a resolution suggesting that Lindbergh stay away from Texas.[48]

In sum, the Des Moines address represents the nadir of Lindbergh's career as an antiwar leader, and marks the end of the course of events that propelled him from, as one columnist put it, "Public Hero No. 1" to "Public Enemy No. 1."[49] The man who had been met in 1927 by a ticker-tape parade of four-million cheering supporters in New York City after his record-breaking transatlantic flight in the *Spirit of St. Louis* was, by 1941, having his writings pulled from libraries across America[50] and having his name literally whitewashed from his home town's water tower.[51]

But though his speech was by almost all accounts a failure—for Lindbergh, for America First, and for the anti-intervention movement generally—the "Lone Eagle's" diatribe against "the British, the Jewish and the Roosevelt administration" is still memorable, as a piece of antiwar literature, for its attempt to demonize—and, by the process of "naming," exorcise—the real or imaginary forces leading the country to war. Indeed, because of the speech's clearly recognizable structure, its strong though not strident tone, and its clear and concise use of language, the speech remains a model of its kind.[52]

IT IS NOW TWO YEARS since this latest European war began. From that day in September, 1939, until the present moment, there has been an ever-increasing effort to force the United States into the conflict.

That effort has been carried on by foreign interests, and by a small minority of our own people; but it has been so successful that, today, our country stands on the verge of war.

At this time, as the war is about to enter its third winter, it seems appropriate to review the circumstances that have led us to our present position. Why are we on the verge of war? Was it necessary for us to become so deeply involved? Who is responsible for changing our national policy from one of neutrality and independence to one of entanglement in European affairs? . . .

When this war started in Europe, it was clear that the American people were solidly opposed to entering it. Why shouldn't we be? We had the best defensive position in the world; we had a tradition of independence from Europe; and the one time we did take part in a European war left European problems unsolved, and debts to America unpaid.

National polls showed that when England and France declared war on Germany, in 1939, less than 10 per cent of our population favored a similar course for America.

But there were various groups of people, here and abroad, whose interests and beliefs necessitated the involvement of the United States in the war. I shall point out some of these groups tonight, and outline their methods of procedure. In doing this, I must speak with the utmost frankness, for in order to counteract their efforts, we must know exactly who they are.

The three most important groups who have been pressing this country toward war are the British, the Jewish, and the Roosevelt administration.

Behind these groups, but of lesser importance, are a number of capitalists, Anglophiles, and intellectuals, who believe that their future, and the future of mankind, depend upon the domination of the British empire.

Add to these the Communistic groups who were opposed to intervention until a few weeks ago, and I believe I have named the major war agitators in this country.

I am speaking here only of war agitators, not of those sincere but misguided men and women who, confused by misinformation and frightened by propaganda, follow the lead of the war agitators.

As I have said, these war agitators comprise only a small minority of our people; but they control a tremendous influence. Against the determination of the American people to stay out of war, they have marshalled the power of their propaganda, their money, their patronage.

Let us consider these groups, one at a time.

First, the British: It is obvious and perfectly understandable, that Great Britain wants the United States in the war on her side.

England is now in a desperate position. Her population is not large enough and her armies are not strong enough to invade the continent of Europe and win the war she declared against Germany.

Her geographical position is such that she cannot win the war by the use of aviation alone, regardless of how many planes we send her. Even if America entered the war, it is improbable that the Allied armies could invade Europe and overwhelm the Axis powers.

But one thing is certain. If England can draw this country into the war, she can shift to our shoulders a large portion of the responsibility for waging it, and for paying its cost. . . .

We know that England is spending great sums of money for propaganda in America during the present war. If we were Englishmen, we would do the same.

But our interest is first in America; and, as Americans, it is essential for us to realize the effort that British interests are making to draw us into their war.

The second major group I mentioned is the Jewish.

It is not difficult to understand why Jewish people desire the overthrow of Nazi Germany. The persecution they suffered in Germany would be sufficient to make bitter enemies of any race.

No person with a sense of the dignity of mankind can condone the persecution of the Jewish race in Germany. But no person of honesty and vision can look on their pro-war policy here today without seeing the dangers involved in such a policy, both for us and for them.

Instead of agitating for war, the Jewish groups in this country should be opposing it in every possible way, for they will be among the first to feel its consequences.

Tolerance is a virtue that depends upon peace and strength. History shows that it cannot survive war and devastation.

A few far-sighted Jewish people realize this, and stand opposed to intervention. But the majority still do not.

Their greatest danger to this country lies in their large ownership and influence in our motion pictures, our press, our radio and our government.

I am not attacking either the Jewish or the British people. Both races, I admire.

But I am saying that the leaders of both the British and the Jewish races, for reasons which are as understandable from their viewpoint as they are inadvisable from ours, for reasons which are not American, wish to involve us in the war.

We cannot blame them for looking out for what they believe to be their own interests, but we also must look out for ours. We cannot allow the natural passions and prejudices of other peoples to lead our country to destruction. [*Applause.*]

The Roosevelt administration is the third powerful group which has been carrying this country toward war. [*Boos.*]

Its members have used [*boos*] the war emergency [*boos*] to obtain a third presidential term for the first time in American history. They have used the war to add unlimited billions to a debt which was already the highest we have ever known.

And they have just used the war to justify the restriction of congressional power, and the assumption of dictatorial procedures on the part of the president and his appointees. [*Applause and boos.*]

The power of the Roosevelt administration depends upon the maintenance of a wartime emergency.

The prestige of the Roosevelt administration depends upon the success of Great Britain to whom the president attached his political future at a time when most people thought that England and France would easily win the war.

The danger of the Roosevelt administration lies in its subterfuge.

While its members have promised us peace, they have led us to war—heedless of the platform upon which they were elected.

In selecting these three groups as the major agitators for war, I have included only those whose support is essential to the war party.

If any one of these groups—the British, the Jewish, or the administration—stops agitating for war, I believe there will be little danger of our involvement.

I do not believe that any two of them are powerful enough to carry this country to war without the support of the third. And to these three, as I have said, all other war groups are of secondary importance.

When hostilities commenced in Europe, in 1939, it was realized by these groups that the American people had no intention of entering the war. They knew it would be worse than useless to ask us for a declaration of war at that time. But they believed that this country could be enticed into the war in very much the same way we were enticed into the last one. [*Applause.*]

They planned: First, to prepare the United States for foreign war under the guise of American defense; second, to involve us in the war, step by step, without our realization; third, to create a series of incidents which would force us into the actual conflict. . . .

Men and women of Iowa: Only one thing holds this country from war today. That is the rising opposition of the American people.

Our system of democracy and representative government is on test today as it has never been before.

We are on the verge of a war in which the only victor would be chaos and prostration.

We are on the verge of a war for which we are still unprepared, and for which no one has offered a feasible plan for victory—a war which cannot be won without sending our soldiers across the ocean to force a landing on a hostile coast against armies stronger than our own.

We are on the verge of war, but it is not yet too late to stay out.

It is not yet too late to show that no amount of money, or propaganda, or patronage can force a free and independent people into war against its will. It is not yet too late to retrieve and to maintain the independent American destiny that our forefathers established in this new world.

The entire future of America rests upon our shoulders. It depends upon our action, our courage, and our intelligence. If you oppose our intervention in this war, now is the time to make your voice heard.

Help us to organize these meetings; and write to your representatives in Washington. I tell you that the last stronghold of democracy and representative government in this country is in our house of representatives and our senate.

There, we can still make our will known. And if we, the American people, do that, independence and freedom will continue to live among us, and there will be no foreign war.

# Korean War (1950-1953)

Two major world powers emerged from the Second World War: the United States and the Soviet Union. The contrasting political ideologies represented by these two regimes, democracy on the one hand and Communism on the other, would play out on the world's stage over the next forty-five years. Indeed, it was the threat of Communism that drove U.S. postwar foreign policy until the collapse and subsequent dissolution of the Soviet government in 1991. Almost immediately after World War II ended, the Cold War began.

Though direct war between the United States and the Soviet Union never occurred, many indirect conflicts took place in which the United States attempted to contain its rival's influence. These indirect conflicts pitted the United States against a Soviet proxy. Thus, in Korea, the United States fought the Communist Democratic People's Republic of Korea; in Vietnam it fought the Communist Democratic Republic of Vietnam; and in Grenada it fought the Communist People's Revolutionary Government.

These indirect armed conflicts (and, for that matter, those in which the United States participated by supplying funds, military training, or weapons) constituted a particularly important objective to the United States because of their dual meaning. In one sense, the United States was simply trying to win local wars and support democratic governments abroad. On another, it was endeavoring to fend off the Soviet Union's worldwide influence. The Soviet Union's exertion of soft power over satellite nations troubled the United States because, as the theory went, if one country came under the influence of Communism, other countries would soon follow like dominos.

Though the United States supplied economic and military aid to Greece and Turkey during the Greek Civil War (1946–1949), it was the Korean War (1950–1953) that marked the country's first full-scale military involvement in the Cold War. Since 1945, Korea had been divided by the 38th parallel. The North was sympathetic to the Soviets; the South, to the United States and the newly formed United Nations. Both the Soviet Union and the United States withdrew their respective militaries from Korea in 1949, but on June 25, 1950, the North Korean People's Army crossed the 38th parallel to invade the South.

Two days later, President Harry S. Truman ordered the U.S. Air Force and Navy to aid South Korea.

Over the next three years, 1,789,000 Americans served in the Korean theater. Of these, approximately 35,000 soldiers died.[1] The Koreans suffered at least 2 million civilian casualties, and probably more than 1 million combat casualties.[2] The Chinese, who intervened in the war on behalf of North Korea in 1950, lost between 382,000 (Chinese estimate) and 1 to 1.5 million (U.S. estimate).[3] Though the United States and South Korea provided over 90 percent of the manpower under the UN command, the fifteen other countries that contributed suffered more than 17,000 casualties.[4] An armistice was signed by the UN command, the North Koreans, and the Chinese on July 27, 1953.

America's second "Red Scare" muted most antiwar dissent before and during the Korean War. Through such investigatory bodies as the House Un-American Activities Committee (HUAC) in the House of Representatives, the anti-Communist leader Joseph McCarthy in the Senate, mandatory loyalty boards, and the passage of the McCarran Internal Security Act of 1950,[5] the government brought to bear substantial resources to find, silence, and punish those deemed to be disloyal or subversive. The chilling effect on free speech was severe and pervasive, because even activities that did not rise to the level of illegality could lead to one's undoing. Though periodic "witch hunts" did not necessary result in convictions or even prosecutions, for example, they nevertheless ruined their targets' professional and personal lives. Paul Robeson and W. E. B. Du Bois are cases in point. Both men chose to speak out against, among other things, the military conflict in Korea. And even though their actions were never deemed to be criminal, the consequences of their dissent were disastrous. Robeson gave a scathing prewar address on June 19, 1949, approximately one year before North Korea crossed the 38th parallel. His pro-Soviet and antiwar activities effectively destroyed his career. For his part, the eighty-two-year-old Du Bois began campaigning for a seat in the U.S. Senate on a peace platform on September 24, 1950. His maiden campaign speech is included below. A few months after Du Bois lost the election, the government began prosecuting him in federal court, arguing that an antiwar organization he chaired was a "principal of a foreign agent." Although the government's case against Du Bois was dismissed, the trial marked another alienating moment for Du Bois, who eventually left the United States to live in Ghana.


## Paul Robeson Declares that Blacks Will Never Fight the Soviet Union

If we must die, let it be in Mississippi or Georgia.


Cold War tensions were high in April 1949. The Chinese Communists had captured Nanking and were advancing on Shanghai, East Asia's preeminent symbol of the West. The U.S. Senate Foreign Relations Committee was considering the North Atlantic Treaty, which would establish a military alliance aimed at protecting Western nations from the Soviet bloc. The Russians were about to detonate their first atomic bomb and bring the possibility of bilateral nuclear war to the world's doorstep.

As the superpowers militarized, Paul Robeson, then the most popular black entertainer in America, traveled to Paris during an international concert tour to attend the World Congress of the Partisans of Peace.[6] Gathering on April 20 with other world peace leaders—including Irène Joliot-Curie, Pablo Picasso, and W. E. B. Du Bois—Robeson sang to two thousand delegates before uttering some extemporaneous remarks that, as his biographer Martin Bauml Duberman puts it, "were to reverberate around the world, marking a fateful divide in his life."[7]

The Associated Press quoted Robeson as follows: "It is unthinkable that American Negroes would go to war on behalf of those who have oppressed us for generations against a country [the Soviet Union] which in one generation has raised our people to the full dignity of mankind."[8] The *New York Times* noted that Robeson declared, "We colonial peoples have contributed to the building of the United States and are determined to share in its wealth. We denounce the policy of the United States Government which is similar to that of Hitler and of Goebbels. We want peace and liberty and will combat for them along with the Soviet Union, the democracies of Eastern Europe, China and Indonesia."[9]

Robeson's remarks were reprinted widely across the United States. The white press called him a traitor, the black press claimed he spoke merely for himself, and government agencies brainstormed about how to oust the "black and red" Robeson from the United States.[10] Robeson did not back down; when he returned to the United States from his European concert tour, he greeted a predominantly hostile public with a vicious counter-attack. On June 19, he criticized his detractors at a four-and-a-half-hour "Welcome Home Rally" at Rockland Palace in Harlem. W. E. B. Du Bois, Congressman Vito Marcantonio, and air force colonel (later general) Ben Davis Jr., among others, gave formal addresses to a crowd of five thousand, about half of whom were white, but it was Robeson who provided the evening's "real fireworks."[11] Incensed by the mob of reporters who had disrupted the wedding ceremony of his son earlier that day (an event not without drama of its own, because Robeson's son was marrying a white woman), Robeson "threw the full weight of his enormous emotional gravity into one of the most powerful polemics of his career, the passionate eloquence of his voice washing over the occasional patches of rhetoric."[12]

After an ethos-driven introduction in which he described his impoverished youth, forecast his theme of the importance of racial equality, and praised the Soviet Union's commitment "human dignity," Robeson reiterated his antiwar statement in Paris: "At the Paris Peace Conference I said it was unthinkable that Negro people of America or elsewhere in the world could be drawn into war with the Soviet Union. I repeat it with a hundred-fold emphasis. THEY WILL NOT." Then, in the middle of the speech, Robeson laid out his argument that the Soviet Union posed no threat to blacks in America or throughout the world; on the contrary, Robeson stated, the Soviets were among blacks' "friends and allies." Finally, in a rousing peroration, Robeson channeled the Harlem Renaissance poet Claude McKay and, like Richard Wright, used war abroad to highlight injustices at home: "If we must die, let it be in Mississippi or Georgia. Let it be wherever we are lynched and deprived of our rights as human beings. Let this be a final answer to the warmongers. Let them know that we will not help to enslave our brothers and sisters and eventually ourselves. Rather, we will help to insure peace in our time."

Even as Robeson criticized the "warmongers" and expressed heretical sympathies with the Soviet Union, he reserved his most ferocious words for the African Americans who had, in his view, betrayed their race by supporting the United States. More than the advent of war, it seems, Robeson was concerned that black leadership in America was selling out to powerful white interests and willfully blinding themselves to the "indefensible truth about our degradation and exploitation":

> What a travesty is this supposed leadership of a great people . . . this spectacle of a craven, fawning, despicable leadership, able to be naught but errand boys, and at the lowest level, stooges and cowardly renegades, a disgrace to the Negro people and to the real and true America of which they so glibly talk. Let them get their crumbs from their Wall Street masters who long ago figure[d] out how to corrupt. Let them snatch their bit of cheese and go scampering rat-like into their holes, where, by heaven, the Negro people will keep them, left to their dirty consciences, if any they have.

Robeson's career was ruined. The next day, a *New York Times* headline blared, "Loves Soviet Best, Robeson Declares."[13] The next week, a front-page editorial carried by Hearst newspapers declared that "it was an accident unfortunate for America that Robeson was born here."[14] The FBI, which sent agents to the Rockland Palace event, dutifully added pages to Robeson's "Loyalty" file.[15] The Senate Judiciary Committee decided to investigate Robeson, and in July the House Un-American Activities Committee invited prominent African Americans to testify against him. One witness was ex-Communist Manning Johnson, who testified that Robeson dreamed of becoming a "Black Stalin."[16] Another was Jackie Robinson, the first African American to break the racial line in major league baseball.

The anti-Robeson hysteria soon turned violent. In August, the Veterans of Foreign Wars, the Jewish War Veterans, the Catholic War Veterans, and others scheduled an anti-Robeson parade to coincide with a concert he was to give in Peekskill, New York. Robeson fans heading to the event were met by a jeering mob of men in military uniforms. Many carried sticks and rocks.[17] The concert was canceled, but Robeson, undeterred, planned to return in September. The "Peekskill Riots" that resulted from that September visit left hundreds of Robeson supporters injured.[18] The city's police force turned a blind eye to, and in some cases encouraged, the violence on the part of the five thousand people who lined the exit roads with stones and rocks.[19]

This pattern of repression continued for at least a decade. The State Department rescinded Robeson's passport in 1950 and refused to issue a new one until he signed a non-Communist oath and pledged not to give political speeches abroad.[20] Because he was blacklisted at home and unable to perform to eager crowds abroad, his income fell from over one hundred thousand dollars in 1947 to six thousand dollars in 1952. In 1956, Robeson, still fighting back, appeared before HUAC to tell the senators, "You are the Un-Americans."[21] In 1958, Robeson published his autobiography, *Here I Stand,* but despite the fact that he was still a worldwide sensation, it was not reviewed by any major American newspaper until the 1970s.

In short, Robeson's life was an "American tragedy"—awesome potential suffocated an environment hostile to blacks and designed to snuff out dissent.[22] In 1919, Robeson had graduated from Rutgers as valedictorian. The class prophesized that by 1940 he would be governor of New Jersey, would have "dimmed the fame of Booker T. Washington," and would be "the leader of the colored race in America."[23] Robeson graduated from Columbia Law School in 1923, but decided to pursue a career in theater after a stenographer at his law firm refused to take down a memorandum. "I never take dictation from a nigger," she said.[24] Robeson then made theater history by being the first black man to perform Shakespeare's *Othello.* He sang "'Ol' Man River" to great acclaim on Broadway in the musical *Show Boat.* In 1940, *Collier's* magazine called Robeson "the favorite male Negro singer" of concertgoers and "America's No. 1 Negro entertainer."[25]

Years of harassment took its toll on Robeson's physical and mental health. Toward the end of his life, Robeson was frequently hospitalized for exhaustion, a circulatory ailment, and what his doctor called "endogenous depression in a manic depressive personality."[26] Robeson attempted suicide twice, and submitted to drug and electric shock therapy that, his son claims, caused permanent brain damage.[27] In 1963, at the age of sixty-five, Robeson went into seclusion, and he died thirteen years later.

As James Baldwin observed of the American who had been both prince and pariah, "In the days when it seemed that there was no possibility in raising the individual voice and no possibility of applying the rigors of conscience, Paul Robeson spoke in a great voice which creates a man."[28]

. . . [T]ODAY I DEFY any part of an insolent, dominating America, however powerful. I defy any errand boys, Uncle Toms of the Negro people, to challenge my Americanism, because by word and deed, I challenge this vicious system to the teeth; because I refuse to let my personal success, as part of a fraction of one-percent of the Negro people, to [*sic*] explain away the injustices to fourteen million of my people. Because with all the energy at my command, I fight for the right of the Negro people and other oppressed labor-driven Americans to have decent homes, decent jobs, and the dignity that belongs to every human being. . . .

. . . What a travesty is this supposed leadership of a great people! And in this historic time, when their people need them most. How Sojourner Truth, Harriet Tubman, Fred Douglass must be turning in their graves at this spectacle of a craven, fawning, despicable leadership, unable to be naught but errand boys, and at the lowest level, stooges and cowardly renegades, a disgrace to the Negro people and to the real and true America of which they so glibly talk. Let them get their crumbs from their Wall Street masters who long ago figure[d] out how to corrupt. Let them snatch their bit of cheese and go scampering rat-like into their holes, where, by heaven, the Negro people will keep them, left to their dirty consciences, if any they have. . . .

. . . I love this Soviet people more than any other nation, because of their suffering and sacrifices for us, the Negro people, the progressive people, the people of the future in this world. At the Paris Conference, I said it was unthinkable that the Negro people of America or elsewhere in the world could be drawn into war with the Soviet Union. I repeat it with a hundred-fold emphasis. THEY WILL NOT. And don't ask a few intellectuals who are jealous of their comfort. As[k] the sugar worker[s] whom I saw starving in Louisiana, the workers in the cotton lands and the tobacco belts in the South. Ask the sugar worker[s] in Jamaica. As[k] the Afric[ans] in Malan's South Africa. Ask them if they will struggle for peace and friendship with the Soviet people, with the peoples of China and the new democrac[ies] or help their imperialist oppressors to return them to an even worse slavery. The answer lies there in the [m]illions of my struggling people, not only 14 million in America, but 40 million in the Caribbean and Latin America—one hundred million in Africa. No wonder all the excitement. For one day this mighty mass will strike for freedom, and a new strength like that of gallant China will add its decisive weight to insuring a world where all men can be free and equal. I am born and bred in this America of ours. I want to love it. I love a part of it. But it's up to the rest of America when I shall love it with the same intensity that I love the Negro people from whom I spring,—in the way that I love progressives in the Caribbean, the black and Indian peoples of South and Central America, the peoples of China and Southeast Asia. Yes, suffering people the world over—in the way that I deeply and intensely love the Soviet Union. That burden of proof rests upon America. . . .

. . . The so-called Western democracies, including our own[,] which so fiercely exploit us and daily deny us our simple constitutional guarantees, can find no answer before the bar of world justice for their treatment of the Negro people—Democracy, indeed! We must have the courage to shout at the top of our voices about our injustices and we must lay the blame where it belongs and where it has belonged for over 300 years of slavery and misery[:] right here on our own doorstep[,] not in any far away place. This is the very time when we can win our struggle.

And we cannot win it by being lured into any kind of war with our closest friends and allies throughout the world. For any kind of decent life—we need, we want, and we demand our constitutional rights—RIGHT HERE in America. We do not want to die in vain anymore on foreign battlefields for Wall Street and the greedy supporters of domestic fascism. If we must die, let it be in Mississippi or Georgia. Let it be wherever we are lynched and deprived of our rights as human beings. Let this be a final answer to the warmongers. Let them know that we will not help to enslave our brothers and sisters and eventually ourselves. Rather, we will help to insure peace in our time—the freedom and liberation of the Negro and other struggling peoples and the building of a world where we can all walk in full equality and full human dignity.

## W. E. B. Du Bois Runs for Congress on a Peace Platform

War is Big Business and a business immensely profitable to a
few, but of measureless disaster and death of dream to the
many.

The first African American to earn a Ph.D. from Harvard, a cofounder of the National
Association for the Advancement of Colored People (NAACP), a leading exponent of
Pan-Africanism, a historian, an economist, a sociologist, a teacher, a magazine editor, a
novelist, a governmental envoy, a poet, W. E. B. Du Bois devoted his prodigious talents
and entire life to actualizing his race's longing for full freedom and dignity. "Undoubt-
edly the most important modern African-American intellectual," wrote Thomas C. Holt,
Du Bois "gave form to the consciousness animating the work of practically all other
modern African-American intellectuals to follow."[29]

Du Bois's gradual alienation from American society—which would culminate in his
joining the American Communist Party in 1961 and becoming a citizen of Ghana two
years later—is well documented and often discussed with respect to his views on domestic
policy and colonialism.[30] But less attention has been paid to Du Bois's gradual disillusionment with the United States as seen through the lens of America's major wars. In fact,
Du Bois's critiques of U.S. involvement in World War I, World War II, and the Korean
conflict exemplify his declining faith in the promise of American democracy, and they
offer support for the proposition that radicals are made, not born.

For example, soon after the United States declared war on Germany in 1917, Du Bois
penned "Close Ranks," a prowar editorial that offered the government his active support.
"While this war lasts," he wrote in the July 1918 issue of the *Crisis,* "let us . . . forget our
special grievances and close our ranks shoulder to shoulder with our own white fellow
citizens and with the allied nations that are fighting for democracy."[31] After the publication of "Close Ranks," Du Bois was criticized for giving Wilson's war program *too much*
support.[32] And when the public learned that Du Bois was considering a captaincy in the
U.S. Army, the black *Cleveland Gazette* called Du Bois a "traitor" and a "Benedict
Arnold" to his race.[33]

After Pearl Harbor in 1941, Du Bois again backed the government and endorsed the
war.[34] But, recalling his editorial twenty-four years earlier, this time he did so wearily: "We
close ranks again, but only, now as then, to fight for democracy not only for white folk but
for yellow, brown, and black. We fight not in joy but in sorrow with no feeling of uplift;
but under the sad weight of duty and in part, as we know to our sorrow, because of the
inheritance of a slave psychology which makes it easier for us to submit rather than to rebel.
Whatever all our mixed emotions are, we are going to play the game."[35] Thus, even though
Du Bois acknowledged the blight of racial discrimination and violence during the twenties
and thirties—as early as 1920 Du Bois had characterized World War I as "the jealous and
avaricious struggle for the largest share in exploiting darker races"[36]—he was willing to
suspend temporarily his doubts and rally behind the American flag.

By the end of World War II, though, Du Bois appeared fed up with American democracy. It had failed to end racism at home—Du Bois himself was still carrying his lunch to work at the NAACP in New York because no restaurant in the area would serve him[37]—and it had done little to stem colonialism abroad. Influenced by Karl Marx, Du Bois fused the plight of blacks and laborers throughout the world, and became a vocal defender of Russian Communism. Thus, when Winston Churchill inaugurated the Cold War in Fulton, Missouri, on March 5, 1946, by declaring that an "iron curtain" had descended between Russia and Western Europe, Du Bois moaned that Churchill's speech was "one of the most discouraging occurrences of modern times."[38] And in an essay published that August, Du Bois wrote that in attempting to abolish "race or class discrimination,"[39] Russia was the "most hopeful country on earth."[40]

Du Bois found himself thrust into the crucible of Cold War justice. As founder of the Peace Information Center (PIC) in 1950, Du Bois helped distribute the Stockholm Peace Appeal, a "ban the bomb" petition that received at least 2.5 million signatures in the United States and more than 150 million worldwide.[41] Secretary of State Dean Acheson attacked the petition in the *New York Times*,[42] UN Ambassador Warren Austin termed petition signers "traitors,"[43] and the Justice Department put enough pressure on Du Bois and the PIC that by the end of October the organization decided to terminate its activities and dissolve.[44]

Meanwhile, Du Bois decided to accept an offer from the American Labor Party to run for United States Senator from New York. Du Bois had initially laughed at the idea of running for public office, but he reconsidered the offer after the government threatened him with indictment. "I do not expect to be elected as United States Senator," he claimed early in the campaign, "but I do expect to get a chance to talk. It is about the only way one can express one's opinion these days."[45] Du Bois gave the speech that appears below at a press conference on September 24, 1950, the first day of his senatorial campaign. It was reprinted in the *Guardian* the following week.[46] He ultimately lost, of course, but not before closing his campaign with the warning that "we are voting for our lives" and summoning voters "to your tents, O Israel." Du Bois won two hundred thousand votes, or 3.9 percent of the total.[47]

Later events provide an interesting historical coda to Du Bois's antiwar activities. In order to avert prosecution by the Justice Department, Du Bois and the PIC dissolved their antiwar organization on October 12, 1950, one month into his Senate campaign.[48] The government refused to relent, however, and a federal grand jury handed down an indictment against Du Bois in Washington, D.C., on February 9, 1951. The following week, Du Bois was arraigned and briefly handcuffed in Federal Court. On February 23, Du Bois turned eighty-three and, to his humiliation, many of his friends and acquaintances declined to attend the celebration and speak on his behalf for fear of guilt by association. Thus, a man who in 1948 headed the *Negro Digest* list of "The Big Ten Who Run America,"[49] and whom Henry Steele Commager, a popular historian, compared to Benjamin Franklin and Thomas Jefferson in his 1948 list "Men Who Make Up Our Minds,"[50] became a social pariah. Du Bois's autobiographical quip about his experience in the early forties, when he stood accused by the FBI of being a socialist, was prescient: "I would have been hailed with approval if I had died at fifty. At seventy-five my death was practically requested."[51]

Du Bois's trial began on November 8, 1951, and attracted national and international criticism. Langston Hughes wrote of the trial, "The Accusers' Name Nobody Will Remember but History Records Du Bois." The *Chicago Defender* published Hughes's work, and the Du Bois Defense Committee set about distributing it widely in barber-shops and beauty parlors. "If W. E. B. Dubois goes to jail," Hughes wrote, "a wave of wonder will sweep around the world."[52] Vito Marcantonio, an antiwar congressman, gave the opening defense argument. Albert Einstein was scheduled to appear on behalf of Du Bois as a character witness. As Gerald Horne writes, "There may not have been a larger protest against a political prosecution since the Scottsboro or Sacco-Vanzetti cases."[53] On November 13, 1951, a federal judge dismissed the *United States v. Peace Information Center* case and chided the government for failing to provide any solid evidence of wrongdoing. To let the case go to the jury, the judge declared, would be to "permit them to speculate on a speculation."[54] Most major Du Bois biographers agree that the prosecution was politically motivated, and unfounded as a matter of law. Thus the Du Bois trial stands as a curious historical footnote: an unusual victory for free speech in a relatively restrictive moment in United States history.[55]

THE GREAT ISSUE, of this time, of this nation, of this world, is peace; and the central theme of this campaign is peace, no more war. There are in this nation today powerful interests which are determined on war. To this end they are suppressing the Bill of Rights so as to stop discussion and stampede the nation through the hysteria of groundless fear.[56] Who is it among us who wants war and why do they want it?

The American Labor Party knows who and why, and there are many others who also know. But the American Labor Party not only knows but it is going to do something about it. . . .

Our party . . . has selected candidates for governor and lieutenant-governor; for comptroller and attorney-general, for members of the legislature and of the federal Congress and for local offices.

It has asked me to run for the United States Senate. This is for me a new role. Only once in my life have I held public office, and that was when for a month I was, in 1928 [*sic;* 1923], made Special Minister Plenipotentiary to Liberia. My political activity has been almost wholly confined to writing. In this writing, with some speaking, I tried first to put the Negro vote in proper and effective relation to the national needs. In the first election of Woodrow Wilson, I sought to end Negro subserviency to the Republican Party. I tried to induce the Bull Moose movement to make Negro rights a main plank and fought it when it refused. I opposed Taft's "lily-white" Southern policy and supported the third party movements of La Follette and Henry Wallace. I have never been an active party worker, but I have been an enrolled member of the Socialist Party, of the Democratic Party under the New Deal, and lately of the American Labor Party.

The basic motive of my political thought and activity has been the securing for all Americans, civil and political rights regardless of race or color. I assumed, and assumed too easily, that once color discrimination was done away with, the nation and the world would be free to attack and solve certain basic problems of human progress which I knew full well cried for solution. Behind and beneath this demand for rights therefore lay always the assumption that with the right to vote, the right to think and speak, and the right to know, would come through the very exercise of these fundamental privileges: the basic right of human beings to live, to work; to eat and be sheltered, to be shielded from disease and have their children educated.

But to my amazement and fright, I have lived to see the era of peace to which I was trained to look forward to as the goal of civilization transformed into plans for universal world war; and a theory of progress by war and more war, each more savage and destructive than the last. I now realize that I, as well as you, am facing a crisis in which no considerations of ease or age, suffice to hold us back from a great duty. That duty is the one of trying to bring reason and past experience to bear upon those of us who have gone temporarily insane.

The basic cause of this insanity is the effort of powerful interests, armed by control of press and radio, school and platform, backed by almost unlimited money, to turn the attention of the world from the fundamental problem of our age. That problem is *that in our unprecedented organization of industry, with its marvellous technique and world-wide extent, the vast majority of mankind remain sick, ignorant and starved, while a few have more income in goods and services than they can use.*

It is no sufficient answer to this fundamental problem, to point out that the present degradation of the worker is not so great as it once was, or is much less in some lands than in others. The point is that it is far too great than is necessary or decent and calls for drastic cure now and not a thousand years hence.

This is the basic problem of our culture, no matter how much we try to conceal and ignore it; or try to divert attention from it to other matters. There are no other matters so important or so pressing. We may be led to yell our heads off to convince ourselves that the problem of this world today is the Soviet Union and Communism. That is deliberate deception. The problem of economic justice to working men existed before the Russian revolution and would remain if Russia were swept from the face of the earth tomorrow. Proposals to solve this problem by socialism and communism, did not originate in Russia and will not end there. What Russia did was to attempt to solve this problem in a systematic way, at a time when the 19th century had bequeathed to the world the dogma that the problem of economic justice was insoluble; that most men must always be poor, ignorant and sick, because most men were so inferior in gift and morals that this was inevitable; that civilization depended on making the few masters of the many, the Rich the rulers of the Poor, and thus in this way, and only in this way, could civilization be built and maintained.

Is this true? Whether it is true or not, we have no right to stop people and nations from denying its truth—from denying the necessity of poverty, disease and ignorance, and from experimenting in their own way to make a better world. Moreover, our own duty is clear and that is not to pull down others but rather to build ourselves up; to prove to the world that the economic condition of mankind can be bettered and that we know how to do this and that we propose to prove our belief by action. Instead of this, what are we up to? We are trying to fight an idea. We are going to make nations agree with us and our way of life by using atom bombs, bomber planes, battleships and artillery. And while we are wasting time, wealth and strength in doing this we are doing almost nothing to implement our own idea of progress.[57]

Why? Why do we propose to make the Russian experiment fail, to throttle China and to throw the world into continuous war? The reason is clear: we fear that any success of socialism or communism will interfere with our money-making. We have become a nation of money-makers. We think that money-making is the great end of man. Our whole ideology bows to this fantastic idea. Religion, science, art and morals in America tend to be measured by the profit they bring, and the true vocation of American manhood is regarded as profit-making business enterprise and not social service.

War is big business and a business immensely profitable to a few, but of measureless disaster and death of dream to the many. Big business wants war in order to keep your mind off social reform; it would rather spend your taxes for atom bombs than for schools because in this way it makes more money; it would rather have your sons dying in Korea than studying in America and asking awkward questions. The system which it advocates depends on war and more war.

In order to have war, big business must have hate; so its press and newspapers ask you to hate communists and if not communists, hate all who do not hate communists; indeed hate all who do not take orders from those who now rule America. . . .

It is the theory of democratic government, that when a situation like this arises, two political parties will examine, debate and dispute issues and acts, until the people can make intelligent choice of the problems before them. Today we have only one political party which shares power for the same ends. Men like Dewey and Hanley can only try to outdo what the Democrats have already done; if the Democrats are for war, they are for more war; if the Democrats repudiate the New Deal, the Republicans loathe and despise it; the one point of agreement between the two so-called chief parties is war on any nation or movement which stands in the way of American profit; and the suppression of all discussion of the merits of the present crisis. I try to spread in America news of the peace movement in Europe and I am threatened with jail. Paul Robeson advises Negroes never to fight against people who are striving for a better world for black and white, and he is denied the right to make a living.

In this situation the American Labor party takes its stand on the proposition "There can be no progress without peace." We are the only nation in the civilized world advocating war and compelling other nations to fight. For this we are hated and feared. Our party calls for the immediate settlement of the war in Korea, which an American soldier has directly characterized when he said "I never saw such a useless damned war in all my life." Mediation with both North and South Korea in conference, and China represented in the United Nations, is the only solution. We ask resumption of the free flow of trade between East and West and the utter overthrow of colonialism even when masked under Point Four.

To stop this program of reason and progress, the allied and associated political profit-makers, called the Republican and Democratic parties, have adopted the last tactics of despair. They have made not only truth but civil rights a casualty of war. . . . They have turned your attention from progress and peace to hate and fear. They are making it illegal to think of progress or to advocate peace. Every path to reform like taxation of great wealth; land division; federal aid to education;[58] effective rent control; river development and forest planning are all called communistic or socialistic and their promoters threatened with disgrace, jail or loss of livelihood.

And now as a last exercise of tyranny, we are presented with the McCarran Act—the Fugitive Slave Law of 1950. You know what the Fugitive Slave Law of 1850 was: capital invested in human beings began to run away; foolish northerners, black and white, helped it hide. The slave power ruled the nation as Wall Street rules it today; they passed a bill that made kidnapping of any Negro possible without trial, that made a man prove his freedom instead of forcing masters to prove property; and tried to make abolitionism in itself a crime. This law was so successful that in a decade it brought Civil War and slavery was abolished three years later.

So today, we are bidden to hate communism when what we must hate is war; we are called subversive when we try to think and act as human beings and not as puppets. If we attack segregation in the army or civil life, we are called traitors to America. Against this the American Labor Party protests and fights. And as its candidate for the United States Senate, I ask your vote to curb Big Business and War as represented by Herbert Lehman; War and Big Business as represented by that eminent veteran, Joe Hanley, and to uphold peace and civil rights, sabotaged by Harry Truman.

To the support of this program I welcome everybody: white and black, Jew and Gentile, Democrat, Communist and even Republican.[59]

# Vietnam War (1964-1973)

By the time Congress passed the Gulf of Tonkin Resolution in 1964,[1] Vietnam had already endured two decades of war. After World War II, the Vietnamese nationalist Ho Chi Minh took the opportunity to declare independence from a weakened France. France, however, refused to capitulate to Ho Chi Minh's demands, and opted instead to fight for the colony it had controlled since the mid- to late nineteenth century. The United States, which viewed the conflict in Vietnam in the context of its own opposition to Communism, supported France. In fact, after 1950 the United States funded up to 80 percent of France's war.[2]

When France was defeated in 1954, Vietnam slid into civil war. The United States sided with the fledgling anticommunist government of the South, and provided its leader, Ngo Dinh Diem, with military and economic aid. The U.S. rationale was the same as that used in Korea: to help the South withstand the rising tide of Soviet-inspired Communism in the North. Unfortunately for the United States, though, the Communist National Liberation Front of South Vietnam was able to effectively destabilize the South's government. After Diem was overthrown and murdered, the government of South Vietnam deteriorated rapidly.

Faced with a decision whether to effectively acquiesce to the North Vietnamese and allow the entire country to be swept by Communism, or to head off the Communist threat with more aggressive military action, President Lyndon B. Johnson chose the latter. After the president reported publicly that North Vietnam had conducted "further deliberate attacks against U.S. naval vessels operating in international waters,"* Congress

---

* The "attacks" that occurred in the Gulf of Tonkin in early August 1964, and that precipitated a significantly more expansive military commitment, are the subject of considerable debate and controversy. It is widely thought that information upon which Johnson relied was incomplete and inaccurate. Johnson himself expressed doubt about the substance of the purported attacks when, six weeks later, he instructed Secretary of Defense Robert McNamara to investigate the events further. "You just came in a few weeks ago and said that—'Damn, they are launching an attack on us—they are firing on us.' When we got through with all the firing, we concluded maybe they hadn't fired at all." Michael Beschloss, *Reaching for Glory: Lyndon Johnson's Secret White House Tapes, 1964–1965* (New York: Simon and Schuster, 2002), 39. The next year, Johnson also reportedly said, "For all I know, our Navy was shooting at whales out there." Joseph C.

passed the Gulf of Tonkin Resolution nearly unanimously.[3] In doing so, the legislative branch gave the executive branch wide-ranging power to use "all necessary measures to repel any armed attack against the armed forces of the United States and to prevent further aggression."[4] Though never formally declared, the country's most controversial war had begun.

After President Johnson first committed combat troops to Vietnam in 1965, the intensity of the conflict escalated steadily. American troops, many of whom were drafted, numbered only six thousand at the beginning of the conflict, but swelled to over five hundred and thirty-six thousand in 1968.[5] The United States was also aided by some eight hundred thousand South Vietnamese troops and sixty-eight thousand troops provided by other countries.[6] Communist troops, including those in the South as well as in the North, numbered three hundred thousand in 1963, but one million a decade later.[7]

American casualties were significant. The National Liberation Front waged systemic guerilla warfare against the U.S. military. More than fifty-eight thousand Americans died during the war.[8] Approximately one hundred and fifty thousand were nonmortally wounded.[9] Vietnamese casualties were much greater. The U.S. use of massive bombing campaigns,[10] air strafing, and Agent Orange produced carnage among the Vietnamese population. Widespread use of carpet bombing incinerated large tracts of land and extracted a particularly large toll on the civilian population.[11] In 1995, the Vietnamese government announced that during the twenty-one-year "American period" of the conflict, some 1.1 million Communist soldiers and some 4 million civilians died.[12]

More antiwar dissent took place during the Vietnam War than any other previous war in American history. It is also the first war during which antiwar speeches appear to have been compiled and disseminated widely. *We Accuse* (1965) and *Teach-ins, U. S. A.* (1967) represent some of the earliest attempts to record antiwar speeches in book form.[13]

This anthology provides a varied, but no by means comprehensive, collection of the most significant antiwar speeches during the Vietnam era. Martin Luther King's relatively early "Beyond Vietnam" speech in New York on April 4, 1967, was a seminal speech for King and the country. After giving the speech, King was attacked by those who believed that his vocal antiwar stance would delegitimize his leadership role in American society

---

Goulden, *Truth Is the First Casualty: The Gulf of Tonkin Affair: Illusion and Reality* (New York: Rand McNally, 1969), 160.

In 2005, the National Security Agency (NSA) released hundreds of pages of long-secret documents on the Gulf of Tonkin incident. Scott Shane, "Vietnam War Intelligence 'Deliberately Skewed,' Secret Study Says," *New York Times*, December 2, 2005. The documents are not inconsistent with the theory that the president's justification for the Gulf of Tonkin Resolution was overstated, if not misleading. Among the declassified documents was a detailed fifty-five-page report by NSA Historian Robert J. Hanyok, "Skunks, Bogies, Silent Hounds, and the Flying Fish: The Gulf of Tonkin Mystery, 2–4 August 1964," *Cryptologic Quarterly* 19, no. 4 / 20, no. 1 (2000/2001): 1–55. Analyzing previously unreleased "signals intelligence," Hanyok concludes that the outright existence of an "attack" on August 4, 1964, was "based on very thin evidence" and that the president "indulged in a very selective use of information." "If the administration had not lied exactly, it had not been exactly honest with the public" (47). But see Louis F. Giles, "The Gulf of Tonkin Mystery: The SIGINT Hounds were Howling," December 5, 2005 (noting that the absence of a "communications intelligence" attack message cannot conclusively prove there was not an attack"). Giles's article is readily available via the NSA website, http://www.nsa.gov.

and sacrifice the burgeoning civil rights movement. Eugene McCarthy's December 2, 1967, antiwar speech in Chicago presaged much of the hotly contested 1968 Democratic primaries. Robert F. Kennedy's March 18, 1968, antiwar speech at Kansas State University, the first formal speech of his presidential campaign, exemplifies the primary importance of the war in the 1968 election. It also implies the important role that college-age individuals, many of whom were or could be drafted into the war, played in the national debate. Shirley Chisholm's speech in Congress on March 26, 1969, and Fannie Lou Hamer's speech in Berkeley on October 15, 1969, illustrate the emergent voice of women in antiwar discourse. Not since World War I, the days of Socialists Kate Richard O'Hare and Helen Keller, had women played such an important role in the national debate over war. The last antiwar speech in this section is John Kerry's April 22, 1971, testimony before the Senate Foreign Relations Committee in Washington, D.C. The speech captures, among other things, the psychological scarring brought about by the war in Vietnam and Cambodia, and the growing belief that the U.S. policies in the region had been a "mistake." Within the following two years, almost all U.S. forces had left Vietnam.

## Martin Luther King Urges Americans to Go "Beyond Vietnam"

If we do not act, we shall surely be dragged down the long,
dark, and shameful corridors of time reserved for those who
possess power without compassion, might without morality,
and strength without sight.

On April 4, 1967, at Riverside Church in New York City, the Reverend Martin Luther King Jr. questioned the morality and the politics of the war in Vietnam. The Riverside address was not King's first antiwar speech—as early as March 9, 1965, he had called for a negotiated settlement between the United States and the Viet Cong—but it was the fullest and most pointed public condemnation of the war he had yet given.[14]

In addition to being a breakthrough for King the antiwar leader, the speech has come to represent an important tactical turning point for King the civil rights leader. His decision to oppose the war, so the argument goes, put the entire mainstream, nonradical civil rights movement in jeopardy. Indeed, the threat that King posed to the movement was as real as racial tensions were high. The summer of 1967 marked the apex of a pattern of urban unrest in America. During the so-called Summer of Love, 164 "civil disorders" were reported in 128 American cities.[15] Little more than a week after King spoke in New York, a riot erupted in Newark that claimed twenty-three lives and destroyed over $10 million in property.[16] Only one week later, Detroit burned—the city experienced the death of forty-three people and some $22 million in property damage over a period of five days.[17] On April 19, Stokely Carmichael talked of "black power" in Seattle,[18] and on April 25, the first issue of the *Black Panther,* that party's official news organ, went into print.

Riots and militancy aside, King's critics did have a point: freedom actually appeared to be on the march. Blacks had made significant gains in American society in recent years. The passage of the Twenty-Fourth Amendment in early 1964 abolished the poll tax. The Civil Rights Act of 1964 prohibited major forms of racial discrimination, and granted the federal government the power to enforce desegregation. The Voting Rights Act of 1965 outlawed the literacy test and other discriminatory voting practices. President Johnson's Executive Order 11246 enforced affirmative action for the first time, and the Supreme Court's landmark decision in *Loving v. Virginia* declared antimiscegenation laws unconstitutional.

In short, the precarious balance between black and white America in the mid-sixties, combined with the fact that blacks had recently won significant legislative victories, led many to argue that King's inclusion of another unpopular cause to African Americans' agenda could upend the civil rights movement. In this way, King's critics argued that King's antiwar activities were myopic, destructive, and overambitious. King was, his critics contended, attempting to bite off more than he could chew.

Reactions to King's speech in the summer of 1967 were accordingly quick and severe. The mainstays of the national media immediately attacked him for speaking out against the war. The *Washington Post* accused King of "grave injury to those who are his natural allies" and "an even graver injury to himself." The *Post* continued, "Many who have listened to him with respect will never against accord him the same confidence. He has diminished his usefulness to his cause, to his country and to his people. And that is a great tragedy."[19] In an editorial entitled "Dr. King's Error," the *New York Times* decried King's linkage of the civil rights and peace movements and rebuked him for "recklessly comparing American military methods to those of the Nazis."[20] *Life* magazine printed some of the worst criticism, calling the Riverside speech "a demagogic slander that sounded like a script for Radio Hanoi." King "goes beyond his personal right to dissent," the magazine said, "when he connects progress in civil rights here with a proposal that amounts to abject surrender in Vietnam." By doing so, *Life* concluded, "King comes close to betraying the cause for which he has worked so long."[21]

Many of King's activist allies also sought to distance themselves from King's antiwar position. Agreeing with the *New York Times,* the NAACP quickly adopted a resolution that labeled any attempt to merge the civil rights and peace movements "a serious tactical mistake."[22] After King rehashed his views at an April 15 rally in front of United Nations Headquarters—at that time the most massive antiwar demonstration in American history[23]—a spokesman for the Urban League wrote off King's future role in the struggle for civil rights: "The Movement is back where it began," the spokesman said, "it's us and the NAACP."[24]

King's remarks at Riverside caused the Federal Bureau of Investigation in particular and the executive branch generally to examine King with a hostility fiercer than at any time since late 1964.[25] J. Edgar Hoover, the director of the FBI, communicated to President Lyndon Johnson in April that "based on King's recent activities and public utterances, it is clear that he is an instrument in the hands of subversive forces seeking to undermine our nation."[26] In a separate communication, Hoover told Johnson that King was a Communist mouthpiece.[27] For his part, the president circulated anti-King material to U.S. senators.[28]

King's opposition to war continued until his death. In King's last sermon, "I've Been to the Mountaintop," King was adamantly antiwar: "Men, for years now, have been talking about war and peace. But now, no longer can they just talk about it. It is no longer a choice between violence and nonviolence in this world; it's nonviolence or nonexistence."[29] These were the last words he spoke on the subject of war; King was assassinated the following evening.

On the day he was killed, a scrap of paper was found in King's pocket that listed the "Ten Commandments on Vietnam"—parts of a speech he intended to give at an antiwar rally in New York later that month. King's wife, Coretta Scott King, spoke in his place.[30] She used the opportunity to present part of the speech that never came to pass:

> Thou shalt not believe in a military victory.
> Thou shalt not believe in a political victory.
> Thou shalt not believe that they—the Vietnamese—love us.
> Thou shalt not believe that the Saigon government has the support of the people.
> Thou shalt not believe that the majority of the South Vietnamese look upon the Viet Cong as terrorists.
> Thou shalt not believe the figure of killed enemies or killed Americans.
> Thou shalt not believe that the generals know best.
> Thou shalt not believe that the enemy's victory means communism.
> Thou shalt not believe that the world supports the United States.
> Thou shalt not kill.[31]

Though the scope of this short commentary primarily involves King's "Beyond Vietnam" speech and its consequences, a short discussion of another of King's antiwar speeches is irresistible. In Atlanta on Christmas Eve, 1967, King delivered "A Christmas Sermon on Peace" in Ebenezer Baptist Church, where he was an associate minister. The speech was broadcast by the Canadian Broadcasting Corporation and was the fifth and final speech in a series. Because it did not produce anywhere near the reaction that the Riverside speech did, and because it is more a sermon for peace than a speech against war, it is not necessary to reprint the speech in full here. King's peroration, or conclusion, however, exemplifies the prophetic, poetic, and hopeful-in-spite-of-it-all nature of King's oratory—features that appear often in King's Riverside address. More importantly, King's "Christmas Sermon" peroration exemplifies the quintessentially "intertextual" nature of his rhetoric. The reader will hear echoes of another, more famous speech in the following small excerpt:

> In 1963, on a sweltering August afternoon, we stood in Washington, D.C., and talked to the nation about many things. Toward the end of that afternoon, I tried to talk to the nation about a dream that I had had, and I must confess to you today that not long after talking about that dream I started seeing it turn into a nightmare

. . . I saw that dream turn into a nightmare as I watched the war in Vietnam escalating, and as I saw so-called military advisers, 16,000 strong, turn into fighting soldiers until today over 500,000 American boys are fighting on Asian soil. Yes, I am personally the victim of deferred dreams, of blasted hopes, but in spite of that I close today by saying I still have a dream, because, you know, you can't give up in life. If you lose hope, somehow you lose that vitality that keeps life moving, you lose that courage to be, that quality that helps you to go on in spite of all. And so today I still have a dream.

. . . I still have a dream today that one day war will come to an end, that men will beat their swords into plowshares and their spears into pruning hooks, that nations will no longer rise up against nations, neither will they study war any more. I still have a dream today that one day the lamb and the lion will lie down together and every man will sit under his own vine and fig tree and none shall be afraid. I still have a dream today that one day every valley shall be exalted and every mountain and hill will be made low, the rough places will be made smooth and the crooked places straight, and the glory of the Lord shall be revealed, and all flesh shall see it together. I still have a dream that with this faith we will be able to adjourn the councils of despair and bring new light into the dark chambers of pessimism. With this faith we will be able to speed up the day when there will be peace on earth and goodwill toward men. It will be a glorious day, the morning stars will sing together, and the sons of God will shout for joy.[32]

King is recalling his "I Have a Dream" speech, which he famously delivered five years earlier on the steps of the Lincoln Memorial in Washington, D.C. This time the words arise in the context of the war in Vietnam, not the battle for civil rights. Nevertheless, by using the same words, King connects the two events. By evoking his earlier address, King asks his audience to recall his hopefulness and share his vision of a better post-Vietnam world.

In his Riverside address, King proves that he is a great borrower of others' works, as well as his own. In his speech, large segments of which were drafted by others,[33] King provides a pregnant set of literary sources for his listeners to consider: Langston Hughes's "Let America Be America Again,"[34] Thich Nhat Hanh's *Vietnam: Lotus in a Sea of Fire*,[35] Saint John's First Epistle,[36] and James Russell Lowell's "The Present Crisis." King's speech remains more political than literary, but his heightened language and artistic sources illustrate a central feature of "literary politics"—employing great literature to cope with periods of great political strife.

MR. CHAIRMAN, LADIES AND GENTLEMEN,

I need not pause to say how very delighted I am to be here tonight, and how very delighted I am to see you expressing your concern about the issues that will be discussed tonight by turning out in such large numbers. . . .

I come to this magnificent house of worship tonight because my conscience leaves me no other choice. I join you in this meeting because I am in deepest agreement with the aims and work of the organization which has brought us together, Clergy and Laymen Concerned About Vietnam. The recent statements of your executive committee are the sentiments of my own heart, and I found myself in full accord when I read its opening lines: "A time comes when silence is betrayal." That time has come for us in relation to Vietnam.

The truth of these words is beyond doubt, but the mission to which they call us is a most difficult one. Even when pressed by the demands of inner truth, men do not easily assume the task of opposing their government's policy, especially in time of war. Nor does the human spirit move without great difficulty against all the apathy of conformist thought within one's own bosom and in the surrounding world. Moreover, when the issues at hand seem as perplexing as they often do in the case of this dreadful conflict, we are always on the verge of being mesmerized by uncertainty. But we must move on.

Some of us who have already begun to break the silence of the night have found that the calling to speak is often a vocation of agony, but we must speak. We must speak with all the humility that is appropriate to our limited vision, but we must speak. And we must rejoice as well, for surely this is the first time in our nation's history that a significant number of its religious leaders have chosen to move beyond the prophesying of smooth patriotism to the high grounds of a firm dissent based upon the mandates of conscience and the reading of history. . . .

Over the past two years, as I have moved to break the betrayal of my own silences and to speak from the burnings of my own heart, as I have called for radical departures from the destruction of Vietnam, many persons have questioned me about the wisdom of my path. At the heart of their concerns, this query has often loomed large and loud: "Why are you speaking about the war, Dr. King?" "Why are you joining the voices of dissent?" "Peace and civil rights don't mix," they say. "Aren't you hurting the cause of your people?" they ask. And when I hear them, though I often understand the source of their concern, I am nevertheless greatly saddened, for such questions mean that the inquirers have not really known me, my commitment, or my calling. Indeed, their questions suggest that they do not know the world in which they live. In the light of such tragic misunderstanding, I deem it of signal importance to try to state clearly, and I trust concisely, why I believe that the path from Dexter Avenue Baptist Church—the church in Montgomery, Alabama, where I began my pastorate—leads clearly to this sanctuary tonight.

I come to this platform tonight to make a passionate plea to my beloved nation. This speech is not addressed to Hanoi or to the National Liberation Front. It is not addressed to China or to Russia. Nor is it an attempt to overlook the ambiguity of the total situation and the need for a collective solution to the tragedy of Vietnam. Neither is it an attempt to make North Vietnam or the National Liberation Front paragons of virtue, nor to overlook the role they must play in the successful resolution of the problem. While they both may have justifiable reasons to be suspicious of the good faith of the United States, life and history give eloquent testimony to the fact that conflicts are never resolved without trustful give and take on both sides. Tonight, however, I wish not to speak with Hanoi and the National Liberation Front, but rather to my fellow Americans.

Since I am a preacher by calling, I suppose it is not surprising that I have seven major reasons for bringing Vietnam into the field of my moral vision. There is at the outset a very obvious and almost facile connection between the war in Vietnam and the struggle I and others have been waging in America. A few years ago there was a shining moment in that struggle. It seemed as if there was a real promise of hope for the poor, both black and white, through the poverty program. There were experiments, hopes, new beginnings. Then came the buildup in Vietnam, and I watched this program broken and eviscerated as if it were some idle political plaything of a society gone mad on war. And I knew that America would never invest the necessary funds or energies in rehabilitation of its poor so long as adventures like Vietnam continued to draw men and skills and money like some demonic, destructive suction tube. So I was increasingly compelled to see the war as an enemy of the poor and to attack it as such.

Perhaps a more tragic recognition of reality took place when it became clear to me that the war was doing far more than devastating the hopes of the poor at home. It was sending their sons and their brothers and their husbands to fight and to die in extraordinarily high proportions relative to the rest of the population. We were taking the black young men who had been crippled by our society and sending them eight thousand miles away to guarantee liberties in Southeast Asia which they had not found in southwest Georgia and East Harlem. So we have been repeatedly faced with the cruel irony of watching Negro and white boys on TV screens as they kill and die together for a nation that has been unable to seat them together in the same schools. . . .

My third reason moves to an even deeper level of awareness, for it grows out of my experience in the ghettos of the North over the last three years, especially the last three summers. As I have walked among the desperate, rejected, and angry young men, I have told them that Molotov cocktails and rifles would not solve their problems. I have tried to offer them my deepest compassion while maintaining my conviction that social change comes most meaningfully through nonviolent action. But they asked, and rightly so, "What about Vietnam?" They asked if our own nation wasn't using massive doses of violence to solve its problems, to bring about the changes it wanted. Their questions hit home, and I knew that I could never again raise my voice against the violence of the oppressed in the ghettos without having first spoken clearly to the greatest purveyor of violence in the world today: my own government. . . .

For those who ask the question, "Aren't you a civil rights leader?" and thereby mean to exclude me from the movement for peace, I have this further answer. In 1957, when a group of us formed the Southern Christian Leadership Conference, we chose as our motto: "To save the soul of America." We were convinced that we could not limit our vision to certain rights for black people, but instead affirmed the conviction that America would never be free or saved from itself until the descendants of its slaves were loosed completely from the shackles they still wear. In a way we were agreeing with Langston Hughes, that black bard of Harlem, who had written earlier:

> O, yes, I say it plain,
> America never was America to me,

And yet I swear this oath.
America will be!

Now it should be incandescently clear that no one who has any concern for the integrity and life of America today can ignore the present war. If America's soul becomes totally poisoned, part of the autopsy must read "Vietnam." It can never be saved so long as it destroys the deepest hopes of men the world over. So it is that those of us who are yet determined that "America will be" are led down the path of protest and dissent, working for the health of our land.

As if the weight of such a commitment to the life and health of America were not enough, another burden of responsibility was placed upon me in [1964].* And I cannot forget that the Nobel Peace Prize was also a commission, a commission to work harder than I had ever worked before for the brotherhood of man. This is a calling that takes me beyond national allegiances.

But even if it were not present, I would yet have to live with the meaning of my commitment to the ministry of Jesus Christ. To me, the relationship of this ministry to the making of peace is so obvious that I sometimes marvel at those who ask me why I am speaking against the war. Could it be that they do not know that the Good News was meant for all men—for communist and capitalist, for their children and ours, for black and for white, for revolutionary and conservative? Have they forgotten that my ministry is in obedience to the one who loved his enemies so fully that he died for them? What then can I say to the Vietcong or to Castro or to Mao as a faithful minister of this one? Can I threaten them with death or must I not share with them my life?

Finally, as I try to explain for you and for myself the road that leads from Montgomery to this place, I would have offered all that was most valid if I simply said that I must be true to my conviction that I share with all men the calling to be a son of the living God. Beyond the calling of race or nation or creed is this vocation of sonship and brotherhood. Because I believe that the Father is deeply concerned, especially for his suffering and helpless and outcast children, I come tonight to speak for them. This I believe to be the privilege and the burden of all of us who deem ourselves bound by allegiances and loyalties which are broader and deeper than nationalism and which go beyond our nation's self-defined goals and positions. We are called to speak for the weak, for the voiceless, for the victims of our nation, for those it calls "enemy," for no document from human hands can make these humans any less our brothers.

And as I ponder the madness of Vietnam and search within myself for ways to understand and respond in compassion, my mind goes constantly to the people of that peninsula. I speak now not of the soldiers of each side, not of the ideologies of the Liberation Front, not of the junta in Saigon, but simply of the people who have been living under the curse of war for almost three continuous decades now. I think of them, too, because it is clear to me that there will be no meaningful solution there until some attempt is made to know them and hear their broken cries.

*King inadvertently said "1954."

They must see Americans as strange liberators. The Vietnamese people proclaimed their own independence in 1954—in 1945 rather—after a combined French and Japanese occupation and before the communist revolution in China. They were led by Ho Chi Minh. Even though they quoted the American Declaration of Independence in their own document of freedom, we refused to recognize them. Instead, we decided to support France in its reconquest of her former colony. Our government felt then that the Vietnamese people were not ready for independence, and we again fell victim to the deadly Western arrogance that has poisoned the international atmosphere for so long. With that tragic decision we rejected a revolutionary government seeking self-determination and a government that had been established not by China—for whom the Vietnamese have no great love—but by clearly indigenous forces that included some communists. For the peasants this new government meant real land reform, one of the most important needs in their lives.

For nine years following 1945 we denied the people of Vietnam the right of independence. For nine years we vigorously supported the French in their abortive effort to recolonize Vietnam. . . .

After the French were defeated, it looked as if independence and land reform would come again through the Geneva Agreement. But instead there came the United States, determined that Ho should not unify the temporarily divided nation, and the peasants watched again as we supported one of the most vicious modern dictators, our chosen man, Premier Diem. . . . When Diem was overthrown they may have been happy, but the long line of military dictators seemed to offer no real change, especially in terms of their need for land and peace.

The only change came from America as we increased our troop commitments in support of governments which were singularly corrupt, inept, and without popular support. All the while the people read our leaflets and received the regular promises of peace and democracy and land reform. Now they languish under our bombs and consider us, not their fellow Vietnamese, the real enemy. They move sadly and apathetically as we herd them off the land of their fathers into concentration camps where minimal social needs are rarely met. They know they must move on or be destroyed by our bombs.

So they go, primarily women and children and the aged. They watch as we poison their water, as we kill a million acres of their crops. They must weep as the bulldozers roar through their areas preparing to destroy the precious trees. They wander into the hospitals with at least twenty casualties from American firepower for one Vietcong-inflicted injury. So far we may have killed a million of them, mostly children. They wander into the towns and see thousands of the children, homeless, without clothes, running in packs on the streets like animals. They see the children degraded by our soldiers as they beg for food. They see the children selling their sisters to our soldiers, soliciting for their mothers.

What do the peasants think as we ally ourselves with the landlords and as we refuse to put any action into our many words concerning land reform? What do they think as we test out our latest weapons on them, just as the Germans tested out new medicine and new tortures in the concentration camps of Europe? Where are the roots of the independent Vietnam we claim to be building? Is it among these voiceless ones? . . .

Perhaps a more difficult but no less necessary task is to speak for those who have been designated as our enemies. What of the National Liberation Front, that strangely anonymous group we call "VC" or "communists"? What must they think of the United States of America when they realize that we permitted the repression and cruelty of Diem, which helped to bring them into being as a resistance group in the South? What do they think of our condoning the violence which led to their own taking up of arms? How can they believe in our integrity when now we speak of "aggression from the North" as if there were nothing more essential to the war? How can they trust us when now we charge them with violence after the murderous reign of Diem and charge them with violence while we pour every new weapon of death into their land? Surely we must understand their feelings, even if we do not condone their actions. Surely we must see that the men we supported pressed them to their violence. Surely we must see that our own computerized plans of destruction simply dwarf their greatest acts. . . .

Here is the true meaning and value of compassion and nonviolence, when it helps us to see the enemy's point of view, to hear his questions, to know his assessment of ourselves. For from his view we may indeed see the basic weaknesses of our own condition, and if we are mature, we may learn and grow and profit from the wisdom of the brothers who are called the opposition. . . .

At this point I should make it clear that while I have tried in these last few minutes to give a voice to the voiceless in Vietnam and to understand the arguments of those who are called "enemy," I am as deeply concerned about our own troops there as anything else. For it occurs to me that what we are submitting them to in Vietnam is not simply the brutalizing process that goes on in any war where armies face each other and seek to destroy. We are adding cynicism to the process of death, for they must know after a short period there that none of the things we claim to be fighting for are really involved. Before long they must know that their government has sent them into a struggle among Vietnamese, and the more sophisticated surely realize that we are on the side of the wealthy, and the secure, while we create a hell for the poor. . . .

I would like to suggest five concrete things that our government should do immediately to begin the long and difficult process of extricating ourselves from this nightmarish conflict:

Number one: End all bombing in North and South Vietnam.

Number two: Declare a unilateral cease-fire in the hope that such action will create the atmosphere for negotiation.

Three: Take immediate steps to prevent other battlegrounds in Southeast Asia by curtailing our military buildup in Thailand and our interference in Laos.

Four: Realistically accept the fact that the National Liberation Front has substantial support in South Vietnam and must thereby play a role in any meaningful negotiations and any future Vietnam government.

Five: Set a date that we will remove all foreign troops from Vietnam in accordance with the 1954 Geneva Agreement. [*sustained applause*]

Part of our ongoing commitment might well express itself in an offer to grant asylum to any Vietnamese who fears for his life under a new regime which included the Liberation Front. Then we must make what reparations we can for the damage we have done. We must provide the medical aid that is badly needed, making it available in this country if necessary. Meanwhile [*applause*], meanwhile, we in the churches and synagogues have a continuing task while we urge our government to disengage itself from a disgraceful commitment. . . .

As we counsel young men concerning military service, we must clarify for them our nation's role in Vietnam and challenge them with the alternative of conscientious objection. [*sustained applause*] . . . Moreover, I would encourage all ministers of draft age to give up their ministerial exemptions and seek status as conscientious objectors. [*applause*] These are the times for real choices and not false ones. We are at the moment when our lives must be placed on the line if our nation is to survive its own folly. Every man of humane convictions must decide on the protest that best suits his convictions, but we must all protest.

Now there is something seductively tempting about stopping there and sending us all off on what in some circles has become a popular crusade against the war in Vietnam. I say we must enter that struggle, but I wish to go on now to say something even more disturbing.

The war in Vietnam is but a symptom of a far deeper malady within the American spirit, and if we ignore this sobering reality [*applause*], and if we ignore this sobering reality, we will find ourselves organizing "clergy and laymen concerned" committees for the next generation. They will be concerned about Guatemala and Peru. They will be concerned about Thailand and Cambodia. They will be concerned about Mozambique and South Africa. We will be marching for these and a dozen other names and attending rallies without end unless there is a significant and profound change in American life and policy. [*sustained applause*] So such thoughts take us beyond Vietnam, but not beyond our calling as sons of the living God.

In 1957 a sensitive American official overseas said that it seemed to him that our nation was on the wrong side of a world revolution. During the past ten years we have seen emerge a pattern of suppression which has now justified the presence of U.S. military advisors in Venezuela. This need to maintain social stability for our investment accounts for the counterrevolutionary action of American forces in Guatemala. It tells why American helicopters are being used against guerrillas in Cambodia and why American napalm and Green Beret forces have already been active against rebels in Peru.

It is with such activity in mind that the words of the late John F. Kennedy come back to haunt us. Five years ago he said, "Those who make peaceful revolution impossible will make violent revolution inevitable." [*applause*] Increasingly, by choice or by accident, this is the role our nation has taken, the role of those who make peaceful revolution impossible by refusing to give up the privileges and the pleasures that come from the immense profits of overseas investments. I am convinced that if we are to get on the right side of the world revolution, we as a nation must undergo a radical revolution of values. We must rapidly begin [*applause*], we must rapidly begin the shift from a thing-oriented society to a person-oriented society. When machines and computers, profit motives and property rights, are considered more important than people, the giant triplets of racism, extreme materialism, and militarism are incapable of being conquered.

A true revolution of values will soon cause us to question the fairness and justice of many of our past and present policies. On the one hand we are called to play the Good Samaritan on life's roadside, but that will be only an initial act. One day we must come to see that the whole Jericho Road must be transformed so that men and women will not be constantly beaten and robbed as they make their journey on life's highway. True compassion is more than flinging a coin to a beggar. It comes to see that an edifice which produces beggars needs restructuring. [*applause*]

A true revolution of values will soon look uneasily on the glaring contrast of poverty and wealth. . . .

A true revolution of values will lay hands on the world order and say of war, "This way of settling differences is not just." This business of burning human beings with napalm, of filling our nation's homes with orphans and widows, of injecting poisonous drugs of hate into the veins of peoples normally humane, of sending men home from dark and bloody battlefields physically handicapped and psychologically deranged, cannot be reconciled with wisdom, justice, and love. A nation that continues year after year to spend more money on military defense than on programs of social uplift is approaching spiritual death. [*sustained applause*]

America, the richest and most powerful nation in the world, can well lead the way in this revolution of values. . . .

This kind of positive revolution of values is our best defense against communism. [*applause*] War is not the answer. Communism will never be defeated by the use of atomic bombs or nuclear weapons. Let us not join those who shout war and, through their misguided passions, urge the United States to relinquish its participation in the United Nations. These are days which demand wise restraint and calm reasonableness. We must not engage in a negative anti-communism, but rather in a positive thrust for democracy [*applause*], realizing that our greatest defense against communism is to take offensive action in behalf of justice. We must with positive action seek to remove those conditions of poverty, insecurity, and injustice, which are the fertile soil in which the seed of communism grows and develops. . . .

It is a sad fact that because of comfort, complacency, a morbid fear of communism, and our proneness to adjust to injustice, the Western nations that initiated so much of the revolutionary spirit of the modern world have now become the arch antirevolutionaries. This has driven many to feel that only Marxism has a revolutionary spirit. Therefore, communism is a judgment against our failure to make democracy real and follow through on the revolutions that we initiated. Our only hope today lies in our ability to recapture the revolutionary spirit and go out into a sometimes hostile world declaring eternal hostility to poverty, racism, and militarism. With this powerful commitment we shall boldly challenge the status quo and unjust mores, and thereby speed the day when "every valley shall be exalted, and every mountain and hill shall be made low [*Audience:*] (*Yes*); the crooked shall be made straight, and the rough places plain." . . .

We are now faced with the fact, my friends, that tomorrow is today. We are confronted with the fierce urgency of now. In this unfolding conundrum of life and history, there is such a thing as being too late. Procrastination is still the thief of time. Life often leaves us standing bare, naked, and dejected with a lost opportunity. The tide in the affairs of men does not remain at flood—it ebbs. We may cry out desperately for time to pause in her passage, but time is adamant to every plea and rushes on. Over the bleached bones and jumbled residues of numerous civilizations are written the pathetic words, "Too late." There is an invisible book of life that faithfully records our vigilance or our neglect. Omar Khayyam is right: "The moving finger writes, and having writ moves on."

We still have a choice today: nonviolent coexistence or violent coannihilation. We must move past indecision to action. We must find new ways to speak for peace in Vietnam and justice throughout the developing world, a world that borders on our doors. If we do not act, we shall surely be dragged down the long, dark, and shameful corridors of time reserved for those who possess power without compassion, might without morality, and strength without sight.

Now let us begin. Now let us rededicate ourselves to the long and bitter, but beautiful, struggle for a new world. This is the calling of the sons of God, and our brothers wait eagerly for our response. Shall we say the odds are too great? Shall we tell them the struggle is too hard? Will our message be that the forces of American life militate against their arrival as full men, and we send our deepest regrets? Or will there be another message—of longing, of hope, of solidarity with their yearnings, of commitment to their cause, whatever the cost? The choice is ours, and though we might prefer it otherwise, we must choose in this crucial moment of human history.

As that noble bard of yesterday, James Russell Lowell, eloquently stated:

> Once to every man and nation comes a moment to decide,
> In the strife of Truth and Falsehood, for the good or evil side;
> Some great cause, God's new Messiah offering each the bloom or blight,
> And the choice goes by forever 'twixt that darkness and that light.
> Though the cause of evil prosper, yet 'tis truth alone is strong
> Though her portions be the scaffold, and upon the throne be wrong
> Yet that scaffold sways the future, and behind the dim unknown
> Standeth God within the shadow, keeping watch above his own.

And if we will only make the right choice, we will be able to transform this pending cosmic elegy into a creative psalm of peace. If we will make the right choice, we will be able to transform the jangling discords of our world into a beautiful symphony of brotherhood. If we will but make the right choice, we will be able to speed up the day, all over America and all over the world, when justice will roll down like waters, and righteousness like a mighty stream. [*sustained applause*]

## Eugene J. McCarthy Celebrates the "Spirit of 1963"

None of us here seek peace at any price. But we are willing to pay a high price for it.

The first antiwar candidate to enter the race for the Democratic presidential nomination in 1968, Eugene McCarthy helped crystallize opposition to President Lyndon Johnson's policies in Vietnam. McCarthy's effectiveness as a political candidate stemmed from what commentators have identified as his "stabilizing force,"[37] his "sober personal style,"[38] and his campaign's "moderate tone."[39] The antiwar movement arguably needed some level-headedness in the late 1960s, because important voices in the mainstream press found the prevailing antiwar movement to be scattered and strident. In 1967, *Time* summed up the movement: "Dissenters ranging from Maoists to hippies, from middle-aged sub-urbanites in SANE to adolescent hotspurs in the Students for a Democratic Society have stormed Pentagon and draft board, marched and picketed and advertised. . . . The peace movement has too often degenerated into caterwaul and caricature and, even worse, non-communication." But McCarthy's candidacy, *Time* predicted, "will at last give legitimate dissenters a civilized political voice."[40] McCarthy served as an antidote to the perceived excesses of the antiwar left. He was a level-headed leader who could bring the antiwar movement an earnest and reputable voice. Even Barry Goldwater, the Republican Party's nominee for president in the 1964 election, was impressed by McCarthy's composure and apparent respectability. McCarthy was "a gentleman and a scholar who has done things in a calm and reasonable way," said Goldwater.[41] If there had to be a Democratic president in 1969, Goldwater admitted, "I would pick McCarthy."[42]

The same measured approach to politics that earned McCarthy praise among some earned him criticism among others. The speech below, which McCarthy presented on December 2, 1967, two days after announcing his intention to seek the Democratic presidential nomination, is a case in point. *Life* called the speech "oblique." "Detached. Philosophic. Cynical. Moral. Learned. Lazy," editorialized the *Wall Street Journal*. E. W. Kenworthy wrote in the *New Republic* that McCarthy's speech "lacked . . . fervor and eloquence." Even McCarthy's supporters bemoaned the candidate's lack of flair. Advisor Joseph Rauh, upon hearing the speech, wrote that McCarthy must "put more fire into the campaign." Two of senator's major financial backers implored him to alter his style and "go for the jugular."[43]

But, as biographer Dominick Sandbrook has pointed out, McCarthy's low-key speeches arose out of a longstanding philosophy of crisis leadership that avoided excited, aggressive, or declamatory rhetoric. Sandbrook's conclusion is amply supported by McCarthy's established views. In 1960, McCarthy, who was a devout Catholic, admonished the "Christian in politics" not to rouse the people's emotions, passions, or prejudices in times of crisis: ."The Christian in politics should shun the devices of the demagogue at all times, but especially at a time when anxiety is great, when tension is high, when uncertainty prevails, and emotions tend to be in the ascendancy."[44] Later, on March 7, 1968, days before he would earn 42.2 percent of the vote as a write-in candidate to President Johnson's 49.5 percent in the New Hampshire primary, McCarthy expressed his distaste for campaign belligerence to a radio station: "I haven't really chosen to campaign in that way [i.e., belligerently]; that's the way I campaign. I think it's natural to me, and I think also if it weren't, if I had the gift or disposition to campaign in some other way, more violently, perhaps more aggressively, I wouldn't do it because I think that the issues with which we are dealing are the kind that ought to be considered with some reservation, and some restraint—somewhat moderately instead of in the atmosphere of shouting and emotion."[45] In 1970, well after his presidential campaign had ended, McCarthy echoed these views, stating matter-of-factly that there was a "danger really in stirring people up on an emotional basis."[46]

McCarthy's December 2, 1967, speech in Chicago to the Conference of Concerned Democrats, the first major speech of the campaign, is a prime example of the measured tone and calm demeanor for which McCarthy's antiwar campaign was known. In introducing McCarthy, activist Allard Lowenstein had brought the crowd to a "fever pitch" with a twenty-minute diatribe aimed squarely at President Johnson.[47] McCarthy, who had arrived during Lowenstein's speech, was furious at his lack of restraint. According to one reporter, "people standing near McCarthy saw the blood drain from his face, then watched as he paced back and forth like a caged animal, muttering and angrily kicking a paper cup against the wall."[48] But whatever emotions McCarthy expressed in private, he held them back in public. As McCarthy walked "grim-faced" to the podium, he demeanor changed, and he began reading his speech "quickly and quietly."[49]

McCarthy's speech is the exact opposite of Lowenstein's. Instead of bashing President Johnson's policies in Vietnam, he asks his audience to aspire to greatness; instead of asking his audience to hate President Johnson, he asks them to love Adlai Stevenson and John F. Kennedy. McCarthy refuses to attack, and chooses instead to ennoble. This was not, as McCarthy later wrote of the opening days of his campaign, "a time for storming the walls, but for beginning a long march."[50]

There are two noteworthy rhetorical features of McCarthy's speech. First, McCarthy makes use of *anaphora,* or the repetition of the same groups of words at the beginnings of successive clauses. Vietnam, says McCarthy, is "a war in which progress is reported not in terms of the capture of a village or of crossing a border or a river, but rather in terms of the kill ratio," "a war of questionable legality and of questionable constitutionality," "[a] war which is not dipolomatically defensible," and "[a] war which is out of the context of the history of this century." Anaphora is one of the most common rhetorical devices used in speeches. When McCarthy's address was published in book form two years later, he tightened the anaphoras and added additional ones, presumably to make it read even more like a speech.[51]

Second, McCarthy makes use of *antithesis,* or the juxtaposition of contrasting ideas. Antithesis usually appears in a parallel structure, as it does in McCarthy's speech:

> [I]n the place of what appears to be doubt, we will establish that the spirit of America is one of trust, and instead of expediency what this nation seeks is right judgment; instead of ghettos that what we want are neighborhoods and communities in America [*applause*]; instead of disunity or what it sometimes masquerades under consensus, we have dedication of purpose [*applause*]; instead of incredibility, let us have integrity [*applause*]; and instead of murmuring let us have clear speech and, we hope, America singing again [*applause*]; and in place of that fear of fear, if any have come close to it which is on the edge of despair, let us have hope again. [*Applause.*]

In this passage, the antithetical elements are not only parallel in structure, but similar in length, employing the rhetorical scheme called *isocolon*. This added symmetry is an important part of the rhythm of McCarthy's sentences, and McCarthy polished it in the subsequently published version of the speech's peroration:

> This is not the real spirit of America. I do not believe that it is. This is a time to test the mood and spirit:
>> To offer in place of doubt—trust.
>> In place of expediency—right judgment.
>> In place of ghettos, let us have neighborhoods and communities.
>> In place of incredibility—integrity.
>> In place of murmuring, let us have clear speech; let us again hear America singing.
>> In place of disunity, let us have dedication of purpose.
>> In place of near despair, let us have hope.[52]

In *Classical Rhetoric for the Modern Student,* Edward P. J. Corbett and Robert J. Connors write that the repeated use of isocolon can "approach the recurrent beat of verse."[53] McCarthy thus wedded form to theme in the final words of the speech by matching his his call to "respond to . . . the steady drum" with the rhetorical analogue to drumming—the isocolon.

. . . [F]IFTEEN YEARS AGO in this city in 1952, the Democratic party nominated Adlai Stevenson to lead in the campaign of that year. [*Applause.*]

He opened that campaign by saying that he was going to talk sense to the American people. And he proceeded to do that in the clearest tones in which anyone has spoken to the people of the country in this century. He did not talk above the people but he spoke to them. He asked all the hard questions and he was prepared to give as best he could the most difficult answers. . . .

And then came John Kennedy, who spoke to us with a new voice and new language, but of the same substance. Added to the clear horn of Adlai Stevenson was the certain drum, a call to action which John Kennedy gave to us in the spirit of honest optimism: knowing what was wrong with the world but still believing that much good could be accomplished. He brought to the problems of the world a quiet courage which was what we needed then and is what we need today. And all of this—difficult problems and difficult proposals—he presented to the country with the greatest civility.

With him came the Peace Corps—what it meant to America. Giving the lie to those who said there was no idealism in the young people of this country. He spoke of the Alliance for Progress. Words to believe in in this country and words to believe in in Latin America.

He presented the first great program for equal rights for all Americans. It was not just a promise but it was a performance. And [he] brought for the first time in this century a new reasoned and rational approach to the economic problems of America. And all the world looked to us, because after the war there was a period of quiet in this country.

This was a new resurgence of hope and of confidence, demonstrated in his voice and his leadership, demonstrating to all the world that this country was not going to be held by the dead hand of the past, but more important than that, that we were not afraid of the violent hand of the future which was reaching back for all of the Western world and for that matter for the entire world in the year 1960.

All of this was the spirit of 1963. Of openness and of confidence and of courage and of daring.

But what, I ask you, is the spirit of 1967 in America only four years later?

A spirit of joylessness; a spirit of frustration; a spirit of anxiety; a time in which the enthusiasm which greeted the Peace Corps has been replaced by demonstrations and protests; a time in which the enthusiasm which greeted the Alliance for Progress has been replaced by disappointment and lack of confidence in America.

A time in which we have a new scripture really. We accept that the vision of a good land was that in which the old men saw visions and the young men dream dreams. This was the hope of America then and the promise of America.

But today the young men have nightmares and the old men—if we consider the Secretary of State in that class—is seeing specters and hallucinations. [*Laughter and applause.*]

The very language of promise and of hope which marked that year and those years has been changed to a new language.

Nearly every program with which we deal and every problem with which we deal is presented now in the context of war. War on poverty. War on crime. War on pollution. War on ignorance. But all of us know that no one of these problems will be solved by the application of either the instruments or the methods of war. But each calls for most careful attention, most careful study, and not just a general commitment but a commitment which is personal, which involves everyone in this country. [*Applause.*]

There is one war today which is properly called a war—and that is the war in Vietnam. Different from any war in which this nation has been involved. In the last two weeks, it's concentrated on the matter of Hill 875. Not even a name for the place, only a number.

A new conception of war and one requiring a new definition of victory if such a definition is possible.

A war in which progress is reported not in terms of the capture of a village or of crossing a border or a river, but rather in terms of the kill ratio. If the ratio is up, we count it progress. If the ratio is down, reports are said to be pessimistic.

[A] war of questionable legality and of questionable constitutionality. [*Applause.*]

A war which is not diplomatically defensible. And this is of particular significance for the United States because this nation had its beginning in the Declaration of Independence in an appeal for what was called "respect to the decent opinion of mankind." And today we are afraid to present our case to that decent opinion. [*Applause.*]

A war which is out of the context of the history of this century which those who defend it and those who advocate it explain it in terms of comparisons beginning with Munich or later than that.

Well there is much history running through this century which goes beyond Munich. There was a time when we thought we could set aside whole nations and whole continents and whole races as though they were not a part of contemporary history. We thought the United States could step into the world for a short time and set it right and then step out again. But this is not the case in 1967.

We are a part of the movement of history itself and the resort to the old devices of covenants and treaties, which were really not effective even in the eighteenth century to say nothing of the nineteenth century, or to accept that in some strange way we can adopt as our responsibility that of policing the planet, is to misread the history of this century and of the next [*applause*] and certainly to misread our role in that history.

We accept that we have military responsibilities, but these are secondary. Our great purpose must be to see to it that our knowledge, our economic power, and our goodwill be brought to bear upon this world in which we live. [*Applause.*]

This is a war which is not even defensible on military grounds [*applause*], running contrary as we know to the advice of men who were said to be great military experts, those who said, "do not become involved in a ground war in Asia." Dwight Eisenhower, General MacArthur, Matthew Ridgway, General Gavin all say this is not the way in which America can be a force for good.

A war which every day proves itself to be ill-advised; as estimate after estimate proves to be false; as escalation after escalation fails to achieve the declared objectives and the promised objectives; as intensification and extension of the war—intensification of weapons and extension to new areas and to new targets—all of these going on at the same time, of necessity a kind of overleaping of escalation of the objectives for which the war is supposedly being waged, beginning with the declaration that we were there to protect what was said to be a viable society in South Vietnam requiring from us only a limited commitment. Of course, when we reached the point where we had one hundred thousand men or two hundred thousand men, the military commitment had run far beyond the objective. So we then escalated the objective to say we are now building a nation in South Vietnam. When that didn't hold and we had to put in more troops, we then said we were saving all of Southeastern Asia. And most recently with a half a million men, we were told that the United States and its security—that *this* is what is at stake in Vietnam.

Escalation of military commitment and escalation of objectives without end. And finally we reach the point, I think, where we must say that putting all of these things together that this war is no longer morally justifiable. [*Sustained applause.*] . . .

Less and less certain, less and less sure, disappearing always as we approach it, becoming hopeless almost to the point of despair. And in this circumstance we are called upon to make new judgments: one a judgment of individual conscience, and the other a community judgment, a judgment for our nation.

And the individual judgment I think must be made in these terms, best described I think by a man talking about the responsibility of the French citizen at the time of the Dreyfus case. He said: "No citizen can escape responsibility. One single injustice, one single crime, one single illegality, if it is officially recorded, nationally accepted and confirmed is sufficient to shatter the whole social contract, to bring about the loss not only of one's honor but the dishonor of a whole people." This is the challenge to the individual conscience of every American today.

The second is the moral challenge in a broader context—that of history itself. And for this judgment, let me say that I believe there is a kind of judgment of nations as there is of men. I will cite the warning sounded for us by Arnold Toynbee in writing about Rome's war with Carthage. He said, "Of course Rome could not lose that war." Rome had set itself upon an empire which was to surround the Mediterranean when he said the price of that effort was to drain off her manpower, to drain off her physical resources, to drain off the moral reserve of Rome so that the internal problems of the empire were neglected and the external problems so neglected that the way was prepared for the fall of the Republic and the rise of the dictators. And then he said, "Remember the nemesis of war." That "war results in vengeance of the dead on the survivors, and the vanquished on the victors."

None of us here seek peace at any price. But we are willing to pay a high price for it. [*Applause.*] What we seek is an honorable and a rational and a political settlement of this war. [*Applause.*] One which will enhance our world position, which will permit us to give proper attention to other problems in other parts of the world, which will permit us to use our physical and our human and our moral energy to deal with the pressing problems here in the United States itself. [*Applause.*]

I have watched for signs that the administration may have set some limit on the price they will pay for victory and I see no such limits indicated. The words of the administration have become empty and hollow. Their message is one of apprehension and fear and even worse than that, I think, they come very close to expressing that which Franklin Roosevelt warned us against: the fear of fear.

This is not, in my judgment, the spirit of the United States of America. [*Applause.*] And we must not let the impression go out in this country that we believe that this is the spirit of this country. And certainly not let the impression go out to the world that we live in this "fear of fear."

The time has come—and this is what we're here to begin tonight—to test the spirit of the people of this country. To determine within the process of politics what the mood and the desire and the commitment of America is.

I say to you at this point that I am ready to be your candidate. [*Cheers and applause.*]

In every primary in which I can reasonably be entered and I would hope that in every kind of party fight my nomination may be advanced. [*Applause.*] And in the course of this effort, not just mine because I speak for you and I hope speak for America [*applause*] that our direction be that in the place of what appears to be doubt, we will establish that the spirit of America is one of trust, and instead of expediency what this nation seeks is right judgment; instead of ghettos that what we want are neighborhoods and communities in America [*applause*]; instead of disunity or what it sometimes masquerades under consensus, we have dedication of purpose [*applause*]; instead of incredibility, let us have integrity [*applause*]; and instead of murmuring let us have clear speech and, we hope, America singing again [*applause*]; and in place of that fear of fear, if any have come close to it which is on the edge of despair, let us have hope again. [*Applause.*]

This is the promise of America. This has always been the promise of America. Stated again by Adlai Stevenson, brought to force and positive action by John Kennedy.

Let us pick up again the lost and severed strands, weave them again into the fabric of America. Let us sort out the sound and the music from the noise and the confusion so that this nation may again respond to the sound of the trumpet and to the steady drum. [*Sustained applause.*]

## Robert F. Kennedy Says of the War in Vietnam, "It Must Be Ended"

They made a desert, and called it peace.

When he was assassinated on June 5, 1968, Robert Kennedy was one of the Senate's foremost antiwar dissidents. His "maiden formal campaign address," delivered at 9 a.m. on March 18, 1968, in Kansas State University's Ahearn Field House, illustrates how the candidate created the excitement that sustained his antiwar campaign until its premature end.[54]

When he arrived at Kansas State to introduce himself to America as a presidential candidate, and also to galvanize opposition to the war in Vietnam, Kennedy was greeted as a celebrity. The *Kansas Collegian,* the university's daily newspaper, reported that people came because they "were attracted by the magnetism of the man and by the name and legend that first captivated the country in the New Frontier days of John Kennedy."[55] High school students, or "bobby-hoppers,"[56] waved signs like "Kiss me Bobby," "Bobby is groovy," "Sock it to 'em Bobby," and "Bamba for Bobby."[57] On the dirt floor, a record crowd of 14,500 packed the field house. Students sat on stairs and hung off rafters.[58]

Not all members of the audience were filled with as much youthful enthusiasm. Supporters of Senator Eugene McCarthy, encouraged by the recent New Hampshire primary, in which he trailed President Johnson by a scant 230 votes,[59] waved "Eugene for Integrity" and "McCarthy '68" placards.[60] Backers of New York Republican governor Nelson Rockefeller were also plentiful, and when Kennedy started to speak, students unfurled large "Rocky" banners directly behind him.[61]

Kennedy's rock-star welcome was surprising, to say the least. As Jack Newfield, a reporter for the *Village Voice,* put it, "This is not a campus where there have been student protests. The students are mostly from rural Kansas. The girls wear short hair, little makeup, and skirts below the knees. The boys had ties and crew cuts."[62] Kennedy himself worried that the first formal speech of his presidential campaign would not be well received. After examining a first draft of the speech, he instructed his head speechwriter,

Adam Walinsky, to elaborate on the justifications for his antiwar position. "These people are conservative," the candidate explained.[63]

But whatever trepidations Kennedy might have had at the beginning of his speech completely disappeared by the end. After fifty minutes of a trenchant critique of the president's policies in Vietnam, *Newsweek* reported that Kennedy "brought down the house" and received a "wild ovation"[64] with his short peroration: "If you will give me your help, if you will give me your hand, I will work with you and we will have a new America!" Newfield, who attended the event, wrote that "the field house sounded as though it was inside Niagara Falls; it was like a soundtrack gone haywire."[65] Stanley Tretick of *Look* magazine saw the "hysteria" and exclaimed, "This is Kansas, fucking Kansas! He's going all the fucking way!"[66]

Kennedy began his speech bizarrely. In his unscripted remarks, the candidate "set off waves of laughter" with ten minutes of shtick.[67] In joke after joke, some prepared and some extemporaneous, the candidate surprised the young audience with self-effacing and irreverent humor. Describing his differences with President Johnson over a proposed commission with the power to change policies in Vietnam, Kennedy quipped, "Really, the only difference between us is that I wanted Senator Mansfield, Senator Fulbright and Senator Morse appointed to the commission. And President Johnson, in his own inimitable style, wanted to appoint General Westmoreland, John Wayne and Martha Raye."[68] Kennedy then began his scripted remarks with equally surprising defiance: "The more riots that come on college campuses, the better the world for tomorrow." One wonders if Kennedy's irreverence, even impertinence, was the product of a man who "does not have to make speeches to win the vote of a young couple . . . who occasionally tell their children why they keep a small bronze statue of the elder Kennedy on their mantle," or, instead, precisely the reason young crowds responded to him so favorably.[69] In any case, to his detractors these flip remarks undercut the seriousness of his later arguments. To those less hostile, however, the humor helped establish Kennedy as a likable figure.

The speech proper has a basic analytical structure. Kennedy first identifies a problem: the existence of a "crisis of confidence" brought about, in part, by the Johnson administration's policies in Vietnam. He then analyzes the problem by describing the consequences of four "true facts." Finally, Kennedy offers two solutions: "negotiate and announce our willingness to negotiate with the National Liberation Front," and, of course, vote for Kennedy.

Along this basic argumentative route, Kennedy sometimes engages in what Roman rhetoricians called *refutatio* (refutation), or answering the counterarguments of one's opponents. Twice Kennedy contests the claim that his proposed strategy of negotiation is equivalent to a "simple withdrawal" or "a radical program of surrender." In addition, Kennedy preemptively refutes the charge of hypocrisy or political opportunism by taking responsibility for some of the policies that brought the United States into Vietnam in the first place. "I was involved in many of the early decisions on Vietnam, decisions which helped set us on our present path," Kennedy admits, adding that "I am willing to bear my share of the responsibility, before history and before my fellow citizens." But, he says, "past error is no excuse for its own perpetuation."

One can interpret Kennedy's speech in a variety of ways. First, it may be thought of as an essay on the distinction between appearance and reality.[70] Kennedy starts by praising political commentator William Allen White, a man who "did not conceal his concern in comforting words." He then urges his audience "to learn the harsh facts that lurk behind the mask of official illusion." Throughout the speech, Kennedy contrasts the administration's confident rhetoric with the sobering realities of war. He offers an insider's exposé of the conflict.

Secondly, one can interpret the speech as one senator's delicate attempt to broach the sensitive topic of his country's defeat, and to promote negotiation as a viable political strategy in light of military failures. In the clearest exposition of his position, Kennedy explains: "The president has offered to negotiate, yet this weekend he told us again that he seeks not compromise but victory, 'at the negotiating table if possible . . . on the battlefield if necessary.' But at a real negotiating table, there can be no victory for either side, only a painful and a difficult compromise." One can fault Kennedy for beating around the bush—"defeat" is never explicitly discussed; only the absence of victory. On the other hand, approaching the topic more directly could likely have added insult to injury. Such a confession from a United States senator would have incensed rather than soothed the nation's already aching psyche. Moreover, Kennedy's audience knew that Vietnam was becoming a stalled conflict at best, and a quagmire at worst. Three days earlier, the military issued widely reported figures indicating that American casualties in the war—139,801, of whom 19,670 were killed and 120,131 wounded—had exceed those in the Korean conflict.[71] The sudden and massive Tet offensive earlier in the year had also made it clear that the United States would face a long and costly war.

Third, one can understand the Kansas State address in the context of Kennedy's strategy to gain the presidency. On the first day of the campaign, for example, Adam Walinsky stated, "Our strategy is to change the rules of nominating a President. We're going to do it a new way. In the street."[72] Kennedy would later tell Helen Dudar of the *New York Post,* "I have to win through the people. Otherwise I'm not going to win."[73] With party bosses pledged to President Johnson and many idealists lost to McCarthy, "winning through the people" may very well have been necessary, but what exactly did Kennedy mean? The following speech establishes fairly certainly that "winning through the people" meant relying on "nostalgia, celebrity and emotion, and being"—as Ronald Steel puts it—"his brother's brother, the anointed heir of the now-beloved and idealized JFK."[74]

Steel's interpretation is compelling. Kennedy recasts his brother's words and makes them his own through both the speech's text and the manner of its presentation. Kennedy frames the speech neatly by invoking the late President Kennedy, both in his introduction and conclusion.* Robert's request that voters give him "their help, their hands, and their

---

* Kennedy began his address with some remarks about the one-time governor of Kansas and Republican presidential nominee: "I am delighted to be here. I'm very pleased because of Governor Landon, who President Kennedy had the greatest affection for. Governor Landon, I know, was at the White House and visited with President Kennedy. President Kennedy talked about it frequently afterwards. And he told me after he visited with Governor Landon that he asked the Governor: "Why aren't there more Democrats in Kansas?" And I don't think we ever got an answer to this day. [*Laughter.*] But I know how highly regarded he was by President Kennedy."

hearts" is borrowed almost verbatim from his brother's vintage 1960 campaign speeches.[75] Robert's admission of "responsibility" is akin to President Kennedy's acceptance of responsibility for the Bay of Pigs disaster.[76] Robert's advocacy of "negotiation" with the National Liberation Front hearkens back to his brother's inaugural advice to "never negotiate out of fear, but never fear to negotiate."[77] Speaking of the first weeks of Kennedy's campaign, *Newsweek* remarked that Kennedy "makes the same effective use of statistics" as his brother did, and also "sprinkles his talks with erudite quotations."[78]

Robert Kennedy used nonverbal techniques to evoke his martyred brother as well. As *Newsweek* pointed out, "almost everything about Bobby's style and presence strengthen the association. He makes a child's fist, thumb on top, pointed out; the gesture was often Jack's. Bobby's voice is normally thinner and higher; but at the height of his delivery of late, it has gained body and begun to resemble that earlier voice. The Harvard-trained Boston diction, the rhetorical, rising cadence—these are hauntingly similar."[79]

In short, the audience saw Robert, but heard John. The "magic ability to captivate"[80] that one Kansas student saw in the young candidate was not magic after all—the "delirious crowds"[81] that met him and the "crescendo of roaring support"[82] that followed his speech were the products of careful speechwriting and speech giving. The deliberate evocation of a martyred brother lay at the heart of Robert Kennedy's appeal.


. . . I AM . . . GLAD TO COME to the home of a great Kansan who wrote, "If our colleges and universities do not breed men who riot, who rebel, who attack life with all the youthful vision and vigor, then there is something wrong with our colleges. The more riots that come on college campuses, the better the world for tomorrow."

That's what he said. And the man who wrote these words was that notorious man, William Allen White—the late editor of the *Emporia Gazette*. [*Applause.*] He is an honored man today, but when he lived and when he wrote, he was often reviled as an extremist or worse on your campus and across this nation. For he spoke—for he spoke as he believed. He did not conceal his concern in comforting words. He did not delude his readers or himself with false hopes or with illusions. It is in this spirit—is in this spirit that I wish to talk with you today.

For this is a year of choice—a year when we choose not simply who will lead us, but where we wish to be led, the country we want for ourselves, and the kind that we want for our children. If in this year of choice we fashion new policies out of old illusions, we ensure for ourselves nothing but crises for the future, and we bequeath to our children the bitter harvest of those crises.

For with all we have done, with all of our immense power and with our immense richness, our problems seem to grow not less, but greater. We are in a time of unprecedented turbulence, of danger, and of questioning. It is at its root really a question of the national soul of this country. The president—the president calls it "restlessness," while cabinet officers and commentators tell us that America is deep in a malaise of the spirit, discouraging initiative, paralyzing will and action, and dividing Americans from one another by their age, by their views, and by the color of their skin.

There are many causes. Some are in the failed promise of America itself, in the children that I have seen starving in Mississippi, idling their lives away in the ghettos, committing suicide in the despair of Indian reservations, or watching their proud fathers sit without work in the ravaged lands of eastern Kentucky. Another cause is our inaction in the face of danger. We seem equally unable to control the violent disorder within our cities, or the pollution and the destruction of the country, of the water and land that we use and that our children must inherit. And a third great cause of discontent is the course that we are following today in Southeast Asia in Vietnam [*applause*], in a war that has divided Americans as they have not been divided since your state was called "bloody Kansas."

All this—questioning and uncertainty at home, divisive war abroad—has led us into a deep crisis of confidence: in our leadership, in each other, in our very selves, and as a nation.

Today I would speak to you of the third of those crises. I would speak to you of the war in Vietnam. I come here to this serious forum in the heart of the nation to discuss this war with you—not on the basis of emotion, but on the basis of fact, not, I hope, in clichés, but with a clear and discriminating sense of where the national interest of this country really lies. It may be that our views on this war will not be in agreement, but what is important is that we discuss our views, that we discuss the facts, and then seek strength in the enduring impulses which have always united this nation, in the strength that we as Americans together can master and bring to our service the enormous forces that rage across the world in which we live.

I do not want—as I believe most Americans do not want—to sell out America's interests, to simply withdraw, to raise the white flag of surrender. I am not suggesting that, and I don't think any other reasonable and responsible American is suggesting that. [*Applause.*] But I also say—but I also say that the only course of action that we can take in Southeast Asia, that we can take in Vietnam, is not necessarily and in my judgment is not the action that we are taking at the moment under the leadership of President Lyndon Johnson. [*Shouts and applause.*] But I am concerned, as Senator Mansfield and Senator Cooper and Senator Fulbright are concerned, as General Shoup and General Norstad and General Ridgway are concerned, and as Eugene McCarthy's brilliant New Hampshire campaign [*applause*] and the words of those associated with him have shown, most Americans are concerned that the course we are following at the present time is deeply wrong. I am concerned, as I believe most Americans are concerned, that we are acting as if no other nation existed, against the judgment and desires of neutrals and our historic allies alike.

I am concerned that at the end of it all, there will be only more Americans killed, more of our treasure spent, and because of the bitterness and because of the hatred on every side of this war, more hundreds of thousands of Vietnamese slaughtered, so that they may say, as Tacitus said of Rome, "They made a desert, and they called it peace."[83] I don't think that's satisfactory for the United States of America. [*Prolonged applause.*] I do not think—I do not think that that is what the American spirit is really about. I do not think that that is what this country stands for.

Let me begin this discussion with a note both personal and public. I was involved in many of the early decisions on Vietnam, decisions which helped set us on our present path. It may be that the effort was doomed from the start; that it was never really possible to bring all the people of South Vietnam under the rule of the successive governments that we supported—governments, one after another, riddled with corruption, inefficiency, and greed; governments which did not and could not successfully capture and energize the national feeling of their people. If that is the case, as it well may be, then I am willing to bear my share of the responsibility, before history and before my fellow citizens. But past error is no excuse for its own perpetuation.[84] Tragedy is a tool for the living to gain wisdom, not a guide by which to live. Now as ever, we do ourselves best justice when we measure ourselves against ancient tests, as in Sophocles: "All men make mistakes, but a good man yields when he knows his course is wrong, and he repairs the evils. The only sin," he said, "is pride." [*Applause.*]

The reversals of the last several months have led our military to ask for two hundred and six thousand more troops. This weekend it was announced that some of them—a "moderate" increase, as it was described—would soon be sent. But isn't this exactly what we have always done in the past? If we examine the history of this conflict, we find the dismal story repeated time after time. Every time—at every crisis—we have first denied that anything was wrong. And then we have sent more troops. And then we have issued more confident communiqués. Every time we have been assured that this one last step— that this one last step—would bring victory. And every time, the predictions and the promises have failed and been forgotten, and the demand has been made again for just one more step up the latter.

But for all of the escalation, all of the last steps, they have brought us no closer to success than we were before. At every occasion, at every time, we have responded to the crisis in Vietnam with military action. We have looked upon the conflict in South Vietnam as just a military conflict. It is not just a military conflict. It is a political and a diplomatic conflict, and we have ignored those two areas, and that's why we're in the trouble we are today in March of 1968. [*Applause.*]

Rather, as the scale of the fighting has increased, as we have as sent more money, as we have escalated, South Vietnamese society has become less and less capable of organizing and defending itself, and we have more and more assumed the whole burden of the war. In just three years, we have gone from sixteen thousand advisers to over five hundred thousand troops; from no American bombing of the North or the South, to an air campaign against both, greater than that waged in all the European theater in World War II; from less than three hundred American dead in all the years prior to 1965, to more than five hundred dead in a single week of combat in 1968. Five hundred and nine this past week.

And once again—and once again—the president tells us, as we have been told for twenty years, that we are going to win; that victory is coming.

But I ask you, what are the true facts? What is our present situation?

First, our control over the rural population—so long described as the key to our efforts—has evaporated. The vice president tells us that the pacification program has stopped. . . . Like it or not the government of South Vietnam is pursuing an enclave policy. Its writ runs where American arms protect it—that far and no further. To extend the power of the Saigon government over its own country, we now can see, will be in essence equivalent to the reconquest and the occupation of most of the entire nation.

Let us clearly understand the full implications of that fact. The point of our pacification operations was always described as winning the hearts and the minds of the people. We recognized that giving the countryside military security against the Viet Cong would be futile—indeed, that it would be impossible—unless the people of the countryside themselves came to identify their interest with ours, and to assist not the Viet Cong, but the Saigon government. For this we recognized that their minds would have to be changed, that their natural inclination would be to support the Viet Cong, or at best to remain passive, rather than to sacrifice themselves for the foreign white man, or for the remote Saigon government.

It is this effort that has been most gravely set back over the period of the last several months. We cannot change the minds of people in villages controlled by the enemy. The fact is, as we all recognize, that we cannot reassert control over those villages now in enemy hands without repeating the whole bloody process of destruction which has ravaged the countryside of South Vietnam throughout the last three years. Nor could we thus keep control without the presence of millions—of millions—of American troops. . . .

The second evident fact of the last two months is that the Saigon government is no more or better an ally than it was before—that it may even be less—and that the war inexorably is growing more, not less, an American effort. American officials continue to talk about a government newly energized, moving, they say, with "great competence," taking, as they say and they describe it, hold "remarkably well," doing "a very, very good piece of work of recovery." I was in the executive branch of the government from 1961 to 1964. In all those years, we heard the same glowing promises about the South Vietnamese government: corruption would soon be eliminated, land reform would soon come, programs were being infused for the first time with new energy. But those statements, those claims, were not the facts. They were not the facts then, and when they are stated today, they are not the facts now. The facts are that there is still no total mobilization, no price or wage controls, no rationing, no overtime work. The facts are, as a committee of the House of Representatives has told us, that land reform is moving backwards with the government forces helping landlords to collect exorbitant back rents from the peasants whom they expect to fight this war. [*Applause.*] And the facts, again the facts, the facts are that eighteen-year-old South Vietnamese are still not being drafted, though now, as many times as in the past, we are assured that this will happen very, very soon. The facts are that thousands of young South Vietnamese buy their deferments from military service while American marines die today at Khe Sanh. I don't accept that. I don't think that's acceptable. [*Prolonged applause.*] If the South Vietnamese government—if the South Vietnamese government feels that Khe Sanh is so important, let them put South Vietnamese soldiers up there and take the marines out. [*Applause, cheers, and whistles.*] . . .

Third, it is becoming more evident with every passing day that the victories we achieve will only come at the cost of the destruction of the nation we once hoped to help. Even before this winter, Vietnam and its people were disintegrating under the blows of war. Now hardly a city in Vietnam has been spared from the new ravages of the past two months. Saigon officials say that nearly three-quarters of a million new refugees have been created, to add to [an] existing refugee population of two million or more. . . . No one really knows the number of civilian causalities. The city of Hue, with most of the country's cultural and artistic heritage, lies in ruins. Of its population of one hundred and forty-five thousand, it has been reported that fully one hundred and thirty thousand are said to be homeless. There is not enough food, not enough shelter, and not enough medical care. There is only death, there is only misery, and there is only destruction.

An American commander said of the town of Ben Tre, "It became necessary to destroy the town in order to save it."[85] That kind of salvation is not, in my judgment, an act that we here in the United States can presume to perform for them. But we must ask our government—we must ask ourselves—for we are responsible. Not just those in Washington, not just those in the executive branch of the government, but all of us in this country. I'm responsible and you are responsible because this action is taking place in Vietnam in our name, in the name of the United States of America, and we have the right to ask questions, and we must ask questions of our government and of ourselves. [*Applause.*]

Where does this logic end? Where does it end? If it becomes "necessary" to destroy all of South Vietnam in order to "save" it, will we here in the United States, will we do that too? Is that what we want? Is that what we stand for? I can't believe that's true. [*Applause.*]

And if we care so little about South Vietnam that we are willing to see the land destroyed and its people dead, then I ask, "Why are we there in the first place?" [*Applause.*]

Can we ordain to ourselves—can we ordain to ourselves the awful majesty of God, to decide what cities and villages are to be destroyed, who will live and who will die, and who will join the refugees wandering in a desert of our own creation? If it is true that we have made a commitment to the South Vietnamese people, we must ask, "Are they being consulted, in Hue, or Ben Tre, or in the villages from which the three million refugees have fled?" If they believe that all the death and all of this destruction are a lesser evil than the Viet Cong, why did they not warn us when the Viet Cong came into Hue, and the dozens of other cities, before the Tet Offensive? And why, I ask you, did they not join the fight? . . .

Let us have no misunderstanding. The Viet Cong are a brutal enemy indeed. Time and time again, they have shown their willingness to sacrifice innocent civilians, to engage in torture and murder and despicable terror to achieve their ends. There can be no easy moral answer to this war, no one-sided condemnation of American actions. I don't believe that the people of South Vietnam want domination and control by the Viet Cong, the National Liberation Front, or the Communists, or North Vietnam. But neither do

I believe that they want to be dominated by the United States of America or by any foreign power. [*Prolonged applause.*]

What we must ask ourselves is whether we have a right to bring so much destruction of another land without clear and convincing evidence that this is what its people want. But that is precisely the evidence that we do not have. What they want is peace, not domination by any outside force. And that is what we are really committed to help bring them, not in some indefinite future, but while some scraps of life remain still to be saved from the holocaust.

The fourth fact that is now more clear than ever is that the war in Vietnam, far from being the last critical test of the United States, is in fact weakening our position in Asia and around the world, and eroding the structure of international cooperation that has directly supported our security for the past three decades. In purely military terms the war has already stripped us of our graduated response capabilities that we have labored so hard to build over the period of the last seven years beginning in 1961. Surely the North Koreans were emboldened to seize the *Pueblo* because they knew that the United States simply cannot afford to fight another Asian war while we are so tied down in Vietnam. We set out to prove our willingness to keep our commitments everywhere in the world. What we are ensuring instead is that it is most unlikely that the American people would ever again be willing to engage in this kind of struggle. Meanwhile our oldest and strongest allies pull back to their own shores, leaving us alone to police all of Asia, while Mao and his Chinese comrades sit patiently by, fighting us to the last Vietnamese, watching us weaken a nation which might have provided a stout barrier against Chinese expansion southward. As Secretary Rusk said just last week when one member of the Foreign Relations Committee asked him, "What do you think about the Chinese coming in and helping the North Vietnamese?" And he said the Chinese will never come into North Vietnam because the people and the government of North Vietnam don't want the Chinese there—a most interesting, and in my judgment a significant, response in view of the efforts and the struggle that we are conducting in Southeast Asia.

There they are, the Chinese, hoping that the war in South Vietnam will further tie us down and perhaps [result] in protracted war in Cambodia, Laos, and Thailand, confident, as it is reported from Hong Kong, that the war in Vietnam will increasingly bog down the United States, sap its resources, discredit its power pretensions, alienate its allies, fraying its ties with the Soviet Union and at the same time aggravating dissensions among American at home. As one American observer puts it, truly: "We seem to be playing the script the way Mao wrote it."

All this bears directly and heavily on whether more troops should now be sent to Vietnam, and if more are sent, what their mission will be. We are entitled to ask—we are required to ask—how many more men, how many more lives, how much more destruction will be asked, to provide the military victory that is always just around the corner, to pour into this bottomless pit of our dreams.

But this question the administration does not and cannot answer. It has no answer— none but the ever-expanding use of military force and the lives of our brave soldiers, in a conflict where military force has failed to solve anything in the past. The president has offered to negotiate, yet this weekend he told us again that he seeks not compromise but victory, "at the negotiating table if possible," it was said, "on the battlefield if necessary." But at a real negotiating table, there can be no victory for either side, only a painful and a difficult compromise. To seek victory at the conference table is to ensure that you will never reach it. Instead the war will go on. The war will go on year after terrible year— until those who sit in the seats of high policy are men who seek another path. And I believe that that must be done this year. [*Prolonged applause.*] And it is for that reason—and it is for that reason—that I offer myself for candidate of president of the United States. [*Prolonged applause.*]

For it is long past time to ask, "What is this war doing to us?" Of course it is costing us money—fully one-fourth of our federal budget—but that is the smallest price that we pay. The cost is our young men, the tens of thousands of their lives cut off and ended forever. The cost is our world position—with neutrals and allies alike, every day more baffled and estranged from a policy they cannot understand.

Higher yet is the price that we pay in our own innermost lives, and in the spirit of this country, and in the soul and the heart of the United States. For the first time in a century, we have open resistance to service in the cause of our nation. For the first time perhaps in our history, we have desertions from our army on political and moral grounds. The front pages of our newspapers show photographs of American soldiers torturing prisoners. Every night we watch horror on the evening news. Violence spreads inexorably across this nation, filling our streets and crippling our lives. And whatever the costs to us, let us think of the young men that we have sent there. Not just the killed, but those who have to kill. Not just the maimed, but all those who must look upon the results of what are forced and have to do.

It may be asked, "Is not such degradation the cost of all wars?" And of course it is. That is why war is not an enterprise lightly to be undertaken, nor prolonged one moment past its absolute necessity. All this—the destruction of South Vietnam, the destruction of the North, the cost to ourselves, the danger to the world—all this we would be willing to stand if it seemed to serve some worthwhile end. But the costs of the war's present course far outweigh anything we can reasonably hope to gain by it for ourselves or for the people of Vietnam. It must be ended, and in my judgment it can be ended, in a peace of brave men who have fought each other with a terrible fury, each believing that he and he alone was in the right. We have prayed to different gods, and the prayers of neither have been answered fully. Now, while there is still time for some of them to be partly answered, now is the time to stop.

And the fact is that much can be done. And it does not involve giving up, but it does involve not continuing to follow the bankrupt policy that we are following at the present time. [*Applause.*] We can—as I have urged for two years, but as we have never done— negotiate and announce our willingness to negotiate with the National Liberation Front. [*Applause.*] We can—as we have never done—assure the Front a genuine place in the political life of South Vietnam. [*Applause.*] We can—as we are refusing to do today—

begin to de-escalate the war, concentrate on protecting populated areas, and thus save American lives and slow down the destruction of the countryside. [*Applause.*] We can stop the bombing and we can go to the negotiating table as the North Vietnamese have said that they will do [*applause*] and we can end the search and the destroy missions. We can—as we have never done—insist that the government of South Vietnam broaden its base, institute real reforms, and seek an honorable settlement with their fellow countrymen. [*Applause.*]

This is no radical program of surrender. This is no sellout of American interests. This is a modest and a reasonable program, a program that I have been discussing over the period of the last two years, which would have been easier two years ago than it is now, which would have been easier a year ago than it is now, which would have been easier three months ago than it is now, but which will be more difficult six months from now than it is at the present time, and I think we should move ahead now. [*Applause.*]

This program would be far more effective than the present course of this administration, whose only response to failure is to repeat it on a larger scale. [*Applause.*] This program, with its more limited costs, would indeed be far more likely to accomplish our true objectives.

And therefore even this modern, modest, and reasonable program is impossible while our present leadership, under the illusion that military victory is just ahead, plunges deeper into the swamp that is our present course.

So I come here today to this great university to ask for your help, not for me, but for your country and for the people of Vietnam and for the peace of all mankind. [*Prolonged applause.*] You are the people, as President Kennedy said, who have "the least ties to the present and the greatest stake in the future." I urge you to learn the harsh facts that lurk behind the mask of official illusion with which we have concealed our true circumstances even from ourselves. Our country is in danger, not just from foreign enemies, but above all, from our own misguided policies and what they can do to this nation that Thomas Jefferson once told us was the last great hope of mankind.

There is a contest on, not for the rule of America, but for the heart of America. In these next eight months we are going to decide what this country will stand for and what kind of men we are. So I ask for your help in the cities and the homes of this state, in the towns and on its farms, contributing your concern and your action, warning of the danger of what we are doing, and the promise—and the promise of what we can do in the future. I ask for your help. [*Prolonged applause.*] I ask you—I ask you as tens of thousands of young men and women are doing all over this land, to organize yourselves and then go forth and work for new policies, not just in Southeast Asia, but here at home as well. In the state of Kansas, across the United States, in our cities, in our rural areas, in our towns, so that we have a new birth for this country, so that we have a new light to guide us. And I pledge that if you give me your help, if you give me your hand, that I will work with you and we will have a new America.

Thank you very much. [*Shouts, whistles, and sustained applause.*]

## Shirley Chisholm Demands "People and Peace, and Not Profits and War"

I intend to vote "No" on every money bill that comes to the
floor of this House that provides any funds for the
Department of Defense . . . until the monstrous waste and the
shocking profits in the defense budget have been eliminated
and our country starts to use its strength, its tremendous
resources, for people and peace, not for profits and war.

The first African American congresswoman, Shirley Chisholm made a career for herself as a "woman warrior" and a champion of underrepresented Americans. Having earned a reputation in the New York State Assembly as a maverick who voted her conscience, in 1968 Chisholm ran successfully for the United States House of Representatives from Brooklyn's newly created black-majority Twelfth District. Her maiden speech in the House, which Chisholm delivered on March 26, 1969, and which is reprinted below, provided Chisholm's colleagues with clear evidence that she planned to live up to her campaign slogan: "Unbought and Unbossed."

Chisholm's description of congressional speech-making in her 1970 autobiography, *Unbought and Unbossed,* illustrates the principle of strategic restraint: "Sometimes it is like a poker game, in which each side reveals some of the strength it has, trying to make it just enough to convince a waverer that there is a lot more being held back and he'd better join the winning side."[86] Chisholm's antiwar speech is a model of such restraint. She believed in many of the antiwar arguments that appear elsewhere in this anthology, but chose not to deploy them. In *Unbought and Unbossed,* for example, Chisholm questions the justice and necessity of the conflict in Southeast Asia and impugns the motives of those who were responsible for perpetuating it: "The war in Southeast Asia was neither just nor unavoidable; it was an unnecessary war into which we stumbled, led by short-sighted, stubborn men who could not admit at any point that they were wrong but who, on the contrary, concealed their mistakes by systematically lying to the country about the nature of the war and the prospects of ending it."[87] During her 1969 speech to Congress, though, Chisholm argues simply that the House should prioritize domestic issues over international ones: "Apart from all other considerations, and they are many, the main fact is that we cannot squander there the lives, the money, the energy that we need desperately here, in our cities, in our schools."

Chisholm's restraint is strategic because the terms of her argument were designed to resonate with her colleagues in Congress. Just as she campaigned for a House seat in Brooklyn's Twelfth District by addressing Puerto Rican voters in Spanish, Chisholm campaigned to end the war in Congress by speaking in a language her audience would understand. The central assumption of Chisholm's speech is that Congress should prioritize the interests of its constituents—that is, Americans—over the interests of foreigners abroad. Congress has a mandate, in other words, to "do something for [the American] people first." This approach appears to have been calculated to garner a broader base of support than would be possible with a speech that, to use just one example, focused on the devastating impact the war had on the Vietnamese.[88] In addition, Chisholm's America first argument helps insulate her from the common prowar refrain that wartime dissent is unpatriotic.

Chisholm had another choice description of congressional speech-making: "It is seldom that anyone listens to what is being said on the floor of the House."[89] If this is true, then the attention Chisholm's 1969 antiwar speech garnered is rare: while her immediate audience was not enormous, it was significant. As Chisholm and her fellow antiwar congressmen spoke, hundreds of women, many clad in black and waving black balloons, protested outside the Capitol building.[90] According to the *New York Times,* the protest "was reported to be the first antiwar demonstration since President Nixon's inauguration" in January.

Chisholm's speech also had lasting consequences for her political career. It struck a chord with college students, who deluged the representative with invitations to speak out against war on campuses across the nation. The support and exposure Chisholm gained as an antiwar leader helped her launch her spirited bid for the presidency three years later.[91]

MR. SPEAKER, on the same day President Nixon announced he had decided the United States will not be safe unless we start to build a defense system against missiles, the Headstart [*sic*] program in the District of Columbia was cut back for the lack of money.

As a teacher, and as a woman, I do not think I will ever understand what kind of values can be involved in spending $9 billion—and more, I am sure—on elaborate, unnecessary, and impractical weapons when several thousand disadvantaged children in the Nation's Capital get nothing.

When the new administration took office, I was one of the many Americans who hoped it would mean that our country would benefit from the fresh perspectives, the new ideas, the different priorities of a leader who had no part in its mistakes of the past. Mr. Nixon had said things like this:

> If our cities are to be livable for the next generation, we can delay no longer in launching new approaches to the problems that beset them and to the tensions that tear them apart.

And he said:

> When you cut expenditures for education, what you are doing is short-changing the American future.

But frankly, I have never cared too much what people say. What I am interested in is what they do. We have waited to see what the new administration is going to do. The pattern now is becoming clear.

Apparently launching those new programs can be delayed for a while, after all. It seems we have to get some missiles launched first.

Recently the new Secretary of Commerce spelled it out. The Secretary, Mr. Stans, told a reporter that the new administration is "pretty well agreed it must take time out from major social objectives" until it can stop inflation.

The new Secretary of Health, Education, and Welfare, Robert Finch, came to the Hill to tell the House Education and Labor Committee that he thinks we should spend more on education, particularly in city schools. But, he said, unfortunately we cannot "afford" to, until we have reached some kind of honorable solution to the Vietnam war. I was glad to read that the distinguished Member from Oregon (Mrs. Green) asked Mr. Finch this:

> With the crisis we have in education, and the crisis in our cities, can we wait to settle the war? Shouldn't it be the other way around? Unless we can meet the crisis in education, we really can't afford the war.

Secretary of Defense Melvin Laird came to Capitol Hill, too. His mission was to sell the anti–ballistic-missile insanity to the Senate. He was asked what the new administration is doing about the war. To hear him, one would have thought it was 1968, that the former Secretary of State was defending the former policies, that nothing had ever happened—a President had never decided not to run because he knew the Nation would reject him in despair, over this tragic war we have blundered into. Mr. Laird talked of being prepared to spend at least 2 more years in Vietnam.

Two more years, 2 more years of hunger for Americans, of death for our best young men, of children here at home suffering the life-long handicap of not having a good education when they are young. Two more years of high taxes, collected to feed the cancerous growth of a Defense Department budget that now consumes two-thirds of our Federal income.

Two more years of too little being done to fight our greatest enemies, poverty, prejudice, and neglect here in our own country. Two more years of fantastic waste in the Defense Department and of penny pinching on social programs. Our country cannot survive 2 more years, or 4, of these kinds of policies. It must stop—this year—now.

Now I am not a pacifist. I am, deeply, unalterably opposed, to this war in Vietnam. Apart from all the other considerations, and they are many, the main fact is that we cannot squander there the lives, the money, the energy that we need desperately here, in our cities, in our schools.

I wonder whether we cannot reverse our whole approach to spending. For years, we have given the military, the defense industry, a blank check. New weapons' [sic] systems are dreamed up, billions are spent, and many times they are found to be impractical, inefficient, unsatisfactory, even worthless. What do we do then? We spend more money on them. But with social programs, what do we do? Take the Job Corps. Its failures have been mercilessly exposed and criticized. If it had been a military research and development project, they would have been covered up or explained away, and Congress would have been ready to pour more billions after those that had been wasted on it.

The case of Pride, Inc., is interesting. This vigorous, successful black organization, here in Washington, conceived and built by young, inner-city men, has been ruthlessly attacked by its enemies in the Government, in this Congress. At least six auditors from the General Accounting Office were put to work investigating Pride. They worked 7 months and spent more than $100,000. They uncovered a fraud. It was something less than $2,100. Meanwhile, millions of dollars—billions of dollars, in fact—were being spent by the Department of Defense, and how many auditors and investigators were checking into their negotiated contracts? Five.

We Americans have come to feel that it is our mission to make the world free. We believe that we are the good guys, everywhere, in Vietnam, in Latin America, wherever we go. We believe we are the good guys at home, too. When the Kerner Commission told white America what black America has always known, that prejudice and hatred built the Nation's slums, maintains them, and profits by them, white America would not believe it. But it is true. Unless we start to fight, and defeat, the enemies of poverty and racism in our own country and make our talk of equality and opportunity ring true, we are exposed as hypocrites in the eyes of the world when we talk about making other people free.

I am deeply disappointed at the clear evidence that the No. 1 priority of the new administration is to buy more and more and more weapons of war, to return to the era of the cold war, to ignore the war we must fight here—the war that is not optional. There is only one way, I believe, to turn these policies around. The Congress can respond to the mandate that the American people have clearly expressed. They have said, "End this war. Stop the waste. Stop the killing. Do something for our own people first." We must find the money to "launch the new approaches," as Mr. Nixon said. We must force the administration to rethink its distorted, unreal scale of priorities. Our children, our jobless men, our deprived, rejected, and starving fellow citizens must come first.

For this reason, I intend to vote "No" on every money bill that comes to the floor of this House that provides any funds for the Department of Defense. Any bill whatsoever, until the time comes when our values and priorities have been turned right-side up again, until the monstrous waste and the shocking profits in the defense budget have been eliminated and our country starts to use its strength, its tremendous resources, for people and peace, not for profits and war.

It was Calvin Coolidge I believe who made the comment that "the Business of America is Business." We are now spending $80 billion a year on defense—that is two-thirds of every tax dollar. At this time, gentlemen, the business of America is war and it is time for a change.

## Fannie Lou Hamer Rallies Antiwar Students at Berkeley

*I am sick of the racist war in Vietnam when we don't have*
*justice in the United States!*

The life of civil rights activist Fannie Lou Hamer was one of remarkable hardship. She was born in 1917, the last of twenty children. Two years later, her sharecropper parents moved to Ruleville, Mississippi, where they fed their family on $1.25 a day. Hamer started picking cotton when she was six years old, and eventually picked hundreds of pounds of cotton each day at a penny a pound. In 1929, when Hamer's parents were finally able to rent land and buy animals of their own, a jealous white neighbor poisoned their mules and cows, sending the family back into abject poverty.[92]

Hardship and abuse followed Hamer into her forties. In 1961, she was hospitalized for the removal of a uterine tumor, and the surgeons performed a hysterectomy without her consent. In 1962, when she had passed Mississippi's literacy test on her third try, the owner of the plantation on which Hamer worked as a timekeeper offered her a hard choice: withdraw her voting registration or be fired. With characteristic boldness, Hamer quit her job and decided to become more politically active.[93]

Some of the worst abuses, however, were yet to come. In the summer of 1963, a year before the "Freedom Summer" campaign attempted to register as many African American voters as possible in Mississippi, Hamer was returning home by bus to Mississippi from a voter registration workshop. Arrested unexpectedly at rest stop in Montgomery County, she was taken to a jail cell, where white officers told her, "We are going to make you wish you was dead." The officers then forced two black male prisoners to beat Hamer with a metal-studded blackjack.[94]

In spite of this extreme adversity, Hamer led a remarkably successful life as a grassroots political activist, a candidate for the United States Congress, and a popular speaker. Despite her many successes, though, she was clearly held back by her lack of formal education. As the U.S. senator from Mississippi Henry Kirksey put it, "If Fannie Lou Hamer had had the same opportunities that Martin Luther King had, then we would have had a female Martin Luther King."[95]

Hamer gave the following speech before thousands of students at a Vietnam moratorium rally on October 15, 1969, in Lower Sproul Plaza at the University of California, Berkeley. Structurally disjointed, argumentatively repetitive, and grammatically nonstandard, Hamer's speech is, by conventional standards, imperfect. In its imperfections, though, lie its authenticity and persuasive force. Whatever Hamer lacked in education, she made up for by conveying an unpretentious earnestness through folksy language, religious quotation, and humor. Delivered at a rally, almost certainly without notes, the following speech is best understood as a patchwork of antiwar arguments interspersed with personal rebukes and gag lines. The effect is to create an aural collage—something that bursts with energy even as it fails to develop fully its central claims.

Hamer's introduction is short and sarcastic: "If this society of yours is a 'Great Society,'" she says, referring to President's Lyndon Johnson's social programs, "God knows I would hate to live in a bad one." Hamer then introduces her two chief grounds for opposing the war in Vietnam: that the people of the United States do not support it, and that it is racist. From this point on, Hamer engages in attack after blistering attack—on the Secretary of Defense's allegedly draft-dodging son, on the black ministers who "made a deal with the power structure," and even on the audience itself. "Don't kid yourself," Hamer tells her Berkeley audience: "You can say 'up-South' and 'down-South.' The only difference in Mississippi and California, Berkeley, is we know what them white folks think about us, and some of you don't know what they think about you here. They will shoot me in the face and as soon as you turn around they will shoot you in the back. So you ain't doin' some big thing here."

Hamer's jabs are not merely cheap *ad hominem* attacks, or humorous gambits to soften her audience; rather, they suggest to the audience that ending the war abroad and empowering blacks at home requires an understanding of the way race and class function in American society. Though Hamer leaves Berkeley with unanswered questions (Do poverty and racism help produce war? If so, how?), she does at least point the way for further analysis.

Focusing on the completeness of Hamer's speech, though, can obscure its best qualities. The most important aspect of her speech is the effectiveness with which she communicates her own deep exasperation with American foreign policy and the disdain she has for the individuals who were carrying it out. The words for which Hamer is best known, "I'm sick and tired of being sick and tired," arose in the context of civil rights, but capture her opposition to the war as well. As an expression of one woman's profound discontent, the speech thus takes on ceremonial proportions and effectively galvanizes antiwar dissent.

GOOD EVENING, women and men—black, brown, white, green, and polka-dot. [*Laughter.*] I'm very happy to be here this afternoon [*"Glad to have ya!"*], and I really feel grateful that what has happened here is something I said in front of Lafayette Park in Washington, D.C., in 1965, after I had sent President Johnson a telegram tellin' him to bring the people home from the Dominican Republic and Vietnam. And I said to President Johnson at that time: "If this society of yours is a 'Great Society,' God knows I would hate to live in a bad one." [*Laughter and applause.*]

But at that time, at that time we felt very alone because when we start sayin' "the war is wrong in Vietnam," well, people looked at us like we were something out of space. But when they talked about, the other day, of the Gallup poll bein' 58 percent of the people against the war in Vietnam, then we see if you are right you have to stand on that principle, and, if it's necessary, to die on the principle because I am sick of the racist war in Vietnam when we don't have justice in the United States! [*Cheers and applause.*]

I've heard, I've heard several comments from people that was talkin' about "with the people, for the people, and by the people." Bein' a black woman from Mississippi, I've learned that long ago that that's not true. It's "with a handful, for a handful, by a handful." [*Cheers.*] But we gon' change that, baby. [*Applause.*] We are going to change that because we going to make democracy a reality for all of the people of this country. [*Cheers and applause.*]

A couple of Sundays ago I was in Washington at the cathedral there, and I read in the *Post* magazine that here was Secretary of Defense Melvin Laird's son had been classified as 4-F. And he had been classified because he had a tendency of a "purine malativination" that would sometimes result in the "gout." I said, "What in the world is 'the gout?'" So we got the dictionary and looked this word up, and what it was sayin' [was that] sometimes his joints *might* swell up and it resulted in a painful swellin' of the big toe. Now ain't that ridiculous? [*Laughter.*] Look it up! The "gout," that's what the man has! And it didn't say he *would* have it, said he *may* have it! And you see, the strange and the awful thing about it, the people that's conducting this war in Vietnam don't have sons to go do it.

And we are sick and tired of seein' people lynched and raped and shot down all across the country in the name of law and order, and not even feedin' the hungry across the country. [*Applause.*] There's something—there's something else funny, too. There's something very funny when a man like Senator James O. Eastland, the biggest welfare recipient in the whole country, [*shouts*] there's something wrong when he can help to set policies for Vietnam and own five thousand, eight hundred acres in the state of Mississippi and people on the plantation sufferin' from malnutrition. ["*Right on.*"] There's something wrong with that.

And we got to go a long way back, people, and talk about real conspiracy. Because it was something wrong in New York City when Malcolm X was shot down through conspiracy. [*Shouts of "right on," applause.*] And it was something wrong in America when again—Kennedy hadn't been a very liberal man but when he seen there was so much wrong that he had to do something about it, *he* was shot down. [*Shouts of support.*] And again on the fourth of April a couple years ago one of the most unviolent souls of our time, Dr. Martin Luther King, was shot down through conspiracy. I want you to know what's happenin' to us today. America is *sick* and man is on the critical list. [*Applause.*]

We want a change throughout the country. And the only way we can have a change is to bring those men home from Vietnam.

People have been greatly punished. They have been criticized because we are in a racist war that don't give a man a chance, that carry 'em to Vietnam. And I don't believe—you know, the first scapegoat this country got to get away on is communism. Now I know about as much about communism as a horse know about New Year. But nobody, and that mean nobody, have to tell me that it's not something wrong with the system, and no communist has to tell me that I'm without food and clothing and a decent place to live in this country.

And I think that charity really began at home. And we are not dealing—you know, some people don't like for you to call them a devil. But we are not dealing with men today. The sixth chapter of Ephesians, in eleventh and twelfth verse, says, "Put on the whole armor of God, that ye may be able to stand against the wiles of the devil." The twelfth verse say, "For we wrestle not against flesh and blood but against powers, against principalities, against the rulers of darkness of *this* world, spiritual weakness in high places." That's when the ministers will stand behind the podium and make a deal with the power structure. So we are telling the ministers we are going to start singing some songs for them. And some of the songs is gon' be "Shall We Gather at the River?" And we gon' leave 'em there. [*Laughter and applause.*]

Because people now no longer believe in a lot of the stuff they been reading. You know, I was really shocked. I got to go into a little of our history to come back to Vietnam and our policies. The truth hadn't been told to us no way! 'Cause I was really shocked when I found out that Columbus didn't discover America. When he got here there was some black brothers said, "Get on off, honey, and tell us where you want to go." [*Laughter.*] You've kept too many things hid not only from my kids, but you've kept 'em from your kids. That's the reason why your own kids is rebellin' against you—because of a sick system. [*Shouts of "that's right" and applause.*]

But we want the boys—you know, I don't think that we have time to say, "Well, we can get 'em out after another billion is killed." We want the fellas to come home *now.* And you know I do believe with this kind of audience—and I think it's this kind of audience in other places—I think a man should be *impeached* when they are not really dealing with the people. [*Applause.*] And I want to say—I want to say to you white Americans, "You can't destroy me because I'm black to save your life without destroying yourself." [*Shout from the crowd: "We don't want to destroy you."*]

All right, well, we want to have peace! We want to have peace and the only way that we can have peace is to bring the boys home from Vietnam, start dealing with the problems in the United States, stop all of this "urban renewal" and "model cities" that's pushin' people out of a place to stay, and start dealin' with facts of life. [*"Right on!"* *Applause.*]

It's a lot of people—it's a lot of people that said, "Well, forget about politics." But baby, what we eat is politics. And I'm not gon' forget no politics. Because in 1972, when I go to Washington as Senator Hamer from Mississippi, [*shouts of support*] you gon' know it's gon' be some changes made. . . .

And people, whether you believe it or not, you better remember this today: "A house divided against itself cannot stand." A nation that's divided against itself cannot stand. And it's two past midnight, and we on our way out.

But we have to have a change. And the change is gon' first start in bringin' the boys home from Vietnam.

And I don't want you to think that you have to pick out a way for me to exist in this society. You know, black people has caught a lot of hell too. We first been told that we wasn't fit to—we got to get the kind of education to fit in this society. But as sick as it is, I wonder, "Do I want the kind of education [*shouts*] that's gon' really rob me of having real love and compassion for my fellow man?" ["*Right on!*"] We got to start ["*Yeah!*"]—we got to start in every institution in this country because the history that we been gettin', baby, has never happened and it never will.

And we got to change some curriculums. And in makin' the change we can have more peace and real democracy when we bring the boys home and some of the billions of dollars that's bein' spent in Vietnam can go into rural areas like Mississippi.

And I want you to know something. Don't kid yourself, baby. You can say "up-South" and "down-South." The only difference in Mississippi and California, Berkeley, is we know what them white folks think about us, and some of you don't know what they think about you here. [*Brief applause.*] They will shoot me in the face there, and as soon as you turn around they will shoot you in the back. So you ain't doin' no big thing here. [*Shouts and laughter.*]

The problem here is like the problem all over the country. And decent people. I'm not talking about I'm going to attack somebody, because it look foolish to me to come out of my house and throw a bottle at my brother's house. I'm not talkin' about that kind of crap. I'm talkin' about some *real* changes that's going to help people throughout the country. And the only way we can do that is, stop engaging ourselves (and I have to say "us") in this racist war. . . .

But we need a change, and the only way we are going to have a change—don't you think that this is not important: one man's feet can't walk across the land; two men's feet can't walk across the land; but if two and two and fifty make a million, we'll see the day come round. And we keep on sayin', "We're against the war." One crowd of people can't change the status quo. But if two and two and fifty make a million, we'll see the day come round that we will have our boys home and we'll be able to stand and fight together for the things that we rightfully deserve—not in Vietnam, not in Biafra, but right here in the United States—to make democracy a reality for all of the people of the world regardless of race or color. [*Sustained applause.*]

Thank you.


## John Kerry Testifies on Behalf of Vietnam Veterans Against the War

[H]ow do you ask a man to be the last man to die in Vietnam?
How do you ask a man to be the last man to die for a mistake?

The speech that a twenty-seven-year-old John Kerry gave to the Senate Foreign Relations Committee on April 22, 1971, introduced a young, eloquent veteran to the American people, single-handedly captured the pain and frustration of thousands of Vietnam veterans, and launched a long-lasting career in politics. As Douglas Brinkley put it, Kerry's 1971 speech was the "point of origin" of Kerry's public life.[96]

Though Kerry's visibility as an antiwar activist peaked during and immediately after his Senate testimony in 1971, a notable strain of antiwar sentiment extended back at least to his senior year at Yale in 1966. Chosen to deliver the class oration, Kerry warned his classmates about the dangers of military action: "An excess of isolationism has become an excess of interventionism. . . . The United States must, I think, bring itself to understand that the policy of intervention that was right for Western Europe does not and cannot find the same application to the rest of the world." And commenting on "service"—a theme that hearkened back to his idol John F. Kennedy's 1961 inaugural address—Kerry added: "We have not really lost the desire to serve. We question the very roots of what we are serving."[97]

After college, Kerry continued his antiwar advocacy. On January 3, 1970, at the end of a brief but distinguished stint in the navy, Kerry formally asked his supervising officer for an early discharge so that he could run for Congress on an antiwar platform. Though the request was granted, Kerry's attempt to run for office proved abortive. He did, however, manage to attract the attention of a fledgling organization called Vietnam Veterans Against the War (VVAW).

With his ironed shirts, pressed pants, refined manners, and well-spoken earnestness, Kerry soon became the Kennedyesque front man for the VVAW. When antiwar senators J. William Fulbright of Arkansas, Edward Kennedy of Massachusetts, and others invited the protesters to a cocktail party in the Capitol, it was Kerry who gave a short, informal speech on behalf of the VVAW and Kerry whom the antiwar senators invited to speak the next day to the Senate Committee on Foreign Affairs.

Few of the addresses in this anthology, at the time they were given, were as critically successful as Kerry's. Literally overnight, the young antiwar activist became a political icon. Almost immediately, calls began to arrive from throughout the country requesting interviews or offering invitations to speak at rallies and commencements. The following week, Helen Dudar of the *New York Post* provided one of the most enthusiastic reviews of the "performance." Kerry, Dudar wrote, is "the man of the hour, a political star born out of the ferment of this season's antiwar protest." His speech "imprinted [itself] on the national consciousness" and "mesmerized members of the Senate Foreign Relations Committee." She continued with her unabashed praise: "Flaming rhetoric combined with cool, cool delivery; very classy." The next day, Dudar added, "people all over town were asking friends whether they'd seen it and wondering when Kerry could start running for President."[98]

The White House was listening. "Destroy the young demagogue before he becomes another Ralph Nader," wrote Charles Colson, Special Council to the President, in a secret memo.[99] Chief of Staff H. R. "Bob" Haldeman remarked to President Nixon and Security Advisor Henry Kissinger that Kerry "did a hell of a great job."[100] Nixon himself thought that Kerry was the hearing's "real star"[101] and agreed with Haldeman: "He was extremely effective."[102]

In the decades since Kerry spoke, his testimony has continued to come under attack, even as it helped define the mood of an era. First, the speech used evidence from the Winter Soldier investigation, some of which was later questioned.[103] Additionally, some accuse Kerry of using a ghostwriter.[104] The most lasting criticism of the speech, though, arises out of Kerry's accusation that war crimes existed at "all levels of command." After he was nominated by the Democrats to challenge President George W. Bush in 2004, a highly publicized organization named Swift Boat Veterans for Truth upbraided Kerry for this later accusation. Composed of veterans who had served with or near Kerry in Vietnam, and led by Kerry's long-time nemesis John O'Neill, the Swift Boat Veterans succeeded in raising Kerry's "disservice" to his country as an important issue in the presidential campaign.[105]

Kerry's speech has three textual features that make it memorable. First, he poses two effective rhetorical questions: "[H]ow do you ask a man to be the last man to die in Vietnam? How do you ask a man to be the last man to die for a mistake?" Rhetorical questions are useful literary devices because they ask the audience to participate—albeit silently—in the speaker's train of logic and, in this way, serve to emphasize the speaker's point. In addition, the questions together are phrased as an *anaphora*. One of the most commonly used (and overused) rhetorical devices, anaphora is the use of the same word or phrase at the beginning of successive clauses or sentences. In moderation, it is an effective means of emphasis. Thus armed with two powerful rhetorical techniques, Kerry produces memorable phrases—the stuff of which headlines are made. To this day, these two sentences constitute the most famous part of the entire speech.

Kerry also makes fine use of *pathos* when he reports in grisly detail the findings of the Winter Soldier investigation, which the VVAW conducted in late January and early February 1971. Many veterans who participated in those proceeding offered harrowing personal accounts: "They told the stories at times they had personally raped, cut off ears, cut off heads, taped wires from portable telephones to human genitals and turned up the power, cut off limbs, blown up bodies, randomly shot at civilians, razed villages in fashion reminiscent of Genghis Khan, shot cattle and dogs for fun, poisoned food stocks, and generally ravaged the countryside of South Vietnam." I have mentioned that the veracity of some testimony from the Winter Soldier investigation has been called into question. Later, Kerry himself conceded that he "wouldn't be surprised" if some Winter Soldier accounts were phony.[106] Truthfulness aside, though, the graphic nature of the narrative is indelible—and therein lies its effectiveness. Like Kerry's rhetorical questions, this narrative serves as a focal point of the speech even today; virtually every edition of Kerry's speech known to this editor includes this passage.

Third and finally, Kerry's peroration evokes two much more famous speeches in American history, and one even more famous speech in British literature. As Kerry puts it: "[We are determined] to undertake one last mission, to search out and destroy the last vestige of this barbaric war . . . so that when, in 30 years from now, our brothers go down the street without a leg, without an arm, or a face, and small boys ask why, we will be able to say 'Vietnam' and not mean a desert, not a filthy obscene memory but mean instead the place where America finally turned and where soldiers like us helped it in the turning." Even Kerry's most forceful detractors acknowledge the power of these words. Responding to the young upstart in his commencement address at United States Military Academy in West Point on June 8, 1971, conservative pundit William F. Buckley Jr. conceded that Kerry's words did have a "haunting resonance" which "moved the audience."[107] This editor would like to suggest that the "resonance" that Buckley identifies, but does not explain, arises out of Kerry's adoption of a motif much older than perhaps even Kerry knew. In fact, the speech's final moment, is aligned squarely with the great speeches of Patton, Napoleon, and Shakespeare's Henry V. What makes Kerry's peroration so remarkable, though, is that unlike these famous speakers, Kerry *opposed* war.

General George Patton, exhorting his troops before D-Day in 1944, said,

> There is one great thing that you men will all be able to say after this war is over and you are home once again. You may be thankful that twenty years from now when you are sitting by the fireplace with your grandson on your knee and he asks you what you did in the great World War II, you won't have to cough, shift him to the other knee and say, "Well, your Granddaddy shoveled shit in Louisiana." No, Sir, you can look him straight in the eye and say, "Son, your Granddaddy

rode with the Great Third Army and a Son-of-a-Goddamned-Bitch named Georgie Patton!"[108]

Napoleon spoke similarly to his soldiers in 1796:

> To you, soldiers, will belong the immortal honor of redeeming the fairest portion of Europe. The French people, free and respected by the whole world, shall give to Europe a glorious peace, which shall indemnify it for all the sacrifices which it has borne the last six years. Then, by your own firesides you shall repose; and your fellow citizens, when they point out any one of you, shall say: "He belonged to the army of Italy!"[109]

Finally, consider Shakespeare's Henry V's "Saint Crispian's Day" speech. Writing in 1599, Shakespeare has Henry V rally his troops on the morning of battle with the following words:

> He that shall see this day and live old age
> Will yearly on the vigil feast his neighbours,
> And say "To-morrow is Saint Crispian."
> Then will he strip his sleeve and show his scars,
> And say "These wounds I had on Crispin's day."
> Old men forget, yet all shall be forgot
> But he'll remember, with advantages,
> What feats he did that day. Then shall our names,
> Familiar in his mouth as household words,
> Harry the king, Bedford and Exeter,
> Warwick and Talbot, Salisbury and Gloucester,
> Be in their flowing cups freshly remember'd.
> This story shall the good man teach his son.[110]

The lesson to draw from these similarities is that Kerry employs what might be called a "universal motif," one that transcends an individual point of view and can be used to serve diverse, even opposite, ends. In contrast to Patton, Napoleon, and Henry V, Kerry is waging—to borrow W. E. B. Du Bois's phrase—a battle for peace.[111] His words are less belligerent than those of his military antecedents, but just as strong; they are less violent, but just as provocative. In short, Kerry's inspiring words of compassionate and peaceful defiance make the speech as a whole the preeminent illustration of its kind.[112]

THE CHAIRMAN [SENATOR FULBRIGHT].

The committee will come to order.

The committee is continuing this morning its hearings on proposals relating to the ending of the war in Southeast Asia. This morning the committee will hear testimony from Mr. John Kerry and, if he has any associates, we will be glad to hear from them.

These are men who have fought in this unfortunate war in Vietnam. I believe they deserve to be heard and listened to by the Congress and by the officials in the executive branch and by the public generally. You have a perspective that those in the Government who make our Nation's policy do not always have and I am sure that your testimony today will be helpful to the committee in its consideration of the proposals before us.

I would like to add simply on my own account that I regret very much the action of the Supreme Court in denying the veterans the right to use the Mall. [Applause.]

I regret that. It seems to me to be but another instance of an insensitivity of our Government to the tragic effects of this war upon our people.

I want also to congratulate Mr. Kerry, you, and your associates upon the restraint that you have shown, certainly in the hearing the other day when there were a great many of your people here. I think you conducted yourselves in a most commendable manner throughout this week. Whenever people gather there is always a tendency for some of the more emotional ones to do things which are even against their own interests. I think you deserve much of the credit because I understand you are one of the leaders of this group.

I have joined with some of my colleagues, specifically Senator Hart, in an effort to try to change the attitude of our Government toward your efforts in bringing to this committee and to the country your views about the war.

I personally don't know of any group which would have both a greater justification for doing it and also a more accurate view of the effect of the war. As you know, there has grown up in this town a feeling that it is extremely difficult to get accurate information about the war and I don't know a better source than you and your associates. So we are very pleased to have you and your associates, Mr. Kerry

At the beginning if you would give to the reporter your full name and a brief biography so that the record will show who you are.

Senator JAVITS. Mr. Chairman, I was down there to the veterans' camp yesterday and saw the New York group and I would like to say I am very proud of the deportment and general attitude of the group.

I hope it continues. I have joined in the Hart resolution, too. As a lawyer I hope you will find it possible to comply with the order even though, like the chairman, I am unhappy about it. I think it is our job to see that you are suitably set up as an alternative so that you can do what you came here to do. I welcome the fact that you came and what you are doing.

[Applause.]

The CHAIRMAN. You may proceed, Mr. Kerry.

Mr. KERRY. Thank you very much, Senator Fulbright, Senator Javits, Senator Symington, Senator Pell. I would like to say for the record, and also for the men behind me who are also wearing the uniforms and their medals, that my sitting here is really symbolic. I am not here as John Kerry. I am here as one member of the group of 1,000, which is a small representation of a very much larger group of veterans in this country, and were it possible for all of them to sit at this table they would be here and have the same kind of testimony.

I would simply like to speak in very general terms. I apologize if my statement is general because I received notification yesterday you would hear me and I am afraid because of the injunction I was up most of the night and haven't had a great deal of chance to prepare.

I would like to talk, representing all those veterans, and say that several months ago in Detroit, we had an investigation at which over 150 honorably discharged and many very highly decorated veterans testified to war crimes committed in Southeast Asia, not isolated incidents but crimes committed on a day-to-day basis with the full awareness of officers at all levels of command.

It is impossible to describe to you exactly what did happen in Detroit, the emotions in the room, the feelings of the men who were reliving their experiences in Vietnam, but they did. They relived the absolute horror of what this country, in a sense, made them do.

They told the stories at times they had personally raped, cut off ears, cut off heads, taped wires from portable telephones to human genitals and turned up the power, cut off limbs, blown up bodies, randomly shot at civilians, razed villages in fashion reminiscent of Genghis Khan, shot cattle and dogs for fun, poisoned food stocks, and generally ravaged the countryside of South Vietnam in addition to the normal ravage of war, and the normal and very particular ravaging which is done by the applied bombing power of this country.

We call this investigation the "Winter Soldier Investigation." The term "Winter Soldier" is a play on words of Thomas Paine in 1776 when he spoke of the Sunshine Patriot and summertime soldiers who deserted at Valley Forge because the going was rough.

We who have come here to Washington have come here because we feel we have to be winter soldiers now. We could come back to this country; we could be quiet; we could hold our silence; we could not tell what went on in Vietnam, but we feel because of what threatens this country, the fact that the crimes threaten it, not reds, and not redcoats but the crimes which we are committing that threaten it, that we have to speak out.

I would like to talk to you a little bit about what the result is of the feelings these men carry with them after coming back from Vietnam. The country doesn't know it yet, but it has created a monster, a monster in the form of millions of men who have been taught to deal and to trade in violence, and who are given the chance to die for the biggest nothing in history; men who have returned with a sense of anger and a sense of betrayal which no one has yet grasped.

As a veteran and one who feels this anger, I would like to talk about it. We are angry because we feel we have been used in the worst fashion by the administration of this country.

In 1970 at West Point, Vice President Agnew said "some glamorize the criminal misfits of society while our best men die in Asian rice paddies to preserve the freedom which most of those misfits abuse," and this was used as a rallying point for our effort in Vietnam.

But for us, as boys in Asia whom the country was supposed to support, his statement is a terrible distortion from which we can only draw a very deep sense of revulsion. Hence the anger of some of the men who are here in Washington today. It is a distortion because we in no way consider ourselves the best men of this country, because those he calls misfits were standing up for us in a way that nobody else in this country dared to, because so many who have died would have returned to this country to join the misfits in their efforts to ask for an immediate withdrawal from South Vietnam, because so many of those best men have returned as quadriplegics and amputees, and they lie forgotten in Veterans' Administration hospitals in this country which fly the flag which so many have chosen as their own personal symbol. And we cannot consider ourselves America's best men when we are ashamed of and hated what we were called on to do in Southeast Asia.

In our opinion, and from our experience, there is nothing in South Vietnam, nothing which could happen that realistically threatens the United States of America. And to attempt to justify the loss of one American life in Vietnam, Cambodia, or Laos by linking such loss to the preservation of freedom, which those misfits supposedly abuse, is to us the height of criminal hypocrisy, and it is that kind of hypocrisy which we feel has torn this country apart.

We are probably much more angry than that and I don't want to go into the foreign policy aspects because I am outclassed here. I know that all of you talk about every possible alternative of getting out of Vietnam. We understand that. We know you have considered the seriousness of the aspects to the utmost level and I am not going to try to dwell on that, but I want to relate to you the feeling that many of the men who have returned to this country express because we are probably angriest about all that we were told about Vietnam and about the mystical war against communism.

We found that not only was it a civil war, an effort by a people who had for years been seeking their liberation from any colonial influence whatsoever, but also we found that the Vietnamese whom we had enthusiastically molded after our own image were hard put to take up the fight against the threat we were supposedly saving them from.

We found most people didn't even know the difference between communism and democracy. They only wanted to work in rice paddies without helicopters strafing them and bombs with napalm burning their villages and tearing their country apart. They wanted everything to do with the war, particularly with this foreign presence of the United States of America, to leave them alone in peace, and they practiced the art of survival by siding with whichever military force was present at a particular time, be it Vietcong, North Vietnamese, or American.

We found also that all too often American men were dying in those rice paddies for want of support from their allies. We saw first hand how money from American taxes was used for a corrupt dictatorial regime. We saw that many people in this country had a one-sided idea of who was kept free by our flag, as blacks provided the highest percentage of casualties. We saw Vietnam ravaged equally by American bombs as well as by search and destroy missions, as well as by Vietcong terrorism, and yet we listened while this country tried to blame all of the havoc on the Vietcong.

We rationalized destroying villages in order to save them. We saw America lose her sense of morality as she accepted very coolly a My Lai and refused to give up the image of American soldiers who hand out chocolate bars and chewing gum.

We learned the meaning of free fire zones, shooting anything that moves, and we watched while America placed a cheapness on the lives of orientals.

We watched the U.S. falsification of body counts, in fact the glorification of body counts. We listened while month after month we were told the back of the enemy was about to break. We fought using weapons against "oriental human beings," with quotation marks around that. We fought using weapons against those people which I do not believe this country would dream of using were we fighting in the European theater or let us say a non-third-world people theater, and so we watched while men charged up hills because a general said that hill has to be taken, and after losing one platoon or two platoons they marched away to leave the high [sic; hill] for the reoccupation by the North Vietnamese because we watched pride allow the most unimportant of battles to be blown into extravaganzas, because we couldn't lose, and we couldn't retreat, and because it didn't matter how many American bodies were lost to prove that point. And so there were Hamburger Hills and Khe Sanhs and Hill 881's and Fire Base 6's and so many others.

Now we are told that the men who fought there must watch quietly while American lives are lost so that we can exercise the incredible arrogance of Vietnamizing the Vietnamese.

Each day—

[Applause.]

The CHAIRMAN. I hope you won't interrupt. He is making a very significant statement. Let him proceed.

Mr. KERRY. Each day to facilitate the process by which the United States washes her hands of Vietnam someone has to give up his life so that the United States doesn't have to admit something that the entire world already knows, so that we can't say that we have made a mistake. Someone has to die so that President Nixon won't be, and these are his words, "the first President to lose a war."

We are asking Americans to think about that because how do you ask a man to be the last man to die in Vietnam? How do you ask a man to be the last man to die for a mistake? But we are trying to do that, and we are doing it with thousands of rationalizations, and if you read carefully the President's last speech to the people of this country, you can see that he says, and says clearly:

> But the issue, gentlemen, the issue is communism, and the question is whether or not we will leave that country to the Communists or whether or not we will try to give it hope to be a free people.

But the point is they are not a free people now under us. They are not a free people, and we cannot fight communism all over the world, and I think we should have learned that lesson by now.

But the problem of veterans goes beyond this personal problem, because you think about a poster in this country with a picture of Uncle Sam and the picture says "I want you." And a young man comes out of high school and says, "That is fine. I am going to serve my country." And he goes to Vietnam and he shoots and he kills and he does his job or maybe he doesn't kill, maybe he just goes and he comes back, and when he gets back to this country he finds that he isn't really wanted, because the largest unemployment figure in the country—it varies depending on who you get it from, the VA Administration 15 percent, various other sources 22 percent. But the largest corps of unemployed in this country are veterans of this war, and of those veterans 33 percent of the unemployed are black. That means 1 out of every 10 of the Nation's unemployed is a veteran of Vietnam.

The hospitals across the country won't, or can't meet their demands. It is not a question of not trying. They don't have the appropriations. A man recently died after he had a tracheotomy in California, not because of the operation but because there weren't enough personnel to clean the mucous [sic] out of his tube and he suffocated to death.

Another young man just died in a New York VA hospital the other day. A friend of mine was lying in a bed two beds away and tried to help him, but he couldn't. He rang a bell and there was nobody there to service that man and so he died of convulsions.

I understand 57 percent of all those entering the VA hospitals talk about suicide. Some 27 percent have tried, and they try because they come back to this country and they have to face what they did in Vietnam, and then they come back and find the indifference of a country that doesn't really care, that doesn't really care.

Suddenly we are faced with a very sickening situation in this country, because there is no moral indignation and, if there is, it comes from people who are almost exhausted by their past indignations, and I know that many of them are sitting in front of me. The country seems to have lain down and shrugged off something as serious as Laos, just as we calmly shrugged off the loss of 700,000 lives in Pakistan, the so-called greatest disaster of all times.

But we are here as veterans to say we think we are in the midst of the greatest disaster of all times now because they are still dying over there, and not just Americans, Vietnamese, and we are rationalizing leaving that country so that those people can go on killing each other for years to come.

Americans seem to have accepted the idea that the war is winding down, at least for Americans, and they have also allowed the bodies which were once used by a President for statistics to prove that we were winning that war, to be used as evidence against a man who followed orders and who interpreted those orders no differently than hundreds of other men in Vietnam.

We veterans can only look with amazement on the fact that this country has been unable to see there is absolutely no difference between ground troops and a helicopter crew, and yet people have accepted a differentiation fed them by the administration.

No ground troops are in Laos, so it is all right to kill Laotians by remote control. But believe me the helicopter crews fill the same body bags and they wreak the same kind of damage on the Vietnamese and Laotian countryside as anybody else, and the President is talking about allowing that to go on for many years to come. One can only ask if we will really be satisfied only when the troops march into Hanoi.

We are asking here in Washington for some action, action from the Congress of the United States of America which has the power to raise and maintain armies, and which by the Constitution also has the power to declare war.

We have come here, not to the President, because we believe that this body can be responsive to the will of the people, and we believe that the will of the people says that we should be out of Vietnam now.

We are here in Washington also to say that the problem of this war is not just a question of war and diplomacy. It is part and parcel of everything that we are trying as human beings to communicate to people in this country, the question of racism, which is rampant in the military, and so many other questions also, the use of weapons, the hypocrisy in our taking umbrage in the Geneva Conventions and using that as justification for a continuation of this war, when we are more guilty than any other body of violations of those Geneva Conventions, in the use of free fire zones, harassment interdiction fire, search and destroy missions, the bombings, the torture of prisoners, the killing of prisoners, accepted policy by many units in South Vietnam. That is what we are trying to say. It is part and parcel of everything.

An American Indian friend of mine who lives in the Indian Nation of Alcatraz put it to me very succinctly. He told me how as a boy on an Indian reservation he had watched television and he used to cheer the cowboys when they came in and shot the Indians, and then suddenly one day he stopped in Vietnam and he said "My God, I am doing to these people the very same thing that was done to my people." And he stopped. And that is what we are trying to say, that we think this thing has to end.

We are also here to ask, and we are here to ask vehemently, where are the leaders of our country? Where is the leadership? We are here to ask where are McNamara, Rostow, Bundy, Gilpatric and so many others. Where are they now that we, the men whom they sent off to war, have returned? These are commanders who have deserted their troops, and there is no more serious crime in the law of war. The Army says they never leave their wounded.

The Marines say they never leave even their dead. These men have left all the casualties and retreated behind a pious shield of public rectitude. They have left the real stuff of their reputations bleaching behind them in the sun in this country.

Finally, this administration has done us the ultimate dishonor. They have attempted to disown us and the sacrifice we made for this country. In their blindness and fear they have tried to deny that we are veterans or that we served in Nam. We do not need their testimony. Our own scars and stumps of limbs are witnesses enough for others and for ourselves.

We wish that a merciful God could wipe away our own memories of that service as easily as this administration has wiped their memories of us. But all that they have done and all that they can do by this denial is to make more clear than ever our own determination to undertake one last mission, to search out and destroy the last vestige of this barbaric war, to pacify our own hearts, to conquer the hate and the fear that have driven this country these last 10 years and more, and so when, in 30 years from now, our brothers go down the street without a leg, without an arm, or a face, and small boys ask why, we will be able to say "Vietnam" and not mean a desert, not a filthy obscene memory but mean instead the place where America finally turned and where soldiers like us helped it in the turning.

Thank you. [Applause.]

# War on Terror (2003-Present)

On September 11, 2001, nineteen terrorists from the militant al-Qaeda network hijacked four planes in midflight. The terrorists did not intend to take hostages. Instead, they altered the planes' flight paths and, transforming the civilian aircrafts into massive missiles, aimed them at key symbols of American military and economic strength. One plane, heading for Washington, D.C., crashed in rural Pennsylvania. Another hit the Pentagon. Two hit the Twin Towers in the World Trade Center complex in New York City. All told, more than three thousand people, nearly all of whom were civilians, died.

The United States responded immediately. On September 13, the White House announced that Osama bin Laden was responsible for the attacks. On September 14, Congress authorized the president "to use all necessary and appropriate force against those nations, organizations, or persons he determines planned, authorized, committed, or aided the terrorist attacks that occurred on September 11, 2001, or harbored such organizations or persons, in order to prevent any future acts of international terrorism against the United States by such nations, organizations or persons."[1] Only one member of Congress opposed the resolution. In the House, the bill passed 420-1, with Barbara Lee casting the lone dissenting vote. In the Senate, it passed 98-0.

With Congress's blessing, President George W. Bush attacked al-Qaeda targets in Afghanistan beginning October 2001. Over the course of the next year, however, the focus of the "War on Terror" gradually shifted to Iraq. In October 2002, Congress passed the Authorization for Use of Military Force Against Iraq Resolution of 2002.[2] The resolution passed in the House on October 10, 2002 by a vote of 296-133, and in the Senate the next day by a vote of 77-23. On March 20, 2003, the United States began its "Shock and Awe" military campaign in Iraq, and Baghdad fell about one month later. On May 1, Bush declared that "major combat operations" in Iraq were over. Another phase of the battle, however, was just beginning. As of Bush's speech, the United States had suffered only 140 casualties in Iraq. By mid-2008, the total military casualties there had risen to over 4,000.[3]

Statistics for Iraqi combatant and civilian casualties are difficult to ascertain. One study in late 2003 pegged the number of Iraqi combatant casualties at approximately 9,000.[4] Civilian casualty figures vary widely. The British medical journal the *Lancet*, which based its conclusions on a sampling of pre- and postinvasion mortality rates, found that as of July 2006 some 600,000 Iraqi deaths were due to violence, the most common cause being gunfire.[5] On the other hand, the *Associated Press* put the number much lower, reporting in 2009 that more than 110,600 Iraqi civilians had "died in violence" since the 2003 U.S.-led invasion.[6]

After September 11, President Bush's approval ratings peaked at nearly 90 percent,[7] and patriotism flared throughout the country. When the United States invaded Iraq in March 2003, Americans were more circumspect about the war, but in May almost 80 percent of the American public still thought the Iraq War was justified, with or without conclusive evidence of illegal weapons.[8]

At the same time, a vigorous antiwar movement began to take shape in the United States and throughout the world. For the first time since Vietnam, large rallies sprouted up throughout the country. Facilitated by the Internet and the availability of alternative media, antiwar organizations coordinated demonstrations worldwide. A Gallup International poll conducted in January 2003 showed that approximately half of the citizens in the world were not in favor of military action against Iraq under any circumstances.[9] The study found that even if the military action were authorized by United Nations, only about one-third of those interviewed stated that they would favor it.[10] On February 15, 2003, only weeks before the invasion, more than 10 million people across the world, including the United States, marched against the war.[11]

I include five antiwar speeches since September 11 in this anthology. The first, by Representative Barbara Lee, is the first major American antiwar speech of the twenty-first century. Lee's September 14 admonition "Let us not become the evil that we deplore" presaged the morality-based critiques of the War on Terror, and thus serves as an important milestone in the public debate. Barack Obama's "Dumb War" speech, given on October 2, 2002, in Chicago's Federal Plaza, showcases the rhetorical virtuosity and intemperate tone of a then little-known state senator from Illinois. The speech later became a centerpiece of Obama's successful presidential campaign. In "Why Iraq?," delivered on November 4, 2002, at Harvard University's Kennedy School of Government, Massachusetts Institute of Technology linguist and political activist Noam Chomsky addressed the alleged connection between the events of September 11 and Iraq. Robert Byrd's "We Stand Passively Mute" speech, delivered on February 12, 2003, in the U.S. Senate, was one of the most popular antiwar speeches of the Senate's foremost war critic. In the epilogue, Arundhati Roy's "Instant-Mix Imperial Democracy" represents what I have called the globalization of dissent. Roy gave the speech on May 13, 2003 in New York City not as an Indian citizen, but as "a subject of the American Empire."

## Barbara Lee Pleads with the House Not to "Become the Evil That We Deplore"

As we act, let us not become the evil that we deplore.

When Representative Barbara Lee of California voted against House Joint Resolution 64, the September 14, 2001, resolution granting the president authority to use "all necessary and appropriate force" against those responsible for the attacks launched at the United States days earlier, she had no idea she would be standing alone.[12] "It never dawned on me that I would cast the only vote against this resolution," Lee reflected on the 420-1 vote. "I could not believe it. It was an awesome feeling. And a lonely feeling."[13]

The public's response to the vote was fast and furious. Lee was "a deeply disturbed and deluded woman," one letter to the editor declared.[14] On September 17, California talk radio was abuzz with callers denouncing Lee as a Communist.[15] A website called DumpBarbaraLee.com soon appeared, calling Lee "un-American" and a "traitor."[16] "Dump the America-hating Barbara Lee from Congress," blared a banner headline.[17] On June 16, 2002, an article in the *Los Angeles Times Magazine* stated that Lee "might just rank as the single most vilified elected official in America."[18] Lee received so many death threats in the days after she cast her dissenting vote that two Capitol police officers were called in to guard her Washington, D.C., office, and a plainclothes bodyguard was assigned to protect the congresswoman twenty-four hours a day.[19] Lee's schedule was kept secret even from some members of her staff.[20]

Still, most of the negative feedback Lee received originated outside of her congressional district. Indeed, the reaction to Lee's vote from her actual constituents was in large part supportive. In mid-October, two thousand people participated in a pro-Lee rally in downtown Oakland.[21] In November, a popular poster in the Bay Area read, "Barbara Lee Speaks for Me." By December, fifty-thousand e-mails, phone calls, and faxes deluged Lee's offices, 73 percent of which were encouraging.[22]

The disparity between the national and local reaction to Lee's speech was a function of the peculiar politics of California's Ninth Congressional District. Drawn from the cities of Berkeley and Oakland, Lee's constituents were among the most liberal in the nation. In the 2000 presidential election, for example, Democrat Al Gore carried the Ninth District with 79 percent of the vote, while Republican George W. Bush earned 12 percent, barely edging out the Green Party's Ralph Nader, who received 9 percent.

The Ninth District also had a history of antiwar dissent extending back at least as far as the Vietnam War. The University of California at Berkeley was a hotbed of activism in the 1960s. It was in Berkeley that Diabolo Press published *We Accuse* in 1965, and in which Fannie Lou Hamer rallied students in 1969. In 1971, the voters elected Ronald V. Dellums to Congress on an antiwar platform. In 1998, during Lee's first term in Congress, she voted against the Iraq Liberation Act of 1998. Passed 360-38 in the House and unanimously in the Senate, this act was the precursor to President Clinton's commencement of military strikes in Iraq in 1998.[23] In 1999, Lee also cast the sole vote against a House resolution stating simply that the "House of Representatives supports the members of the United States Armed Forces who are engaged in military operations against the Federal Republic of Yugoslavia and recognizes their professionalism, dedication, patriotism, and courage."[24] Notably, Lee's vote came *after* the United States military became engaged in Kosovo.[25] Questioned in 1999 whether she was a conscientious objector, Lee responded that "this district—the Ninth Congressional District—would have it no other way."[26]

In her short speech on September 14, 2001,[27] Lee outlines her major objections to the war resolution and frames her remarks with self-proclaimed "restraint." First, Lee argues that the events of September 11, 2001, raised issues concerning "national security, foreign policy, public safety, intelligence gathering, economics, and murder." As a result of the varied issues at play, Lee states, the U.S. response should be "equally multi-faceted." "We are not dealing with a conventional war," she says, and "we cannot respond in a conventional manner." Second, Lee argues that the country's present militancy is rash. Any "rush to judgment" will inevitably increase the risk that innocent noncombatants will be killed. Lee's third argument involves ethnic discrimination: we cannot "let our anger . . . inflame prejudice against all Arab Americans, Muslims, [or] Southeast Asians." In the tradition of Carl Schurz, who criticized the United States's part in the Filipino Insurrection by documenting the racism that that conflict engendered, Lee suggests that military retaliation might produce an irrational hatred of innocent people on account of their race, ethnicity, or religion. Fourth and finally, Lee warns Congress that an endorsement of the war resolution would represent an abandonment of its constitutional responsibility to limit the president's war-making power. Quoting Senator Wayne Morse, one of two senators who opposed the 1964 Gulf of Tonkin Resolution,[28] Lee declares that history will redeem her vote: "I believe that within the next century, future generations will look with dismay and great disappointment upon a Congress which is now about to make such a historic mistake."

Judging by the reaction to Lee's widely reported speech in magazines and newspapers throughout the country, one sentence stood out above all others: "Let us not become the evil that we deplore." Why did reporters almost uniformly choose this particular phrase for sound-bite status? Lee's statement evokes the rhetorical trope of *paradox* because her words imply a contradiction: a war to end evil could perpetuate it. Compare Lee's statement to, for example, that of Carl Schurz in the context of the Philippine-American War: "The more complete our success, the greater will be our disgrace." A good, short paradox can be particularly quotable because it is thought-provoking and tends to involve the listener in a shared experience of discovery.

The power of paradox finds additional support in the origin of Lee's dissent. Lee herself grabbed the phrase from the Very Reverend Nathan D. Baxter, whose speech Lee had heard earlier that day at the National Cathedral in Washington. Baxter, the dean of the National Cathedral, delivered a short invocation at the ceremony, saying in part, "Let us also pray for Divine wisdom as our leaders consider the necessary actions for national security—wisdom of the grace of God that despite our grief we may not become the evil we deplore."* In fact, it was when Lee heard these words that she decided to oppose the resolution then pending in the House. As Lee later put it, "I listened to the remarks of the clergy. Many of them made profound statements. But I was struck by what one of them said: 'As we act, let us not become the evil that we deplore.' That was such a wise statement, and it reflected not only what I was feeling but also my understanding of the threats we continue to face. When I left the cathedral, I was fairly resolved."[29]

MR. SPEAKER,

I rise today with a heavy heart, one that is filled with sorrow for the families and loved ones who were killed and injured in New York, Virginia, and Pennsylvania. Only the most foolish or the most callous would not understand the grief that has gripped the American people and millions across the world.

This unspeakable attack on the United States has forced me to rely on my moral compass, my conscience, and my God for direction.

September 11 changed the world. Our deepest fears now haunt us. Yet I am convinced that military action will not prevent further acts of international terrorism against the United States.

I know that this use-of-force resolution will pass although we all know that the President can wage a war even without this resolution. However difficult this vote may be, some of us must urge the use of restraint. There must be some of us who say, let's step back for a moment and think through the implications of our actions today—let us more fully understand its consequences.

* The full text of Baxter's invocation is as follows:

"When ancient Israel had suffered the excruciating pain and tragedy of militant aggression and destruction, God said to them through the prophet Jeremiah:

"A voice is heard in Ramah, lamenting and bitter weeping, Rachel is weeping for her children, and she refuses to be comforted, because they are no more.

"Today we gather to be reassured that God hears the 'lamenting and bitter weeping' of Mother America, because so many of her children are no more. Let us now seek that assurance in prayer, for the healing of our grief stricken hearts, for the souls and sacred memory of those who have died. Let us also pray for Divine wisdom as our leaders consider the necessary actions for national security, wisdom of the grace of God that despite our grief we may not become the evil we deplore. Let us stand and pray together,

"God of Abraham and Mohammed and Father of our Lord, Jesus Christ: we are today a people of heavy and distraught hearts. The evil hand of hate and cowardly aggression, which has devastated the innocent in many other lands, has visited America this week and too many of her children are no more. But we know you are not the God of hate and cowardice, but of courage and of justice. So we gather this day asking that you provide us healing as a nation. Heal our grief. Soothe our suffering hearts. Save us from blind vengeance, from random prejudice and from crippling fear.

"Guide our leaders, especially George our President. Let the deep faith that he and they share guide them in the momentous decisions they must make for our national security.

"We also thank you for the courage of flight crews and passengers in the face of certain death; we thank you for the brave volunteers, police and emergency workers who labor tirelessly, even as we pray. We thank you for the outpouring of generosity by businesses, unions, agencies, spiritual communities and individual citizens. Yes, Lord, Your Spirit is at work. Grant us wisdom, grant us courage, grant us peace for the facing of this hour.

"Amen."

We are not dealing with a conventional war. We cannot respond in a conventional manner. I do not want to see this spiral out of control. This crisis involves issues of national security, foreign policy, public safety, intelligence gathering, economics, and murder. Our response must be equally multi-faceted.

We must not rush to judgment. Far too many innocent people have already died. Our country is in mourning. If we rush to launch a counter-attack, we run too great a risk that women, children, and other non-combatants will be caught in the crossfire.

Nor can we let our justified anger over these outrageous acts by vicious murderers inflame prejudice against all Arab Americans, Muslims, Southeast Asians, or any other people because of their race, religion, or ethnicity.

Finally, we must be careful not to embark on an open-ended war with neither an exit strategy nor a focused target. We cannot repeat past mistakes.

In 1964, Congress gave President Lyndon Johnson the power to "take all necessary measures" to repel attacks and prevent further aggression. In so doing, this House abandoned its own constitutional responsibilities and launched our country into years of undeclared war in Vietnam.

At that time, Senator Wayne Morse, one of two lonely votes against the Tonkin Gulf Resolution, declared, "I believe that history will record that we have made a grave mistake in subverting and circumventing the Constitution of the United States. . . . I believe that within the next century, future generations will look with dismay and great disappointment upon a Congress which is now about to make such a historic mistake."

Senator Morse was correct, and I fear we make the same mistake today. And I fear the consequences.

I have agonized over this vote. But I came to grips with it in the very painful yet beautiful memorial service today at the National Cathedral. As a member of the clergy so eloquently said, "As we act, let us not become the evil that we deplore."


## Barack Obama Criticizes a "Dumb War"

I am not opposed to all wars. I'm opposed to dumb wars.


Barack Obama mesmerized the media and much of America in the run-up to the presidential election of 2008. Beginning in the fall of 2006, people throughout the country hailed the then first-term United States senator from Illinois as one of the most captivating American leaders in recent history. "Obama is certainly the party's most magnetic leader since Bill Clinton, and perhaps since Robert F. Kennedy," wrote *Harper's Magazine*.[30] The *National Review* observed in early 2008 that Obama was the subject of over three thousand Google hits for the phrase "black JFK,"[31] and *Ebony* quoted a seventy-one-year-old man who claimed that Obama "could possibly be a Dr. King."[32] Edward McClelland in *Salon* puzzled over how Obama "got to be Elvis, Lord Byron and Bobby Kennedy, all in the same dark suit."[33]

What is perhaps most remarkable about Obama, however, is not how comfortable many were in comparing Obama to the great leaders of twentieth-century America; rather, it is the consistency with which members of the media and the public stated that he possessed "charisma." *Harper's Magazine* wrote of Obama's "sheer charisma."[34] The *Economist* editorialized about Obama's "striking political talents, most notably a public charisma.[35] The *Seattle Post-Intelligencer* commented that Obama "is charismatic and has some kind of youth mojo thing going on."[36] Reporters in the United States wrote that Obama "oozed" charisma,[37] while reporters as far as way as Ireland wrote that he "dripped" it.[38] A newspaper in Tennessee said that Obama had "rock-star charisma,"[39] and one in Washington claimed that the candidate was "charisma-drenched."[40] An *Associated Press* writer in New York wrote that Obama was "the charisma king of the 2008 presidential fields."[41] *Time* wrote that he had "drop-dead charisma"[42] The *Atlantic Monthly* wrote of Obama's "charisma, intelligence and ambition, tempered by a self-deprecating wit."[43] And Cindy Richards of the *Chicago Sun Times* opined that Obama had "the charisma and panache to sit behind the desk in the Oval Office."[44]

Firsthand accounts of Obama's speeches support the media's conclusion. In Seattle in October 2006, for example, reporters Neil Modie and Scott Gutierrez captured the crowd's excitement at an Obama rally: "As far as 2,500 people stuffed into a gymnasium were concerned, Barack Obama, Superstar, lived up to the hurricane of hype surrounding him. The Illinois Democratic senator, author, potential presidential candidate, cover-boy celebrity and political phenomenon had a partisan crowd cheering almost his every word Thursday, even though they missed a lot of what he said because they were cheering so loudly. He could have read pages from the phone directory and they'd have applauded."[45] In Missouri the next month, reporters Deirdre Shesgreen and Jo Mannies found the same energy and enthusiasm: "In St. Louis, he was greeted with whoops and cheers. Asked why she came to see Obama speak, Lynette Wilson, a 47-year-old office administrator, said, 'I think he's hot!' And, she added, 'very intelligent.' 'He's going to put her over the edge,' Wilson said. 'He's such a whirlwind. He's energizing and people feel the connection to him.'"[46] Regardless of McClelland's suggestion that many reporters covering the candidate were "drinking the Obama juice,"[47] and his quip that "when reporters go one on one with Barack Obama, they end up writing things they'll regret in the morning papers," the phenomenon of "Obamamania"[48] was clear, distinct, and unlike anything the American public had seen in recent years.

When reflecting upon Obama's charisma, it is easy to forget that he is a rhetorical leader. In other words, Obama is primarily known and understood through the vehicle of speech. Just as William Jennings Bryan is best known for his "Cross of Gold" speech at the 1896 Democratic National Convention in Chicago, Eugene V. Debs for his 1918 antiwar speech in Canton, Martin Luther King for his 1963 "I have a dream" speech in Washington, D.C., or Robert F. Kennedy for his 1968 impromptu eulogy for Martin Luther King in Indianapolis, Barack Obama is probably best known for his 2002 antiwar speech in Chicago and his 2004 "Audacity of Hope" speech at the Democratic National Convention in Boston. The latter speech catapulted him onto the world's stage,[49] and the former, as it turned out, cemented his status as one of the foremost critics of the Iraq War.[50]

Before considering Obama's antiwar speech itself, though, it is important to underscore the pervasiveness of the public's understanding of Obama as a *merely* rhetorical leader. As a reporter for the *New York Times* put it (on the front page) in late 2006, "it remains unclear whether an Obama candidacy would present a slate of new ideas or just offer a fresh way of articulating familiar ideology."[51] Mario Cuomo, the former governor of New York, was more blunt: "Pure, glorious rhetoric about hope and aspiration. Just lacking specifics."[52] New York's *Daily News* was more denunciatory: "Obama must show he understands that charisma cannot produce consensus, candidates are not prophets and speechifying isn't leading."[53] Across the Atlantic, some in London expressed similar misgivings. The *Independent* published one op-ed that asked rhetorically, "This talented newcomer may drip charisma from his pores, but does he have substance?"[54] In the London *Times,* another author called Obama a "passing American Idol," and suggested that the Illinois senator was something akin to the "cads, chancers or charlatans" of history.[55]

The alleged vacuity of Obama's speeches did not go unnoticed at the events at which Obama spoke. Even as reporters Shesgreen and Mannies recognized the overwhelming excitement felt by those at the Obama rally in St. Louis, they also pointed out that at least some attendees were less enraptured. They quoted a seventy-six-year-old retired postal worker who compared Obama to a "snake Baptist preacher" who used his charms "to get people's emotions up to a pitch."[56]

In Obama, then, one sees how one individual's rhetoric forged an extraordinarily charismatic persona and helped transform a relatively little-known politician into a political leader on the world stage. At the same time, one sees how susceptible rhetorical leaders are to the charge that their speeches lack substance. Obama was criticized for the alleged emptiness of his message, or for somehow pulling the wool over his audience's eyes, but even his strongest detractors admit the power of such a charm, the effectiveness of such a hoax. Thus, while Peggy Noonan, a former speechwriter for presidents Ronald Reagan and George H. W. Bush, concluded that Obama "doesn't have an issue, he has a thousand issues, which is the same as having none, in the sense that a speech about everything is a speech about nothing," she nevertheless acknowledged Obama's "obvious appeal," "sudden rise," and "wild popularity."[57]

Barack Obama's first significant public denunciation of the War in Iraq occurred on October 2, 2002, in Chicago's Federal Plaza at a rally organized by the ANSWER Coalition.[58] The speech is significant for four reasons. First, from a rhetorical point of view, it exemplifies many of the common literary devices used by American antiwar speakers. Second, it has concrete historical importance, because it was Obama's first formal public statement against the war and because it served as the genesis of his antiwar views.[59] Third, it represents a manifestation of political courage, because Obama's future as a political leader was by no means cemented in 2002, and he had little political capital to spend on unpopular viewpoints.[60] Fourth and finally, there is some evidence that the speech represents a uniquely unvarnished specimen of Obama's true and impromptu thoughts about the War in Iraq, as Obama appears to have made some efforts, which he later abandoned, to dampen the speech's tone and remove one of its most forceful messages. I consider the first and last point in detail.

With respect to the speech's rhetoric, one of the first rhetorical techniques Obama uses is what I have called *hereditary ethos*.[61] Obama starts his speech by claiming, "I don't oppose all wars," and cites World War II as the one war he supported, or rather would have supported had he been alive. In the process, Obama invokes his soldier-grandfather: "My grandfather signed up for a war the day after Pearl Harbor was bombed, fought in Patton's army. He saw the dead and dying across the fields of Europe; he heard the stories of fellow troops who first entered Auschwitz and Treblinka. He fought in the name of a larger freedom, part of that arsenal of democracy that triumphed over evil, and he did not fight in vain." Compare Obama's introductory remarks with Moorfield Storey's at the Naval War College in 1897: "I sympathize with you and understand your hopes. I could not spring from ancestors who for five successive generations died at sea, without some of a sailor's instincts, some comprehension of his feelings. I appreciate therefore the difficulties of my position, perhaps my own audacity, in undertaking to speak as I propose to speak to-day."[62]

Obama and Storey's impulse to assert their hereditary ethos stems from the fact that both men had very successful legal and academic careers (both graduated, for example, from Harvard Law School), but neither spent any time in the military. Unlike, for example, John Kerry, who earned two Purple Hearts in Vietnam before testifying against the war to the Senate Armed Services Committee in 1971, neither Obama nor Storey had experience in international affairs, much less military service. The lack of authoritativeness with which each could speak on the subject of war or the military may have compelled both to fish for evidence of some military relationship, however attenuated or even irrelevant.

In a larger sense, though, ethos does not simply have to do with one's résumé; it has to do with one's courage. Speakers who are not afraid of conflict will appear more convincing than those who fear confrontation. It may be for this reason—the fear of being labeled a sissy—that antiwar speakers often go to great lengths to distance themselves from any sort of pacifism, and compensate with a little belligerency of their own. Thus, Obama claims that he would go to war himself if such a step would help prevent another attack: "After September 11th, after witnessing the carnage and destruction, the dust and the tears, I supported this Administration's pledge to hunt down and root out those who would slaughter innocents in the name of intolerance, and I would willingly take up arms myself to prevent such tragedy from happening again." Compare these remarks with those of Charles Eliot Norton, who began his "Counterfeit Patriotism" speech in 1898 by quoting the advice of Sir Philip Sidney to his younger brother Robert: if there were any good wars in which to fight, Philip said, by all means he should go to them.[63] Of course, whether there were any highly recommended wars in which to fight was unclear.

Another antiwar rhetorical technique Obama employs is a vicious tone. Questioning the expertise of the administration's top war hawks, he states, "What I am opposed to is the cynical attempt by Richard Perle and Paul Wolfowitz and other armchair, weekend warriors in this administration to shove their own ideological agendas down our throats, irrespective of the costs in lives lost and in hardships borne." Obama also attacks the motivations of Karl Rove, then senior advisor to President Bush. Dubbing Rove a "political hack," Obama claims that he is using the war "to distract us" from other, more important social programs. Still, Obama stops short of attacking the president himself. At least in this very limited sense, there is a current of temperance in a sea of invective. Nevertheless, he taunts President Bush in a series of refrains throughout the speech ("You want a fight, President Bush?") to great effect.

There is a final piece to the story of Barack Obama's 2002 antiwar speech. On June 5, 2003, a weekly Internet magazine, the *Black Commentator*, criticized Obama for removing the entirety of his antiwar speech from his website and replacing it with something more temperate:

> Then, a few weeks ago, Barack Obama's heartfelt statement of principled opposition to lawless militarism and the rule of fear was stricken without explanation from his campaign web site, and replaced with mild expressions of "anxiety":
>
>> But I think [people are] all astonished, I think, in many quarters, about, for example, the recent Bush budget and the prospect that, for example, veterans benefits might be cut. And so there's discussion about that, I think, among both supporters and those who are opposed to the war. What kind of world are we building?
>>
>> And I think that's—the anxiety is about the international prospects and how we potentially reconstruct Iraq. And the costs there, then, tie in very directly with concerns about how we're handling our problems at home.
>
> His passion evaporated, a leading black candidate for the US Senate mouths bland generalities on war, peace and the US role in the world. . . . For a black candidate who is utterly reliant upon a fired up base among African American and progressive voters, who must distinguish himself from a crowded Democratic field, this is strange behavior, indeed. Polls show Blacks have consistently opposed administration war policies by at least two to one, as does the white progressive "base" of the party. Yet Obama appears determined to contain, rather than amplify, these voices.[64]

Obama responded to the *Black Commentator* with a letter, which the magazine published two weeks later.[65] He wrote that he was "proud of the fact that I stood up early and unequivocally in opposition to Bush's foreign policy (and was the only U.S. Senate candidate in Illinois to do so)." Obama continued that his "opposition hasn't changed, and I continue to make it a central part of each and every one of my political speeches.[66] As to the removal of the speech from his website, Obama wrote,

The only reason that my original anti-war speech was removed from my website was a judgment that the speech was dated once the formal phase of the war was over, and my staff's desire to continually provide fresh news clips. The "bland" statement that Bruce offers up as an example of my loss of passion wasn't an official statement or speech at all, but a 30 second response to a specific question by Aaron Brown on CNN about the mood of Illinois voters a few days after the war started. . . .

. . . I've always preached the need for elected officials and candidates to be held accountable for their views. I don't exempt myself from that rule. I'd simply ask that folks take the time to find out what my views are before they start questioning my passion for justice or the integrity of my campaign effort. I'm not hard to reach.

In the meantime, I'll talk to my staff about sprucing up the website![67]

Obama's explanation seems reasonable and forthcoming, and at some point before December 2006 he did once again make the speech available to the public online via his website.[68] At least as late as December 2006, however, when it became much more likely that Obama would seek the presidency,[69] he was displaying a truncated version of his speech online, even as an unabridged copy of the speech was available elsewhere on the Internet.[70] The truncated version omitted the entirety of Obama's powerful peroration: "The consequences of war are dire, the sacrifices immeasurable. We may have occasion in our lifetime to once again rise up in defense of our freedom, and pay the wages of war. But we ought not—we will not—travel down that hellish path blindly. Nor should we allow those who would march off and pay the ultimate sacrifice, who would prove the full measure of devotion with their blood, to make such an awful sacrifice in vain." These are most wrenching lines of the speech, and are reminiscent of Charles Eliot Norton's painful expression of national guilt in 1898, when he concluded his antiwar address with the following words: "We mourn the deaths of our noble youth fallen in the cause of their country when she stands for the right; but we may mourn with a deeper sadness for those who have fallen in a cause which their generous hearts mistook for one worthy of the last sacrifice." Obama would, of course, ultimately include his entire speech, including his dramatic conclusion, on his website. But he has never stated publicly why he chose originally to omit it.

GOOD AFTERNOON.

Let me begin by saying that although this has been billed as an anti-war rally, I stand before you as someone who is not opposed to war in all circumstances.

The Civil War was one of the bloodiest in history, and yet it was only through the crucible of the sword, the sacrifice of multitudes, that we could begin to perfect this union, and drive the scourge of slavery from our soil.

I don't oppose all wars.

My grandfather signed up for a war the day after Pearl Harbor was bombed, fought in Patton's army. He saw the dead and dying across the fields of Europe; he heard the stories of fellow troops who first entered Auschwitz and Treblinka. He fought in the name of a larger freedom, part of that arsenal of democracy that triumphed over evil, and he did not fight in vain.

I don't oppose all wars.

After September 11th, after witnessing the carnage and destruction, the dust and the tears, I supported this administration's pledge to hunt down and root out those who would slaughter innocents in the name of intolerance, and I would willingly take up arms myself to prevent such tragedy from happening again.

I don't oppose all wars. And I know that in this crowd today, there is no shortage of patriots or of patriotism.

What I am opposed to is a dumb war. What I am opposed to is a rash war. What I am opposed to is the cynical attempt by Richard Perle and Paul Wolfowitz and other armchair, weekend warriors in this administration to shove their own ideological agendas down our throats, irrespective of the costs in lives lost and in hardships borne.

What I am opposed to is the attempt by political hacks like Karl Rove to distract us from a rise in the uninsured, a rise in the poverty rate, a drop in the median income—to distract us from corporate scandals and a stock market that has just gone through the worst month since the Great Depression.

That's what I'm opposed to. A dumb war. A rash war. A war based not on reason but on passion, not on principle but on politics.

Now let me be clear—I suffer no illusions about Saddam Hussein. He is a brutal man. A ruthless man. A man who butchers his own people to secure his own power. He has repeatedly defied UN resolutions, thwarted UN inspection teams, developed chemical and biological weapons and coveted nuclear capacity.

He's a bad guy. The world, and the Iraqi people, would be better off without him.

But I also know that Saddam poses no imminent and direct threat to the United States, or to his neighbors, that the Iraqi economy is in shambles, that the Iraqi military is a fraction of its former strength, and that in concert with the international community he can be contained until, in the way of all petty dictators, he falls away into the dustbin of history.

I know that even a successful war against Iraq will require a US occupation of undetermined length, at undetermined cost, with undetermined consequences.

I know that an invasion of Iraq without a clear rationale and without strong international support will only fan the flames of the Middle East, and encourage the worst, rather than best, impulses of the Arab world, and strengthen the recruitment arm of Al Qaeda.

I am not opposed to all wars. I'm opposed to dumb wars.

So for those of us who seek a more just and secure world for our children, let us send a clear message to the president today.

You want a fight, President Bush? Let's finish the fight with Bin Laden and Al Qaeda, through effective, coordinated intelligence and a shutting down of the financial networks that support terrorism, and a homeland security program that involves more than color-coded warnings.

You want a fight, President Bush? Let's fight to make sure that the UN inspectors can do their work, and that we vigorously enforce a non-proliferation treaty, and that former enemies and current allies like Russia safeguard and ultimately eliminate their stores of nuclear material, and that nations like Pakistan and India never use the terrible weapons already in their possession, and that the arms merchants in our own country stop feeding the countless wars that rage across the globe.

You want a fight, President Bush? Let's fight to make sure our so-called allies in the Middle East, the Saudis and the Egyptians, stop oppressing their own people, and suppressing dissent, and tolerating corruption and inequality and mismanaging their economies so that their youth grow up without education, without prospects, without hope, the ready recruits of terrorist cells.

You want a fight, President Bush? Let's fight to wean ourselves off Middle East oil, through an energy policy that doesn't simply serve the interests of Exxon and Mobil.

Those are the battles that we need to fight. Those are the battles that we willingly join. The battles against ignorance and intolerance. Corruption and greed. Poverty and despair.

The consequences of war are dire, the sacrifices immeasurable. We may have occasion in our lifetime to once again rise up in defense of our freedom, and pay the wages of war. But we ought not—we will not—travel down that hellish path blindly. Nor should we allow those who would march off and pay the ultimate sacrifice, who would prove the full measure of devotion with their blood, to make such an awful sacrifice in vain.

## Noam Chomsky Asks, "Why Iraq?"

[T]he Bush administration . . . is following "the classic modern strategy of an endangered right-wing oligarchy, which is to divert mass discontent to nationalism" inspired by fear of enemies about to destroy us.

While some contend that Massachusetts Institute of Technology linguist and activist Noam Chomsky's political theories lie beyond "the publicly tolerated spectrum of discussion,"[71] and others argue that he has been "banished to the margins of political debate,"[72] Chomsky was certainly the most prolific and widely listened to American opponent of the War on Terror.[73] In the six-year period after September 11, 2001, Chomsky published a book a year devoted in whole or in part to U.S. foreign policy. *9-11*, a collection of interviews conducted largely via e-mail that Chomsky published in 2001, was published in twenty-six countries, translated into twenty-three languages, and found its way onto best-seller lists in the United States, Canada, Germany, India, Italy, Japan, and New Zealand.[74] During the same period, he also gave dozens of antiwar lectures or speeches throughout the world,[75] which were attended by thousands, sometimes tens of thousands, of people.[76]

No stranger to dissent, Chomsky was already "one of the most articulate spokesmen of the resistance against the Vietnam war" in the 1960s.[77] In fact, Chomsky's outspoken criticism of the war in Vietnam through books, articles, and speeches earned him a place on Nixon's "Enemies List," and, later, arrest and a night in jail.[78] Throughout the 1980s and '90s, Chomsky continued to express concern over America's allegedly perfidious influence overseas. Today, he may still be, as Christopher Lehmann-Haupt put it 1973, "the foremost gadfly of our national conscience."[79]

In the months leading up to the invasion of Iraq, President George W. Bush and his administration provided increasingly alarming statements to the public that Saddam Hussein posed a clear and present danger to the United States. "There is no doubt that Saddam Hussein now has weapons of mass destruction," Vice President Richard Cheney told the Veterans of Foreign Wars on August 26, 2002.[80] The people of the United States "cannot wait for the final proof—the smoking gun—that could come in the form of a mushroom cloud," Bush declared on October 7, adding that "we have every reason to assume the worst."[81]

Chomsky challenged the Bush administration's views in a speech on November 4, 2002, at Harvard University's Kennedy School of Government. Speaking under the auspices of Harvard's Institute of Politics, Chomsky addressed an overflow crowd of college and graduate students, professors, and community activists. Institute of Politics director Daniel R. Glickman noted that the audience was one of the biggest of the year.[82]

Chomsky presents three antiwar arguments. First, he claims that the administration had not adequately proven that a connection existed between Iraq and terrorist networks such as al-Qaeda. The war could not lessen a terrorist threat, he said, because a country cannot eliminate a danger that did not exist in the first place. Secondly, Chomsky argues that war would *produce* the very threat that the administration feared. The conflict in Iraq, Chomsky predicts, would spawn a generation of terrorists committed to exacting revenge.

Having quickly described the consequences of war, Chomsky next proceeds to analyze its causes. In the section of the speech beginning "So, Why Iraq?" Chomsky begins his third argument in true antiwar fashion: by impugning the Bush administration's motives. Quoting Anatol Lieven of the Carnegie Endowment for International Peace, Chomsky contends that the Bush administration is following "'the classic modern strategy of an endangered right-wing oligarchy, which is to divert mass discontent to nationalism' inspired by fear of enemies about to destroy us." As evidence, Chomsky points to governmental actions that are consistent with such a strategy: the demonization of Saddam Hussein; comments by key administration officials broaching the possibility of a nuclear "mushroom cloud"; and the erosion of social policies designed to protect the poor and police the rich.

Chomsky's distinct style, a matter-of-fact sarcasm, is particularly noticeable toward the end of the speech, where Chomsky refers to the Bush administration as "recycled Reaganites," President Reagan as "another brave cowboy," and Saddam Hussein as a "sort of Martian foe." Chomsky's comparisons are evocative of Eugene V. Debs's hard-hitting rants against President Theodore Roosevelt who, Debs claimed, traipsed around Germany before the outbreak of World War I "check by jowl" with Kaiser Wilhelm II of Hohenzollern, the "Beast of Berlin." To Chomsky, Saddam Hussein is the "Beast of

Baghdad." Chomsky's and Debs's targets are different, of course, but their bitterness and contempt are one and the same.

THANKS.

After the introduction I think maybe I ought to give a campaign talk for Jill Stein. Well, I'm disciplined so I'll talk about what I was asked to talk about, which is Iraq and the connection between Iraq and the so-called War on Terror. There is a connection. It's pretty thin, but it's been drawn. Intelligence agencies have pointed out that they can't detect any real connection between Iraq and the terrorist networks—al-Qaeda and the rest—which isn't too surprising.

But there is a connection nevertheless, and it's been pointed out: namely, we can create a link if we want. And the best way to create a link would be by attacking Iraq. It's expected widely that if we do attack Iraq, that's very likely to ignite terrorist attacks maybe that are being planned as a possible deterrent, and it's very likely to spawn a new generation of terrorist who will be seeking revenge and also deterrence. And the deterrence is not a slight matter. Those of you who have been following the international relations literature—I'm going to be very establishment in this talk and I'm only going to quote people right in the mainstream—people who have been following it know that leading scholars, respected figures in international relations have been pointing out for some time—in fact, well before Bush—that U.S. adventurism is stimulating the proliferation of weapons of mass destruction as a deterrent. That's not just countries that are being specifically targeted for attack, but others who are concerned about deterring a state that seeks "unilateral world domination through absolute military superiority," and is "becoming a menace to itself and the world under a radical nationalist leadership." I've been quoting Kenneth Waltz, a well-known figure in international relations, and Anatol Lieven, who is the Senior Associate of the Carnegie Endowment for International Peace.

In fact, even real hard-liners are expressing pretty serious concerns. So one of the leading military and strategic analysts concerned primarily with the Middle East, Anthony Cordesman—who's about as hard-line as you can get within anything that might be called the spectrum of sanity [*laughter*]—warned recently against what he called "the neo-conservative fantasies of the sillier armchair strategists and their plans for reconstructing the Middle East and maybe the world." He was referring to Richard Perle and Douglas Feith, but that also includes Wolfowitz, Rumsfeld, [and] others who all happen to be very close to the extreme right-wing in Israel. So you're getting quite a lot of clear and good reporting from the mainstream Israeli press about them. As maybe you know, Richard Pearle—who's very close to the center of planning now—and Douglas Feith were writing position papers for Benjamin Netanyahu, Israel's new Foreign Minister who's well to the right of Ariel Sharon. They were doing that in the 1990s, and that's their connections and context. And it's not understandable that even a hard-line military analyst like Cordesman is worried about their sillier proposals, which are in fact being thought about and maybe implemented. Well, that's about the only connection I know of between Iraq and the terrorism at the moment. We can stimulate terrorism if we really intend to.

So, why Iraq? Obviously it's not in order to stimulate terrorism. Well, before going into that I'll begin with a truism that should be unnecessary to mention: in the case of either a threat of or resort to violence, the burden of proof is always on those who advocate it. So that's true whether it's domestic abuse or international affairs. And it's a heavy burden. Maybe there's an argument for it, but it's those who advocate force and violence who have to bear the burden. And it's a heavy one. You never need any arguments against the use of violence; it's automatic. You need an argument for it. It has to be a very strong one. That should be obvious and I'll just put it in back.

So why do they want to do it? Just to simplify, since time is brief, I'll pick two views that are expressed pretty prominently in the mainstream, and I'll quote mainstream analysts. So here's the first interpretation. I'll start with Youssef Ibrahim in the *International Herald Tribune* a couple days ago. He's a senior fellow in the Council on Foreign Relations, and was a senior Middle East correspondent for the *New York Times* and the *Wall Street Journal* for about thirty years. He moved to the CFR recently. His interpretation is that the goals of the Bush administration are basically two: (1) gaining short-term political advantage, and (2) "turning Iraq into a private, American oil-pumping station." Well, there's a counterargument against that in the *New York Times* yesterday, and maybe a response to it I don't know, by Serge Thion, who disparages the oil relationship on the grounds that there's not going to be an instant bonanza for Iraqi oil. And it's true. But it's not a very persuasive argument. By the same argument you can prove nobody was interested in Iraqi oil eight years ago, or Texas oil, or Saudi Arabian oil, or Venezuelan oil, or certainly not Alaskan or North Sea oil [that's] really expensive to get at. So by that argument, yeah, it's true you're not going to get billions of dollars tomorrow, and it will take development funds, but the argument is very weak, in fact, much weaker in the case of Iraqi oil, which is vast and relatively easily accessible than it was in numerous other cases. So I think we can dismiss the counterargument, which was, I think, a front page story in the *Times'* Week in Review yesterday. Well that's Youssef Ibrahim.

Lieven, whom I quoted before, has a more detailed analysis along the same lines. He suggests that the Bush administration . . . is following "the classic modern strategy of an endangered right-wing oligarchy, which is to divert mass discontent to nationalism" inspired by fear of enemies about to destroy us. And he speaks for many people in the world when he regards that as the U.S. government's policies now as a menace to itself, meaning the country, and to the world. Well, September 11 provided a pretext for resort to force, not just for the United States, that's worldwide and it was predicted at once. So the Russians in Chechnya, the Chinese and their western minorities, the Indonesian Punjabis, Israel and the occupied territories, and all over the world repressive governments that were engaged in violent repression used September 11 as a pretext to intensify it under the guise of a "war on terror," and assuming, correctly, that they get a nod of approval from the boss in Washington. And it's not surprising that the U.S. itself would adopt the same idea.

So, yes, 9-11 was a pretext. And it was also used as a pretext to discipline populations throughout the world, again, under the guise of a war on terror. And that ranges from the Central Asian dictatorships all the way over to the more democratic countries, including our own. So the fact that September 11 would prove a pretext for a war in Iraq is not a great surprise.

And in fact this was pointed out also to pursue the domestic political agenda, as Lieven points out, is natural for an endangered right-wing oligarchy to do that, especially when it's carrying out quite an extensive attack against the domestic population. That's not a big secret, or it shouldn't be.

In the U.S. that was pointed out right away by, for example, Paul Krugman, a well-known economist in one of his regular *New York Times* columns, who reported right away that "literally before the dust had settled" over the World Trade Center ruins, influential Republicans signaled that they were "determined to use terrorism as an excuse to pursue a radical right-wing agenda." And he and other have been documenting how they've been following that course ever since. Again, shouldn't be a secret, so I won't pursue it.

The Beast of Baghdad was then brought in to be an even more terrifying threat. And there are also independent reasons. There is a longstanding goal, Ibrahim and others are surely correct and it's kind of obvious, it's been a longstanding goal to restore to U.S. control the second largest oil reserves in the world. It's been recognized ever since the mid-forties. The State Department in 1945 [said] that this was a major component in what they called a "stupendous force in strategic power, and one of the greatest material prizes in world history." And a major theme of U.S. foreign policy since the Second World War has been to make sure that the U.S. dominates it. France was expelled on the interesting grounds that it was an enemy state since it had been occupied by Germany, and so therefore its contracts were void. And England was slowly reduced to what the British Foreign Office calls a "junior partner."

The U.S. puts it differently. Forty years ago a senior statesman, probably Dean Acheson, in internal discussion described Britain as "our lieutenant"—the fashionable word is "partner," and they like to hear the fashionable word. But [that in] reality was the actual word. And control over Middle East oil has been a very large part from the Second World War.

Let me stress that it's control; it's not access. There's a lot of confusion about that. The United States really doesn't care much about access to Middle East oil. From up until 1970 it didn't care at all. North America was the biggest producer; but it didn't affect the need to control the region. Since then the biggest importer has usually been Venezuela. If you look at U.S. intelligence projections, for example the National Intelligence Council's projections for the next fifteen years, they predict and suggest that the U.S. should rely on a more secure Atlantic basin resources—West Africa and Latin America. But that has absolutely nothing to do with control of Middle East oil. That has to do with being "one of the greatest material prizes in world history," which means that whoever controls it and can have an effect on setting price and production levels can also determine that the wealth, the vast amount of the wealth, flows right back here. And it does. It's independent of access to oil.

A "stupendous source of strategic power" has nothing to do with access; that has to do—that translates as a lever of world control, and that's been recognized clearly since the 1940s, and it remains true today.

Well, September 11 gave the pretext, the domestic politics effects the timing, and the strategy has been working quite brilliantly. You see it right now in the midterm elections. It's going to be even more important next year. Presumably if you put yourselves in Karl Rove's shoes, Bush's campaign manager, when the presidential campaign begins in a little over a year, do you really want people to be thinking about what's happening to their pensions, or how they're going to take care of their elderly mother, or what about their job, or why can't they get health care, or what about an environment that their children might live in? Things like that are certainly not what they want people to be paying attention to. They'll want people to be singing praises to the brave cowboy who saved them from destruction at the hands of a colossal foe, sort of Martian foe [*laughter*], and we'll by then be marching off to some new adventure, exactly as Lieven says. That's the tradition, that's the classic strategy of an endangered right-wing oligarchy which wants to divert mass content, which has plenty of ground, into nationalism and fear. And it takes a lot of work to overlook the fact that the only people who are afraid of Condoleezza Rice's mushroom cloud—which is going to consume us imminently—the only people who are afraid of it are Americans, not the people of the region, for example. I mean, they're afraid—afraid of the United States more than they are of Iraq.

Of course, Iraqis are afraid of Saddam Hussein—and they have every right to be—but that can't possibly be the reason for the U.S. war. The U.S. was supporting Saddam right through his worst atrocities, [and] helping him develop weapons of mass destruction right up to day of the invasion of Kuwait. It's the same people who are running Washington right now, so whatever the reasons are, it's not that.

So, yeah, they're afraid of Saddam Hussein, but they also know they can't do very much; in fact, very little. If he made a move anywhere, Iraq would be obliterated. He knows that and the people of the region know that, but even the U.S. press, the national press, which is usually highly supportive of power, now recognizes that "the world is more concerned with the unbridled use of American power than it is about the threat posed by Saddam Hussein." It's a lead story in the *Christian Science Monitor* a couple days ago, and it's been pointed out by others.

So there definitely is a security issue: there's a problem of securing the agenda of the radical right-wing oligarchy, and making sure that they can continue for another four years to undermine living standards, destroy social policy, concentrate the wealth of a very narrow sector of an unusually corrupt part of the business establishment as Krugman and many others have been pointing out. And to secure that agenda is very serious. And it's a security problem. And that's about the only security problem anyone can seem to conjure up. But it's real, of course.

Well, that's one interpretation. One interpretation well within the mainstream establishment is what I just said: there's a long-term goal of regaining control over the second largest resources in the Middle East, and ensuring domination of one of the greatest material prizes in world history, and a stupendous source of strategic power. September 11 gave a pretext, as it gave a pretext around the world, for an intensification of violence and disciplining of the populations, and domestic considerations in that very important security problem probably accounts for the timing. So it has to be *this* winter, not next winter. That'll be too late. By then we'll have been consumed by the mushroom cloud, which will avoid everyone else but hit us. And of course it's kind of like an accident that that will be right in the middle of the presidential campaign, just as it's an accident that the people of the region are afraid—but mostly of us, and joining most of the world in that. Well, that's one interpretation.

Incidentally, all of this is not only the classic strategy of an endangered right-wing oligarchy under a radical nationalistic leadership as Lieven points out, but it's also second nature to the people in Washington. Remember that the people running the show are recycled Reaganites almost entirely. They come out of the Reagan administration, when they were doing precisely the same thing. When the Reagan administration came into office 20 years ago in 1981, the first thing it did was declare a war on terror with pretty much the same rhetoric as today. At that time Americans had to be terrified by Libyan hit men who were wandering the streets of Washington planning to kill our leader, another brave cowboy [*laughter*], who was hiding in the White House surrounded by tanks. If you're old enough you'll remember that, or your parents will. That was twenty years ago. And they had to be worried about the Sandinistas who were "only two days marching time from Texas" [*laughter*], the brave cowboy told us. And they were following a script, the script of *Mein Kampf,* in their plan to conquer the hemisphere, if not beyond—that was George Schultz, the administration moderate, the Colin Powell of the day. And there was a national emergency called, [and] renewed every year because of the threat to the U.S.'s security and survival posed by people like Qaddafi who was planning to "expel America from the world," according to Reagan, or at least his speech writers. [*Laughter.*]

And people were afraid. This is traditionally a very frightened society. You can ask about the reasons, but it's well-known. Americans happen to be more frightened of almost anything than most other people [*laughter*] for all kinds of historical reasons, but it's clearly true. It can be crime, aliens [*laughter*], drugs, you name it. There's a lot of fear. And it's not hard to stir up fear among the population, and it was going on right through the eighties. So all of this is absolutely second nature to the guys making policy today, and it wouldn't be too surprising if that's what they're planning.

Well, my time is just about running out, which is fine, because there is another view, which I can fortunately skip because there's no time. [*Laughter.*] . . .

## Robert Byrd Chastises the Senate for Standing "Passively Mute"

War must always be a last resort, not a first choice.

During the months surrounding the U.S. invasion of Iraq on March 20, 2003, Senator Robert C. Byrd, Democrat of West Virginia, established himself as the Senate's foremost antiwar dissident, giving dozens of antiwar speeches up to and after the 2003 invasion. Adding credibility to his criticism was the fact over the course of his fifty-year congressional career, Byrd had proven he was no pacifist. Indeed, he had been a staunch supporter of the wars in Korea and Vietnam.[83]

Byrd's rhetorical style is always classical, often ornate, and sometimes anachronistic. He is fond—perhaps too fond—of alliteration: the nation, he says, stands "at the brink of battle," terrorists occupy "dark dens" in "devastated" Afghanistan, the U.S. has "massive military might," and the war in Iraq is a "destabilizing and dangerous . . . debacle." He uses anaphora ("This administration has squandered . . . This administration has ignored . . . This administration has failed . .), metaphor ("we are truly sleepwalking through history," rhetorical questions ("Have we not learned that after winning the war, one must also secure the peace?"), and a host of other devices throughout his speeches.

Most of Byrd's prewar rhetoric was either admired or dismissed. John Tierney of the *New York Times* called Byrd's antiwar speeches "extraordinary even for the maestro of senatorial rhetoric."[84] John Dicker of the *Rocky Mountain News,* in contrast, wrote that even though Byrd's denunciations of the Bush administration were "eloquent," his rhetoric ultimately "does not merit a close reread" because "Byrd's oratory is married to its context."[85] Most of the nation tended to agree with Dicker. Though Byrd delivered over sixty preinvasion speeches that criticized the Bush administration's bellicosity, his statements were, at first, largely ignored by the mainstream media.

Byrd's address in the Senate on February 12, 2003, however, captured the attention of the nation and the world. MoveOn.org, an antiwar advocacy group, received fifteen copies of the speech from activists within seventy-two hours of its delivery.[86] Within ten days, the speech was published on countless websites, discussed on Internet blogs, and reprinted in newspapers throughout the world.[87] As it ricocheted around the globe, it was translated into several languages.[88] Interest in the eighty-four-year-old opponent of the War on Terror increased exponentially as well. In the month preceding Byrd's speech, the Senator's congressional website received some four hundred and thirty-six thousand hits; the month after, that number increased to 3.7 million.[89] Two of Byrd's own postinvasion books, one bearing the speech's name, feature his February 12 remarks.

Byrd employs numerous arguments questioning the war's morality, its practicality, its cost, and its unprecedented nature. His most significant argument, though, involves the extent to which Senate was—or was not—limiting the power of the executive branch to launch a preemptive attack on a sovereign nation. In an interview conducted on July 27, 2004, on National Public Radio, Byrd summarized his position.

> We've got to take that power back from the president. You see the framers wrote the Constitution. And when they gave to the Congress the power to declare war they were giving to the Congress the power to declare war and they were not thinking in terms of one person or even one body.
>
> It takes two bodies, the House and the Senate, to declare war and it takes many people. And here we were, here we were acquiescing to an administration that doesn't really understand the role of the Senate and we were shifting to one man

this awesome power. And then we were relegating to ourselves the position of doing nothing. We relegated ourselves to the sidelines and that's where we are today.[90]

When Byrd accuses Congress of remaining "ominously, dreadfully silent" in the lead-up to war, he is not accusing them of mere timidity. Byrd believes that Congress has a responsibility to test and limit the executive's war powers. Any other understanding of Congress's duty is, Byrd suggests, inconsistent with the spirit of the Founding Fathers and the Constitution.

Thus, Byrd's conclusion leads him to blame not only the president for using the war power to apply a "revolutionary doctrine . . . in an extraordinary way at an unfortunate time," but also the Senate for standing down when faced with presidential initiative. As Raymond Smock, director of the Robert C. Byrd Center for Legislative studies at Shepherd University, observed of Byrd, "He's just as mad at the Senate as he is at the president."[91]

There is one section of Byrd's speech that is significant both in the narrow context of the War on Terror and in the broader context of American moral philosophy. At one point in his speech, Byrd implies that the United States, like all countries, is at least partially "evil":

> This administration has turned the patient art of diplomacy on its head. It has turned the patient art of diplomacy into threats, labeling, and name calling of the sort that reflects quite poorly on the intelligence and sensitivity of our leaders and which will have consequences for years to come, calling heads of state pygmies, labeling whole countries as evil—as though we are not evil, as though there is no country that is not evil—denigrating powerful European allies as irrelevant. These types of crude insensitivities can do our great Nation no good.

In the context of the War on Terror, Byrd is referring to President George W. Bush's State of the Union Address in 2002. There, President Bush spoke of an "axis of evil" that threatened world peace: "States like these [i.e., North Korea, Iran and Iraq], and their terrorist allies, constitute an axis of evil, arming to threaten the peace of the world. By seeking weapons of mass destruction, these regimes pose a grave and growing danger. They could provide these arms to terrorists, giving them the means to match their hatred. They could attack our allies or attempt to blackmail the United States. In any of these cases, the price of indifference would be catastrophic."[92] By implying that the United States itself was partially "evil," Byrd turns Bush's speech on its head. Byrd's humility—his willingness to acknowledge his own country's faults—doubtless added to his personal appeal among members of the antiwar movement and contributed to the speech's attractiveness as an antidote to the president's earlier address.

At the same time, Byrd the speech historian must have been aware that by mentioning the word "evil," he was setting his address up against an iconic phrase of Republican speechifying. For just as Byrd was referencing Bush, Bush was referencing President

Ronald Reagan. In 1983, Reagan gave an address at the National Association of Evangelicals in which he coined the phrase "evil empire":

> Yes, let us pray for the salvation of all of those who live in that totalitarian darkness—pray they will discover the joy of knowing God. But until they do, let us be aware that while they preach the supremacy of the state, declare its omnipotence over individual man, and predict its eventual domination of all peoples on the Earth, they are the focus of evil in the modern world. . . .
>
> . . . I urge you to speak out against those who would place the United States in a position of military and moral inferiority. . . . In your discussions of the nuclear freeze proposals, I urge you to beware the temptation of pride—the temptation of blithely declaring yourselves above it all and label both sides equally at fault, to ignore the facts of history and the aggressive impulses of an evil empire, to simply call the arms race a giant misunderstanding and thereby remove yourself from the struggle between right and wrong and good and evil.[93]

The moral absolutism of Bush and Reagan were extremely effective, as they provided a clear dichotomy between what was good and what was bad. Moral relativism, what Reagan decried in the context of the communism and what Bush disdained in the context of terrorism, plays a central role in Byrd's speech. One wonders whether Bush or Reagan's speech would have been more effective if either speaker had found less wrong with the values of another culture, or whether Byrd's speech would have been more effective if he had found less wrong with the values of his own.

MADAM PRESIDENT, to contemplate war is to think about the most horrible of human experience. On this February day, as this Nation stands at the brink of battle, every American on some level must be contemplating the horrors of war.

My wife says to me at night: Do you think we ought to get some of those large bottles, the large jugs, and fill them with water? She says: Go up to the attic and see if we don't have two or three there. I believe we have two or three there.

And so I went up to the attic last evening and came back to report to her that, no, we didn't have any large jugs of water, but we had some small ones, perhaps some gallon jugs filled with water. And she talked about buying up a few things, groceries and canned goods to put away.

I would suspect that kind of conversation is going on in many towns across this great, broad land of ours. And yet this Chamber is for the most part ominously, dreadfully silent. You can hear a pin drop. Listen. You can hear a pin drop. There is no debate. There is no discussion. There is no attempt to lay out for the Nation the pros and cons of this particular war. There is nothing.

What would Gunning Bedford of Delaware think about it? What would John Dickinson of Delaware think about it? What would George Read think about it? What would they say?

We stand passively mute in the Senate today, paralyzed by our own uncertainty, seemingly stunned by the sheer turmoil of events. Only on the editorial pages of some of our newspapers is there much substantive discussion concerning the prudence or the imprudence of engaging in this particular war. I can imagine hearing the walls of this Chamber ring just before the great war between the States, a war that tore this Nation asunder and out of which the great State of West Virginia was born.

But today we hear nothing, almost nothing, by way of debate. This is no small conflagration that we contemplate. It is not going to be a video game. It may last a day or 6 days. God created Earth, and man, the stars, the planets, and the Moon in 6 days. This war may last 6 days. It may last 6 weeks. It could last longer. This is no small conflagration that we contemplate. This is no simple attempt to defang a villain. No, this coming battle, if it materializes, represents a turning point in U.S. foreign policy and possibly a turning point in the recent history of the world.

This Nation is about to embark upon the first test of a revolutionary doctrine applied in an extraordinary way, at an unfortunate time—the doctrine of preemption, no small matter—the idea that the United States or any other nation can legitimately attack a nation that is not imminently threatening but which may be threatening in the future.

The idea that the United States may attack a sovereign government because of a dislike for a particular regime is a radical, new twist on the traditional idea of self-defense. It appears to be in contravention of international law and the U.N. Charter. And it is being tested at a time of worldwide terrorism, making many countries around the globe wonder if they will soon be on our hit list, or some other nation's hit list.

High-level administration figures recently refused to take nuclear weapons off the table when discussing a possible attack on Iraq. What could be more destabilizing? What could be more world shattering? What could be more future shattering? What could be more unwise than this kind of uncertainty, particularly in a world where globalism has tied the vital economic and security interests of so many nations so closely together?

There are huge cracks emerging in our time-honored alliances. One wonders what is going to happen, and about what is happening to the United Nations. One should pause to reflect on what is happening there at the United Nations, formed 54 years ago. And we say: If you are not with us, you are against us. That is a pretty hard rule to lay down to the United Nations. If you are not with us, you are against us. If you don't see it our way, take the highway. We say to Germany and we say to France—both of whom have been around longer than we—if you don't see it our way, we will just brush you to the side.

Do we fail to think about a possible moment down the road, a bit further on, when we may wish to have Germany and France working with us and thinking with us, standing with us, because there is a larger specter, at least in my mind, looming behind the specter of Saddam Hussein and Iraq. There looms a larger specter, that of North Korea, which has one or two nuclear weapons now, and others within reach within a few weeks. So there are huge cracks, I say, emerging in our time-honored alliances, and U.S. intentions are suddenly subject to damaging worldwide speculation.

Anti-Americanism based on mistrust, misinformation, suspicion, and alarming rhetoric from U.S. leaders is fracturing the once solid alliance against global terrorism which existed after September 11, 2001.

Here at home, people are warned of imminent terrorist attacks, with little guidance as to when or where such attacks might occur. Family members are being called to active duty, with no idea of the duration of their stay away from their hearthside, away from their homes, away from their loved ones, with no idea of the duration of their stay or what horrors they may have to face, perhaps in the near future. Communities are being left with less than adequate police and fire protection, while we are being told that a terrorist attack may be imminent. What about those communities like little Sophia, WV? . . .

This administration, now in power for a little over 2 years, must be judged on its record. I believe that record is dismal. . . .

In foreign policy, this administration has failed to find Osama bin Laden. In fact, yesterday we heard from him again marshaling his forces and urging them to kill, kill, kill.

This administration has split traditional alliances, possibly crippling for all time international order, crippling entities such as the United Nations and NATO. This administration has called into question the traditional worldwide perception of the United States as being a well-intentioned peacemaking, peace loving, peacekeeping nation.

This administration has turned the patient art of diplomacy on its head. It has turned the patient art of diplomacy into threats, labeling, and name calling of the sort that reflects quite poorly on the intelligence and sensitivity of our leaders and which will have consequences for years to come, calling heads of state pygmies, labeling whole countries as evil—as though we are not evil, as though there is no country that is not evil— denigrating powerful European allies as irrelevant. These types of crude insensitivities can do our great Nation no good. . . .

While we may have massive military might today, we cannot fight a global war on terrorism alone. We need the cooperation and the friendship of our time-honored allies, as well as the newer found friends whom we can attract with our wealth. Our awesome military machine will do us little good if we suffer another devastating attack on our homeland which severely damages this economy.

Our military manpower is already stretched thin, and they are taking them from our States every day. Yesterday, I talked to the Senate about the vacancies, about the empty seats at the dinner tables in the homes of many West Virginians, because of the National Guard and Reserve departures every day from the State of West Virginia. Yes, there they come. They are law enforcement officers. They are State troopers. They are road builders. They are doctors. They are teachers. They are Sunday school teachers. These are the men and women who keep the lights burning when the snows fall and darkness comes. But on whom will we depend when these men and women are gone to foreign lands to fight a war if a war faces us here at home, a different kind of war.

Our awesome military machine will do us little good if we suffer another devastating attack on our homeland which severely damages our economy.

As I say, our military forces are already being stretched thin and we will need the augmenting support of those nations that can supply troop strength, not just sign letters cheering us on.

The war in Afghanistan has cost us $37 billion so far. Yes, we bombed those caves. We ran them into the holes, but they could not hide. We ran them out of the holes, and we ran behind them to get them. But there is evidence that terrorism may already be starting to regain its hold in that region. We have not found Bin Laden, and unless we secure the peace in Afghanistan, the dark dens of terrorism may yet again flourish in that remote and devastated land.

Pakistan, as well, is at risk of destabilizing forces. This administration has not finished the first war against terrorism, and yet it is eager to embark on another conflict with perils much greater than those in Afghanistan. Is our attention span that short? Have we not learned that after winning the war, one must also secure the peace?

Yet we hear little, precious little, about the aftermath of war in Iraq. In the absence of plans, speculation abroad is rife. Will we seize Iraq's oil fields, becoming an occupying power which controls the price and supply of that nation's oil for the foreseeable future? There are some who think so.

To whom do we propose to hand the reins of power in Iraq after Saddam Hussein? Will our war inflame the Muslim world, resulting in devastating attacks on Israel? Will Israel retaliate with its own very potent nuclear arsenal? What are we about to unleash here? The genie is getting out of the bottle. Can it ever be put back? Will the Jordanian and Saudi Arabian Governments be toppled by radicals, bolstered by Iran, which has much closer ties to terrorism than Iraq? Could a disruption of the world's oil supply lead to a worldwide recession? Has our senselessly bellicose language and our callous disregard for the interests and opinions of other nations increased the global race to join the nuclear club and make proliferation an even more lucrative practice for nations which need the income?

In only the space of 2 short years, this reckless and arrogant administration has initiated policies which may reap disastrous consequences for years.

We have heard it asked, Are you better off today than you were 4 years ago? The question can be shortened: Are we better off than we were 2 years ago?

One can understand the anger and the shock of any President after the savage attacks of September 11. One can appreciate the frustration of having only a shadow to chase and an amorphous, fleeting enemy on which it is nearly impossible to exact retribution. But to turn one's frustration and anger into the kind of extremely destabilizing and dangerous foreign policy debacle that the world is currently witnessing is inexcusable from any administration charged with the awesome power and responsibility of guiding the destiny of the greatest superpower on the planet.

Frankly, many of the pronouncements made by this administration are outrageous. There is no other word. Yet this Chamber is hauntingly silent—silent. What would John Langdon of New Hampshire say about that? What would Nicholas Gilman of New Hampshire say about that? What would Rufus King and Nathaniel Gorham of Massachusetts say? What would Alexander Hamilton, who signed the Constitution, from the

State of New York, say about the silence in this Chamber? What would Dr. Samuel Johnson of Connecticut say about the silence in this Chamber? What would William Paterson or William Livingston or David Brearley or Jonathan Dayton of New Jersey, the signers of the Constitution, have to say about the silence in this Senate which they created? What would Benjamin Franklin, Thomas Mifflin, James Wilson, Robert Morris, of Pennsylvania, have to say? What would Thomas FitzSimons or Gouverneur Morris, who signed the Constitution on behalf of the State of Pennsylvania, have to say about the silence that rings and reverberates from these walls today, the silence with respect to the war on which we are about to enter? What would they have to say? What would their comments be? Gunning Bedford, George Read of Delaware, Daniel Carroll, Dan of St. Thomas Jenifer of Maryland. These and more.

What would these signers of the Constitution have to say about this Senate which they created when they note the silence, that is deafening, that emanates from that Chamber on the great subject, the great issue of war and peace? Nothing. Nothing is being said except by a few souls. Yet this Chamber is hauntingly silent—hauntingly silent on what is possibly the eve of horrific infliction of death and destruction on the population of the nation of Iraq. Think about that.

Oh, I know Saddam Hussein is the person who is primarily responsible. But how about us? How about ourselves?

Yes, there are going to be old men dying. There will be women dying. There will be children, little boys and girls dying if this war goes forward in Iraq. And American men and women will die, too.

Iraq has a population, I might add, of which over 50 percent is under age 15. Over 50 percent of the population in Iraq is under age 15. What is said about that? This Chamber is silent—silent. When it is possibly only days before we send thousands of our own citizens to face unimagined horrors of chemical and biological warfare, this Chamber is silent. The rafters should ring. The press galleries should be filled. Senators should be at their seats listening to questions being asked about this war, questions to which the American people out there have a right to expect answers. The American people are longing for information and they are not getting it. This Chamber is silent. On the eve of what could possibly be a vicious terrorist attack in retaliation for our attack on Iraq, it is business as usual here in the Senate, and business as usual means it is pretty quiet. There is not much going on in the Senate. Business as usual.

Oh, I know it may be scare talk to talk about what may happen in the event of a terrorist attack. But when the Twin Towers fell, it wasn't scare talk. When hundreds of local firefighters and police officers, law enforcement officers died as the walls of the Twin Towers came tumbling down, it wasn't scare talk. It wasn't scare talk.

We are truly sleepwalking through history. In my heart of hearts I pray that this great Nation and its good and trusting citizens are not in for a rudest of awakenings. To engage in war is always to pick a wild card. And war must always be a last resort, not a first choice.

But I truly must question the judgment of any President who can say that a massive unprovoked military attack on a nation which is over 50 percent children is in the highest moral traditions of our country. This war is not necessary at this time. Pressure appears to be having a good result in Iraq. Our mistake was to put ourselves in a corner so quickly. Our challenge is now to find a graceful way out of a box of our own making. Perhaps—just perhaps—there is still a way, if we allow more time.

Madam President, I yield the floor.

# Epilogue: The Globalization of Dissent

## Arundhati Roy Rails Against "Imperial Democracy"

Empire's conquests are being carried out in your name.

Worldwide popular opposition to the U.S. invasion of Iraq was considerable. As mentioned above, in a Gallup International Poll in January 2003 approximately half of all global interviewees said they were not in favor of military action against Iraq under any circumstances, and even if the war were first approved by the United Nations, only about one-third of those interviewed stated that they would affirmatively support it.[1] In the weeks before the United States commenced Operation Shock and Awe in March 2003, more than 10 million people across the world marched against the war.[2]

The sheer size of organized antiwar activity directed at the United States from abroad warrants the inclusion of at least one speech in this anthology. But the speech below is included for more than the sake of diversity. While it demonstrates many of the standard features of American antiwar speeches, it also helps illustrate the provenance of Americans' antiwar dissent and, in that way, sharpens our understanding of the subject. "Empire's conquests are being carried out in your name," Indian activist Arundhati Roy reminds her American audience.

Roy is best known for her first and only novel, *The God of Small Things* (1997), which has been translated into over thirty languages. Her other writings are all political nonfiction. In "The Great Indian Rape Trick" (1994), Roy investigated whether a filmmaker ought to restage the rape of a living woman without her consent.[3] *The Cost of Living* (1999) addressed the effect of India's dams on rural populations, and the implications of India's nuclear arsenal. *Power Politics* (2001) criticized, among other things, privatization in India, and recounted how her criticism of the Indian government earned her a night in jail. In her most recent works, *War Talk* (2003), *An Ordinary Person's Guide to Empire* (2004), and *The Checkbook and the Cruise Missile* (2004), Roy turned her attention wholly toward war, imperialism, and, ever increasingly, the United States.

Roy delivered the following address, entitled "Instant-Mix Imperial Democracy (Buy One, Get One Free)," on May 13, 2003, to a full house of three thousand at New

York City's Riverside Church, where thirty-six years earlier Martin Luther King Jr. had condemned America's involvement in Vietnam. Roy's poised and poetic style, as emotionally charged as King's but infinitely more embittered, is the result of carefully designed rhetorical devices. Early in her remarks, for example, Roy employs simile: "I speak as a slave who presumes to criticize her king." The speech's climax is constructed with a provocative metaphor: "Democracy is the Free World's whore, willing to dress up, dress down, willing to satisfy a whole range of taste, available to be used and abused at will." These classical rhetorical devices are effective because they are memorable, and memorable because they are imaginative. Roy's speech, which contains a rich and venomous vocabulary, is that of a person conscious of the limits of language and the power of metaphor to fill in the gaps of what words cannot convey. "As a writer," Roy says of her craft, "one spends a lifetime journeying into the heart of language, trying to minimize, if not eliminate, the distance between language and thought."[4] Simile and metaphor are the primary vehicles Roy uses to accomplish these ends.

Roy's speech may be easily criticized as style over substance, not because it lacks substance, but because it is so stylized. At the speech's best, Roy speaks with beauty of an artist and the political consciousnesses of a statesman—literary politics itself. In the excerpted portion of the speech, for example, Roy provides a detailed, though starkly partisan, discussion of the war's allegedly faulty justification, its management, and its unpopularity. There, she also discusses (and alleges) who is paying for the war (the poor), who is fighting it (the poor), and who will benefit from it (corporate, military, and governmental leadership). At the speech's worst, though, Roy evidences a complete lack of diplomacy that impedes well-intentioned attempts at political compromise. Even as the speech's allegations are powerful enough to excite and galvanize the doves, her intemperance virtually guarantees that it will be ignored or summarily dismissed by the hawks.


IN THESE TIMES, when we have to race to keep abreast of the speed at which our freedoms are being snatched from us, and when few can afford the luxury of retreating from the streets for a while in order to return with an exquisite, fully formed political thesis replete with footnotes and references, what profound gift can I offer you tonight?

As we lurch from crisis to crisis, beamed directly into our brains by satellite TV, we have to think on our feet. On the move. We enter histories through the rubble of war. Ruined cities, parched fields, shrinking forests, and dying rivers are our archives. Craters left by daisy cutters, our libraries.

So what can I offer you tonight? Some uncomfortable thoughts about money, war, empire, racism, and democracy. Some worries that flit around my brain like a family of persistent moths that keep me awake at night.

Some of you will think it bad manners for a person like me, officially entered in the Big Book of Nations as an "Indian citizen," to come here and criticize the U.S. government. Speaking for myself, I'm no flag-waver, no patriot, and am fully aware that venality, brutality, and hypocrisy are imprinted on the leaden soul of every nation. But when a country ceases to be merely a country and becomes an empire, then the scale of operations changes dramatically. So may I clarify that tonight I speak as a subject of the American Empire? I speak as a slave who presumes to criticize her king.

Since lectures must be called something, mine tonight is called "Instant-Mix Imperial Democracy (Buy One, Get One Free)." [*Laughter and applause.*]

Way back in 1988, on the 3rd of July, the U.S.S. *Vincennes,* a missile cruiser stationed in the Persian Gulf, accidentally shot down an Iranian airliner and killed 290 civilian passengers. George Bush the First, who was at the time on his presidential campaign, was asked to comment on the incident. He said quite subtly, "I will never apologize for the United States. I don't care what the facts are."

*I don't care what the facts are.* What a perfect maxim for the New American Empire. Perhaps a slight variation on the theme would be more apposite: *The facts can be whatever we want them to be.*

When the United States invaded Iraq, a New York Times/CBS News survey estimated that 42 percent of the American public believed that Saddam Hussein was directly responsible for the September 11th attacks on the World Trade Center and the Pentagon. And an ABC News poll said that 55 percent of Americans believed that Saddam Hussein directly supported al-Qaeda. None of this opinion is based on evidence (because there isn't any). All of it is based on insinuation, auto-suggestion, and outright lies circulated by the U.S. corporate media, otherwise known as the "Free Press," that hollow pillar on which contemporary American democracy rests. [*Applause.*]

Public support in the U.S. for the war against Iraq was founded on a multi-tiered edifice of falsehood and deceit, coordinated by the U.S. government and faithfully amplified by the corporate media.

Apart from the invented links between Iraq and al-Qaeda, we had the manufactured frenzy about Iraq's Weapons of Mass Destruction. George Bush the Lesser [*laughter, shouts, and applause*] went to the extent of saying it would be "suicidal" for the U.S. *not* to attack Iraq. We once again witnessed the paranoia that a starved, bombed, besieged country was about to annihilate almighty America. (Iraq was only the latest in a succession of countries—earlier there was Cuba, Nicaragua, Libya, Grenada, Panama.) But this time it wasn't just your ordinary brand of friendly neighborhood frenzy. It was Frenzy with a Purpose. It ushered in an old doctrine in a new bottle: the Doctrine of Pre-emptive Strike, also known as The United States Can Do Whatever The Hell It Wants, And That's Official.

The war against Iraq has been fought and won and no Weapons of Mass Destruction have been found. Not even a little one. [*Laughter.*] Perhaps they'll have to be planted before they're discovered. [*Applause.*] And then, the more troublesome amongst us will need an explanation for why Saddam Hussein didn't use them when his country was being invaded.

Of course, there'll be no answers. True Believers will make do with those fuzzy TV reports about the discovery of a few barrels of banned chemicals in an old shed. There seems to be no consensus yet about whether they're really chemicals, whether they're actually banned and whether the vessels they're contained in can technically be called barrels. [*Laughter.*] (There were unconfirmed rumors that a teaspoonful full of potassium permanganate and an old harmonica were found there too.) [*Laughter.*]

Meanwhile, in passing, an ancient civilization has been casually decimated by a very recent, casually brutal nation.

Then there are those who say, so what if Iraq had no chemical and nuclear weapons? So what if there is no al-Qaeda connection? So what if Osama bin Laden hates Saddam Hussein as much as he hates the United States? Bush the Lesser has said Saddam Hussein was a "Homicidal Dictator." And so, the reasoning goes, Iraq needed a "regime change."

Never mind that forty years ago, the CIA, under President John F. Kennedy, orchestrated a regime change in Baghdad. In 1963, after a successful coup, the Ba'ath party came to power in Iraq. Using lists provided by the CIA, the new Ba'ath regime systematically eliminated hundreds of doctors, lawyers, teachers, and political figures known to be leftists. An entire intellectual community was slaughtered. (The same technique was used to massacre hundreds of thousands of people in Indonesia and East Timor.) The young Saddam Hussein was said to have had a hand in supervising the bloodbath. But in 1979, after factional infighting within the Ba'ath Party, Saddam Hussein became the president of Iraq. In April 1980, while he was massacring Shias, the U.S. National Security Adviser Zbigniew Brzezinksi declared, "We see no fundamental incompatibility of interests between the United States and Iraq." Washington and London overtly and covertly supported Saddam Hussein. They financed him, equipped him, armed him, and provided him with dual-use materials to manufacture weapons of mass destruction. They supported his worst excesses financially, materially, and morally. They supported the eight-year war against Iran and the 1988 gassing of Kurdish people in Halabja, crimes which 14 years later were re-heated and served up as reasons to justify invading Iraq. After the first Gulf War, the "Allies" fomented an uprising of Shias in Basra and then looked away while Saddam Hussein crushed the revolt and slaughtered thousands in an act of vengeful reprisal.

The point is, if Saddam Hussein was evil enough to merit the most elaborate, openly declared assassination attempt in history (the opening move of Operation Shock and Awe), then surely those who supported him ought at least to be tried for war crimes? [*Applause.*] Why aren't the faces of U.S. and U.K. government officials on the infamous pack of cards of wanted men and women? [*Applause.*]

Because when it comes to Empire, facts don't matter.

Yes, but all that's in the past we're told. Saddam Hussein is a monster who must be stopped *now*. And only the U.S. can stop him. It's an effective technique, this use of the urgent morality of the present to obscure the diabolical sins of the past and the malevolent plans for the future. Indonesia, Panama, Nicaragua, Iraq, Afghanistan—the list goes on and on. Right now there are brutal regimes being groomed for the future—Egypt, Saudi Arabia, Turkey, Pakistan, the Central Asian Republics.

U.S. Attorney General John Ashcroft recently declared that U.S. freedoms are "not the grant of any government or document, but . . . our endowment from God." (Why bother with the United Nations when God himself is on hand?) [*Applause.*]

So here we are, the people of the world, confronted with an Empire armed with a mandate from heaven (and, as added insurance, the most formidable arsenal of weapons of mass destruction in history). Here we are, confronted with an Empire that has conferred upon itself the right to go to war at will, and the right to deliver people from corrupting ideologies, from religious fundamentalists, dictators, sexism, and poverty by the age-old, tried-and-tested practice of extermination. Empire is on the move, and Democracy is its sly new war cry. Democracy, home-delivered to your doorstep by daisy cutters. Death is a small price for people to pay for the privilege of sampling this new product: Instant-Mix Imperial Democracy (bring to a boil, add oil, then bomb). [*Applause.*]

But then perhaps Chinks, Negroes, dinks, gooks, and wogs don't really qualify as real people. Perhaps our deaths don't qualify as real deaths. Our histories don't qualify as history. They never have.

Speaking of history, in these past months, while the world watched, the U.S. invasion and occupation of Iraq was broadcast on live TV. Like Osama bin Laden and the Taliban in Afghanistan, the regime of Saddam Hussein simply disappeared. This was followed by what analysts called a "power vacuum." Cities that had been under siege, without food, water, and electricity for days, cities that had been bombed relentlessly, people who had been starved and systematically impoverished by the UN sanctions regime for more than a decade, were suddenly left with no semblance of urban administration. A seven-thousand-year-old civilization slid into anarchy. On live TV.

Vandals plundered shops, offices, hotels, and hospitals. American and British soldiers stood by and watched. They said they had no orders to act. In effect, they had orders to kill people, but not to protect them. Their priorities were clear. The safety and security of Iraqi people was not their business. The security of whatever little remained of Iraq's infrastructure was not their business. But the security and safety of Iraq's oil fields were. Of course they were. The oil fields were "secured" almost before the invasion began.

On CNN and BBC the scenes of the rampage were played and replayed. TV commentators, army and government spokespersons portrayed it as a "liberated people" venting their rage at a despotic regime. U.S. Defense Secretary Donald Rumsfeld said: "It's untidy. Freedom's untidy and free people are free to commit crimes and make mistakes and do bad things." Did anybody know that Donald Rumsfeld was an anarchist? [*Laughter and applause.*] I wonder—did he hold the same view during the riots in Los Angeles following the beating of Rodney King? [*Applause.*] Would he care to share his thesis about the Untidiness of Freedom with the two million people being held in U.S. prisons right now? [*Applause.*] (The world's "freest" country has the highest number of prisoners in the world.) Would he discuss its merits with young African American men, 28 percent of whom will spend some part of their adult lives in jail? Could he explain why he serves under a president who oversaw 152 executions when he was governor of Texas? [*Applause.*] . . .

Television tells us that Iraq has been "liberated" and that Afghanistan is well on its way to becoming a paradise for women [*laughter*]—thanks to Bush and Blair, the twenty-first century's leading feminists. [*Laughter, shouts, and applause.*] In reality, Iraq's infrastructure has been destroyed. Its people brought to the brink of starvation. Its food stocks depleted. And its cities devastated by a complete administrative breakdown. Iraq is being ushered in the direction of a civil war between Shias and Sunnis. Meanwhile, Afghanistan has lapsed back into an era of anarchy, and its territory has been carved up into fiefdoms by hostile warlords.

Undaunted by all this, on the 2nd of May, Bush the Lesser launched his 2004 campaign hoping to be finally elected U.S. president. [*Laughter, shouts, and applause.*] In what probably constitutes the shortest flight in history [*laughter*], a military jet landed on an aircraft carrier [*laughter*], the U.S.S. *Abraham Lincoln* [*laughter*], which was so close to shore that, according to the Associated Press, administration officials acknowledged "positioning the massive ship to provide the best TV angle for Bush's speech, with the sea as his background instead of the San Diego coastline." [*Laughter.*] President Bush, who never served his term in the military, emerged from the cockpit in fancy dress—a U.S. military bomber jacket, combat boots, flying goggles, helmet. Waving to his cheering troops, he officially proclaimed victory over Iraq. He was careful to say that it was "just one victory in a war on terror . . . [which] still goes on."

It was important to avoid making a straightforward victory announcement, because under the Geneva Convention a victorious army is bound by the legal obligations of an occupying force, a responsibility that the Bush administration does not want to burden itself with. And also, closer to the 2004 elections, in order to woo wavering voters, another victory in the "War Against Terror" might become necessary. Syria is being fattened for the kill.

It was Herman Goering, that old Nazi, who said, "People can always be brought to the bidding of the leaders. . . . All you have to do is tell them they're being attacked and denounce the pacifists for a lack of patriotism and exposing the country to danger. It works the same way in any country."

He's right. It's dead easy. That's what the Bush regime banks on. The distinction between election campaigns and war, between democracy and oligarchy, seems to be closing fast. . . .

As soon as the war began, the governments of France, Germany, and Russia, which refused to allow a final resolution legitimizing the war to be passed in the UN Security Council, fell over each other to say how much they wanted the United States to win. President Jacques Chirac offered French airspace to the Anglo-American air force. U.S. military bases in Germany were open for business. German Foreign Minister Joschka Fischer publicly hoped for the "rapid collapse" of the Saddam Hussein regime. Vladimir Putin publicly hoped for the same. These are governments that colluded in the enforced disarming of Iraq before their dastardly rush to take the side of those who attacked it. Apart from hoping to share the spoils, they hoped Empire would honor their pre-war oil contracts with Iraq. Only the very naive could expect old Imperialists to behave otherwise.

Leaving aside the cheap thrills and the lofty moral speeches made in the UN during the run up to the war, eventually, at the moment of crisis, the unity of Western governments—despite the opposition from the majority of their people—was overwhelming.

When the Turkish government temporarily bowed to the views of 90 percent of its population, and turned down the U.S. government's offer of billions of dollars of blood money for the use of Turkish soil, it was accused of lacking "democratic principles." [*Laughter.*] According to a Gallup International poll, in no European country was support for a war carried out "unilaterally by America and its allies" higher than 11 percent. But the governments of England, Italy, Spain, Hungary, and other countries of Eastern Europe were praised for disregarding the views of the majority of their people and supporting the illegal invasion. That, presumably, was fully in keeping with democratic principles. What's it called? New Democracy? (Like Britain's New Labour?)

In stark contrast to the venality displayed by their governments, on the fifteenth of February, weeks before the invasion, in the most spectacular display of public morality the world has ever seen, more than 10 million people marched against the war on five continents. [*Shouts and applause.*] Many of you, I'm sure, were among them. They— *we*—were disregarded with utter disdain. When asked to react to the antiwar demonstrations, President Bush said, "It's like deciding, well, I'm going to decide policy based upon a focus group. The role of a leader is to decide policy based upon the security, in this case the security of the people."

Democracy, the modern world's holy cow, is in crisis. And the crisis is a profound one. Every kind of outrage is being committed in the name of democracy. It has become little more than a hollow word, a pretty shell, emptied of all content or meaning. It can be whatever you want it to be. Democracy is the Free World's whore, willing to dress up, dress down, willing to satisfy a whole range of taste, available to be used and abused at will. . . .

So, as Lenin used to ask: What Is to Be Done? [*Applause.*]

Well . . .

We might as well accept the fact that there is no conventional military force that can successfully challenge the American war machine. Terrorist strikes only give the U.S. government an opportunity that it is eagerly awaiting to further tighten its stranglehold. Within days of an attack you can bet that Patriot II would be passed. To argue against U.S. military aggression by saying that it will increase the possibilities of terrorist strikes is futile. It's like threatening Br'er Rabbit that you'll throw him into the bramble bush. Any one who's read the document called "The Project for the New American Century" can attest to that. The government's suppression of the congressional committee report on September 11th, which found that there was intelligence warning of the strikes that was ignored, also attests to the fact that, for all their posturing, the terrorists and the Bush regime might as well be working as a team. [*Applause.*] They both hold people responsible for the actions of their governments. They both believe in the doctrine of collective guilt and collective punishment. Their actions benefit each other greatly.

The U.S. government has already displayed in no uncertain terms the range and extent of its capability for paranoid aggression. In human psychology, paranoid aggression is usually an indicator of nervous insecurity. It could be argued that it's no different in the case of the psychology of nations. Empire is paranoid because it has a soft underbelly.

Its "homeland" may be defended by border patrols and nuclear weapons, but its economy is strung out across the globe. Its economic outposts are exposed and vulnerable. Already the Internet is buzzing with elaborate lists of American and British government products and companies that should be boycotted. Apart from the usual targets—Coke, Pepsi, McDonald's—government agencies like USAID, the British DFID, British and American banks, Arthur Andersen, Merrill Lynch, and American Express could find themselves under siege. [*Applause.*] These lists are being honed and refined by activists across the world. They could become a practical guide that directs the amorphous but growing fury in the world. Suddenly, the "inevitability" of the project of Corporate Globalization is beginning to seem more than a little evitable.

It would be naive to imagine that we can directly confront Empire. Our strategy must be to isolate Empire's working parts and disable them one by one. [*Applause.*] No target is too small. No victory too insignificant. We could reverse the idea of the economic sanctions imposed on poor countries by Empire and its allies. We could impose a regime of peoples' sanctions on every corporate house that has been awarded with a contract in postwar Iraq [*shouts and applause*], just as activists in this country and around the world targeted and exposed institutions of apartheid. Each one of them should be named, exposed, and boycotted. Forced out of business. [*Applause.*] That could be our response to the Shock and Awe campaign. It would be a great beginning.

Another urgent challenge is to expose the corporate media for the boardroom bulletin that it really is. We need to create a universe of alternative information. We need to support independent media like Democracy Now! [*applause*], alternative radio, South End Press.

The battle to reclaim democracy is going to be a difficult one. Our freedoms were not granted to us by any governments. They were wrested *from* them by us. And once we surrender them, the battle to retrieve them is called a revolution. [*Shouts and applause.*] It's a battle that must range across continents and countries. It must not acknowledge national boundaries but, if it is to succeed, it has to begin here. In America. The only institution more powerful than the U.S. government is American civil society. [*Applause.*] The rest of us are subjects of slave nations. We are by no means powerless, but you have the power of proximity. You have access to the Imperial Palace and the Emperor's chambers. [*Laughter and applause.*] Empire's conquests are being carried out in your name, and you have the right to refuse. You could refuse to fight. Refuse to move those missiles from the warehouse to the dock. [*Shouts and applause.*] Refuse to wave that flag. [*Applause.*] Refuse the victory parade. [*Continued applause.*]

You have a rich tradition of resistance. You need only read Howard Zinn's *A People's History of the United States* [*applause*] to remind yourself of this.

Hundreds of thousands of you have survived the relentless propaganda you have been subjected to, and are actively fighting your own government. In the ultra-patriotic climate that prevails in the United States, that's as brave as any Iraqi or Afghan or Palestinian fighting for his or her homeland.

If you join the battle, not in your hundreds of thousands, but in your millions, you will be greeted joyously by the rest of the world. And you will see how beautiful it is to be gentle instead of brutal, safe instead of scared. Befriended instead of isolated. Loved instead of hated.

I hate to disagree with your president. Yours is by no means a great nation. But you could be a great people.

History is giving you the chance.

Seize the time.

Thank you. [*Shouts and applause.*]

A list of full-text sources for the speeches in this anthology appears below, including each speech's first publication and other places where it can readily be found. I have also noted the text (or audio recording) from which each excerpt in this anthology is derived. Entries are presented in chronological order.

Full-text versions of many of the speeches in this anthology are available online. Google, including Google Books, is an excellent place to start one's research, particularly for nineteenth-century, nongovernmental speeches. The Library of Congress's online resources are also superb; many of the speeches delivered before Congress can be found there. See *A Century of Lawmaking for a New Nation: U.S. Congressional Documents and Debates, 1774–1875,* http://memory.loc.gov/ammem/amlaw/, and THOMAS, http://thomas.loc.gov/. The former includes speeches through 1875 published in, successively, the *Annals of Congress,* the *Register of Debates,* the *Congressional Globe,* and the *Congressional Record.* The latter includes speeches published since 1989 in the *Congressional Record.* Speeches published between 1875 and 1989 can be accessed online through fee-based ·services such as ProQuest and HeinOnline.

The speeches in this anthology have been edited in varying degrees: La Follette, Vallandigham, Schurz, Debs, Robeson, and O'Hare (less than 25 percent excerpted); Long, Bryan, Norris, Parker, Storey, Lincoln, Thomas, and Wright (less than 50 percent excerpted); Roy, Lindbergh, Kennedy, and Sumner (more than 50 percent excerpted); Byrd, and Hamer (more than 75 percent excerpted); Norton, Du Bois, King, Kerry, Chisholm, Lee, Obama, Chomsky, and McCarthy (more than 95 percent excerpted).

## Mexican-American War

### Theodore Parker

Text from the first publication, *A Sermon of War, Preached at the Melodeon, on Sunday, June 7, 1846* (Boston: Little, Brown, 1846). A slightly revised version appears in Parker, *Speeches, Address, and Occasional Sermons* (Boston: W. Crosby and H. P. Nichols, 1852), 46–80, and in *The Collected Works of Theodore Parker* (London: Trübner, 1863), 1–31. The speech is included in a recent anthology, *American Sermons: The Pilgrims to Martin Luther King, Jr.* (New York: Literary Classics of the United States, 1999), 600–29.

### Charles Sumner

Text from *The Works of Charles Sumner,* vol. 1 (Boston: Lee and Shepard, 1870), 374–82. The speech was first printed in the *Liberator,* February 19, 1847, 30.

### Abraham Lincoln

Text from Remarks on January 12, 1848, Cong. Globe, 30th Cong., 1st Sess., appendix 93–95 (1847–48). The speech also appears in *The Collected Works of Abraham Lincoln,* ed. Roy Prentice Basler, vol. 1 (New Brunswick: Rutgers University Press, 1953), 432.

## Civil War

### Clement Vallandigham

Text from Remarks on January 14, 1863, Cong. Globe, 37th Cong., 3d sess., appendix 52–60. The speech also appears in *The Record of Hon. C. L. Vallandigham on Abolition, the Union, and the Civil War* (Cincinnati: J.

Walter, 1863), 168–204; and *Speeches, Arguments, Addresses, and Letters of Clement L. Vallandigham* (New York: J. Walter, 1864), 418–53.

### Alexander Long

Text from Remarks on April 8, 1864, Cong. Globe, 38th Cong., 1st Sess. 1499–1503 (1863–64). The speech also appears in Long, *The Present Condition and Future Prospects of the Country: Speech of Hon. Alexander Long, of Ohio, Delivered in the House of Representatives, April 8, 1864* (N.p.: n.d., 1864).

## Spanish-American War and Philippine Insurrection

### Moorfield Storey

Text from *A Civilian's View of the Navy: Lecture Delivered September 6, 1897* (Washington, D.C.: Government Printing Office, 1897).

### Charles Eliot Norton

Text from "Professor Norton's View," *Boston Evening Transcript,* June 8, 1898, 12. The speech also appears in *Letters of Charles Eliot Norton*, ed. Sara Norton and M. A. De Wolfe Howe, vol. 2 (Boston: Houghton Mifflin, 1913), 261–69.

Text of "Counterfeit Patriotism" from "Half Free; Half Despotic . . . Prof. Norton Presides Today at Ashfield," *Boston Evening Transcript,* August 21, 1902, 2.

### Carl Schurz

Text from *Speeches, Correspondence and Political Papers of Carl Schurz,* ed. Frederic Bancroft, vol. 6 (New York: G. P. Putnam's Sons, 1913), 77–120. The speech was originally printed as *The Policy of Imperialism: Address by Hon. Carl Schurz at the Anti-Imperialist Conference in Chicago, October 17, 1899* (Chicago: American Anti-imperialistic League, 1899). It is also included in a recent anthology, *American Speeches: Political Oratory from Abraham Lincoln to Bill Clinton* (New York: Library of America, 2006), 161–94.

## World War I

### William Jennings Bryan

Text from *America and the European War: Address by William Jennings Bryan at Madison Square Garden, New York City, February 2, 1917* (New York: Emergency Peace Federation, 1917).

### George Norris

Text from Remarks on April 4, 1917, 55 Cong. Rec. pt. 1 S212–14 (1917).

### Robert M. La Follette

Text from Remarks on April 4, 1917, 55 Cong. Rec. pt. 1 S223–36 (1917). The speech was also published as *War with Germany: Speech of Hon. Robert M. La Follette of Wisconsin in the Senate of the United States, Wednesday, April 4, 1917* (Washington, D.C.: Government Printing Office, 1917).

### Kate Richards O'Hare

Text from *Socialism and the World War* (St. Louis: Frank P. O'Hare, 1919). The speech also appears in O'Hare, *Selected Writings and Speeches,* ed. Philip S. Foner and Sally M. Miller (Baton Rouge: Louisiana State University Press, 1982).

*Eugene V. Debs*

Text from Exhibit 8, U.S. District Court, Northern District of Ohio, Eastern Division, Cleveland, Criminal Case Files, Case 5057, Record Group 21. For a virtually identical version, see *Eugene V. Debs, Plaintiff in Error, vs. the United States of America, in Error to the District Court of the United States for the Northern District of Ohio* (Washington, D.C.: Judd and Detweiler, 1918), 194–215.[1] The speech was reprinted in various Socialist Party publications over the next few years: *Eugene V. Debs' Canton Speech* (Chicago: Socialist Party of the United States, 1918); *The Debs Case: A Complete History* (Chicago: National Socialist Office, 1919), 2–31; *The Debs White Book* (Girard, Kansas: Appeal to Reason, 1920), 3–36; *Debs and the War* (Chicago: National Office Socialist Party, n.d.), 5–33.[2]

## World War II

*Norman Thomas*

Text from "War or Democracy," radio address over NBC and Mutual (September 21, 1940), Norman Thomas Papers, Manuscripts and Archives Division, The New York Public Library, Astor, Lenox and Tilden Foundations. The speech also appears in *Norman Thomas on War: An Anthology,* ed. Bernard K. Johnpoll (New York: Garland, 1974).

*Richard Wright*

Text from "Not My People's War," *New Masses,* June 17, 1941, 8–9, 12.

*Charles Lindbergh*

Text from *Des Moines Register,* September 12, 1941, 6, with audience reactions inserted by the editor based on a sound recording: "Address on U. S. Neutrality—Charles Lindbergh," in *Great Speeches of the 20th Century,* vol. 4 ([Santa Monica, CA?]: Rhino Word Beat, 1991). Early versions of the speech can be found in the Charles Augustus Lindbergh Papers, Manuscripts and Archives, Yale University Library.

## Korean War

*Paul Robeson*

Text from news release, "Address by Paul Robeson: Welcome Home Rally for Paul Robeson, New York, June 19: Auspices of the Council on African Affairs," Council on African Affairs, New York, [1949]. The speech also appears in a pamphlet, *For Freedom and Peace: Address at Welcome Home Rally, New York, June 19, 1949* (New York: Council on African Affairs, 1949); and as "For Freedom and Peace," in *Paul Robeson Speaks: Writings, Speeches, Interviews, 1918–1974,* ed. Philip S. Foner (New York: Brunner/Mazel, 1978), 201–11.

*W. E. B. Du Bois*

Text from "The Campaign of 1950," speech, Series 2, Box 200, folder 19, W. E. B. Du Bois Papers (MS 312), Special Collections and University Archives, University of Massachusetts Amherst Libraries. This typescript contains handwritten and typed revisions by Du Bois, and is probably closer than any other version to the speech as Du Bois actually delivered it. The first published version of Du Bois's speech appears to be "I Speak for Peace," leaflet, Series 7, W. E. B. Du Bois Papers (MS 312). I have noted the more significant differences between the typescript and leaflet versions of the speech. The printed version, with minor corrections, is reprinted in *W. E. B. Du Bois Speaks: Speeches and Addresses,* vol. 2, ed. Philip S. Foner (New York: Pathfinder Press, 1970), 287–91.

## Vietnam War

### Martin Luther King Jr.

Text from a transcription posted online by the Martin Luther King, Jr., Research and Education Institute, http://mlk-kpp01.stanford.edu/index.php/encyclopedia/documentsentry/doc_beyond_vietnam. I made slight, nonmaterial revisions to the transcription based on an audio recording of the speech, "Beyond Vietnam," in *A Call to Conscience: The Landmark Speeches of Dr. Martin Luther King, Jr.* (audio CD) (New York: Intellectual Properties Management, in association with Warner Books, 2001). A print version of the CD is also available (same title, same publication information). The speech also appears in *Landmark Speeches on the Vietnam War,* ed. Gregory Allen Olson (College Station: Texas A&M University Press, 2010), 93–113.

### Eugene J. McCarthy

Text transcribed from a sound recording: Remarks of December 2, 1967, to the Conference of Concerned Democrats, Eugene J. McCarthy Papers, University of Minnesota Libraries, Special Collections and Rare Books, McCarthy Historical Project, Oral History Project (Miscellaneous), 711-, T.6 (Box 27-GU 185) (dicta-belt). The speech is published in *The Year of the People* (Garden City, N.Y.: Doubleday, 1969), app. 5, 284–89.

### Robert F. Kennedy

Text transcribed from an audio recording posted at Kansas State University's Landon Series Lectures website, http://ome.ksu.edu/lectures/landon/past.html. An edited version of the speech appears in "Conflict in Vietnam and at Home," in *Issues 1968* (Lawrence: University Press of Kansas, 1968), 29–45, and in *The Landon Lectures on Public Issues,* ed. Diana B. Carlin and Meredith A. Moore (Lanham, Md.: University Press of America, 1990), 55–66, and transcriptions can be found online: "Remarks of Robert F. Kennedy at the University of Kansas [*sic*; Kennedy spoke at Kansas State University, not the University of Kansas], March 18, 1968," John F. Kennedy Presidential Library and Museum, http://www.jfklibrary.org/Research/Ready-Reference/RFK-Speeches/R emarks-of-Robert-F-Kennedy-at-the-University-of-Kansas-March-18–1968.aspx (accessed October 25, 2011); "Conflict in Vietnam and at Home," Kansas State University, http://ome.ksu.edu/lectures/landon/trans/Kennedy68.html (accessed October 25, 2011).

### Shirley Chisholm

Text from Remarks on March 26, 1969, 115 Cong. Rec. H7765 (1969).

### Fannie Lou Hamer

Text transcribed from a sound recording, *Vietnam Moratorium Rally at UCB October Sixty-Nine* (Los Angeles: Pacifica Radio Archive), record # BB2435. The recording can also be heard on *Collected Speeches of Fannie Lou Hamer* (North Hollywood, Cal.: Pacifica Radio Archive, 2000), and at the end of the October 7, 2002, War and Peace Report, archived on the Democracy Now website: http://www.democracynow.org/2002/10/7/fannie_lou_hamer_a_ memorial_broadcast. An alternative transcription of the speech has recently been published as "To Make Democracy a Reality," in *The Speeches of Fannie Lou Hamer: To Tell It Like It Is* (Jackson: University Press of Mississippi, 2011), 98–103.

### John F. Kerry

Text from *Legislative Proposals Relating to the War in Southeast Asia: Hearings Before the Committee of Foreign Relations, United Senate, Ninety-Second Congress, First Session on S. 376, S. 974, S.J. Res. 82, S.J. Res. 89, S. Cong. Res. 17, S. Res. 62, S. Res. 66; April 20, 21, 22, and 28, May 3, 11, 12, 13, 25, 26, and 27, 1971* (Washington, D.C.: Government Printing Office, 1971). The speech also appears in John Kerry et al., *The New Soldier* (New York: Collier Books, 1971). An audio version of Kerry's speech is available through the Pacifica Radio Archive: *John Kerry's Senate Testimony,* record # BC0019.10 (Los Angeles: Pacifica Radio Archive). A video of the speech was aired on C-Span on August 26, 2004: *Vietnam War Hearing 1971* program # 181065–1, available at http://www.c-spanvideo.org/program/181065-1.

## War on Terror

*Barbara Lee*

Text from Remarks on September 14, 2001, 147 Cong. Rec. H5672 (2001). The original, shorter version of the speech—the one Lee actually delivered—appears at 147 Cong. Rec. H 5642–43 (2001).

*Barack Obama*

Text from Barack Obama, "Weighing the Costs of Waging War in Iraq," *Hyde Park Herald,* October 30, 2002, 4. Obama's Senate campaign website, on which the speech was posted, is no longer maintained, but can be accessed through the Internet Archive: see "Obama: I'm Not Against Wars but . . . ," press release, October 23, 2002, http://web.archive.org/web/20021217033809/www.obamaforillinois.co m/news.shtml (accessed September 28, 2011). This version of the speech contains numerous typographical errors. An Obama presidential campaign ad that includes a fourteen-second video clip of the speech is posted on YouTube: http://www.youtube.com/watch?v = AUV69LZbCNQ (accessed September 29, 2011). Audio of the same clip accompanies a transcript of the speech on the NPR website: http://www.npr.org/templates/story/story.php? storyId = 99591469. The speech also appears in two anthologies of Obama's speeches: *Barack Obama: Speeches on the Road to the White House,* ed. Maureen Harrison and Steve Gilbert (Carlsbad, Cal.: Excellent Books, 2009); *Power in Words: The Stories Behind Barack Obama's Speeches, from the State House to the White House,* ed. Mary Frances Berry and Josh Gottheimer (Boston : Beacon Press, 2010), 1–9.

*Noam Chomsky*

Text transcribed from a sound recording, "Why Iraq?," which is available online at the Harvard University Institute of Politics website, http://www.iop.harvard.edu/Multimedia-Center/All-Videos/WHY-IRAQ2 (streaming video) (accessed September 29, 2011), and from Turning Tide Productions, Wendell, Mass.

*Robert Byrd*

Text from "On the Brink of War," Remarks on February 12, 2003, 149 Cong. Rec. S2268–71.

## Epilogue: The Globalization of Dissent

*Arundhati Roy*

Text transcribed from the DVD *Instant-Mix Imperial Democracy: Buy One, Get One Free* (Oakland, Cal.: AK Press, 2004). The speech also appears in *An Ordinary Person's Guide to Empire* (Cambridge, Mass.: South End Press, 2004), 41–68.

While the rhetorical devices described and illustrated below are not unique to the genre of American antiwar speeches, they are found in abundance there, and so the vast majority of examples below are taken from speeches in this anthology. Here I follow the classical model that distinguishes clearly between tropes and figures or schemes—one that remained substantially intact in most rhetoric handbooks through at least 1960.[1] I avoid classifications and subclassifications as much as possible—first, because many such classifications are debatable, and second, because an excessive classification scheme will not serve my purpose. The reader should nevertheless be mindful that each of the entries below is a summary, and that each trope, figure, or scheme has spawned a body of scholarship in its own right.[2]

*Tropes*

**Metaphor**. An implicit comparison between two things that, though fundamentally different, have a common feature. Metaphors usually appear in the form X *is* Y.

> War is hell.
> > —General William Tecumseh Sherman, as quoted by Charles Eliot Norton during the Spanish-American War

> Military glory—that *attractive rainbow* that rises in showers of blood, that *serpent's eye* that charms to destroy.
> > —Abraham Lincoln, during the Mexican-American War

**Simile**. An explicit comparison between two things that, though fundamentally different, have a common feature. Similes usually appear in the form X *is like* Y.

> His mind, tasked beyond its power, is running hither and thither, *like an ant on a hot stove,* finding no position on which it can settle down, and be at ease.
> > —Abraham Lincoln on President Polk's vacillating justifications for the Mexican-American War; Lincoln changed his simile in his published speech, which has Polk's mind running "like some tortured creature on a burning surface"

> If we will but make the right choice, we will be able to speed up the day, all over America and all over the world, when justice will roll down *like waters,* and righteousness *like a mighty stream.*
> > —Martin Luther King Jr., encouraging listeners to oppose the Vietnam War

Closely related to the tropes of metaphor and simile are the tropes of **allegory** and **parable**. For our purposes, an allegory is a continued or sustained metaphor. A parable can be thought of as a condensed allegory, and though both tropes are often used to teach lessons, a parable is often associated specifically with religious or moral instruction.

> A crown of stars is on that giant's head, some glorious with flashing, many-colored light; some bloody red; some pale and faint, of most uncertain hue. His right hand lies folded in his robe; the left rests on the Bible's opened page, and holds these sacred words—All men are equal, born with equal rights from God. The old man says to the young, "Brother, BEWARE!" and Alps and Rocky Mountains say "BEWARE!" That stripling giant, ill-bred and scoffing, shouts amain: "My feet are red with the Indian's blood; my hand has forged the negro's chain. I am strong; who dares assail me? I will drink his blood, for I have made my covenant of lies and leagued with hell for my support. There is no Right, no Truth; Christianity is false, and God a name." His left hand rends those sacred scrolls, casting his Bibles underneath his feet, and in his right he brandishes the negro-driver's whip—crying again—"Say, who is God, and what is Right." And all his mountains echo

RIGHT. But the old Genius sadly says again: "Though hand join in hand, the wicked shall not prosper." The hollow tomb of Egypt, Athens, Rome, of every ancient State, with all their wandering ghosts, replies "AMEN."
—Theodore Parker on Uncle Sam during the Mexican-American War

Go out into an agricultural community; you may select the best that you have. Pick out two men living side by side on farms, with nothing but an imaginary line between their land. Pick out two farmers, who are honest and well meaning, and, to make it as strong as you can, take two belonging to the same church and sitting in adjoining pews under the same interpretation of the Scripture. Suppose they try to preserve peace on the European plan, how will they go at it? One of them will go to town and get the best gun he can find, and then he will go to the newspaper office and put in a notice like this: "I love peace, and I have no thought of trespassing on my neighbor's rights, but I am determined to protect my own rights and defend my honor at any cost, and I now have the best gun that money will buy, and it is only fair that my neighbor should know that if he ever interferes with my rights I will blow his head off, in a neighborly way."
—William Jennings Bryan on militarism during World War I

**Metonymy**. The substitution of an attribute of a thing for the thing itself.

What union is there between Russia and Poland, between Austria and Hungary, between England and Catholic Ireland, where the *sword* and the *bayonet* for centuries have been employed?
—Alexander Long, suggesting that cultural differences between the North and South during the Civil War could not be resolved militarily

*Pulpit* and *press* lent themselves to the task of exalting war.
—Charles Eliot Norton on religious leaders' and publishers' support of the Spanish-American War

We are going into war upon the command of *gold*.
—George Norris on the financial interests behind the U.S. entrance into World War I

In the first example, Long substitutes two tools of war (swords and bayonets) for the war itself. In the second example, Norton substitutes the location from which members of the clergy speak for the clergymen themselves, and the physical presses by which journalists' articles are published for the journalists themselves. The second example also illustrates how common a rhetorical device metonymy actually is, even though its technical name is obscure. Consider, for example, another extremely common metonymic term in politics: "White House." Though it can be used to describe the presidential mansion, it is often used as a substitute for the word "president," as in "the White House announced today the end of peace negotiations."[3] In the third example, Norris substitutes a possession of the wealthy (gold) for the wealthy themselves.

**Periphrasis**. Substitution of a descriptive word or phrase for a name, or of a name for a quality associated with the name.

The ground is muddy with the *life of men*.
—Theodore Parker, referring to blood

[T]hey had to be worried about the Sandinistas who were "only two days marching time from Texas," the *brave cowboy* told us.
—Noam Chomsky on President Ronald Reagan's attempt to manufacture political fear

The literal meaning of the Greek term *periphrasis* is "roundabout of words," and, as José Antonio Mayoral has pointed out, this trope can be used in practically an unlimited number of ways, because almost every word can be substituted by several words that convey its meaning.[4] Euphemism (e.g., "he passed away" instead of "he died" ) is a common type of periphrasis.

**Personification** or **Prosopopoeia**. Investing abstractions or inanimate objects with human qualities or abilities.

The waves which mercifully *receive* the dead and *wash away* the stains of conflict, the ocean air which blows away the smoke of battle, make us forget that in the sea fight also there are horrors and that the sailor knows hardship and suffering at least as great as the soldier's.
—Moorfield Storey, reminding students at the Naval War College in Newport of the costs of naval war

> It is the *object* of the sword to cut and cleave asunder, but never to unite.
> —Alexander Long, arguing that the Civil War would destroy the Union

In the first example, the "waves" are given the human qualities of "receiving" and "washing away," and the ability to accomplish both "mercifully." In the second example, the "sword" is given the human qualities of intention, agency, or purpose. Incidentally, these examples might also have been used to illustrate other tropes as well. One might say that "stains of conflict" is an example of periphrasis, because it is a descriptive way of signifying "blood." One might say that the word "sword" in the second example exemplifies metonymy, because it serves as a substitute for the word "armies" or the phrase "military power" and is a central attribute of both. Likewise, the Theodore Parker example used above to illustrate allegory and parable is also a good illustration of personification. When, in Parker's case, mountains and tombs begin to speak, the trope of personification is obviously at work.

**Hyperbole**. The use of exaggeration or overstatement for the purpose of emphasis or heightened effect.

> There is not one single vestige of the Constitution remaining; every clause and every letter of it has been violated.
> —Alexander Long on the Civil War's effect on civil liberties

> [M]ore glorious than any page of history that has yet been written will be that page that will record our nation's claim to the promise made to the peacemaker.
> —William Jennings Bryan on the United States's opportunity to serve as a neutral mediator during World War I

**Litotes**. A figure of speech that substitutes what is meant by denying its opposite; the use of understatement.

> War is not an enterprise lightly to be undertaken.
> —Robert F. Kennedy, during the Vietnam War

> Deterrence is not a slight matter.
> —Noam Chomsky, arguing that the Iraq War would stimulate the proliferation of weapons of mass destruction as a deterrent against U.S. adventurism

> This is no small conflagration that we contemplate. This is no simple attempt to defang a villain.
> —Robert C. Byrd, arguing that preemptive war with Iraq would represent a revolutionary change in U.S. foreign policy

Again, note how rhetorical devices work together. In the first example, Kennedy inverts the natural or usual word order. Instead of saying "war is not an enterprise to be undertaken lightly," he says "war is not an enterprise lightly to be undertaken." This is the *figure* or *scheme* known as *anastrophe,* and is considered in the subsection on figures and schemes, below.

**Rhetorical Question** or **Erotema**. The asking of a question, not for the purpose of eliciting a response, but for asserting or denying something obliquely.

> And now, sir, can this war continue? Whence the money to carry on? Where the men? Can you borrow? From whom? Can you tax more? Will the people bear it?
> —Clement Vallandigham, during the Civil War

> Shall we say the odds are too great? Shall we tell them the struggle is too hard? Will our message be that the forces of American life militate against their arrival as full men, and we send our deepest regrets? Or will there be another message—of longing, of hope, of solidarity with their yearnings, of commitment to their cause, whatever the cost?
> —Martin Luther King Jr., urging his listeners to practice "nonviolent coexistence" during the Vietnam War

> [H]ow do you ask a man to be the last man to die in Vietnam? How do you ask a man to be the last man to die for a mistake?
> —John Kerry, implying that the war in Vietnam was a mistake

What could be more destabilizing? What could be more world shattering? What could be more future shattering? What could be more unwise than this kind of uncertainty, particularly in a world where globalism has tied the vital economic and security interests of so many nations so closely together?
—Robert C. Byrd on the administration's refusal to rule out a nuclear attack on Iraq

Why bother with the United Nations when God himself is on hand?
—Arundhati Roy, mocking a governmental official for invoking God during the Iraq War

Because the most persuasive speakers are those who speak *with* their audience instead of *to* it, the rhetorical question can be an effective method of inviting members of the audience to participate in the speech, as opposed to merely observing it. In addition, as the examples above show, speakers, when particularly impassioned, will often rope together rhetorical questions to great effect. Thus, rhetorical questions can often be found in a speech's *peroration,* or closing. What can be more effective than a rhetorical question?

**Irony**. The use of a word or phrase in such a way as to express the opposite of what is being said.

September 11 gave the pretext, the domestic politics effects the timing, and the strategy has been working quite brilliantly.
—Noam Chomsky, arguing that the war in Iraq served as a calculated distraction from more important domestic problems

Death is a small price for people to pay for the privilege of sampling this new product: Instant-Mix Imperial Democracy (bring to a boil, add oil, then bomb).
—Arundhati Roy on the importance of Iraqi lives during the War on Terror

**Paradox**. A statement that appears contradictory, but nevertheless contains a measure of truth.

I can imagine no greater calamity to this country than a successful war.
—Moorfield Storey, lamenting the military buildup prior to the Spanish-American War

The more complete our success, the greater will be our disgrace.
—Carl Schurz, arguing that the Philippine-American War was a war of criminal aggression

To conquer a peace.
—The "jargon of the day," as quoted by Robert F. Kennedy

It became necessary to destroy the town in order to save it.
—An anonymous American commander speaking of the town in Ben Tre, Vietnam, as quoted by Robert F. Kennedy

I define paradox as a type of trope in which the meaning of a term is transferred or used in an unintuitive sense. In the first two examples above, it is paradoxical that "success" can be "calamitous" or "disgraceful." Like rhetorical questions, paradox requires a type of silent audience participation. Each listener must unlock the riddle and decide for himself exactly what the sentence means. As a technique that facilitates audience participation, paradox is therefore particularly effective.

*Figures* and *Schemes*

Figures and schemes, as noted above, involve a rearrangement of the expected order of words or of sentences. Scholars of rhetoric have identified dozens of classes and subclasses of such schemes. Schemes of words are formed by adding, subtracting, or transposing letters or syllables of words—and are usually the province of poets, who may need to rhyme particular words or use a certain number of syllables in a given line. Such schemes are rarely seen in antiwar speeches. Schemes of sentences operate in the same way as schemes of words, but the operations of addition, subtraction, and the like are on a larger textual unit—a clause or a sentence, as opposed to an individual word. For example, one can omit a word in a sentence (*asyndeton*) in a similar way to how one can omit a syllable in a word (*aphaeresis* and *apocope*).

*Schemes of Balance*

Schemes of balance are formed by "balancing" clauses in some way.

**Parallelism**. Similarity of structure in a pair or series of related words.

> No language can tell the tale; no brain can grasp the horrors and no soul can sense the degradation that has come to the women of war scarred Europe.
> —Kate Richards O'Hare on the effect of World War I on European women

> The entire future rests upon our shoulders. It depends upon our action, our courage, and our intelligence.
> —Martin Luther King Jr. on the importance of opposing the Vietnam War

> I've heard several comments from people that was talkin' about "with the people, for the people, and by the people." Bein' a black woman from Mississippi, I learned that long ago that that's not true. It's "with a handful, for a handful, by a handful."
> —Fannie Lou Hamer on inequality before and during the Vietnam War

The parallelism in these three examples is obvious. As Corbett observes, the principle of parallelism is "one of the basic principles of grammar and rhetoric."[5] In each example, nouns are matched with nouns, verbs with verbs, and prepositional phrases with prepositional phrases. As these examples also show, parallel phrases ordinarily appear in groups of three.

A special case of parallelism is **isocolon**, or the scheme in which parallel elements are similar in length, as well as in structure. One can see isocolon most easily in the third example, when the three prepositional phrases "with the people, for the people, and by the people" are yoked to the three other prepositional phrases "with a handful, for a handful, by a handful," which contain exactly the same number of syllables. One might say that the second example exemplifies isocolon as well, because the phrases "our action," "our courage," and "our intelligence" contain the same number of words. The similarity here is not as strong, however, as in the third example, because "action" and "courage" have two syllables, while "intelligence" has three.

**Antithesis**. Juxtaposition of contrasting ideas, often in parallel structure.

> The glory of war is not the light of Heaven, but the flames of hell.
> —Charles Eliot Norton on the Spanish-American War

> The master class has always declared the war; the subject class has always fought the battles.
> —Eugene V. Debs, on World War I

> War is Big Business and a business immensely profitable to a few, but of measureless disaster and death of dream to the many.
> —W. E. B. Du Bois on the Korean War

In each of these three examples, the speaker juxtaposes contrasting ideas in parallel structure. In the first, "Heaven" is juxtaposed with "hell"; in the second, "master class" is juxtaposed with "subject class," and "declared the wars" with "fought the battles"; and in the third, Du Bois makes a common juxtaposition between "few" and "many." In all examples, one sees evidence of *parallelism* at work. In the third, one observes *alliteration* as well. Finally, in the first and second, one also sees *isocolon*.

*Schemes of Unusual or Inverted Word Order* (Hyperbaton)

**Hyperbaton** is a deviation from the correct word order.[6] It is an effective rhetorical device because it surprises an audience and thereby gains its attention. Some examples are *parenthesis, apposition,* and *anastrophe.*

**Parenthesis**. The addition of a verbal unit that interrupts the normal syntactical flow of the sentence.

> The enormous expenditures lavished upon this war, now extending to fifty millions of dollars—we have been told recently on the floor of the Senate that they were near one hundred millions—are another reason for its cessation.
> —Charles Sumner on the Mexican-American War

I am concerned, as I believe most Americans are concerned, that we are acting as if no other nation existed, against the judgment and desires of neutrals and our historic allies alike.
—Robert F. Kennedy on the Vietnam War

Parenthesis is a common literary device. Its traditional purpose was to amplify a statement, but a more descriptive and modern purpose is to give an utterance "an additional nuance of meaning and tinge of emotional coloring."[7] In Corbett's view, parenthesis is an effective rhetorical device because "for a brief moment, we hear the author's voice, commenting, editorializing." This voice, this interruption, invests the sentence with "an emotional charge that it would otherwise not have."[8] In the first example above, the speaker uses parenthesis to amplify his point. In the second, the speaker uses parenthesis to editorialize, or color, his statement.

**Apposition**. Placing side by side two coordinate elements, the second of which serves as an explanation or modification of the first.

This is a year of choice, a year when we choose not simply who will lead us, but where we wish to be led.
—Robert F. Kennedy on the year 1968

I am pleading for the cause of American honor and self-respect, American interests, American democracy—aye, for the cause of the American people against an administration of our public affairs which has wantonly plunged this country into an iniquitous war; which has disgraced the Republic by a scandalous breach of faith to a people struggling for their freedom whom we had used as allies; which has been systematically seeking to deceive and mislead the public mind by the manufacture of false news; which has struck at the very foundation of our Constitutional government by an executive usurpation of the war-power; which makes sport of the great principles and high ideals that have been and should ever remain the guiding star of our course; and which, unless stopped in time, will transform this government of the people, for the people and by the people into *an imperial government* cynically calling itself republican—*a government in which the noisy worship of arrogant might will drown the voice of right;* which will impose upon the people a burdensome and demoralizing militarism, and which will be driven into *a policy of wild and rapacious adventure* by the unscrupulous greed of the exploiter—*a policy always fatal to democracy.*
—Carl Schurz on the Spanish-American War

In these examples, one sees how appositive phrases can be used artfully on the one hand, and "wrought by disorder"[9] on the other. In the second example, Schurz uses the scheme of apposition twice, and I have italicized each instance of the scheme for clarity of reading.

**Anastrophe**. Deviation from the natural order of words or phrases.

*"Auferre, trucidare, rapere, falsis nominibus, Imperium; atque, ubi solitudinem faciunt, Pacem appellant"*: With lying names, they call spoliation, murder, and rapine, Empire; and when they have produced the desolation of solitude, they call it *Peace.*
—Charles Sumner, quoting Tacitus, on the Mexican-American War

With grief, with anxiety must the lover of his country regard the present aspect and the future prospect of the nation's life.
—Charles Eliot Norton on the Spanish-American War

How beautiful upon the mountains are the feet of him that bringeth good tidings, that publisheth peace.
—Moorfield Storey, quoting Isaiah 52:7 (King James Version)

The "unnatural" wordings in these examples are memorable and, in some cases, extremely enduring. The first quote has survived almost two thousand years: it was originally spoken by the Caledonian leader Calgacus, referring to the practices of the Roman army. It was recorded by the Roman senator and historian Tacitus around the turn of the first century CE. Charles Sumner used the quote in his antiwar speech in 1846, and Robert F. Kennedy used a loose translation of it in his antiwar speech in 1968 ("They made a desert, and called it peace"). The third quote was used by Charles Russell, Lord Chief Justice of England and Wales, in his 1896 address on international arbitration to the American Bar Association, an address Russell ended by urging his listeners to work in harmony with Britain for the "Peace of the World." Moorfield Storey quoted

Russell Russell (and Isaiah) the following year in his address on militarism just before the outbreak of the Spanish-American War.

## Schemes of Omission

**Ellipsis**. Deliberate omission of a word or words which are readily implied by the context.

> It was not so dark as now; the nation never so false.
> —Charles Eliot Norton on the Spanish-American War

> War results in vengeance of the dead on the survivors, and the vanquished on the victors.
> —Arnold Toynbee as quoted by Eugene J. McCarthy during the Vietnam War

The scheme of ellipsis produces an economy of language. As is usual with schemes of omission, one may more easily see the effect of the device when the omitted words are reinserted. The first quote above, for example, would produce a phrase that still works, but is nevertheless less artful: "It was not so dark as *it is* now, *and* the nation *was* never so false." The second quote sounds unnecessarily wordy in its longer form: "War results in vengeance of the dead on the survivors, *and also results in vengeance of* the vanquished on the victors."

**Asyndeton**. Deliberate omission of conjunctions between a series of related words, phrases, or clauses.

> There writhe the wounded; men who but few hours before were poured over the battle-field a lava-flood of fiery valor—fathers, brothers, husbands, sons.
> —Theodore Parker, imagining a battlefield during the Mexican-American War

> War is demoralizing, uncivilizing, corrupting.
> —Moorfield Storey on the Spanish-American War

The scheme of asyndeton produces "clear-cut brevity,"[10] "celerity of speech,"[11] a "hurried rhythm."[12] As such, asyndeton is often, though certainly not always, used in a speech's *peroration,* or closing. There, more than in other parts of a speech, a speaker often wants to rouse the audience by quickening the pace. Aristotle, in fact, concluded his *Rhetoric* with an example of asyndeton: "I have done. You have heard me. The facts are before you. I ask for your judgment."[13]

## Schemes of Repetition

**Alliteration**. Repetition of initial or medial consonants in two or more adjacent words.

> We should not seek to hide our *b*lunder behind the smoke of *b*attle.
> —Robert M. La Follette, referring to the failure of the United States to maintain neutrality in World War I

> We can escape war and fascism by the vigor of a *d*ynamic *d*emocracy *d*edicated to the conquest of poverty and the brotherhood of men.
> —Norman Thomas on World War II

> The nation stands "at the *b*rink of *b*attle"; Congress is "*s*eemingly *s*tunned"; terrorists occupy "*d*ark *d*ens" in "*d*evastated" Afghanistan; the United States has "*m*assive *m*ilitary *m*ight"; the war in Iraq is a "*d*estabilizing and *d*angerous . . . *d*ebacle."
> —Robert C. Byrd on the War on Terror

> You have the *p*ower of *p*roximity. You have access to the Im*p*erial *P*alace and the Em*p*eror's chambers.
> —Arundhati Roy, urging Americans to oppose the Iraq War

Alliteration is an extremely common and well-known device in politics, poetry, and popular culture. The scheme is often found in slogans and advertising campaigns as well. As with all rhetorical devices, too much alliteration becomes tiresome. After that, it can only be used for comedy.

**Anaphora**. Repetition of the same word or group of words at the beginning of successive clauses.

> *We Negroes have no issues to settle* in Mexico. *We Negroes have no issues to settle* in Brazil. *We Negroes those have no issues to settle* in Martinique. *We Negroes have no issues to settle* in the Argentine. *We Negroes have no issues to settle* in the Azores or the Cape Verde Islands. And, above all, *we Negroes have no issues to settle* in Dakar.
> —Richard Wright during the Korean War

> We are on the verge of war, but *it is not yet too late* to stay out. *It is not too late* to show that no amount of money, or propaganda, or patronage can force a free and independent people into war against its will. *It is not yet too late* to retrieve and to maintain the independent American destiny that our forefathers established in this new world.
> —Charles Lindbergh on World War II

> And *if we will only make the right choice,* we will be able to transform this pending cosmic elegy into a creative psalm of peace. *If we will make the right choice,* we will be able to transform the jangling discords of our world into a beautiful symphony of brotherhood. *If we will but make the right choice,* we will be able to speed up the day, all over America and all over the world, when justice will roll down like waters, and righteousness like a mighty stream.
> —Martin Luther King Jr. on the Vietnam War

Anaphora is one of the most used, and overused, rhetorical schemes. As Corbett writes, because the scheme helps establish a marked rhythm in the sequence of clauses, anaphora "is usually reserved for those passages where the author wants to produce a strong emotional effect."[14]

Anaphoric clauses are usually ordered in increasing importance. Speakers tend to place the most important, abstract, profound, or otherwise memorable phrases at the end of a passage. Rhetoricians called this crescendo "climax," and it is effective because audiences tend to remember the most recent words or ideas to which they are exposed.

**Epistrophe**. Repetition of the same word or group of words at the end of successive clauses.

> The eyes of the North are full of *cotton;* they see nothing else, for a web is before them; their ears are full of *cotton,* and they hear nothing but the buzz of their mills; their mouth is full of *cotton* . . . [T]he talent of the North is blinded, deafened, gagged with its own *cotton.*
> —Theodore Parker on the Mexican-American War

> There's a lot of people that said: "Well, forget about *politics.*" But baby, what we eat is *politics.* And I'm not gon' forget no *politics.*
> —Fannie Lou Hamer on the Vietnam War

Note the similarity of these two antiwar quotes to two quotes far more famous:

> When I was a *child,* I spake as a *child,* I understood as a *child,* I thought as a *child:* but when I became a man, I put away childish things.
> —1 Corinthians 13:11 (King James Version)

> I'll have *my bond!* Speak not against *my bond!*
> I have sworn an oath that I will have *my bond!*
> —*The Merchant of Venice,* 3.3.3–4

Epistrophe is the inverse of anaphora. It is an uncommon scheme, but its strength and rhythm make it memorable. Whenever one hears an instance of epistrophe, one can fairly conclude that the speaker did not employ the device by accident. It is simply not a speech pattern that occurs in everyday discourse.

# NOTES

## Introduction

1. Three recent examples are Harvey A. Averch, *The Rhetoric of War: Language, Argument, and Policy During the Vietnam War* (Lanham, Md.: University Press of America, 2002); John Collins and Ross Glover, *Collateral Language: A User's Guide to America's New War* (New York: New York University Press, 2002); Shawn J. Parry-Giles, *The Rhetorical Presidency, Propaganda, and the Cold War, 1945–1955* (Westport, Conn.: Praeger, 2002).

2. For broad studies, see Peter Brock, *Pacifism in the Twentieth Century* (Syracuse: Syracuse University Press, 1999); Charles F. Howlett, *The American Peace Movement: References and Resources* (Boston: G. K. Hall, 1991); John Lofland, Victoria L. Johnson, and Pamela Kato, *Peace Movement Organizations and Activists in the U.S.: An Analytic Bibliography* (New York: Haworth Press, 1991); Lawrence Wittner, *Rebels Against War: The American Peace Movement, 1933–1983* (Philadelphia: Temple University Press, 1984); Charles DeBenedetti, *The Peace Reform in American History* (Bloomington: Indiana University Press, 1980); Charles Chatfield, *Peace Movements in America* (New York: Schocken Books, 1973); Joseph R. Conlin, *American Anti-War Movements* (Beverley Hills: Glencoe Press, 1968). Narrower antiwar studies are also readily available. Many are part of the Syracuse Studies on Peace and Conflict Resolution series. For the War of 1812, the Mexican-American War, and the Spanish-American War, see Samuel Eliot Morison, Frederick Merk, and Frank Burt Freidel, *Dissent in Three American Wars* (Cambridge, Mass.: Harvard University Press, 1970). For World War I, see Frances H. Early, *A World Without War: How U.S. Feminists and Pacifists Resisted World War I* (Syracuse: Syracuse University Press, 1997); Charles DeBenedetti, *Origins of the Modern American Peace Movement, 1915–1929* (Millwood, N.Y.: KTO Press, 1978). For World War II, see Justus D. Doenecke, *The Battle Against Intervention, 1939–1941* (Malabar, Fla.: Krieger, 1997); Ruth Sarles, *A Story of America First: The Men and Women Who Opposed U.S. Intervention in World War II*, ed. Bill Kauffman (Westport, Conn.: Praeger, 2003). For the Korean War, see Robbie Lieberman, *The Strangest Dream: Communism, Anticommunism,* and the U.S. Peace Movement 1945–1963 (New York: Syracuse University Press, 2000). For the Vietnam War, see Charles Chatfield, *The American Peace Movement: Ideals and Activism* (New York: Twayne, 1992); Charles DeBenedetti, *An American Ordeal: The Antiwar Movement of the Vietnam Era* (Syracuse: Syracuse University Press, 1990). For the Cold War, see John Lofland, *Polite Protesters: The American Peace Movement of the 1980s* (Syracuse: Syracuse University Press, 1993). For the Persian Gulf War, see Robert A. Hackett, *Engulfed: Peace Protest and America's Press During the Gulf War: An Occasional Paper* (New York: Center for War, Peace, and the News Media, New York University, 1993).

3. William Safire, ed., *Lend Me Your Ears: Great Speeches in History* (New York: W. W. Norton, 1992), 7–8. Though Safire's anthology provides the most striking illustration of this point, he is certainly not alone in his skewed distribution of prowar and antiwar speeches. Robert Torricelli and Andrew Carroll's *In Our Own Words* (New York: Kodansha International, 1999) goes slightly further in documenting dissent by including six speeches critical of a war alongside twelve in favor of one. Brian MacArthur includes some rousing antiwar sentiment in *The Penguin Book of Historic Speeches* (London: Viking, 1995) and *The Penguin Book of Twentieth-Century Speeches* (London: Penguin, 1993), but both volumes are ultimately similarly skewed away from antiwar views. In *My Fellow Americans: The Most Important Speeches of America's Presidents, from George Washington to George W. Bush* (Naperville, Ill.: Sourcebooks, 2003), Michael Waldman arguably had his hands tied, for though commanders in chief have occasionally warned of war's dangers, they are not normally prone to criticizing their own actions.

4. Indeed, the only true antiwar speech anthology that this editor could locate is *We Accuse: A Powerful Statement of the New Political Anger in America, as Revealed in the Speeches Given at the 36-Hour "Vietnam Day" Protest in Berkeley, California* (Berkeley: Diablo Press, 1965). The following anthologies include antiwar speeches alongside other forms of antiwar literature: Robert Mann, *Wartime Dissent in America: A History and Anthology* (New York: Palgrave Macmillan: 2010) (speeches, pamphlets, and essays); Murray Polner and Thomas E. Woods Jr., *We*

*Who Dared to Say No to War: American Antiwar Writing from 1912 to Now* (New York: Basic Books, 2008) (speeches, articles, poetry, book excerpts, and political cartoons).

5. In *My Fellow Americans,* Waldman includes President George W. Bush's October 7, 2001, war message: "We will not waver; we will not tire; we will not falter; and we will not fail." This excellent speech is set to become a standard alongside President George H. W. Bush's analogous 1991 address, which Torricelli and Carroll include in *In Our Own Words.*

6. See note 3, above.

7. Michael Cromartie, ed., *Peace Betrayed? Essays on Pacifism and Politics* (Washington, D.C.: Ethics and Public Policy Center, 1989); Andrew W. Cordier and Kenneth L. Maxwell, eds., *Paths to World Order* (New York: Columbia University Press, 1967).

8. Patrick Mannix, *The Rhetoric of Antinuclear Fiction: Persuasive Strategies in Novels and Films* (Lewisburg: Bucknell University Press, 1992).

9. Edward Morrow, ed., *Cry Out: Poets Protest the War* (New York: George Braziller, 2003); Lorrie Goldensohn, *Dismantling Glory: Twentieth-Century Soldier Poetry* (New York: Columbia University Press, 2003); Ruth Harriet Jacobs, ed., *We Speak for Peace* (Manchester, Conn.: KIT, 1993); Michael Harrison and Christopher Stuart-Clark, eds., *Peace and War: A Collection of Poems* (Oxford: Oxford University Press, 1989).

10. J. W. Fenn, *Levitating the Pentagon: Evolutions in the American Theatre of the Vietnam War Era* (Newark: University of Delaware Press, 1992); Ingrid Rogers, ed., *Swords into Plowshares: A Collection of Plays About Peace and Social Justice* (Elgin, Ill.: Brethren Press, 1983).

11. D. J. R. Bruckner, *Art Against War: 400 Years of Protest in Art* (New York: Abbeville Press, 1984); James D. Sullivan, *On the Walls and in the Streets: American Poetry Broadsides from the 1960s* (Urbana: University of Illinois Press, 1997). *On the Walls* includes a chapter on "Ephemeral Broadsides of the Antiwar Movement."

12. John Whiteclay Chambers II and David Culbert, eds., *World War II, Film, and History* (New York: Oxford University Press, 1996); Mannix, *Rhetoric of Antinuclear Fiction;* Robert Hughes, Stanley Brown, and Carlos Clarens, eds., *Films of Peace and War* (New York: Grove Press, 1962); Andrew Buchanan, *Peace Through Film* (London: Peace Book Co., 1940).

13. Various artists, *Celebrate Peace: Songs of Peace and Freedom,* produced by Craig Taubman, 2003, Sweet Louise Music; Marianne Philbin, ed., *Give Peace a Chance: Music and the Struggle for Peace* (Chicago: Chicago Review Press, 1983); Student Peace Union, ed., *Songs for Peace: 100 Songs of the Peace Movement* (New York: Oak, 1966).

14. Michael True, *An Energy Field More Intense than War: The Nonviolent Tradition and American Literature* (Syracuse: Syracuse University Press, 1975).

15. Stewart O'Nan, ed., The *Vietnam Reader* (New York: Anchor Books, 1998). O'Nan includes an "Oral History Boom" chapter, and also documents antiwar films, songs, memoirs, essays, and photographs. He does not include speeches.

16. John Boardman Whitton, *Propaganda Towards Disarmament in the War of Words* (Dobbs Ferry, N.Y.: Oceana, 1964).

17. Howard Zinn, *Artists in Times of War* (New York: Seven Stories Press, 2003); Cynthia Jane Wachtell, "War No More: The Emergence of American Anti-War Literature from the Civil War Through World War I" (Ph.D. thesis, Harvard University, 1998); True, *Energy Field.*

18. The best, and perhaps only, example of a previous American antiwar speech anthology is *We Accuse.* However, it is also starkly partisan and severely limited in scope. In *Teach-ins, U.S.A.: Reports, Opinions, Documents* (New York: Praeger, 1967), Louis Menashe and Ronald Radosh compile, among other things, Vietnam-era teach-ins.

19. See William H. Rehnquist, *All the Laws but One: Civil Liberties in Wartime* (New York: Knopf, 1998).

20. Statement by Senator Robert F. Kennedy, March 18, 1968, Robert F. Kennedy Papers, RFK Presidential Campaign Papers, 1968, Speech Writers' Division, Box 5, File: Vietnam, John Fitzgerald Kennedy Library, Boston, Mass.

21. Paul Potter, "The Incredible War," *National Guardian,* April 29, 1965.

22. Edward P. J. Corbett and Robert J. Connors, *Classical Rhetoric for the Modern Student,* 4th ed. (New York: Oxford University Press, 1999), 17.

23. James Jasinski, *Sourcebook on Rhetoric: Key Concepts in Contemporary Rhetorical Studies* (Thousand Oaks, Cal.: Sage, 2001), 81, notes that "some scholars view the classical canons as a 'paradigm' for all communications theory; hence, they remain present in contemporary thought as an often implicit organizing framework." Jasinski also comments, however, that "shifts in the nature of rhetorical studies seem to require some rather drastic rethinking of the five traditional canons."

24. I have little to say in this anthology about the three classical canons of arrangement, memory, and delivery. While arrangement is mentioned occasionally in various introductions to individual speeches (e.g., by making reference to a given speech's introduction, body, or conclusion), it makes little sense to focus much on this canon given that this anthology is one of excerpts, not entire speeches.

The historical treatment of the canon of memory mostly involves how to memorize one's speech, and is therefore inapplicable here. Finally, the canon of delivery is more properly considered in books about voice, diction, or acting.

25. Walter Watson, "Invention," in *Encyclopedia of Rhetoric*, ed. Thomas O. Sloane (Oxford: Oxford University Press, 2001), 389; see also Corbett and Connors, *Classical Rhetoric*, 17.

26. See Corbett and Connors, *Classical Rhetoric*, 17–19.

27. Ibid., 493.

28. These are highly simplified definitions, and, indeed, each concept has spawned a significant body of scholarship in its own right. I believe that these are fair approximations that well serve this book's pedagogical purpose; and in any case, the definitions that I use make up a useful shorthand for the analysis summarized in this introduction and fleshed out throughout this book. Sloane's *Encyclopedia of Rhetoric* is a good resource for further examination of each of these concepts. It not only provides a comprehensive history of each of these rhetorical concepts, but includes a great deal of bibliographical material as well.

29. Lane Cooper, *The Rhetoric of Aristotle* (New York: Appleton-Century-Crofts, 1932), xvii.

30. Gary Orren, "Gore vs. Bush: Why It's All Greek to Me," *Kennedy School of Government Bulletin* (Autumn 2000): 36–39.

31. "Nothing to Say," in Corbett and Connors, *Classical Rhetoric*, 82.

32. The definition belongs to W. Martin Bloomer, "Topics," in Sloane, *Encyclopedia of Rhetoric*, 779.

33. Corbett and Connors, *Classical Rhetoric*, 84–130.

34. *Ars Rhetorica* 1359b–1360a. This and all subsequent citations to the *Ars Rhetorica* are from the W. Rhys Roberts translation, in Aristotle, *Rhetoric* (New York: Modern Library, 1954).

35. Ibid.

36. Ibid., 1358b, 1366b–1368a. Somewhat unfortunately for the beginning student, this type of discourse goes by many names. At various times it has been called epideictic, demonstrative, declamatory, or panegyrical oratory. Whatever it is called, though, ceremonial oratory stands in contrast to deliberative (aka political) and judicial (aka legal) oratory. Deliberative and judicial oratory have many names as well. Deliberative discourse is sometimes called political, hortative, or advisory oratory, while judicial discourse is sometimes called legal or forensic oratory.

37. The distinction between ceremonial discourse and deliberative discourse is well established. Aristotle classified all rhetoric into three classes, the first two being ceremonial and deliberative and the third being forensic. *Ars Rhetorica* 1358b.

38. *Ars Rhetorica* 1358b, 1366b–1368a.

39. The other "special topic," or what Aristotle calls "War and Peace" (e.g., the extent of a country's military strength), is pervasive in antiwar literature, but not particularly profound. Aristotle's analysis concerns *power* or, in other words, whether one country is stronger than another. Put still another way, Aristotle implied that the central inquiry in antiwar speeches is simply "Can we win?" and not "Should we fight?" While there are at least two excellent examples of antiwar speakers in this anthology whose antiwar speeches are largely about whether the war was winnable (Clement Vallandigham during the Civil War and Charles Lindbergh during World War II), and while Aristotle's proposed framework is therefore a useful analytical tool for those speeches, I argue that such a power-driven analysis is not the best and should certainly not be the exclusive manner of dissecting American antiwar speeches over the last century and a half. This is because the country's military strength over this time has been truly overwhelming, and had antiwar speakers been limited to discussing the relative strength of their country, they would probably have come to the paradoxical conclusion that the United States should have been fighting *more* wars, not less. I therefore devote little space in this anthology to Aristotle's topic of "War and Peace."

40. For the changes in American antiwar poetry over the course of over two hundred years, see Lorrie Goldensohn, ed., *American War Poetry: An Anthology* (New York: Columbia University Press, 2006).

41. Robert F. Kennedy, *RFK: Selected Speeches*, ed. Edwin O. Guthman and C. Richard Allen (New York: Viking, 1993), 270.

42. Compare Lincoln's final speech as it appears in the *Congressional Record* with Lincoln's handwritten manuscript, p. 37. A digital facsimile of Lincoln's handwritten speech can be found in the Abraham Lincoln Papers at the Library of Congress, http://memory.loc.gov/ammem/alhtml/malhome.html.

43. Martin Luther King Jr., "The Domestic Impact of the War in Vietnam, Address Delivered at the National Labor Leadership Assembly for Peace," November 11, 1967 (New York: Clergy and Laymen Concerned About Vietnam), National Labor Leadership Assembly and Peace Collection, State Historical Society of Wisconsin, Madison, Wis., Box 2, folder 9, 67III1–004. An audio recording of this address can be found in the Martin Luther King Jr. Papers, 1950–1968, Martin Luther King Jr. Center for Nonviolent Social Change, Inc., Atlanta, Ga., T-58, 67III1–000.

44. William Hazlitt, "Character of Lord Chatham," in *Political Essays, with Sketches of Public Characters* (London: William Hone, 1819), 358.

45. See Corbett and Connors, *Classical Rhetoric,* 126.

46. *Rhetorica ad Herennium,* trans. H. Caplan (London: Heinemann, 1954), 1.3, quoted in Wolfgang G. Müller, "Style," in Sloane, *Encyclopedia of Rhetoric,* 745.

47. Corbett and Connors, *Classical Rhetoric,* 21.

48. Cicero, *De Oratore* 1.142 ("inventa vestire atque ornare oratione").

49. Müller, "Style," 752.

50. Jeff Zeleny, "Testing the Water, Obama Tests His Own Limits," *New York Times,* December 24, 2006, A1.

51. Mike Lupica, "Mario Sez: It's About Charisma, Money and . . . Predicts '08 Prez Race Will Be More of the Same," *New York Daily News,* February 14, 2007, 6.

52. "Time to Walk the Walk," editorial, *New York Daily News,* May 11, 2007.

53. "Obama Sets Out on His Mission to Excite and Unite a Divided Nation," *Independent* (London), February 10, 2007.

54. Corbett and Connors, *Classical Rhetoric,* 21.

55. My discussion of these classical elements largely follows the discussion that appears in Corbett and Connors, *Classical Rhetoric,* and Sloane, *Encyclopedia of Rhetoric.*

56. On these styles, see Müller, "Style," in Sloane, *Encyclopedia of Rhetoric* (following *Rhetorica ad Herennium*).

57. See ibid.

58. Quintilian, *Institutio Oratoria* 12.10.61.

59. Müller, "Style.

60. See *We Accuse* and *Teach-ins, U.S.A.*

61. Quintilian, *Institutio Oratoria* 12.10.61.

62. The definition belongs to Corbett and Connors, *Classical Rhetoric,* 379.

63. Ibid.

64. Ibid.

65. John Stuart Mill, *On Liberty and Other Essays* (New York: Oxford University Press, 1991), 40.

66. *U.S. v. Debs,* 249 U.S. 211, 212 (1919).

67. Ray Ginger, *The Bending Cross: A Biography of Eugene Victor Debs* (New York: Russell and Russell, 1968), 356.

68. Wayne S. Cole, *Charles A. Lindbergh and the Battle Against American Intervention in World War II* (New York: Harcourt Brace Jovanovich, 1974), 132, citing "'Copperheads' Back Lindy on Anti-war Stand," *Chicago Daily Tribune,* June 5, 1941, 1.

69. William J. Clinton, Remarks at Memorial Service for Eugene McCarthy (January 14, 2006). See Frederick J. Frommer, "Clinton Eulogizes Sen. Eugene McCarthy," *Associated Press,* Saturday, January 14, 2006, 3:48 p.m.; John Files, "Hundreds Honor McCarthy as Man Who Changed History," *New York Times,* January 15, 2006. See also "Eugene

McCarthy (1916–2005): The Legacy of the Former Senator and Anti-War Presidential Candidate," *Democracy Now!,* January 18, 2006, http://www.democracynow.org/article.pl?sid=06/01/18/1442236 (accessed June 6, 2009).

70. *The Trial of Hon. Clement L. Vallandigham by a Military Commission* (Cincinnati: Rickey and Carroll, 1893).

71. *U.S. v. Debs,* 249 U.S. at 214.

72. The government argued in court that Du Bois's organization was a "principal of a foreign agent." Under the McCarran Act, such organizations were required to register with the U.S. government.

73. James Darsey, "The Legend of Eugene Debs: Prophetic Ethos as Radical Argument," *Quarterly Journal of Speech* 74 (1988): 435.

74. In the War on Terror chapter, three of the four speeches concern the war in Iraq. One speech, by Barbara Lee, concerns the war in Afghanistan.

## Chapter 1

1. Seymour V. Connor and Odie B. Faulk, *North America Divided: The Mexican War, 1846–1848* (New York: Oxford University Press: 1971), 182. Connor and Faulk's calculation presumably includes Mexico's loss of Texas, which was annexed by the United States in 1845 but whose independence Mexico refused to recognize until the end of the Mexican-American War.

2. Inaugural Address, Washington, D.C. (March 4, 1845).

3. Ibid.

4. "Annexation," *United States Magazine and Democratic Review* 17 (July 1845): 5–10.

5. Armando C. Alonza, *Tejano Legacy: Ranchers and Settlers in South Texas, 1734–1900* (Albuquerque: University of New Mexico Press, 1998).

6. James K. Polk, Message to Congress, Washington, D.C., May 11, 1846, Cong. Globe, 29th Cong., 1st Sess. 782–83 (1846).

7. Cong. Globe, 29th Cong., 1st Sess. 795 (1846).

8. Ibid., 804.

9. U.S. Department of Veterans Affairs, "Fact Sheet: America's Wars," May 2011, *www.va.gov/opa/publications/factsheets/fs_americas_wars.pdf* (accessed September 8, 2011).

10. Ibid.; see also Robert E. May, "Mexican War," in *The Oxford Companion to United States History,* ed. Paul S. Boyer (Oxford: Oxford University Press, 2001). This document is available on Oxford Reference Online (by subscription).

11. Timothy J. Henderson, *A Glorious Defeat: Mexico and Its War with the United States* (New York: Hill and Wang, 2007), 179.

12. May, "Mexican War."

13. John H. Schroeder, *Mr. Polk's War* (Madison: University of Wisconsin Press, 1973), 113.

14. Robert C. Albrecht, *Theodore Parker* (New York: Twayne, 1971), 72.

15. Ibid.

16. American National Biography Online, s.v. "Parker, Theodore" (by Henry Warner Bowden). Parker's controversial religious views also contributed to his alienation from other Unitarian clergymen. See, for example, Albrecht, *Theodore Parker*, 56–60, and Dean Grodzins, *American Heretic: Theodore Parker and Transcendentalism* (Chapel Hill: University of North Carolina Press, 2002), 129–74.

17. Albrecht, *Theodore Parker*, 72.

18. Henry Steele Commager, *Theodore Parker* (Boston: Beacon Press, 1960), ix.

19. Grodzins, *American Heretic*, 43.

20. Protecting escaped slaves was a federal criminal offense punishable by up to six months in prison and no more than one thousand dollars. Adjusted for inflation, this amount is equivalent to over twenty-five thousand 2010 dollars.

21. The Kansas Crusade generally refers to the agitation that culminated with Kansas entering the Union as a free state in early 1861.

22. Commager, *Theodore Parker*, 199.

23. American National Biography Online, s.v. "Parker, Theodore." Grodzins puts the number significantly lower, writing that "50,000 listened to [Parker] lecture every year, in lyceums from Maine to Illinois." Regardless of the exact number, Grodzins agrees that an astounding number of people heard Parker. In the 1850s, Grodzins notes, weekly audiences in Boston numbered nearly three thousand—almost 2 percent of the city's total population—and thousands more on both sides of the Atlantic bought his published sermons and addresses. Grodzins, *American Heretic*, ix.

24. Octavius Brooks Frothingham, *Theodore Parker: A Biography* (Boston: James R. Osgood, 1874), 340–42.

25. Theodore Parker, *The Effect of Slavery on the American People: A Sermon Preached at the Music Hall, Boston, on Sunday, July 4, 1858* (Boston: W. L. Kent, 1858), 5. Herndon was a great, perhaps even fawning, admirer of Parker, and once wrote the Reverend: "May I say you are my ideal—strong, direct, energetic, charitable." Herndon sent Parker copies of his own speeches: "If you see any expressions in these pieces which are yours in essence, remember you impressed the hard steel upon a softer plate." On Herndon and Parker's friendship, *see* Commager, *Theodore Parker*, 261–66.

26. David Herbert Donald, *Lincoln's Herndon* (New York: Knopf, 1948), 128. For more discussion of Parker's influence on Lincoln speech, with respect to ideas as well as words, see Garry Wills, *Lincoln at Gettysburg: The Words That Remade America* (New York: Simon and Schuster, 1992), 105–20.

27. Schroeder, *Mr. Polk's War*, 115.

28. Ibid.

29. Fuller to the *New York Tribune*, November or December 1847, in *The Writings of Margaret Fuller*, ed. Mason Wade (New York: Viking, 1941), 427, quoted in Schroeder, *Mr. Polk's War*, 116.

30. For an brief overview of these individuals' opinions, see Schroeder, *Mr. Polk's War*, 116–19.

31. Ibid., 115.

32. See the appropriate forms of prayer for that service by the present Bishop of Oxford, in Jay's Address before the American Peace Society, in 1845. [Footnote by Parker.]

33. Sir Walter Scott, *Marmion*.

34. The 1852 edition Parker's speech of the speech changed "unspoken and insupportable" to "unspoken and unspeakable." The revised language is an example of *polyptoton*, a rhetorical trope formed by the repetition of words derived from the same root but having different endings.

35. Lord Byron, *Childe Harold*.

36. Ibid.

37. *Form of Prayer and Thanksgiving to Almighty God*: "O Lord God of Hosts. . . ." [Footnote by Parker (abridged).]

38. In a note to the speech as printed in his *Collected Works*, Parker identifies the man as Charles Sumner.

39. "Abolitionist Charles Sumner Excoriates Two Senate Colleagues on the Issue of 'Bloody Kansas,'" in *Lend Me Your Ears: Great Speeches in History*, ed. William Safire (New York: W. W. Norton, 1992), 278–82.

40. James Shepherd Pike *First Blows of the Civil War: The Ten Years of Preliminary Conflict in the United States, from 1850 to 1860* (New York: American News, 1879), 338–39.

41. Charles Sumner, "The True Grandeur of Nations," in *The Works of Charles Sumner* (Boston: Lee and Shepard, 1870), 1:5–132.

42. Charles Sumner, "Slavery and the Mexican War," in *Works*, 1:333–51.

43. Charles Sumner, "Withdrawal of American Troops from Mexico," in *Works*, 1:374–82.

44. "The speech of Mr. Sumner was characterized by his usual eloquence," the *Boston Daily Whig* editorialized on February 8, 1947. But, the *Whig* continued, Sumner's arguments "disappointed the expectations of his warmest friends."

45. *Liberator*, February [19?], 1847. The speech also appears in the Boston *Daily Courier*, February 6, 1847.

46. Sumner, "Withdrawal."

47. Sumner, *Works*, 374.

48. *Liberator,* February [19?], 1847.

49. *Boston Daily Whig,* February 5, 1847.

50. Adam Smith, *The Theory of Moral Sentiments,* ed. D. D. Raphael and A. L. Macfie (Oxford: Oxford University Press, 1979), 10.

51. Adam Smith, *Lectures on Rhetoric and Belles Lettres,* ed. J. C. Bryce (New York: Oxford University Press, 1983), 25.

52. Life of Josiah Quincy, Jr., p. 320. [Footnote by Sumner.]

53. Tacitus, Agricola, c. 30. [Footnote by Sumner.] Note that Robert F. Kennedy uses the same Tacitus quote in a different translation: "They made a desert, and called it 'peace.'" See the Vietnam War chapter, below.

54. Sumner is referring to Daniel Webster.

55. James D. Richardson, ed., *A Compilation of the Messages and Papers of the Presidents, 1789–1897* (Washington, D.C.: GPO, 1897), 4:542. Polk's December 7, 1857, address can also be found in the Cong. Globe, 30th Cong., 1st Sess. 4–12 (1847–48).

56. For an illustration of the Whigs' strategy, see the House proceedings of January 3, 1848. George Ashmun of Massachusetts moved to amend a resolution of thanks to General Taylor to read "in a war unnecessarily and unconstitutionally begun by the President of the United States." Remarks on January 3, 1848, Cong. Globe, 30th Cong., 1st Sess., appendix 95 (1847–48). The measure, supported by Lincoln, passed in the House along party lines by a margin of 85 to 81 before being rejected by the Senate.

57. Richardson, *Compilation,* 4:534.

58. Abraham Lincoln, "'Spot' Resolutions in the United States House of Representatives," in *The Collected Works of Abraham Lincoln,* ed. Roy P. Basler, vol. 1 (New Brunswick: Rutgers University Press, 1953), 421. The text of Lincoln's December 27, 1848, resolutions as printed in the *Congressional Globe* was considerably altered from the original. Cong. Globe, 30th Cong., 1st Sess. 64 (1847–48).

59. General Taylor "had, more than once, intimated to the War Department that, in his opinion, no such movement [of American troops] was necessary to the defense or protection of Texas." See Lincoln, *Collected Works,* 1:422.

60. Lincoln to William H. Herndon, Washington, January 8, 1848, in *Collected Works,* 1:430. For more on Lincoln's efforts, see David Herbert Donald, *Lincoln* (New York: Simon and Schuster, 1995), 123.

61. For example, Donald W. Riddle argues that Lincoln was "the politician following party policy because he believed that to do so would be of advantage to the party." *Congressman Abraham Lincoln* (Urbana: University of Illinois Press, 1957; repr., Westport, Conn.: Greenwood Press, 1979), 55. Citations are to the 1979 edition.

62. *Sangamo Journal* (Illinois), June 4, 1846, quoted in Albert J. Beveridge, *Abraham Lincoln, 1809–1858,* 2 vols. (Boston: Houghton Mifflin, 1928), 1:381; see also Earl Schenck Miers, ed., *Lincoln Day by Day: A Chronology, 1809–1865,* 3 vols. (Washington, D.C.: Lincoln Sesquicentennial Commission, 1960), 1:273.

63. Lincoln reminds William H. Herndon of this fact in his letter dated February 1, 1848, in *Collected Works,* 1:447.

64. Mark E. Neely Jr., "War and Partisanship: What Lincoln Learned from James K. Polk," *JISHS* 74 (Autumn 1981): 205. Compare Lincoln's comment with Parker's ("I know the Mexicans are a wretched people; wretched in their origin, history, and character"), above.

65. Lincoln, "Speech in United States House of Representatives: The War with Mexico," in *Collected Works,* 1:432.

66. Lincoln to William H. Herndon, Washington, February 15, 1848, in *Collected Works,* 1:451–52.

67. Lincoln's position, like that of many Whigs, was that the necessity and constitutionality of the war have "nothing to do" with the supplies question. Lincoln to Herndon, Washington, February 1, 1848, in *Collected Works,* 1:447.

68. Donald, *Lincoln,* 123. For Lincoln's desire to give a distinguished antiwar speech, see Lincoln to Herndon, Washington, January 8, 1848 ("I expect to make [a speech] within a week or two, in which I hope to succeed well enough to wish you to see it).

69. For excerpted newspaper responses favorable to Lincoln's speech, see Herbert Mitgang, ed., *Lincoln, as They Saw Him: His Life and Times from the Original Newspaper Documents of the Union, the Confederacy, and Europe* (New York: Fordham University Press, 2000), 54–55. For a short summary of those favorable responses, see Donald, *Lincoln,* 124. For the full text of pro-Lincoln responses, see the *Illinois Journal* (formerly the *Sangamo Journal* of Springfield, Illinois), February 3, 1848 (quoting the *Missouri Republican*) and the *Rockford Forum* (Illinois), January 19, 1848 (quoting the *Baltimore Patriot*).

70. John Jamieson of Missouri held that during war, the House should refrain from questioning "whether we are in the right or wrong." Of those, like Lincoln, who did question the nation's course, Jamieson stated, "If they take that ground they will be entombed so deep, and the clods will be so heavy upon them, that they will never be resurrected until the very last trump from the archangel." Remarks on January 18, 1848, Cong. Globe, 30th Cong., 1st Sess. 190 (1847–48). For more on Jamieson and others' reaction to Lincoln's speech, see Riddle, *Congressman Abraham Lincoln,* 50–51.

71. Remarks of John L. Robinson of Indiana on January 18, 1848, Cong. Globe, 30th Cong., 1st Sess.

196 (1847–48) (Lincoln "never ventured to tell the people of Springfield district, Illinois, when electioneering for his seat, that the war was unnecessary and unconstitutional; but after he got here he could venture to declare it!").

72. Remarks of Howell Cobb on February 2, 1848, Cong. Globe, 30th Cong., 1st sess. 289 (1847–48) ("I ask [Lincoln and his party] to say what particular spot of territory it was that the army first placed their foot upon, that constituted the commencement of this 'unnecessary and unconstitutional' war?").

73. The congressional reaction to Lincoln's speech is described fully in Riddle, *Congressman Abraham Lincoln*, 49–51.

74. The newspapers cited below were largely Democratic newspapers, most of which were likely opposed to Lincoln anyway, on other grounds. Journalistic objectivity, even as an ideal, did not exist in Lincoln's time.

75. *Belleville (Illinois) Advocate*, March 2, 1848, quoted in Mitgang, *As They Saw Him*, 56.

76. *Illinois State Register*, January 28, 1848, quoted in Mitgang, *As They Saw Him*, 55.

77. *Illinois State Register*, January 14, 1848, quoted in Riddle, *Congressman Abraham Lincoln*, 36.

78. *Illinois State Register*, February 25, 1948, quoted in Riddle, *Congressman Abraham Lincoln*, 37. The *State Register* was quoting the *Peoria Press*.

79. *Belleville (Illinois) Advocate*, March 2, 1848, quoted in Riddle, *Congressman Abraham Lincoln*, 37–38.

80. *Illinois State Register*, March 10, 1848, quoted in Mitgang, *As They Saw Him*, 57.

81. *Peoria Democratic Press*, May 17, 1848, quoted in Mitgang, *As They Saw Him*, 58.

82. For a complete list of references to the Mexican-American War in the Lincoln-Douglas debates, see the index in the *Collected Works* (186).

83. Abraham Lincoln, "Autobiography Written for John L. Scripps" (ca. June 1860), in Lincoln, *Collected Works*, 4:66.

84. Remarks on February 23, 1863, Cong. Globe, 37th Cong., 3d Sess. appendix 2 174 (1863).

85. On June 11, 1863, Vallandigham supporters presented President Lincoln with a series of resolutions adopted by the Democratic state convention at Columbus on June 11 (a convention that had nominated the exiled Vallandigham for governor). "Matthew Birchard, et al. to Abraham Lincoln, June 26, 1863 (Committee from Ohio Democratic Convention presents resolutions on behalf of Clement Vallandigham)," Abraham Lincoln Papers, Library of Congress, transcribed and annotated by the Lincoln Studies Center, Knox College, Galesburg, Ill. The abridged text of these resolutions, along with Lincoln's complete response, can be found in Lincoln, *Collected Works*, 6:300–301. One resolution states, in part, "When gentlemen of high standing & extensive influence including your Excellency opposed, in the discussions before the people, the policy of the Mexican War, were they 'warring upon the Military' & did this 'give the Military constitutional jurisdiction to lay hands upon them?'" See also Donald, *Lincoln*, 420. Lincoln offered the following public response: "I dislike to waste a word on a merely personal point; but I must respectfully assure you that you will find yourselves at fault should you ever seek for evidence to prove your assumption that I opposed, in discussions before the people, the policy of the Mexican war.'" Lincoln, *Collected Works*, 6:302. Arguably, Lincoln is correct that he did not oppose the "policy" of the Mexican War, in the sense that he did not oppose how the war was being carried out. Lincoln did, though, oppose President Polk's decision to start the war in the first place.

86. *This Fiery Trial: The Speeches and Writings of Abraham Lincoln*, ed. William E. Gienapp (Oxford: Oxford University Press, 2002), xv.

87. James Engell, *The Committed Word* (University Park: Pennsylvania State University Press, 1999), 143–46.

88. Chauncey M. Depew, *My Memories of Eighty Years* (New York: Charles Scribner's Sons, 1922), 57–58, quoted in Engell, *Committed Word*, 145.

89. Engell, *Committed Word*, 145.

90. Ibid., 142–46. See generally chap. 9, "Lincoln's Language, and Ours."

91. Carl Sandburg, *Abraham Lincoln: The Prairie Years and the War Years* (New York: Harcourt, 1954), 96.

92. William Lee Miller, *Lincoln's Virtue: An Ethical Biography* (New York: Knopf, 2002), 169.

93. Again, the exception proves the rule: Charles Sumner's antiwar speech, above, is a ennobling address in an otherwise vicious genre.

94. See Congressional Globe, 1st sess. 30th Cong., page 64. [Footnote by Lincoln]

95. In his original draft, Lincoln wrote, "His mind, tasked beyond its power, is running hither and thither, like an ant on a hot stove, finding no position, on which it can settle down, and be at ease." For Lincoln's softening of his tone, see Beveridge, *Abraham Lincoln*, 1:430.

## Chapter 2

1. U.S. Department of Veterans Affairs, "Fact Sheet: America's Wars," May 2011, www.va.gov/opa/publications/factsheets/fs_americas_wars.pdf (accessed September 8, 2011).

2. Brian Holden Reid, "American Civil War," in *The Oxford Companion to Military History*, ed. Richard Holmes (New York: Oxford University

Press, 2001). This document is available on Oxford Reference Online (by subscription).

3. Judith Schenck Koffler and Bennett L. Gershman, "The New Seditious Libel," 69 *Cornell Law Review* 816 (1984): 829n53.

4. Ibid.

5. James Parker Hall, "Free Speech in Wartime," 21 *Colum. L. Rev.* 526 (1921): 527–28.

6. Lincoln to Erastus Corning, June 12, 1863, in *Abraham Lincoln: Speeches and Writings, 1859–1865,* ed. Don E. Fehrenbacher (New York, 1989), 456–57.

7. Ibid.

8. U.S. Const. Art. I, Sec. 6 ("The Senators and Representatives . . . shall in all cases, except treason, felony and breach of the peace, be privileged from arrest during their attendance at the session of their respective Houses, and in going to and returning from the same; and for any speech or debate in either House, they shall not be questioned in any other place").

9. Frank L. Klement, *The Limits of Dissent: Clement L. Vallandigham and the Civil War* (Lexington: University Press of Kentucky, 1970; repr., New York: Fordham University Press, 1998), 144. Citations are to the 1970 edition. The Copperheads tried to reappropriate their name by wearing a lapel pin made from the Goddess of Liberty on the copper penny to symbolize their defiance of efforts to suppress their antiwar rhetoric. James M. McPherson, foreword to Jennifer L. Weber, *Copperheads: The Rise and Fall of Lincoln's Opponents in the North* (Oxford: Oxford University Press, 2006), ix.

10. Some dissent took place outside of Congress as well. The Democratic press, for example, often gadded Lincoln about the war. In addition, people organized, albeit discreetly. Secret societies, such as the Sons of Liberty, can be thought of as antiwar organizations, though they were arguably more "prowar Confederate" than "antiwar Unionist." Finally, during the election of 1864, there was a particularly large amount of antiwar sentiment within the Democratic party. Indeed, Lincoln's Democratic opponent, George B. McClellan, was chosen by the Democrats to run on an antiwar platform.

11. Joanna D. Cowden, *Heaven Will Frown on Such a Cause as This: Six Democrats Who Opposed Lincoln's War* (Lanham, Md.: University Press of America, 2001), 174; Klement, *Limits of Dissent,* 156–59.

12. Geoffrey R. Stone, *Perilous Times: Free Speech in Wartime from the Sedition Act of 1798 to the War on Terrorism* (New York: W. W. Norton, 2004); William H. Rehnquist, *All the Laws but One: Civil Liberties in Wartime* (New York: Knopf, 1998).

13. Concerned that Vallandigham's imprisonment would be a "constant source of irritation and political discussion," Lincoln ordered Burnside to commute Vallandigham's sentence from imprisonment to banishment to the Confederacy. The president decided that exile would excite far less sympathy for Vallandigham and might even "damage his prestige" among his followers. Stone, *Perilous Times,* 109.

14. Cowden, *Heaven Will Frown.*

15. Remarks on Dec. 15, 1859, Cong. Globe, 36th Cong., 1st Sess. appendix 4:43 (1860). Vallandigham doubtlessly ate up the "laughter and applause" his remark caused in the House.

16. Frank L. Klement has written numerous books about Vallandigham and antiwar movements during the Civil War. See, for example, *Limits of Dissent.* More recently, Cowden has sketched the lives of six antiwar dissenters, including Vallandigham, in *Heaven Will Frown.* I know of no speech anthologies that include any of Vallandigham's speeches, except the recent volume edited by Murray Polner and Thomas E. Woods Jr., *We Who Dared to Say No to War: American Antiwar Writing from 1912 to Now* (New York: Basic Books, 2008). The only other Vallandigham speeches published in the last 130 years are a reprint of his 1863 *The Record of Hon. C. L. Vallandigham on Abolition, the Union, and the Civil War* (Wiggins, Miss.: Crown Rights, 1998) and a reprint of his January 14, 1863, speech in Marion Mills Miller's *Great Debates in American History: From the Debates in the British Parliament on the Colonial Stamp Act (1764–1765) to the Debates in Congress at the Close of the Taft Administration (1912–1913),* vol. 6 (New York: Current Literature, 1913).

17. Vallandigham's May 1, 1863, speech at Mount Vernon may be reconstructed from a report in the *Mount Vernon Democratic Banner,* May 9, 1863, and the account of James T. Irvine, which appears in Vallandigham, *Vallandigham,* 248–49. Reports from two governmental agents who attended the speech appear in "Proceedings of a Military Commission, Convened in Cincinnati, May 6, 1863," Citizens' File, 1861–1865, War Department Collection of Confederate Records, National Archives. This has been reprinted as *The Trial of Hon. Clement L. Vallandigham by a Military Commission* (Cincinnati: Rickey and Carroll, 1893). See especially 13–16 and 21–23.

18. Vallandigham declared in the United States House of Representatives that blacks belonged to a "degraded, inferior and outcast race" and that "no wise people will ever in any manner encourage the attempt to elevate such a race to social or political equality." Remarks on May 22, 1858, Cong. Globe, 35th Cong., 1st Sess., pt. 3 2320–21 (1858).

19. At sixteen, Vallandigham wrote a memorandum to himself in which he expressed certainty that his death would inspire "the tears and regrets of millions." James Vallandigham, *A Life of Clement L. Vallandigham* (Baltimore: Turnbull Brothers, 1872), 17–18.

20. Remarks on January 14, 1863, Cong. Globe, 37th Cong., 2d Sess. pt. 2 appendix 59 (1863).

21. *Cincinnati Gazette* (Republican), quoted in Clement L. Vallandigham, *Speeches, Arguments, Addresses, and Letters of Clement L. Vallandigham* (New York: J. Walter, 1864), 574. The lone Democrat to rise in the House and deny Vallandigham's contentions was Henrick B. Wright of Pennsylvania. See Remarks on January 14, 1863, Cong. Globe, 37th Cong., 2d Sess., pt. 1 318–21 (1863).

22. Ibid

23. *St. Louis Republican,* quoted in Vallandigham, *Speeches,* 575.

24. *Constitutional Union* (Philadelphia), quoted in Vallandigham, *Speeches,* 575.

25. *Cincinnati Enquirer,* quoted in Vallandigham, *Speeches,* 575.

26. *Columbus Crisis,* January 21, 1863. Frank Klement notes that Samuel Medary of the *Crisis* "usually defended Vallandigham, and his weekly newspaper criticized Lincoln, opposed the war, and expressed pro-Western views." Klement, *Limits of Dissent,* 327.

27. *Boston Herald,* quoted in Vallandigham, *Speeches,* 574. The "worst detractors" phrase belongs to Vallandigham's brother. Still, it must be acknowledged that the vast majority of Republican newspapers that mentioned the speech expressed disapproval. See Klement, *Limits of Dissent,* 127.

28. James M. McPherson, *Battle Cry of Freedom: The Civil War Era* (New York: Oxford University Press, 1988), 546–47.

29. "The Reverse at Fredericks," *Harper's Weekly,* December 27, 1862, 818.

30. Donald, *Lincoln,* 417.

31. Klement, "Apostle for Peace," chap. 9 in *Limits of Dissent,* 116–37.

32. William Cullen Bryant, "Seventy-Six," a poem commemorating the heroism of the soldiers in the American Revolution.

33. Paul Potter, "The Incredible War," *National Guardian,* April 29, 1965.

34. Joyce Carol Oates, "Muhammad Ali: The Greatest Second Act," in *ESPN SportsCentury,* ed. Michael MacCambridge (New York: Hyperion, 1999), 210. Later Ali elaborated: "Why should they ask me . . . to put on a uniform and go ten thousand miles from home and drop bombs and bullets on brown people in Vietnam while so-called Negro people in Louisville are treated like dogs? If I thought going to war would bring freedom and equality to twenty-two million of my people, they wouldn't have to draft me; I'd join tomorrow. But I either have to obey the laws of the land or the laws of Allah. I have nothing to lose by standing up and following my beliefs. So I'll go to jail. We've been in jail for four hundred years." Quoted in Thomas Hauser, *Muhammad Ali: His Life and Times* (New York: Simon and Schuster, 1991), 167.

35. Speech to the House of Representatives (April 8, 1864).

36. This portion of Lincoln's speech does not appear in the excerpt chosen for the Mexican-American War chapter.

37. Long was quoting a Senate Committee Report considering a Georgia law that purported to set aside a congressional law regulating commerce with Native Americans. The Committee was chaired by Colonel Benton. Martin van Buren and General William H. Harrison, two senators who later became president, were members. See Senate Documents, 2nd Sess. 19th Congress, Document No. 69.

38. John Quincy Adams, *The Jubilee of the Constitution: A Discourse Delivered at the Request of the New York Historical Society, in the City of New York, on Tuesday, the 30th of April, 1839; Being the Fiftieth Anniversary of the Inauguration of George Washington as President of the United States, on Thursday, the 30th of April, 1789* (Freeport, N.Y.: Books for Libraries Press, 1972).

39. Cong. Globe, 38th Congress, 1st Sess. 1503 (1864).

40. Ibid.

41. Ibid., 1505.

42. Ibid.

43. Ibid.

44. Ibid., 1505–6.

45. Ibid., 1506.

46. Ibid., 1634.

47. Ibid.

48. *Cincinnati Daily Commercial,* April 14, 1864, quoted in Louise Schwallie Heidish, "Alexander Long, Ultraconservative Democrat" (M.A. thesis, Miami University, 1962), 110.

49. "A Union Soldier" to Alexander Long, St. Louis, Missouri, April 12, 1864, in Box B 3, Long Papers, quoted in Heidish, "Alexander Long," 110.

50. "A returned soldier" to Alexander Long, St. Louis, Missouri, April 18, 1864, in Box B 3, Long Papers, quoted in Heidish, "Alexander Long," 110. The envelope in the Long Papers is marked "annonymous [*sic*] scoundrel."

51. Rufus Robinson Dawes, "Memoir of Rufus Dawes," in Dawes, *Service with the Sixth Wisconsin Volunteers* (Marietta, Ohio: E. R. Alderman and Sons, 1890), 319.

52. As mentioned in the introduction to Vallandigham's speech, above, the *Cincinnati Enquirer* remarked of his January 14, 1863, speech, "No speech has been made in congress for years . . . that has been so universally admired. The *Enquirer*'s selective amnesia evidences the partisan—and in this case propagandistic—nature of some Civil War–era newspapers.

53. *Cincinnati Enquirer,* April 10, 1864, quoted in Heidish, "Alexander Long," 106.

54. *Cincinnati Enquirer*, April 12, 1864, quoted in Cowden, *Heaven Will Frown*, 183.

55. *Cincinnati Enquirer*, April 20[?], 1864, quoted in Heidish, "Alexander Long," 109.

56. Heidish, "Alexander Long," 102.

57. Ibid. Heidish reports that Wood later clarified that his views were not quite synonymous with Long's.

58. *Cincinnati Daily Enquirer*, April 11, 1864, quoted in Heidish, "Alexander Long," 116.

59. Ibid.

60. Heidish, "Alexander Long," 118.

61. *Cincinnati Daily Enquirer*, April 11, 1864, quoted in Heidish, "Alexander Long," 118.

62. Ibid.

63. Ibid., quoted in Heidish, "Alexander Long," 119.

64. Ibid., quoted in Heidish, "Alexander Long," 119–20.

65. Ibid., quoted in Heidish, "Alexander Long," 120.

66. Heidish, "Alexander Long," 117.

67. *Cincinnati Daily Times*, April 11, 1864, quoted in Heidish, "Alexander Long," 110.

68. Heidish, "Alexander Long," 112.

69. Ibid.

70. "The Proposition to Expel Representative Long," *New York Times*, April 11, 1864.

## Chapter 3

1. Anne Applebaum, "A History of Horror," *New York Review of Books*, October 21, 2001. Applebaum is also the author of *Gulag: A History* (New York: Doubleday, 2003).

2. Applebaum, "History of Horror."

3. Ibid.

4. Ibid.

5. See, e.g., David Halberstam, *The Making of a Quagmire: America and Vietnam During the Kennedy Era* (New York: Random House, 1965).

6. "Mark Twain, the Greatest American Humorist, Returning Home," *New York World*, quoted in *Mark Twain's Weapons of Satire: Anti-Imperialist Writings on the Philippine-American War*, ed. Jim Zwick (Syracuse: Syracuse University Press, 1992).

7. "Spanish-American War," in *The Oxford Companion to American Literature*, 6th ed., ed. James D. Hart, rev. Phillip W. Leininger (New York: Oxford University Press, 1995). This document is available on Oxford Reference Online (by subscription).

8. Secretary of State John Hay to Theodore Roosevelt ("It has been a splendid little war; begun with the highest motives, carried on with magnificent intelligence and spirit, favored by the fortune which loves the brave. It is now to be concluded, I hope, with that firm good nature which is after all the distinguishing trait of our American character"), quoted in Hugh Thomas, *Cuba: The Pursuit of Freedom*, 2nd ed. (Cambridge, Mass.: Da Capo Press, 1998), 404.

9. U.S. Department of Veterans Affairs, "Fact Sheet: America's Wars," May 2011, *www.va.gov/opa/publications/factsheets/fs_americas_wars.pdf* (accessed September 8, 2011); Hannah Fischer, "American War and Military Operations Casualties: Lists and Statistics," Congressional Research Service Report for Congress, July 13, 2005, http://www.history.navy.mil/library/online/american war casualty.htm (accessed June 7, 2009).

10. U.S. Department of Veterans Affairs, "Fact Sheet: America's Wars"; David F. Trask, "Spanish-American War," in *The Oxford Companion to United States History*, ed. Paul S. Boyer (Oxford: Oxford University Press 2001). This document is available on Oxford Reference Online (by subscription).

11. Ibid.

12. Ibid.

13. See, e.g., Richard E. Welch Jr., "American Atrocities in the Philippines: The Indictment and the Response," *Pacific Historical Review* 43, no. 2 (1974): 233–53.

14. F. Laurison Bullard, "Moorfield Storey, Leader of the Bar, Dies," *New York Times*, October 25, 1929. For the most complete account of Storey's life, see M. A. De Wolfe Howe, *Portrait of an Independent: Moorfield Storey* (Boston: Houghton Mifflin, 1932).

15. Moorfield Storey, *A Civilian's View of the Navy: Lecture Delivered September 6, 1897* (Washington, D.C.: GPO, 1897).

16. Theodore Roosevelt, *Address of Hon. Theodore Roosevelt, Assistant Secretary of the Navy: Before the Naval War College, Newport, R.I., Wednesday, June 2, 1897* (Washington, D.C.: Navy Branch, GPO, 1897), 5, quoted in Howard K. Beale, *Theodore Roosevelt and the Rise of America to World Power* (Baltimore: Johns Hopkins Press, 1956), 40.

17. Aristotle, *Rhetoric* 1.2.1356a.

18. Storey quotes from a speech to the American Bar Association given a year earlier, on August 20, 1896, by Charles Russell, Lord Chief Justice of England and Wales.

19. Most of following information can be found in American National Biography Online, s.v. "Norton, Charles Eliot." The most recent biographies of Norton are James Turner, *The Liberal Education of Charles Eliot Norton* (Baltimore: Johns Hopkins University Press, 1999), and Linda Dowling, *Charles Eliot Norton: The Art of Reform in Nineteenth-Century America* (Durham: University of New Hampshire Press, 2007). Also useful is Kermit Vanderbilt, *Charles Eliot Norton: Apostle of Culture in a Democracy* (Cambridge, Mass.: Belknap Press, 1959).

20. Vanderbilt, *Apostle of Culture*, 134.

21. Ibid.

22. *San Francisco Call*, May 8, 1898, 21.

23. Gargan to Herbert Welsh, April 30, 1898, in *Letters of Charles Eliot Norton*, ed. M. A. De Wolfe Howe, 2 vols. (Boston: Houghton Mifflin, 1913), 2:269–70.

24. See, for example, *San Francisco Call*, cited above.

25. Charles Eliot Norton, "True Patriotism," *Boston Evening Transcript*, June 8, 1898.

26. Charles Eliot Norton to Leslie Stephen, June 24, 1898, in *Letters of Charles Eliot Norton*, 2:271.

27. A large collection of Norton's hate mail, including this letter, can be found in the Norton Papers (NP) in Houghton Library at Harvard University. An especially good reference point is in "Records of the Hour," a two-volume scrapbook (fMS Am 1088.3), hereafter cited as "Records." H. Jenkins to Charles Eliot Norton, May 20, 1898, NP in "Records."

28. *Letters of Charles Eliot Norton*, 2:457–58.

29. Ibid., 2:257–59. The full text of Hoar's address, entitled "Americanism, American Honor" and delivered at the opening of the Clark University summer school session of 1898, can be found in the *Springfield Republican*, July 14, 1898. On July 19, 1898, the *Republican* also published Hoar and Norton's personal correspondence. Both can be found in "Records," vol. 2.

30. To Henry Cabot Lodge, Cincinnati, October 20, 1899, in *The Letters of Theodore Roosevelt*, ed. Elting E. Morison, 8 vols. (Cambridge, Mass.: Harvard University Press, 1951–54), 2:1086.

31. "We must not despair of the Republic."

32. *The Policy of Imperialism: Address by Hon. Carl Schurz at the Anti-Imperialist Conference in Chicago, October 17,1899* (Chicago: American Anti-imperialistic League, 1899). Schurz's speech was later published in *Speeches, Correspondence, and Political Papers of Carl Schurz*, ed. Frederic Bancroft, 6 vols. (New York: G. P. Putnam's Sons, 1913), 6:87–120.

33. For a summary of American brutality, see Howard Zinn, *A People's History of the United States: 1492–Present*, new ed. (New York: HarperCollins, 2003), 307–9. Zinn owes much to the following standard texts: R. L. Beisner, *Twelve Against Empire: The Anti-Imperialists, 1898–1900* (New York: McGraw-Hill, 1968); Philip S. Foner, *The Spanish-Cuban-American War and the Birth of American Imperialism, 1895–1902*, 2 vols. (New York: Monthly Review Press, 1972); and Samuel Eliot Morison, Frederick Merk, and Frank Burt Freidel, *Dissent in Three American Wars* (Cambridge, Mass.: Harvard University Press, 1970). A more balanced account of the war is Stuart Creighton Miller's *Benevolent Assimilation: The American Conquest of the Philippines, 1899–1903* (New Haven: Yale University Press, 1982).

34. "Our fighting blood was up," a volunteer from the state of Washington wrote, "and we all wanted to kill 'niggers.' This shooting human beings is a 'hot game,' and beats rabbit hunting all to pieces." *Public Opinion* 26 (1899): 499.

35. Ernest R. May, *Imperial Democracy: The Emergence of America as a Great Power* (New York: Harcourt Brace, 1961), 91.

36. Edward Cary, "Carl Schurz," *New York Times*, January 24, 1897.

37. George Washington, "General Washington Talks His Officers Out of Insurrection," in *Lend Me Your Ears: Great Speeches in History*, ed. William Safire (New York: W. W. Norton, 1992), 96.

38. Turner, *Liberal Education*, 210.

39. Ibid.

40. Ibid.

41. *Daily Hampshire Gazette*, September 1, 1898. In "Records," 1:15.

42. "Half Free; Half Despotic . . . Prof. Norton Presides Today at Ashfield," *Boston Evening Transcript*, August 21, 1902.

43. Betty Gulick, *Charles Eliot Norton and the Ashfield Dinners, 1879–1930* (Ashfield, Mass.: Ashfield Historical Society), quoted in Turner, *Liberal Education*, 280.

44. "Half Free; Half Despotic."

45. Ibid.

46. Ibid.

47. Ralph Barton Perry, *The Thought and Character of William James: As Revealed in Unpublished Correspondence and Notes, Together with His Published Writings*, 2 vols. (Boston: Little, Brown, 1935; repr., Westport, Conn.: Greenwood Press, 1974), 2:314.

## Chapter 4

1. "World War I," in *Dictionary of Contemporary World History*, ed. Jan Palmowski (New York: Oxford University Press, 2003). This document is available on Oxford Reference Online (by subscription).

2. Ibid.

3. U.S. Department of Veterans Affairs, "Fact Sheet: America's Wars," May 2011, www.va.gov/opa/publications/factsheets/fs_americas_wars.pdf (accessed September 8, 2011).

4. Ibid.

5. David S. Houston, *Eight Years with Wilson's Cabinet, 1913 to 1920; with a Personal Estimate of the President*, 2 vols. (Garden City, N.Y.: Doubleday, Page, 1926) 1:146. Later on, Bryan stated, "I must act according to my conscience."

6. The importance of this debate can scarcely be exaggerated. Arthur Link has called it "one of the fiercest legislative controversies of the decade," and, at least in the early months after Bryan's resignation, it appeared to many that Wilson had lost control of the Democratic Party to Bryan and his allies. As the *New Republic* editorialized, Wilson's opponents "had started him on a slide down hill towards an abyss from which he would never emerge as an influential political leader." Editorial, *New Republic,* February 5, 1916, 1.

7. *New York Times,* November 6, 1915.

8. Arthur S. Link, *Wilson: Confusions and Crises, 1915–1916* (Princeton: Princeton University Press, 1964), 23

9. For example, on June 19, 1915, Bryan spoke to a standing room only audience at Carnegie Hall; the next week, seventy thousand came to hear him at Madison Square Garden. Donald K. Springen, *William Jennings Bryan: Orator of Small Town America,* Great American Orators Series 11 (New York: Greenwood Press, 1991), 47.

10. Link, *Wilson: Confusions and Crises,* 23–33; for Bryan's significance in the eyes of this Wilson scholar, see especially 30–33 ("Democratic insurgents could take courage from the knowledge that one greater than they now fought at their side. He was Bryan, the Great Commoner and apostle of peace, who had given his boundless energy and matchless oratory to the peace crusade since his resignation as Secretary of State").

11. Editorial, *New Republic,* February 5, 1916, 1.

12. *America and the European War: Address by William Jennings Bryan at Madison Square Garden, New York City, February 2, 1917* (New York: Emergency Peace Federation, 1917).

13. For comprehensive coverage of Bryan's speech on February 2, see Paolo E. Coletta, *William Jennings Bryan,* 3 vols. (Lincoln: University of Nebraska Press, 1964–69), 3:49–51.

14. Merle Eugene Curti, "Bryan and World Peace," *Smith College Studies in World History* 16, nos. 3–4 (1931): 241n83.

15. "'Fight,' Says Bryan, 'To Last if Invaded,'" *New York Times,* February 3, 1917.

16. Joseph Tumulty, *Woodrow Wilson as I Know Him* (Garden City, N.Y.: Doubleday, Page, 1924), 255.

17. Springen, *William Jennings Bryan,* 19.

18. Robert Alexander Kraig, "The Second Oratorical Renaissance," in *Rhetoric and Reform in the Progressive Era,* ed. J. Michael Hogan (East Lansing: Michigan State University Press, 2003), 19.

19. Mark Sullivan attributes this remark to Ohio Republican Joseph B. Foraker. Mark Sullivan, *Our Times: The United States, 1900–1925,* 6 vols. (New York: Charles Scribner's Sons, 1926–35), 1:193.

20. Republican Senator David Hill of New York, quoted in *Lend Me Your Ears: Great Speeches in History,* ed. William Safire (New York: W. W. Norton, 1992), 849.

21. At the height of Chautauquas' popularity in the first and second decades of the twentieth century, the events passed through ten thousand communities and reached forty thousand people annually. See Kraig, "Second Oratorical Renaissance," 21.

22. Victoria Case and Robert Ormond Case, *We Called It Culture: The Story of Chautauqua* (New York: Doubleday, 1948), 92.

23. Malcolm Sillars has noted a similarly reductionist technique, writing that "part of Bryan's argumentative approach to speaking was an inclination to narrow the issues to a single question." Malcolm O. Sillars, "William Jennings Bryan: The Jeffersonian Liberal as Progressive," in Hogan, *Rhetoric and Reform in the Progressive Era,* 218.

24. Bryan's use of parable should be compared to Theodore Parker's: both speakers use this rhetorical device—essentially an extended metaphor—to help their audiences understand the war and the basis of their opposition to it.

25. A reporter from the *New York Times* observed that the audience "laughed uproariously at the jocular passages." "'Fight,' Says Bryan."

26. "President Wilson's Letter to Senator Stone Announcing His Stand on Armed Liner Issue," special to the *New York Times,* February 25, 1916.

27. Arthur Link has catalogued many of these. Arthur S. Link, *Wilson: Campaigns for Progressivism and Peace, 1916–1917* (Princeton: Princeton University Press, 1965), 291–93.

28. The resolutions before the American Neutral Conference Committee were as follows:

1. Keep Americans off belligerent ships, and off neutral ships carrying contraband (especially munitions of war).
2. Defer, until the present war is over, settlement for any injuries inflicted by European belligerents. Under no circumstances let our nation become a party to the European quarrel.
3. Let Congress in no case declare war without a previous advisory referendum.

29. Remarks of Senator George Norris of Nebraska on April 4, 1917, 55 Cong. Rec. pt. 1 S212–14 (1917); Remarks of Senator James A. Reed of Missouri on April 4, 1917, 55 Cong. Rec. pt. 1 S215 (1917), pt. 1: S215. Visitors in the galleries applauded Reed's remarks. *New York American,* April 5, 1917, quoted in Richard Lowitt, *George W. Norris: The Persistence of a Progressive, 1913–1933* (Urbana: University of Illinois Press, 1971), 74.

30. John F. Kennedy, *Profiles in Courage* (New York: Harper and Row, 1956), 211.

31. Jay Heinrichs, "How Harvard Destroyed Rhetoric," *Harvard Magazine* (July–August 1995): 37–43.

32. *Fighting Liberal: The Autobiography of George W. Norris* (New York: Macmillan, 1945), 23.

33. Ibid., 23–27. Norris writes in his autobiography that his participation on the debate team "ushered me into a new life" (23) and was "a great privilege, and a great pleasure" (27). Debating "was one of the main things which started me on my political career" (26). On Norris winning a debate in an unanimous decision, see 23.

34. Writers' Program of the Works Projects Administration in the State of Indiana, *Indiana: A Guide to the Hoosier State* (New York: Oxford University Press, 1941), 310.

35. Norris also argued that England and Germany were equally at fault with respect to the United States, in that both nations were violating settled principles of international law that prohibited warring nations from interfering with neutral vessels on the high seas.

36. Mark Twain, "To the Person Sitting in Darkness," http://www.antiimperialist.com/templates/Flat/img/pdf2/PersonSittinginDarkness.pdf (accessed September 22, 2012). Twain's essay, along with other anti-imperialist writings, can also be found in *Mark Twain's Weapons of Satire: Anti-Imperialist Writings on the Philippine-American War*, ed. Jim Zwick (Syracuse: Syracuse University Press, 1992).

37. William Jennings Bryan, "Democratic Candidate William Jennings Bryan Delivers His 'Cross of Gold' Speech," in Safire, *Lend Me Your Ears*, 849–53.

38. See the section on Senator Norris, above.

39. *New York World*, April 5, 1917.

40. *La Follette's*, April 24, 1909.

41. On the *ad populum* strategy, see Marie E. J. Rosenwasser, "Six Senate War Critics and Their Appeal for Gaining Audience Response," *Today's Speech* 17, no. 3 (1969): 45.

42. Remarks of Senator John Sharp Williams of Mississippi on April 4, 1917, 55 Cong. Rec. pt. 1 S237.

43. Ibid., 235.

44. Nancy C. Unger, *Fighting Bob La Follette: The Righteous Reformer* (Chapel Hill: University North Carolina Press, 2000), 250.

45. "Hang an Effigy of 2 Senators," *Washington Post*, April 6, 1917.

46. Ibid. Such actions were not confined to Washington, D.C. In fact, La Follette was strung up and burned in effigy as far away as Cleburn, Texas. "La Follette Burned in Effigy in Texas," *New York Times*, April 6, 1917. The *Times* noted that "cries of derision" erupted from the crowd as the figure was burnt in the town square.

47. Unger, *Fighting Bob*, 43.

48. Ibid., 38.

49. Ibid., 43.

50. Carl R. Burgchardt, *Robert M. La Follette, Sr.: The Voice of Conscience*, Great American Orators Series 14 (New York: Greenwood Press, 1992), xiii.

51. Incidentally, the analysis also applies to La Follette's major wartime address "Free Speech in Time of War." Remarks on October 6, 1918, 55 Cong. Rec. pt. 8 S7878–86 (1918). This remarkable speech was not included in this anthology because its main topic is free speech in times of war, not opposition to the war per se. However, the speech does quote extensively from Mexican-American War dissenters, including Abraham Lincoln, Daniel Webster, Henry Clay, and Thomas Corwin. There are few better examples of an antiwar dissenter looking to his or her ideological ancestors for inspiration.

52. Remarks of Senator John Sharp Williams, pt. 1 238.

53. Edward P. J. Corbett and Robert J. Connors, *Classical Rhetoric for the Modern Student*, 4th ed. (Oxford: Oxford University Press, 1999), 23.

54. Unger, *Fighting Bob*, 44–45.

55. David P. Thelen, *The Early Life of Robert M. La Follette, 1855–1884* (Chicago: Loyola University Press, 1966), 35.

56. Jefferson B. Simpson, interview by Carroll Pollock Lahman, September 7, 1938, in Lahman, "Robert Marion La Follette as Public Speaker and Political Leader, 1855–1905 (Ph.D. diss., University of Washington, 1936), quoted in Thelen, *Early Life*, 35.

57. Belle Case La Follette and Fola La Follette, *Robert M. La Follette, June 14, 1855–June 18, 1925*, 2 vols. (New York: Macmillan, 1953), 1:666.

58. Letter, Martin J. Wade to Attorney General, June 11, 1919, File 9–19–603, Correspondence, Record Group 60, Department of Justice, National Archives, Washington, D.C. (hereafter "DOJ"), quoted in Erling N. Sannes, "'Queen of the Lecture Platform': Kate Richards O'Hare and North Dakota Politics, 1917–1921," *North Dakota History* 58 (Fall 1991): 14.

59. Neil K. Basen, "Kate Richards O'Hare: The 'First Lady' of American Socialism, 1901–1917," *Labor History* 21, no. 2 (1980): 172.

60. Ibid., 176. O'Hare ran for the Senate out of Missouri, where she polled 2 percent of the vote (188). Basen also points out that in 1910 O'Hare became the first woman to run for the U.S. House of Representatives in Kansas (175), where she polled 5% (187). In both cases, she ran on the Socialist ticket. In Missouri she polled on par with other Socialist candidates (188), while in Kansas she generally ran ahead of her ticket (187).

61. Ibid., 174–75. Basen writes that by 1910, O'Hare "had carved a national reputation as a scintillating spellbinder second only to Debs in popularity on the Socialist platform" (174). From 1911 to 1917, O'Hare "enjoyed her most productive years, writing a popular column for the *Rip-Saw* and lecturing on the Socialist lyceum course. . . . During this six year span, the *National Rip-Saw* was transformed into America's second largest Socialist newspaper with a circulation averaging 150,000 paying subscribers" (175).

62. "Speech Delivered in Court by Kate Richards O'Hare Before Being Sentenced by Judge Wade," in O'Hare, *Selected Writings and Speeches,* ed. Philip S. Foner and Sally Miller (Baton Rouge: Louisiana State University Press, 1982), 171. The speech was first published in *Social Revolution* (February 1918): 6–7.

63. Bernard J. Brommel, "Kate Richards O'Hare: A Midwestern Pacifist's Fight for Free Speech," *North Dakota Quarterly* 44 (Winter 1976): 10; Sannes, "Queen of the Lecture Platform," 5. Quoting a local newspaper, Brommel puts the number at 125. Quoting a bulletin published by O'Hare's husband, Sannes puts the number at 147. "Local Happenings," *Bowman Pioneer,* July 12, 1917; *Frank P. O'Hare's Bulletin* (St. Louis), no. 53, May 15, 1920, 1, copy in Swarthmore College Peace Collection, Swarthmore, Pa. In December, the *Bismarck Evening Tribune* put the crowd at 170. *Bismarck Evening Tribune,* December 6, 1917.

64. Kathleen Kennedy, *Disloyal Mothers and Scurrilous Citizens: Women and Subversion During World War I* (Bloomington: Indiana University Press, 1998), 18. The *Bismarck Evening Tribune* wrote of the audience that "half of these people were foreigners, who had come to hear an American lecture." *Bismarck Evening Tribune,* December 6, 1917.

65. *Blue Book* (Bismarck, N.D.: Tribune, State Printers and Binders, 1912), 400–401, quoted in Sannes "Queen of the Lecture Platform," 5. Brommel puts the town's population at 800 (Brommel, "A Midwestern Pacifist," 10). The 2000 U.S. Census lists Bowman Township's population at a scant 1600.

66. Sannes, "Queen of the Lecture Platform," 5. Sannes's article includes a old photograph of the tiny theater in which in O'Hare spoke.

67. Though some secondary accounts have O'Hare giving the same speech almost 150 times, she reports that Bowman was her seventy-sixth appointment. Kate Richards O'Hare, *Socialism and the World War* (St. Louis: Frank P. O'Hare, 1919), 2. This portion of O'Hare's text can be found in *Selected Writings and Speeches,* 121.

68. Sannes, "Queen of the Lecture Platform," 5.

69. Brommel, "Midwestern Pacifist," 6.

70. *Women in World History: A Biographical Encyclopedia,* ed. Anne Commire (Waterford, Conn.: Yorkin, 2001), s.v. "O'Hare, Kate Richards" (by Sally M. Miller).

71. Kennedy, *Disloyal Mothers,* 19.

72. For O'Hare's grueling incarceration, see Stephen M. Kohn, *American Political Prisoners: Prosecutions Under the Espionage and Sedition Acts* (Westport, Conn.: Praeger, 1994), 121.

73. *United States v. Kate Richards O'Hare, District of North Dakota* (December 1917), quoted in Walter Nelles, *Espionage Act Cases: With Certain Others on Related Points* (New York: National Civil Liberties Bureau, 1918), 45.

74. The government's star witness, a Bowman farmer, offered a slightly different version: "Mothers who became pregnant for the purposes of bringing into the world sons to become cannon fodder are no better than the farmer's brood sow. . . . I descended into the doors of death to bring a son into the world. I thank my God tonight he is not old enough to fight. . . . Young men foolish enough to enlist or volunteer are only good enough for German fertilizer." *Bismarck Evening Tribune,* December 6, 1917. For yet more versions of O'Hare's speech, see "Disloyal Utterances in North Dakota," remarks of Senator P. J. McCumber of North Dakota on July 23, 1917, 55 Cong. Rec. pt. 5 S5389–91 (1917). McCumber reads two letters into the *Record,* each decrying O'Hare's speech. Interestingly, both letters were read into the *Record* anonymously, and neither writer attended O'Hare's lecture, but only heard about it secondhand. For an investigation into the political machinations at work in Bowman and in the Senate, see Sannes, "Queen of the Lecture Platform," 2–19.

75. Brommel, "Midwestern Pacifist," 12.

76. Nelles, *Espionage Act Cases,* 46.

77. Ibid., 47.

78. For other female antiwar leaders who indicted "patriotic motherhood" during World War I, see Kennedy, *Disloyal Mothers.* For antiwar speeches by two of O'Hare's notable contemporaries, see Jane Addams, "The Revolt Against War," *Survey,* July 17, 1915, 355–59; and Helen Keller, "Strike Against War," in *Voices of a People's History of the United States,* ed. Howard Zinn and Anthony Arnove (Boston: South End Press, 2004), 284–88.

79. S. Michele Nix, ed., *Women at the Podium: Memorable Speeches in History* (New York: Harper Resource, 2000), 1. Nix's anthology is one of only a handful of anthologies known to this author that are composed solely of speeches by women. See also Karlyn Kohrs Campbell, ed., *Man Cannot Speak for Her: Key Texts of the Early Feminists* (New York: Greenwood Press, 1989); Patricia Scileppi Kennedy and Gloria Hartmann O'Shields, eds., *We Shall Be Heard:*

*Women Speakers in America, 1828–Present* (Dubuque, Iowa: Kendall/Hunt, 1983).

80. Nix, *Women at the Podium,* 5.

81. Paraphrasing Thomas Paine, *The Crisis:* "These are the times that try men's souls: The summer soldier and the sunshine patriot will, in this crisis, shrink from the service of his country; but he that stands by it now, deserves the love and thanks of man and woman." John Kerry refers to the same passage later in this anthology.

82. In 1908, Debs delivered the keynote speech to a large group of ministers at the Third National Conference of the Christian Socialist Fellowship at Carnegie Hall. Revered Ellis Carr, editor of the *Christian Socialist,* introduced Debs as a prophet-leader and compared the persecution of Christ to the treatment strikers had received. Shortly after he started speaking, Carr made reference to "Gene Debs," and then turned around to look at him. The crowd erupted in applause, and one woman in the audience leapt up to deliver a short speech. "The Socialists Deify Debs," *New York Sun,* June 1, 1908; *New York Herald,* June 1, 1908, quoted in Bernard J. Brommel, *Eugene V. Debs: Spokesman for Labor and Socialism* (Chicago: Charles H. Kerr, 1978), 92; also see *New York Times,* June 1, 1908.

83. Ray Ginger, *The Bending Cross: A Biography of Eugene Victor Debs* (New York: Russell and Russell, 1968), 267.

84. Eugene V. Debs, "How I Became a Socialist," in *Debs: His Life, Writings and Speeches* (Chicago: Charles H. Kerr, 1908), 82 (emphasis in original). The article was originally published in the *New York Comrade,* April 1902.

85. Nick Salvatore, *Eugene V. Debs: Citizen and Socialist* (Urbana: University of Illinois Press, 1982), 149.

86. Ibid., 291.

87. Eugene V. Debs, *Writings and Speeches of Eugene V. Debs* (New York: Hermitage Press, 1948), 417–33.

88. *U.S. v. Debs,* 249 U.S. 211, 214 (1919).

89. "Socialist Leader Eugene V. Debs Defends Himself in Court Against Charges of 'Disloyalty' and 'Sedition,'" in *In Our Own Words,* ed. Robert Torricelli and Andrew Carroll (New York: Kodansha International, 1999), 47–51.

90. Eugene Victor Debs, "Statement to the Court," in *Writings and Speeches,* 437. It is this speech that Safire chooses to include in his anthology. See Safire, *Lend Me Your Ears,* 341–44.

91. Ginger, *Bending Cross,* 360.

92. Wilson to Tumulty, April 3, 1919 [cable], Box 699, Section 4, Department of Justice, Subject File, 77175, National Archives, Washington, D.C., quoted in Salvatore, *Eugene V. Debs,* 300.

93. Palmer to Wilson, April 3, 1919, Box 699, Section 4, Department of Justice, Subject File, 77175, National Archives, Washington, D.C., quoted in Salvatore, *Eugene V. Debs,* 300.

94. Salvatore, *Eugene V. Debs,* 310.

95. Ibid.

96. For a chronicle of Debs's difficult prison stay and a brief treatment of the simultaneous fracturing of the Socialist party, see ibid., 308–28.

97. Ginger, *Bending Cross,* 414; Salvatore, *Eugene V. Debs,* 328; newsreel footage of Debs is incorporated into Renner Wunderlich and Margaret Lazarus's documentary *Eugene Debs and the American Movement* (Cambridge, Mass.: Cambridge Documentary Films, 1977).

98. Ginger, *Bending Cross,* 356.

99. *Debs and the War* (Chicago: National Office Socialist Party, n.d.), 13.

100. Near the beginning of the excerpt, when he mentions visiting three "loyal comrades" in the workhouse "over yonder," he is referring to Charles Ruthenberg, Alfred Wagenknecht, and Charles Baker, three leaders of the Socialist movement in Ohio who had been jailed for obstructing registration and the draft.

101. Many later versions of Debs's speech (e.g., *Debs and the War*) include a modified version of this passage: "To whom do the Wall Street junkers in our country marry their daughters? After they have wrung their countless millions from your sweat, your agony and your life's blood, in a time of war as in a time of peace, they invest these untold millions in the purchase of titles of broken-down aristocrats, such as princes, dukes, counts and other parasites and no-accounts. (Laughter) Would they be satisfied to wed their daughters to honest workingmen? (Shouts from the crowd, 'No!') To real democrats? Oh, no! They scour the markets of Europe for vampires who are titled and nothing else. (Laughter) And they swap their millions for the titles, so that matrimony with them becomes literally a matter of money.

"These are the gentry who are today wrapped up in the American flag, who shout their claim from the housetops that they are the only patriots, and who have their magnifying glasses in hand, scanning the country for evidence of disloyalty, eager to apply the brand of treason to the men who dare to even whisper their opposition to junker rule in the United States. No wonder Sam Johnson declared that 'patriotism is the last refuge of the scoundrel.' He must have had this Wall Street gentry in mind, or at least their prototypes, for in every age it has been the tyrant, the oppressor and the exploiter who has wrapped himself in the cloak of patriotism, or religion, or both to deceive and overawe the people. (Applause)."

102. Paraphrase of Alfred, Lord Tennyson, "The Charge of the Light Brigade."

103. Many later versions of Debs's speech (e.g., *Debs and the War*) include a modified version of this passage as well: "Wars throughout history have been waged for conquest and plunder. In the middle ages when the feudal lords who inhabited the castles whose towers may still be seen along the Rhine concluded to enlarge their domains, to increase their power, their prestige and their wealth they declared war upon one another. But they themselves did not go to war any more than the modern feudal lords, the barons of Wall Street go to war. (Applause) The feudal barons of the middle ages, the economic predecessors of the capitalists of our day, declared all wars. And their miserable serfs fought all the battles. The poor, ignorant serfs had been taught to revere their masters; to believe that when their masters declared war upon one another, it was their patriotic duty to fall upon one another and to cut one another's throats for the profit and glory of the lords and barons who held them in contempt. And that is war in a nutshell. The master class has always declared the wars; the subject class has always fought the battles. The master class has had all to gain and nothing to lose, while the subject class has had nothing to gain and all to lose—especially their lives. (Applause)

"They have always taught and trained you to believe it to be your patriotic duty to go to war and to have yourselves slaughtered at their command. But in all the history of the world you, the people, have never had a voice in declaring war, and strange as it certainly appears, no war by any nation in any age has ever been declared by the people.

And here let me emphasize the fact—and it cannot be repeated too often—that the working class who fight all the battles, the working class who make the supreme sacrifices, the working class who freely shed their blood and furnish the corpses, have never yet had a voice in either declaring war or making peace. It is the ruling class that invariably does both. They alone declare war and they alone make peace.

'Yours not to reason why;

Yours but to do and die.'

That is their motto and we object on the part of the awakening workers of this nation.

If war is right let it be declared by the people. You who have your lives to lose, you certainly above all others have the right to decide the momentous issue of war or peace. (Applause)."

Chapter 5

1. U.S. Department of Veterans Affairs, "Fact Sheet: America's Wars," May 2011, www.va.gov/opa/publications/factsheets/fs_americas_wars.pdf (accessed September 8, 2011).

2. Ibid.

3. "World War II," in *A Dictionary of World History* (New York: Oxford University Press, 2000). This document is available on Oxford Reference Online (by subscription).

4. J. Garry Clifford and John W. Jeffries, "World War II," in *The Oxford Companion to United States History,* ed. Paul S. Boyer (Oxford: Oxford University Press 2001). This document is available on Oxford Reference Online (by subscription).

5. Michel Fabre, *The Unfinished Quest of Richard Wright,* trans. Isabel Barzun, 2nd ed. (Urbana: University of Illinois Press,1993), 224.

6. *Socialist Call,* February 13, 1937, quoted in Murray Seidler, *Norman Thomas: Respectable Rebel,* 2nd ed. (Syracuse: Syracuse University Press, 1967), 205.

7. For pacifism as a reason for entering the Socialist Party, see Bernard K. Johnpoll, *Pacifist's Progress: Norman Thomas and the Decline of American Socialism* (Chicago: Quadrangle Books, 1970), 205.

8. Seidler, *Respectable Rebel,* 205.

9. *Socialist Call,* August 27, 1938, quoted in Seidler, *Respectable Rebel,* 205–6.

10. Harry Fleischman, *Norman Thomas: A Biography* (New York: W. W. Norton, 1964), 197. The *Register* argued that Thomas ought to be neutralized in the tradition of Alexander Berkman and Emma Goldman, two dissenters "who got their just desert during the last war" by being arrested, imprisoned, and ultimately deported to Russia. Ibid.

11. Ibid.

12. Ibid.

13. Norman Thomas, *What Is Our Destiny?* (Garden City, N.Y.: Doubleday, 1944), 37.

14. Thomas proposed this policy at the 1942 Milwaukee convention of the Socialist Party. About half the delegates favored Thomas's position, while the other half favored "political non-support." See Fleischman, *Norman Thomas,* 203.

15. Thomas, *What Is Our Destiny?*

16. American National Biography Online, s.v. "Wright, Richard."

17. Richard Wright, "Not My People's War," *New Masses,* June 17, 1941, 8–9, 12.

18. Fabre, *Unfinished Quest,* 223.

19. For example, see *Daily Worker,* September 30, 1940; May 20, 1941. See also "Anniversary Greeting to *New Masses,*" *New Masses,* February 18, 1941, 26.

20. *Domino,* May 8, 1941.

21. Richard Wright, "The Negro People and the War," lecture delivered at Columbia University, New York (April 23, 1941).

22. Wright, along with Vito Marcantonio and Theodore Dreiser, took part in the pacifist demonstration at Randall Stadium in Wisconsin on May 5, 1941. Fabre, *Unfinished Quest,* 222.

23. Richard Wright, "Not My People's War," *Magazine Abstracts* 7 (1941): 7:70.

24. Fabre, *Unfinished Quest,* 222–24.

25. Wright's arrangement of material leaves something to be desired. Later in the speech, in a section which has not been excerpted, Wright completes his comparison between the First and Second World Wars by quoting a recent announcement of the president's press secretary, Stephen T. Early: "The policy of the War Department is not to intermingle colored and white enlisted personnel in the same regimental organizations. This policy has been proven satisfactory over a period of years, and to make changes would produce situations destructive of morale and detrimental to the preparations for national defense."

26. Charles A. Lindbergh, "Aviation, Geography, and Race," *Reader's Digest,* November 1939, 64–67; Charles A. Lindbergh, "What Substitute for War?" *Atlantic Monthly,* March 1940, 304–5.

27. Paul Palmer, "America Speaks to CAL," August 31, 1940, Charles A. Lindbergh Collection (#325), Manuscripts and Archives, Sterling Memorial Library, Yale University, New Haven, Conn., quoted in A. Scott Berg, *Lindbergh* (New York: G. P. Putnam's 1998), 410.

28. Ibid.

29. Palmer, "America Speaks," quoted in Berg, *Lindbergh,* 410. See also Frank Lloyd Wright, *An Autobiography* (New York: Duell, Sloan and Pearce, 1943), 500 ("Now when everywhere is equivocation and cowardice, you not only think straight but you dare speak straight").

30. Charles A. Lindbergh, *The Wartime Journals of Charles A. Lindbergh* (New York: Harcourt Brace Jovanovich, 1970), 274–75.

31. "L and the Like," *Richmond News Leader,* January 28, 1941, quoted in Berg, *Lindbergh,* 416.

32. Dorothy Thompson, "An Open Letter to Anne Morrow Lindbergh," *Look,* March 1940, n.p., quoted in Berg, *Lindbergh,* 397.

33. Berg, *Lindbergh,* 409.

34. Ibid., 412.

35. J. J. Breslin (Post Office Dept. Inspector) to Lindbergh, June 14, 1940, quoted in Berg, *Lindbergh,* 396.

36. Truman Smith, then on active duty as a colonel in the General Staff of the Military Intelligence Division, spoke on behalf of the administration. Berg, *Lindbergh,* 397. Berg notes that Lindbergh stated in 1971 that General Henry H. "Hap" Arnold said that if he did not accept the offer, the government would destroy any record of the conversation (599).

37. Franklin Delano Roosevelt to Stimson, May 21, 1940, quoted in Robert Dallek, *Franklin D. Roosevelt and American Foreign Policy, 1939–1941* (New York: Oxford University Press, 1995), 225.

38. Dallek, *Franklin D. Roosevelt,* 225.

39. Berg, *Lindbergh,* 432.

40. FDR Presidential Press Conference #738, April 25, 1941. See also "President Defines Lindbergh's Niche," *New York Times,* April 26, 1941.

41. Ruth Sarles, *A Story of America First: The Men and Women Who Opposed U.S. Intervention in World War II,* ed. Bill Kauffman (Westport, Conn.: Praeger, 2003), 88. Sarles provides an excellent review of public opinion polls immediately prior to the U.S. entrance into the war.

42. For highlights of the nation's almost uniform attack on Lindbergh's speech, see Berg, *Charles Lindbergh,* 427–30; Wayne S. Cole, *Charles A. Lindbergh and the Battle Against American Intervention in World War II* (New York: Harcourt Brace Jovanovich, 1974), 173–85.

43. Cole, *Charles A. Lindbergh,* 174.

44. "The Un-American Way," *New York Times,* September 26, 1941.

45. "The Shape of Things," Nation, October 11, 1941.

46. "Assail Lindbergh for Iowa Speech," *New York Times,* September 13, 1941.

47. Berg, *Charles Lindbergh,* 428.

48. Walter Hornaday, "Southwest for Action," *New York Times,* September 21, 1941, sec. E.

49. Berg, *Charles Lindbergh,* 428.

50. Ibid., 421.

51. Ibid.

52. Much has been written about Lindbergh's alleged anti-Semitism, both in this speech in particular and in Lindbergh's public career generally. I do not wish to contribute to that debate. One can best confirm or deny the allegation of Lindbergh's public anti-Semitism based upon the texts of Lindbergh's speeches themselves.

## Chapter 6

1. Hannah Fischer, "American War and Military Operations Casualties: Lists and Statistics," Congressional Research Service Report for Congress, July 13, 2005, http://www.history.navy.mil/library/online/americanwarcasualty.htm (accessed June 7, 2009). See also U.S. Department of Veterans Affairs, "Fact Sheet: America's Wars," May 2011, www.va.gov/opa/publications/factsheets/fs_americas_wars.pdf (accessed September 8, 2011).

2. William Stueck, "Korean War," in *The Oxford Companion to United States History,* ed. Paul S.

Boyer (Oxford: Oxford University Press, 2001). This document is available on Oxford Reference Online (by subscription).

3. Ibid.

4. Ibid.

5. 64 Stat. 987 (1950).

6. See chap. 10 of Lawrence S. Wittner, *The Struggle Against the Bomb*, vol. 1 (Stanford: Stanford University Press, 1993).

7. Martin B. Duberman, *Paul Robeson* (New York: Knopf, 1988), 342.

8. The full AP dispatch can be found in the Robeson Archives.

9. "Paris 'Peace Congress' Assails U.S. and Atlantic Pact, Upholds Soviet," *New York Times*, April 21, 1949.

10. Duberman documents the reaction to Robeson's remarks in great detail (342–50).

11. Duberman, *Paul Robeson*, 357.

12. Ibid.

13. "Loves Soviet Best," *New York Times*, June 17, 1949.

14. "An Undesirable Citizen," editorial, *Boston Advertiser*, June 26, 1949. Representative Thomas J. Lane read the article into the *Congressional Record* the next day.

15. FBI file on Robeson, FBIHQ File 100–12304, sect. 3, accessed via the FBI website, http://vault.fbi.gov.

16. Duberman, *Paul Robeson*, 359–60. See generally *Hearings Regarding Communist Infiltration of Minority Groups*, July 13–18, 1949 (Washington, D.C.: GPO, 1949).

17. Charles H. Wright, "Paul Robeson at Peekskill," in *Paul Robeson, the Great Forerunner*, ed. editors of *Freedomways* (New York: Dodd, Mead, 1978), 135.

18. Joseph Walwik, *The Peekskill, New York, Anti-Communist Riots of 1949* (Lewiston, N.Y.: Edwin Mellen, 2002), 3.

19. Ibid.

20. American National Biography Online, s.v. "Robeson, Paul."

21. *Paul Robeson Speaks: Writings, Speeches, Interviews, 1918–1974*, ed. Philip S. Foner (New York: Brunner/Mazel, 1978), 41.

22. The phrase belongs to Larry R. Gerlach.

23. Duberman, *Paul Robeson*, 576n31.

24. Eslanda Goode Robeson, *Paul Robeson, Negro* (London: Gollancz, 1930), 72.

25. Robeson, *Robeson Speaks*, 33.

26. Dr. John Flood to Dr. Morris Perlmutter, January 17, 1964, Robeson Archives, quoted in Duberman, *Paul Robeson*, 503.

27. Duberman reviews the medical implications of Robeson's electroconvulsive therapy (which was administered to him at least twenty-four times), as well as Paul Robeson Jr.'s allegations of foul play by the U.S. government ("Broken Health," chap. 24 in *Paul Robeson*, 498–521 and notes).

28. Robeson, *Robeson Speaks*, 44.

29. American National Biography Online, s.v. "Du Bois, W. E. B."

30. See, e.g., David L. Lewis, "Against the Grain: From the NAACP to the Far Left," chap. 14 in *W. E. B. Du Bois: The Fight for Equality and the American Century* (New York: Henry Holt, 2000), 496–553.

31. *Crisis* 16 (July 1918): 111.

32. Raymond Wolters calls Du Bois's editorial "the most controversial editorial of his long career." Wolters, *Du Bois and His Rivals* (Columbia: University of Missouri Press, 2002), 118. Wolters documents the reaction to Du Bois's editorial (118–19).

33. *Cleveland Gazette*, July 27, 1918, quoted in Wolters, *Du Bois*, 121.

34. Before the United States was attacked by Japan at Pearl Harbor on December 7, 1941, Du Bois was a noninterventionist. See, for example, As the Crow Flies, *Amsterdam News*, January 25, 1941 (arguing against U.S. participation in the war program); "A Chronicle of Race Relations," *Phylon* 2, no. 2 (1941): 172–93 (writing that "perhaps the finest single word in the war controversy has been uttered by Anne Morrow Lindbergh" in her *The Wave of the Future* [New York: Harcourt, Brace, 1940] where she calls for "reform at home rather than crusade abroad"); "Federal Action Programs and Community Action in the South," *Social Forces* 19 (March 1941): 375–80 (urging a Fisk student not to fall victim to war hysteria, and expressing regret for his own mistake in doing so during World War I).

35. W. E. B. Du Bois, As the Crow Flies, *Amsterdam News*, March 14, 1942, in Du Bois, *Newspaper Columns*, ed. Herbert Aptheker, 2 vols. (White Plains, N.Y.: Kraus-Thomson, 1986), 1:415.

36. W. E. B. Du Bois, *Darkwater: Voices Within the Veil* (New York: Harcourt, Brace and Howe, 1920), 49.

37. Jack Moore, *W. E. B. Du Bois* (Boston: Twayne, 1981), 142.

38. Gar Alperovitz and Sanho Tree, *The Decision to Use the Atomic Bomb and the Architecture of an American Myth* (New York: Knopf, 1995), 680.

39. W. E. B. Du Bois, "Common Objectives," *Soviet Russia Today* 15 (August 1946): 15.

40. Ibid., 16. Also in Du Bois, *Writings by W. E. B. Du Bois in Periodicals Edited by Others*, ed. Herbert Aptheker, 4 vols. (White Plains, N.Y.: Kraus-Thomson, 1982), 3:225.

41. Gerald Horne, *Black and Red: W. E. B. Du Bois and the Afro-American Response to the Cold War*,

*1944–1963* (Albany: State University of New York Press, 1986), 127–28, 131.

42. Walter H. Waggoner, "Acheson Derides Soviet 'Peace' Bids," *New York Times,* July 13, 1950.

43. Horne, *Black and Red,* 133.

44. Ibid., 136. The PIC was also financially strapped.

45. Du Bois to Mae Ovings, September 18, 1950, Reel 65, #418, Du Bois Papers, quoted in Horne, *Black and Red,* 137. Du Bois expresses a similar sentiment in an October 27, 1950, letter to his granddaughter at Fisk: "Ordinarily there would be no chance of election, but I do have an opportunity to say to the public what I think about the present situation." *Correspondence of W. E. B. Du Bois,* ed. Herbert Aptheker, 3 vols. (Amherst: University of Massachusetts Press, 1973–78), 3:297.

46. *Guardian,* October 4, 1950. The leftist *Guardian* printed enthusiastic praise of the speech in a letter to the editor the following week: "We hope that all the wary and wobbly, wishy-washy, fagged and fogged liberals will read it and weep for the shame which is theirs in this crucial hour of the history they are helping to write." Clara M. Vincent, letter to the editor, *Guardian,* October 25, 1950.

47. Lewis, *W. E. B. Du Bois,* 552. However, Du Bois won 12.6 percent of Harlem's votes—more than 3 percent more than the American Labor party's gubernatorial nominee, who earned 8.9 percent. See Horne, *Black and Red,* 146.

48. See Horne, "Ban the Bomb," chap. 12 in *Black and Red,* 126–36. Horne quotes minutes from an October 12, 1950, meeting of the Peace Information Center's Executive Board.

49. Roi Ottley, "The Big Ten Who Run America," *Negro Digest,* May 1948. Singer-activist Paul Robeson and NAACP Chairman Walter White were also on the list.

50. Henry Steele Commager, "Men Who Make Up Our Minds," *48* (1948). Commager's list contained sixty-one names, and Du Bois was number sixty-one.

51. *The Autobiography of W. E. B. Du Bois: A Soliloquy on Viewing My Life from the Last Decade of Its First Century* (New York: International, 1971), 414.

52. *Chicago Defender,* October 6, 1951, quoted in Horne, *Black and Red,* 159

53. Horne, *Black and Red,* 157.

54. David L. Lewis, *W. E. B. Du Bois: The Fight for Equality and the American Century, 1919–1963* (New York: Henry Holt, 2000), 552.

55. Ibid.; Horne, "In Battle for Peace," chap. 12 in *Black and Red,* 151–82.

56. The published version (which reflects the typescript before Du Bois's revisions) has a slightly different version of this sentence: "To this end they are suppressing the Bill of Rights so as to stop discussion, distort the facts and stampede the nation through the hysteria of groundless Fear."

57. Du Bois added this sentence to the typescript; it does not appear in the printed version.

58. Du Bois added the phrase "federal aid to education" to the typescript; it does not appear in the printed version.

59. Du Bois added this sentence to the typescript; it does not appear in the printed version.

## Chapter 7

1. H.J. Res. 1145 (August 7, 1964). The congressional resolution gave the executive branch the broad right "to take all necessary measures to repel any armed attack against the forces of the United States."

2. George C. Herring, "Vietnam War," in *The Oxford Companion to United States History,* ed. Paul S. Boyer (Oxford: Oxford University Press, 2001), 806. This document is available on Oxford Reference Online (by subscription)

3. The Resolution was approved by the House 416–0 and by the Senate 88–2. In the House, Eugene Siler of Kentucky opposed the measure, though his vote was not counted in opposition. In the Senate, Wayne Morse of Oregon and Ernest Gruening of Alaska also opposed the measure.

4. H.J. Res. 1145. No more formal declaration of war ever passed.

5. Herring, "Vietnam War," 807.

6. Ibid.

7. Spencer C. Tucker, ed., *Encyclopedia of the Vietnam War: A Political, Social, and Military History* (New York: Oxford University Press, 1998), 453; Military History Institute of Vietnam, *Victory in Vietnam: The Official History of the People's Army of Vietnam, 1954–1975,* trans. Merle L. Pribbenow (Lawrence: University of Kansas Press, 2002) 431, cited in Jeffrey Record and W. Andrew Terrill, "Iraq and Vietnam: Differences, Similarities and Insights," Strategic Studies Institute (U.S. Army War College, 2004), 8, http://www.strategicstudiesinstitute.army.mil/pdffiles/00367.pdf (accessed June 7, 2009).

8. Hannah Fischer, "American War and Military Operations Casualties: Lists and Statistics," Congressional Research Service Report for Congress, July 13, 2005, http://www.history.navy.mil/library/online/americanwarcasualty.htm (accessed June 7, 2009). See also U.S. Department of Veterans Affairs, "Fact Sheet: America's Wars," May 2011, www.va.gov/opa/publications/factsheets/fs_americas_wars.pdf (accessed September 8, 2011). These figures cover November 1, 1955, to May 15, 1975.

9. Fischer, "American War and Military Operations Casualties"; U.S. Department of Veterans Affairs, "Fact Sheet."

10. The weight of bombs dropped during the Vietnam War far exceeded the total weight of all bombs dropped during World War II. "Vietnam War," in *The Oxford Essential Dictionary of the U.S. Military* (New York: Berkley Books, 2001). This document is available on Oxford Reference Online (by subscription).

11. Ibid.

12. Tucker, *Encyclopedia of the Vietnam War,* 64, quoted in Record and Terrill, "Iraq and Vietnam," 20. Record and Terrill note that the 1.1 million figure presumably included the three hundred thousand Communist soldiers who went missing in action. The Vietnamese report was dated April 3, 1995. See also "Vietnam War Casualties," *New York Times,* January 24, 1973, 17.

13. *We Accuse: A Powerful Statement of the New Political Anger in America, as Revealed in the Speeches Given at the 36-Hour "Vietnam Day" Protest in Berkeley, California* (Berkeley: Diablo Press, 1965); Louis Menashe and Ronald Radosh, *Teach-ins, U.S.A.: Reports, Opinions, Documents* (New York: Praeger, 1967).

14. The Martin Luther King, Jr. Research and Education Institute (the "Institute") in Stanford, California, has published a comprehensive chronology. The Institute's King Online Encyclopedia notes that King's antiwar sentiments emerged publicly for the first time in March 9, 1965, when King declared that "millions of dollars can be spent every day to hold troops in South Viet Nam and our country cannot protect the rights of Negroes in Selma" ("Statement on Voter Registration in Alabama," March 9, 1965, Martin Luther King, Jr. Papers, 1950–1968, Martin Luther King, Jr., Center for Nonviolent Social Change, Inc., Atlanta). On August 29, 1965, King told reporters on *Face the Nation* that as a minister he had "a prophetic function" and as "one greatly concerned about the need for peace in our world and the survival of mankind, I must continue to take a stand on this issue" (Institute, citing Robert R. Muntz Library, University of Texas at Tyler, Tyler, Texas). The Institute also notes that in a version of the "Transformed Nonconformist" sermon given in January 1966 at Ebenezer Baptist Church, King voiced opposition to the Vietnam War by describing American aggression as a violation of the 1954 Geneva Accord, which promised self-determination. Finally, the Institute notes that in early 1967 King stepped up his antiwar proclamations, giving similar speeches in Los Angeles and Chicago. The Los Angeles speech, called "The Casualties of the War in Vietnam" and presented by King on February

25, 1967, stressed the history of the conflict and argued that American power should be "harnessed to the service of peace and human beings, not an inhumane power [unleashed] against defenseless people" (Martin Luther King, Jr. Papers, 1950–1968, Atlanta).

15. Max German, "The Newark and Detroit 'Riots' of 1967," http://www.67riots.Rutgers.edu/introduction.html (accessed May 24, 2009).

16. Ibid.

17. Ibid.

18. Stokely Carmichael, Remarks on April 18, 1967, Seattle, Washington, http://courses.washington.edu/spcmu/carmichael/transcript.htm (accessed March 22, 2005).

19. *Washington Post,* April 6, 1967.

20. *New York Times,* April 6, 1967.

21. David J. Garrow, *Bearing the Cross: Martin Luther King, Jr., and the Southern Christian Leadership Conference* (New York: W. Morrow, 1986), 554.

22. "NAACP Decries Stand of Dr. King on Vietnam," *New York Times,* April 11, 1967.

23. "On the March Again: New York," *Nation,* May 1967, 551.

24. *Newsweek,* May 15, 1967, 33.

25. David J. Garrow, *The FBI and Martin Luther King, Jr.: From "Solo" to Memphis* (New York: Norton, 1981), 180.

26. Hoover to Mildred Stegall, "Martin Luther King, Jr., SM-C," April 19, 1967, FBI File # 100–106670–2895, quoted in Garrow, *FBI and MLK,* 182; see also Garrow, *Bearing the Cross,* 555.

27. Garrow, *Bearing the Cross,* 555.

28. Ibid., 556.

29. Martin Luther King, Jr., "I've Been to the Mountaintop," speech in Mason Temple, Memphis, Tennessee (April 3, 1968), in King, *A Testament of Hope: The Essential Writings of Martin Luther King, Jr.,* ed. James M. Washington (San Francisco: HarperSanFrancisco, 1991), 279–86.

30. Coretta Scott King, speech on the Civil Rights Movement at the 27th Peace March in New York, Sheep Meadow, Central Park (April 27, 1968). Speaking only three weeks after the death of her husband, Mrs. King read from the handwritten notes of her husband's incomplete speech. The speech was broadcast by KPFA the same day. *See* Pacific Radio Archive (Los Angeles), Archive # BB1331.

31. Lionel Lokos, *The Life and Legacy of Martin Luther King, Jr.* (New Rochelle, N.Y.: Arlington House, 1968), 402–3, quoted in Henry E. Darby and Margaret N. Rowley, "King on Vietnam and Beyond," in *Martin Luther King, Jr.: Civil Rights Leader, Theologian, Orator,* ed. David J. Garrow, 3 vols. (Brooklyn: Carlson, 1989), 1:48.

32. Martin Luther King Jr., *The Trumpet of Conscience* (New York: Harper and Row, 1968), 75–78.

33. In *Bearing the Cross,* David Garrow writes that "large segments of the speech were drafted by Vincent Harding, smaller portions by John Maguire and Andrew Young" (229). Garrow interviewed all three individuals. Harding's comments also appear in *Visions of History,* ed. Henry Abelove et al. (New York: Pantheon, 1983), 229. Keith D. Miller has argued more recently that "Beyond Vietnam" is a "largely ghostwritten anti-war address," as evidenced by King's "inductive" approach. *Voice of Deliverance: The Language of Martin Luther King, Jr. and Its Sources* (New York: Free Press, 1992), 148–50.

34. "Let America Be America Again," in *The Collected Poems of Langston Hughes* (New York: Alfred A. Knopf, 1994).

35. Thich Nhat Hanh, *Vietnam: Lotus in a Sea of Fire* (New York: Hill and Wang, 1967), 81. King nominated Hanh for the Nobel Peace Prize.

36. 1 John 7:7–8.

37. Contemporary Authors Online, s.v. "Eugene J. McCarthy."

38. Dominic Sandbrook, *Eugene McCarthy: The Rise and Fall of Postwar American Liberalism* (New York: Alfred A. Knopf, 2004), 182.

39. George Rising, *Clean for Gene: Eugene McCarthy's 1968 Presidential Campaign* (Westport, Conn.: Praeger, 1997).

40. *Time,* December 8, 1967, 21.

41. Sandbrook, *Eugene McCarthy,* 183.

42. Ibid.

43. Ibid., 176.

44. Ibid., 179.

45. Ibid., 180.

46. Transcript of BBC interview, March 8, 1970, "Jan 1970–June 1971," Box 5, "McCarthy: By and About," McCarthy Historical Project Archive, Georgetown University, Washington, D.C., quoted in Sandbrook, *Eugene McCarthy,* 183.

47. Albert Eisele, *Almost to the Presidency: A Biography of Two American Politicians* (Blue Earth, Minn.: Piper, 1972), 288.

48. Ibid.

49. Ibid.

50. Ibid., 289.

51. Eugene J. McCarthy, *Year of the People* (Garden City, N.Y.: Doubleday, 1969), 284–89.

52. Ibid., 289.

53. Edward P. J. Corbett and Robert J. Connors, *Classical Rhetoric for the Modern Student,* 4th ed. (Oxford: Oxford University Press, 1999), 382.

54. Robert F. Kennedy, *RFK: Selected Speeches,* ed. Edwin O. Guthman and C. Richard Allen (New York: Viking, 1993), 270.

55. Connie Langland, "A Crowd Reacts to the Magnetism," *Kansas Collegian,* March 19, 1968.

56. *Time,* April 26, 1968, 22.

57. *Manhattan (Kansas) Mercury,* "Kennedy Rides Crest Here," March 18, 1968; *Time,* March 29, 1968, 22; Kennedy, *Selected Speeches,* 270.

58. "Robert F. Kennedy Speaking at Podium to Large Crowd," March 18, 1968, Manhattan, Kansas. Corbis Images: Code: U1586738, Bettmann/CORBIS.

59. *Time,* March 22, 1968, 12.

60. Langland, "Crowd Reacts."

61. "Robert F. Kennedy Speaking at Podium," *Manhattan Mercury,* March 18, 1968.

62. Jack Newfield, *Robert Kennedy: A Memoir* (New York: E. P. Dutton, 1969), 255. On March 19 the *Manhattan Mercury* forewent the candidate himself and instead included a large front-page photograph of his seated wife, clapping and blinking, that conspicuously included her bared knees. The subtly critical caption read, "THAT'S MY MAN—Miniskirted Mrs. Robert Kennedy is obviously in complete accord with something her husband had just said as he spoke yesterday at Kansas State University, where as the audience response rose she joined in every round of applause."

63. Kennedy, *Selected Speeches,* 270.

64. "Bobby on the Run," *Newsweek,* April 1, 1968, 24.

65. Newfield, *Robert Kennedy,* 257.

66. Ibid.

67. "Kennedy All-Star Panel Draws Laugh in Kansas," *New York Times,* March 19, 1968.

68. Ibid.

69. Richard Reeves, "The Making of a Candidate," *New York Times Magazine,* March 21, 1968, 27.

70. On this being a theme of Kennedy's previous antiwar speeches, see John M. Murphy, "Crafting the Kennedy Legacy," *Rhetoric and Public Affairs* 3, no. 4 (2000): 577–601.

71. Gene Roberts, "Casualties of U.S. Top Korea War's," *New York Times,* March 15, 1968.

72. Newfield, *Robert Kennedy,* 253.

73. Helen Dudar, "The Perilous Campaign," *New York Post,* June 5, 1968.

74. Ronald Steel, *In Love with Night: The American Romance with Robert Kennedy* (New York: Simon and Schuster, 2000), 147.

75. "Socking It to 'Em," *Time,* April 5, 1968, 22; Victor S. Navasky, "The Haunting of Robert Kennedy," *New York Times,* June 2, 1968.

76. See Murphy, "Crafting the Kennedy Legacy," 591.

77. John F. Kennedy, Inaugural Address (January 20, 1961). For an analysis of the similarities between two of Robert Kennedy's early antiwar speeches and President Kennedy's rhetoric, see Murphy, "Crafting the Kennedy Legacy," 591.

78. Time, "Socking It to 'Em," April 5, 1968, 22.

79. Ibid.

80. Langland, "Crowd Reacts."

81. Steel, *In Love with Night,* 146.

82. Kennedy, *Selected Speeches,* 270.

83. Note that Charles Sumner uses the same Tacitus quote in a different translation: "When they have produced the desolation of solitude, they call it *Peace.*" See the Mexican-American War chapter, above.

84. In a slip of the tongue, Kennedy said "perpetration."

85. Associated Press correspondent Peter Arnett quoted a U.S. Air Force major saying this in early February. See Peter Arnett, "Ruined Bentre, After 45 Days, Still Awaits Saigon's Aid," *New York Times,* March 15, 1968, 3.

86. Shirley Chisholm, *Unbought and Unbossed* (Boston: Houghton Mifflin, 1970), 96.

87. Ibid.

88. For one example of a speech that describes in graphic detail the effect that American firepower had on local populations throughout Southeast Asia, see Martin Luther King Jr.'s speech, above.

89. Chisholm, *Unbought and Unbossed,* 96.

90. Marjorie Hunter, "White House Pickets, House Speakers Score War," *New York Times,* March 27, 1969.

91. Chisholm, *Unbought and Unbossed,* 99.

92. Chana Kai Lee, *For Freedom's Sake: The Life of Fannie Lou Hamer* (Urbana: University of Illinois Press, 1999); Kay Mills, *This Little Light of Mine: The Life of Fannie Lou Hamer* (New York: E. P. Dutton, 1993).

93. Lee, *For Freedom's Sake;* Mills, *This Little Light of Mine.*

94. For Hamer's own harrowing description of abuse, see her testimony at the Democratic National Convention, Atlantic City, N.J. (July 22, 1964). The text appears in *The Speeches of Fannie Lou Hamer: To Tell It Like It Is,* ed. Maegan Parker Brooks and Davis W. Houck (Jackson: University Press of Mississippi, 2011), 42–45.

95. Mills, *This Little Light of Mine,* 300.

96. Douglas Brinkley, *Tour of Duty: John Kerry and the Vietnam War* (New York: William Morrow, 2004), 1.

97. Michael Kranish, Brian C. Mooney, and Nina J. Easton, *John F. Kerry: The Complete Biography by the* Boston Globe *Reporters Who Know Him Best* (New York: PublicAffairs, 2004), 54. Kerry delivered the class oration on June 12, 1966. An earlier version of the speech was published in the class yearbook. Kranish, Mooney, and Easton call it "serviceable but forgettable, with vapid and airy phrases about the future" (51).

98. Helen Dudar, "Kerry: Man in Demand," *New York Post,* April 30, 1971, 5, 20–21.

99. Michael Kranish, "John F. Kerry, Candidate in the Making, Part 3," *Boston Globe,* June 17, 2003.

100. Ibid.

101. Ibid.

102. Ibid.

103. See Gary Kulik, *"War Stories": False Atrocity Tales, Swift Boaters, and Winter Soldiers—What Really Happened in Vietnam* (Washington, D.C.: Potomac Books, 2009). Kulik's chapter 5, in particular, examines the testimony of the Winter Soldier veterans with a self-styled "skeptical eye." While Kulick acknowledges that "there were men who spoke the truth at the WSI" and that "Americans did commit war crimes in Vietnam," he concludes that those who spoke the truth will nevertheless always be linked to those who "succumbed to the power of rumor, second- and third-hand evidence, 'boot-camp propaganda,' and imputed motive." Ibid., 154.

104. Adam Walinsky, who was also a speechwriter for Robert F. Kennedy, allegedly ghostwrote Kerry's speech. Walinsky denies the charge, while Kerry admits that "Adam might have touched it up a bit." Kranish, Mooney, and Easton, *John F. Kerry,* 242.

105. John E. O'Neill, *Unfit for Command: Swift Boat Veterans Speak out Against John Kerry* (Washington, D.C.: Regnery; Lanham, Md.: National Book Network, 2004).

106. *Los Angeles Times,* May 23, 2004. Kerry, however, stands by the bulk of his claims. "Free-fire zones, women getting blown away, children getting blown away, ears being cut off, rapes—people know this," Kerry says. "These are a matter of record in our history."

107. William F. Buckley Jr., "John Kerry's America: What He Said About Us," *National Review Online,* February 4, 2004, http://www.nationalreview.com/flashback/wfb200402040837.asp (accessed February 23, 2005). Buckley originally spoke these words during a June 8, 1971, commencement address to the United States Military Academy at West Point. The speech was later reprinted in Buckley's *Let Us Talk of Many Things: The Collected Speeches* (Roseville, Cal.: Forum).

108. Torricelli and Carroll, *In Our Own Words,* 143.

109. Napoleon Bonaparte, "Oration Delivered on May 15, 1796, a Few Days After the Battle of Lodi," in Epes Sargent, *Standard Speaker: Containing Exercises in Prose and Poetry for Declamation in Schools, Academies, Lyceums, Colleges . . .* (Philadelphia: Thomas, Cowperthwait, 1852); see also William Safire, ed., *Lend Me Yours Ears: Great Speeches in History* (New York: W. W. Norton, 1992), 102–4.

110. William Shakespeare, *King Henry V,* ed. Emma Smith (Cambridge: Cambridge University Press, 2002), 3.4.44–56.

111. W. E. B. Du Bois, *In Battle for Peace: The Story of My 83rd Birthday* (New York: Masses and Mainstream, 1952).

112. Note Kerry's veiled reference to Robert Kennedy's line "They made a desert, and called it peace." Kennedy was referencing Tacitus: *Auferre, trucidare, rapere, falsis nominibus imperium; atque, ubi solitudinem faciunt, pacem appellant.* The same quote was used by Charles Sumner in 1847 (translated differently), and is discussed in that context in the section on Sumner, above.

## Chapter 8

1. Authorization for Use of Military Force, Pub. L. 107–40, 115 Stat. 225 (September 18, 2001).

2. Pub. L. 107–243, 116 Stat. 1498 (October 16, 2002).

3. See "Iraq Coalition Casualty Count," http://icasualties.org/iraq/index.aspx. The total number of American military fatalities rises to over 4,500 if one includes U.S. military deaths in Afghanistan. However, toward the end of Bush's term as president, the frequency of casualties began to drop. On iCasualties .org, see generally Matthew Bigg, "U.S. 'Joe Blow' Keeps Track of Iraq War Dead," Reuters, December 27, 2006 (reporting that the website's proprietor claims to gets a million hits a day on peak days and at least four million hits a month, and that Web audience measurement firm Hitwise calls it "one of the most visited non-partisan sites aimed at U.S. politics junkies"); Anna Varela, "A Somber Tally in Iraq," *Palm Beach Post*, October 17, 2005 (noting that the website has been cited in the *New York Times*, on the BBC, and in other news outlets, including the U.S. government–run Voice of America).

4. Carl Conetta, "The Wages of War: Iraqi Combatant and Noncombatant Fatalities in the 2003 Conflict," Project on Defense Alternatives, Research Monograph # 8, October 20, 2003, http://www.comw.org/0310rm8.html ("The Iraqi combatant fatality total that most reasonably reflects the existing evidence is 9,200 dead plus/minus 1,600 (or plus/minus 17.5 percent)." The dates Conetta uses in his study are unclear.

5. Gilbert Burnham, Riyadh Lafta, Shannon Doocy, and Les Roberts, "Mortality After the 2003 Invasion of Iraq: A Cross-Sectional Cluster Sample Survey," *Lancet* 368, no. 9545 (2006): 1421–28. This study was also published by the same authors with the title "The Human Cost of the War in Iraq: A Mortality Study, 2002–2006." It was conducted by the Bloomberg School of Public Health at Johns Hopkins University in Baltimore, Maryland, and Al-Mustansiriya University's School of Medicine in Baghdad, Iraq, in cooperation with the Massachusetts Institute of Technology's Center for International Studies in Cambridge, Massachusetts. See http://web.mit.edu/CIS/pdf/Human_Cost_of_War.pdf (accessed June 8, 2009).

6. Associated Press, "Report: 110,600 Iraqis Killed Since Invasion," April 24, 2009, published on http://www.msnbc.com (accessed June 12, 2010). The *Associated Press* also noted that of the 87,215 deaths since 2005, 59,957 came in 2006 and 2007, "when sectarian attacks soared and death squads roamed the streets." It continued, "The period was marked by catastrophic bombings and execution-style killings."

7. "How the Presidents Stack Up," graphic in *Wall Street Journal*, May 5, 2006, http://online.wsj .com/public/resources/documents/info-presapp0605-31.html (accessed June 8, 2009). The *Wall Street Journal* obtained its data from Gallup and the Associated Press.

8. Dana Milbank and Jim VandeHei, "No Political Fallout for Bush on Weapons," *Washington Post*, May 17, 2003, A1. The *Washington Post* obtained its data from a Gallup poll made on behalf of CNN and *USA Today*.

9. Gallup International, "Iraq Poll 2003," http://www.gallup-international.com/ (accessed June 8, 2009). The survey also showed that the Argentines felt most strongly (83 percent) against military action. A large percentage of the Spanish and the French (74 percent and 60 percent, respectively) felt the same way. In general, Gallup International concluded, "a war against Iraq declared unilaterally by the US and its allies does not receive much public support."

10. Ibid. The Gallup International data show that a UN sanction would change the mind of some, but not many. The organization pointed out that if military action were taken, 73 percent of Americans felt that their country should support this action. But apart from citizens in the United States, only in Australia did a majority of the population (53 percent) agree.

11. Angelique Chrisafis et al., "Millions Worldwide Rally for Peace," *Guardian*, February 17, 2003, http://www.guardian.co.uk/international/story/0,,897057,00.html (accessed June 8, 2009).

12. H.J. Res. 64, 107th Cong., 1st Sess. (2001).

13. Barbara Lee, "Barbara Lee's Stand," interview by John Nichols, *Nation*, October 8, 2001, 5.

14. Nicholas Eric Spinner, letter to the editor, *Los Angeles Times*, July 14, 2002.

15. Peter Carlson, "The Solitary Vote of Barbara Lee; Congresswoman Against Use of Force," *Washington Post*, September 19, 2001, sec. C.

16. Gary Rivlin, "Looking-Glass Politics; Rep. Barbara Lee Cast the Sole Vote Against Military Retaliation for the Sept. 11 Terrorist Attacks. Think Her

Career Is Over? You Don't Know the East Bay," *Los Angeles Times,* June 16, 2002.

17. Ibid.

18. Ibid.

19. Ibid.

20. Ibid.

21. Ibid.

22. Susan McHenry, "Barbara Lee: Going Against the Tide," *Essence,* December 2001, 26.

23. H.R. 4655, 105th Cong., 2d Sess. (1998); William J. Clinton, Address to the Nation Announcing Military Strikes on Iraq (December 16, 1998).

24. H.R. 130, 106th Cong., 1st Sess. (1999).

25. Lee's position can be contrasted with that of her Republican colleague Randy Cunningham from California's 51st Congressional District in San Diego. A former TOPGUN pilot, Cunningham originally opposed U.S. involvement in Kosovo, but reconsidered after the president committed troops there. See 145 Cong. Rec. H1660, H1662 ("I am vehemently opposed to us going into Kosovo, and I will explain why. But making that statement, now that we are engaged in Kosovo, I will do everything in my power to support the President"). Unlike Cunningham, Lee did not present a speech in the debate over H.R. 130.

26. Ruth Conniff, "Conscientious Objector in the House," *Progressive* 63, no. 5 (1999): 10.

27. There are two versions of Lee's speech: the first as she delivered it, and the second as revised and extended. The revised and extended version of the speech was the one disseminated to the public, and the one that triggered such strong responses. For the sake of historical accuracy, and to illustrate how significantly speakers can, and sometimes do, alter their speeches after the fact, I include the first version of Lee's speech below:

Mr. Speaker, I want to thank our ranking member and my friend for yielding time.

Mr. Speaker, I rise today really with a very heavy heart, one that is filled with sorrow for the families and the loved ones who were killed and injured this week. Only the most foolish and the most callous would not understand the grief that has really gripped our people and millions across the world.

This unspeakable act on the United States has forced me, however, to rely on my moral compass, my conscience, and my God for direction. September 11 changed the world. Our deepest fears now haunt us. Yet I am convinced that military action will not prevent further acts of international terrorism against the United States. This is a very complex and complicated matter.

This resolution will pass, although we all know that the President can wage a war even

without it. However difficult this vote may be, some of us must urge the use of restraint. Our country is in a state of mourning. Some of us must say, let us step back for a moment. Let us just pause for a minute and think through the implications of our actions today so that this does not spiral out of control.

I have agonized over this vote, but I came to grips with it today and I came to grips with opposing this resolution during the very painful yet very beautiful memorial service. As a member of the clergy so eloquently said, "As we act, let us not become the evil that we deplore."

147 Cong. Rec. H5642 (2001).

28. H.J. Res. 1145, 88th Cong., 2d Sess. (1964). Senator Ernest Gruening also voted against the resolution.

29. Lee, "Barbara Lee's Stand," 5.

30. Ken Silverstein, "Barack Obama Inc.: The Birth of a Washington Machine," *Harper's Magazine,* November 2006, http://www.harpers.org/archive/2006/11/0081275 (accessed May 27, 2007).

31. Mark Hemingway, "Passing a Sputtering Torch: The Kennedys Endorse Obama," *National Review,* January 29, 2008.

32. Sylvester Monroe, "Sen. Barack Obama; On the Outside Looking in, or Part of the Civil Rights Legacy?" *Ebony,* May 2007, 96.

33. Edward McClelland, "How Obama Learned to Be a Natural," Salon.com, February 12, 2007.

34. Silverstein, "Barack Obama Inc."

35. "Her Latest Incarnation . . . Hillary Clinton," *Economist,* May 19, 2007.

36. Heidi Przybyla, "Students Are the Backbone of Barack Obama's Campaign," *Seattle Post-Intelligencer,* May 16, 2007.

37. Mark Phelan, "Obama Talks Conservation, Drives Hemi," *Detroit Free Press,* May 11, 2007 ("The Democratic presidential contender was in Detroit on Monday, oozing charisma"); Michael Paul Williams, "Obama's Hip Status Slips During Visit," *Richmond Times Dispatch,* May 11, 2007 ("Obama, an Illinois senator running for president, oozes charisma and seems aptly cast as The Hip Hope for a New America"); Vincent Moss, "Charismatic Candidate Could Make It to the Top; Is This the Black JFK?," Commentary, *Sunday Mirror* (London), February 11, 2007 ("Oozing charisma and ambition, Barack Obama is the most exciting figure to burst on to the American political scene since a young Bill Clinton").

38. McClelland, "How Obama Learned to Be a Natural" ("Today he drips with charisma and inspires fawning admiration from all quarters"); "Vilsack Backers Remain Confident Despite Obama's

Expected Entry in White House Race," *Frontrunner*, January 17, 2007 ('He literally drips charisma,' said Gordon Fischer, a former Iowa Democratic Party chairman and Vilsack supporter who concedes some caucus-goers will be smitten by Obama's attributes"); "Barack Obama: The Great Black Hope," *Sunday Tribune* (Ireland), February 11, 2007, News, N06 ("This talented newcomer may drip charisma from his pores").

39. "Rock-Star Charisma," *Chattanooga Times Free Press* (Tennessee), January 28, 2007.

40. Tod Lindberg, "Charisma-Drenched Barack Obama," *Washington Times*, January 23, 2007, Op-Ed, A17 ("The entry of the charisma-drenched Barack Obama into the Democratic presidential race has overturned Hillary Rodham Clinton's presumptive smooth sailing to the nomination, and the Clinton people are running scared").

41. David Crary, "Interracial Marriages Surge Across U.S.," *Associated Press*, April 13, 2007.

42. Joe Klein, "How to Build a Bonfire," *Time*, February 26, 2007, 18 ("In fact, given Obama's slim political résumé and drop-dead charisma, his campaign is more candidate-driven than most").

43. Ryan Lizza, "The Natural: Why Is Barack Obama Generating More Excitement Among Democrats than John Kerry?," *Atlantic Monthly*, September 2004, http://www.theatlantic.com/doc/200409/lizza (accessed May 27, 2007).

44. Cindy Richards, "Health Care Needs Dose of Real Reform," *Chicago Sun Times*, January 31, 2007 ("Unlike his predecessors, Sen. Barack Obama is a candidate with the potential to edge out front-runner Clinton for the Democratic nod and the charisma and panache to sit behind the desk in the Oval Office").

45. Neil Modie and Scott Gutierrez, "About 2,500 People Turn out to Hear, Touch Democrats' Rising Star; Obama Thrills Crowd Like Celebrity," *Seattle Post-Intelligencer*, October 27, 2006.

46. Deirdre Shesgreen and Jo Mannies, "Obama Lends a Hand," *St. Louis Post-Dispatch*, November 6, 2006.

47. McClelland, "How Obama Learned to Be a Natural."

48. Garrett M. Graff, "The Legend of Barack Obama," Washingtonian.com, November 1, 2007, http://www.washingtonian.com/articles/mediapolitics/1836.html (accessed June 8, 2009).

49. Ibid. ("Obama's 2004 keynote address at the Democratic convention, delivered in his sonorous baritone voice, transformed him into a rock star—or at least the hottest thing in the Democratic Party"); Silverstein, "Barack Obama Inc." ("Obama ascended to political fame with a 'stirring and widely lauded speech' at the 2004 Democratic Convention"); McClelland, "How Obama Learned to Be a Natural" ("Obama delivered a maiden speech to rival that of Hubert Humphrey in 1948, or William Jennings Bryan in 1896"). As *Harper's* pointed out, the speech was "universally hailed," and even the conservative *National Review* characterized it as "simple," powerful," and deserving of "rapturous critical reception." See Rich Lowry, "Oh Bama!," *National Review*, July 28, 2004, http://www.nationalreview.com/lowry/lowry200407281612.asp (accessed June 8, 2009). Less than two months later, Obama was elected to the U.S. Senate, winning with 70 percent of the vote. See Silverstein, "Barack Obama, Inc."

50. As Hillary Clinton commented on *Meet the Press* during the 2008 presidential campaign, "The story of his campaign is really the story of that speech and his opposition to Iraq." "On Meet the Press, Hillary Examines Sen. Obama on Iraq," Targeted News Service, January 13, 2008.

51. Jeff Zeleny, "Testing the Water, Obama Tests His Own Limits," *New York Times*, December 24, 2006, A1.

52. Mike Lupica, "Mario Sez: It's About Charisma, Money and . . . Predicts '08 Prez Race Will Be More of the Same," *New York Daily News*, February 14, 2007, 6.

53. "Time to Walk the Walk," editorial, *New York Daily News*, May 11, 2007.

54. Rupert Cornwell, "Obama Sets out on His Mission to Excite and Unite a Divided Nation," *Independent* (London), February 10, 2007, 2.

55. Tim Hames, "I've Got the Sauce to Say it: Barack Obama Is a Loser," *Times* (London), February 12, 2007.

56. Shesgreen and Mannies, "Obama Lends a Hand."

57. Peggy Noonan, "Declarations: 'The Man from Nowhere,'" *Wall Street Journal*, December 16, 2006, P14.

58. According to the ANSWER Coalition's website, http://www.answercoalition.org/national/index.html (accessed May 28, 2007), the organization formed on September 14, 2001, and represents "major national organizations that have campaigned against U.S. intervention in Latin America, the Caribbean, the Middle East and Asia, and organizations that have campaigned for civil rights and for social and economic justice for working and poor people inside the United States." The group claims to have "organized the first national demonstration against war and racism following September 11 on September 29, 2001, which brought 25,000 people into the streets of Washington D.C., and 15,000 in San Francisco." Michael Crowley also offers further details about the event's origins. See "Cinderella Story," *New Republic*, February 27, 2008, 14. Crowley writes that on the last weekend of September 2002, BettyLu

Saltzman, "a wealthy political gadfly in her seventies," telephoned Marilyn Katz, "a p.r. maven" and a former aide to Chicago mayor Harold Washington. "We have to do something about Bush's drive to war," Crowley quotes Saltzman as saying. The two women contacted friends on the "local liberal-activist circuit" about staging a demonstration. Ibid. A slew of local politicians were invited to speak, but few accepted, according to Crowley. One of them was Obama; another was Jesse Jackson. Ibid.

59. See Barack Obama, *The Audacity of Hope: Thoughts on Reclaiming the American Dream* (New York: Crown, 2006). Obama returned often to the themes outlined in his 2002 speech. In fact, he would often refer explicitly to it in subsequent addresses. For an almost mirror image of Obama's 2002 speech in 2007, see his remarks on the Iraq War, March 21, 2007, 153 Cong. Rec. S3457. As the powerful genesis of his antiwar views, the speech is often the starting point for politicians, journalists, and others who point to alleged inconsistencies between Obama's *words* on the stump and *votes* on the Senate floor. For example, on *Meet the Press* on January 13, 2007, Hillary Clinton stated that Obama "gave a very impassioned speech against [the War in Iraq] and consistently said that he was against the war, he would vote against the funding for the war. By 2003, that speech was off his website. By 2004, he was saying that he didn't really disagree with the way George Bush was conducting the war. And by 2005, 6, and 7, he was voting for $300 billion in funding for the war. . . . And when he became a senator, he didn't go to the floor of the Senate to condemn the war in Iraq for 18 months. He didn't introduce legislation against the war in Iraq. He voted against timelines and deadlines initially." See also Crowley, "Cinderella Story" (providing a short but nuanced evaluation of the consistency, or lack thereof, of Obama's antiwar stance).

60. In a September 26, 2007, debate at Dartmouth College, Obama congratulated himself for "telling the truth to the American people even when it's tough, which I did in 2002, standing up against this war at a time where it was very unpopular. And I was risking my political career, because I was in the middle of a U.S. Senate race." Crowley, "Cinderella Story." In reality, the courageousness of Obama's stance on the War in Iraq was likely more significant at the national level than at the state level. As Ron Fournier has pointed out, the *Chicago Sun-Times* published a poll in October 2002 under the headline "Illinois Is Not Ready for War." "Analysis: Obama Prescient on Iraq, but 'Courageous Leader' Tag May Be a Stretch," Associated Press, October 2, 2007. Fournier notes that the *Sun-Times* survey found that more than half of voters in the Democratic-leaning

state wanted more proof that Saddam was developing weapons of mass destruction before the United States waged war. Ibid. In addition, Fournier also avers that Obama's strategy for winning the Democratic Senate nomination "hinged on his ability to form a coalition among blacks and so-called lakefront liberals in Chicago, hardly a pro-war constituency." Ibid. "His rivals for the nomination," Fournier writes, "also would criticize the war." Ibid.

61. See the section on Moorfield Storey, above.

62. See ibid.

63. See Charles Eliot Norton's "Counterfeit Patriotism" speech, above.

64. Bruce A. Dixon, "In Search of the Real Barack Obama: Can a Black Senate Candidate Resist the DLC?," *Black Commentator*, Issue 45, June 5, 2003. http://www.blackcommentator.com/45/45_dixon.html (accessed June 8, 2009).

65. "Not 'Corrupted' by DLC, Says Obama, Black U.S. Senate Candidate Response to BC Critique," Issue 47, June 19, 2003, http://www.black commentator.com/47/47_cover.html (accessed June 8, 2009).

66. Ibid.

67. See ibid. The CNN report "U.S. Marine Battalions Engaged in Fierce Fighting of War Against Iraqi Paramilitary Units, Regular Forces in Nasiriyah" aired on March 28, 2003. Transcript # 032802CN.V84.

68. http://www.barackobama.com. Not all were satisfied with Obama's explanation of the removal of the speech from the website. At the January 22, 2008 presidential debate, Hillary Clinton told her opponent, "You gave a great speech in 2002 opposing the war in Iraq . . . by the next year the speech was off your Web site." Hillary Clinton's statement was strenuously objected to by professor of law Lawrence Lessig, who cited evidence from the Internet's "Way-Back Machine." See "Lessig Explains Why He Is for Obama," *Liberal Values,* http://liberalvaluesblog.com/?p = 2852 (accessed February 28, 2009) (stating "the speech that she says was removed from Obama's website *remained* on Obama's website throughout the course of the next year. You can know that by going to this site, The Archive.org's Wayback Machine, and you can actually see copies of the web taken in every couple of month intervals from 1996 on." Obama's own admission of removing the speech from the website, however, belies Lessig's claims.

69. After being elected to the U.S. Senate in November 2004, Obama told the *Chicago Sun Times,* "I can unequivocally say I will not be running for national office in four years." See Scott Fornek, "Obama for President? That's 'Silly,'" *Chicago Sun-Times,* November 4, 2004. By October 2006, Obama's willingness to entertain a potential presidential

bid had changed. Obama admitted to Tim Russert on CNN's *Meet the Press* on October 22, 2006, that he was contemplating running for president.

70. See "Barack Obama's Iraq Speech," Answers.com, http://www.answers.com/topic/barack-obamas-iraq-speech (accessed December 26, 2006).

71. *Times Literary Supplement,* March 27, 1969.

72. *Los Angeles Times Book Review,* December 27, 1981.

73. Samantha Power, "The Everything Explainer," review of *Hegemony or Survival: America's Quest for Global Dominance,* by Noam Chomsky, *New York Times Book Review,* January 4, 2004. Power concludes that Chomsky "may be the most widely read American voice on foreign policy on the planet today."

74. Ibid.

75. *9–11* (New York: Seven Stories Press, 2001); *Hegemony or Survival: America's Quest for Global Dominance* (New York: Metropolitan Books, 2003); *Power and Terror: Post 9/11 Talks and Interviews* (New York: Seven Stories Press, 2003); *Imperial Ambitions: Conversations on the Post 9/11 World* (New York: Metropolitan Books, 2005); *Failed States: The Abuse of Power and the Assault on Democracy* (New York: Metropolitan Books, 2006); *Perilous Power: The Middle East and U.S. Foreign policy: Dialogues on Terror, Democracy, War, and Justice,* with Gilbert Achcar (Boulder: Paradigm, 2007); *Interventions* (San Francisco: City Lights Books, 2007); *What We Say Goes: Conversations on U.S. Power in a Changing World* (New York: Metropolitan Books, 2007).

76. Power, "The Everything Explainer."

77. Jan G. Deutsch, review of *American Power and the New Mandarins,* by Noam Chomsky, *New York Times Book Review,* March 16, 1969.

78. Chomsky's organizational role in the March 1967 march on the Pentagon and subsequent arrest was memorialized by Norman Mailer, who spent the night with Chomsky in jail, and wrote about it in *The Armies of the Night: History as a Novel, the Novel as History* (New York: New American Library, 1968). Chomsky's own account can be found in "On Resistance," an article Chomsky authored in the December 7, 1967, issue of the *New York Review of Books.*

79. Christopher Lehmann-Haupt, "The Burden of Noam Chomsky," *New York Times,* August 2, 1973.

80. "Remarks—Vice-President Richard B. Cheney" (August 26, 2002), in *Proceedings of the 103rd National Convention of the Veterans of Foreign Wars of the United States* (Washington, D.C.: GPO, 2006), 37, available at http://www.gpo.gov/fdsys/pkg/CDOC-109hdoc145/pdf/CDOC-109hdoc145.pdf.

81. "President Bush Outlines Iraqi Threat," news release, http://georgewbush-whitehouse.archives.gov/news/releases/2002/10/20021007-8.html, and in *The Iraq Papers,* ed. John Ehrenberg et al. (Oxford: Oxford University Press, 2010), 88.

82. Yingzhen Zhang, "Chomsky Denounces Bush's Handling of Conflict with Iraq," *Harvard Crimson,* November 5, 2002.

83. Byrd originally opposed the Persian Gulf War in 1991, but after President George H. W. Bush commenced military operations there, Byrd changed positions. See Remarks on U.S. Presence in the Persian Gulf, U.S. Senate, Washington, D.C., January 17, 1991, 137 Cong. Rec. S963, S968 ("Mr. President, the war that we all had hoped to avoid, but feared would come, has come. For those of us who counseled a different strategy in the weeks before the U.N. deadline, it is now time to unite in our support for the brave men and women of our Armed Forces who will prosecute this struggle and carry the alliance to ultimate victory. . . . [T]oday and for the duration of this war, here in this Chamber, there will be no division, no separating aisle, no party line. Together we stand in our support for the men and women on the front line—one President, one Senate, one Nation, one destiny!").

84. John Tierney, "Threats and Responses: The Senate; Byrd, at 85, Fills the Forum with Romans and Wrath," *New York Times,* November 20, 2002, sec. A.

85. John Dicker, "Antiwar Analysis Falls Short," *Rocky Mountain News* (Denver), July 23, 2004, sec. D.

86. Matthew Cooper, "Lionized in Winter: At 85, Robert Byrd Has Become an Overnight Internet Sensation and the Senate's Unlikeliest Liberal," *Time,* June 2, 2003, 33.

87. See, e.g., "We Stand Passively Mute . . . ," *The Guardian* (London), Feb. 18, 2003; "A Way Out of the Box . . . ," *Business Times* (Singapore), February 21, 2003.

88. Robert Byrd, interview on *Fresh Air* (NPR) with Terry Gross, July 27, 2004. A Google search on February 23, 2005, for example, yielded translations in most of the Romance languages.

89. Cooper, "Lionized in Winter."

90. Byrd, interview on *Fresh Air,* July 27, 2004, http://m.npr.org/news/front/128162362?singlePage=true.

91. Gail Russell, "Congress off Track, a Senate Sage Warns," *Christian Science Monitor,* September 22, 2004, 3.

92. George W. Bush, State of the Union Address, Washington, D.C. (January 29, 2002).

93. Ronald Reagan, Address at the National Association of Evangelicals in Orlando, Florida (March 8, 1983).

## Epilogue

1. Angelique Chrisafis and others, "Millions Worldwide Rally for Peace," *Guardian* (London), February 17, 2003, http://www.guardian.co.uk/international/story/0,,897057,00.html (accessed June 8, 2009). See the introduction to the War on Terror chapter, above.

2. Ibid.

3. Arundhati Roy, "The Great Indian Rape Trick," pts. I and II, *Sunday Magazine* (New Delhi), August 22 and September 3, 1994.

4. Robert Hanks, "Doing It for the Voles," *Daily Telegraph* (London), November 16, 2002, 4.

## Appendix A

1. Two independent transcriptions of Debs's Canton, Ohio, speech were read into the record during his trial before the U.S. District Court for the Northern District of Ohio. The first transcription was made by Virgil Steiner, a twenty-year-old stenographer hired by the U.S. Department of Justice. By his own admission Steiner had no prior experience taking speeches. The second transcription was made by Edward R. Sterling, a thirty-two-year-old lawyer and shorthand reporter hired by the Socialist Party. Sterling had a great deal more experience than Steiner. Both versions were submitted by the government and admitted into evidence by the Court. Steiner's version is shorter and cleaner; Sterling's is longer, captures more of Debs's word flow, and includes more audience reactions. When Debs appealed his case to the U.S. Supreme Court, his attorneys included in their brief a modified version of Sterling's transcription. Sometime later, perhaps during Debs's subsequent imprisonment, yet another version of his speech appeared, one based on the Sterling transcription but apparently adapted by the Socialists for mass production. It is this latter version that, in one form or another, editors appear to have published for almost a century. This anthology includes the original Sterling transcription, as introduced into evidence, because it appears to be the most true-to-life account of what Debs actual said. This is not to say the transcription is perfect. As Sterling himself admitted on cross-examination by Debs' lawyer, "[I]t is common for speakers to use a wrong word and think they are using the right word as Mr. Debs did in his speech; and it is also possible that I might have gotten the wrong word here in place of the right word. Experts do not claim to be perfect. The[y] simply claim to be highly skilled."

2. Chronicling the early pamphlets that reproduce Debs's speech is challenging because not all publications are dated. One of the first of these early, undated publications, *Eugene V. Debs' Canton Speech,* leaves Debs's errors as quoted by Sterling intact, explaining, "It is also evident to anyone familiar with Comrade Debs' wide knowledge, fluent style and perfect English, that he could not have committed the grammatical errors or made the incorrect quotations and historical references which this version of his speech contains. We have thought it best however, to publish exactly what the Government claims he said, and upon which they base the justice of his conviction and of his continued imprisonment long after the war is over, rather than a more complete and accurate version."

*Debs and the War* appears to be one of the earliest and most commonly cited corruptions of Debs's Canton speech. While *The Debs Case* and *The Debs White Book* made relatively small corrective changes (e.g., correcting Debs's reference from "Jackson" to "Johnson"), *Debs and the War* inserted language that had not previously been reported. *Debs and the War* is particularly troubling as a source for Debs's speech, because it erroneously states that it was taken "from the court records and is identical with the version submitted in evidence by the Government and upon which Comrade Debs' conviction and sentence were based."

## Appendix B

1. Heinrich F. Plett, "Figures of Speech," in *Encyclopedia of Rhetoric,* ed. Thomas O. Sloane (Oxford: Oxford University Press, 2001), 309–14 (pegging the date at 1960). Plett briefly surveys the attempts to modernize the classical system, focusing on Ferdinand de Saussure's *Cours de linguistique générale,* ed. C. Bally and A. Sechehaye (Paris: Payot, 1916), and Noam Chomsky's *Aspects of the Theory of Syntax* (Cambridge, Mass.: M.I.T. Press, 1965).

2. For further information, consult Edward P. J. Corbett and Robert J. Connors, *Classical Rhetoric for the Modern Student,* 4th ed. (Oxford: Oxford University Press, 1999), and Sloane, *Encyclopedia of Rhetoric.* The definitions of rhetorical devices in this appendix are drawn from those in these two works.

3. Richard Nate, "Metonymy," in *Encyclopedia of Rhetoric,* 496.

4. José Antonio Mayoral, "Periphrasis," trans. A. Ballesteros, in Sloane, *Encyclopedia of Rhetoric,* 569.

5. Corbett and Connors, *Classical Rhetoric,* 381.

6. Heiner Peters, "Hyperbaton," in Sloane, *Encyclopedia of Rhetoric.*

7. I. R. Ga'Perin, *Stylistics,* 2nd ed. (Moscow, 1977), quoted in Heinrich F. Plett, "Parenthesis," in *Encyclopedia of Rhetoric.*

8. Corbett and Connors, *Classical Rhetoric,* 385.

9. Quoted in ibid.

10. Andrea Grun-Oesterreich, "Asyndeton," in *Encyclopedia of Rhetoric,* 57.

11. Ibid.

12. Corbett and Connors, *Classical Rhetoric,* 387

13. *Ars Rhetorica* 1420b.

14. Corbett and Connors, *Classical Rhetoric,* 438.

# BIOGRAPHICAL AND BIBLIOGRAPHICAL NOTES

## Mexican-American War

### Theodore Parker

There are many full-length biographies of Parker. The most recent are Dean Grodzins's *American Heretic: Theodore Parker and Transcendentalism* (Chapel Hill: University of North Carolina Press, 2002) and David B. Chesebrough's *Theodore Parker: Orator of Superior Ideas* (Westport, Conn.: Greenwood Press, 1999). Chesebrough focuses on Parker's rhetoric. Older biographies include Robert C. Albrecht's *Theodore Parker* (New York: Twayne, 1971), Henry Steele Commager's *Theodore Parker* (Boston: Beacon Press, 1936), and John Chadwick's *Theodore Parker: Preacher and Reformer* (Boston: Houghton Mifflin, 1900). Nineteenth-century biographies include Octavius Brooks Frothingham's *Theodore Parker: A Biography* (Boston: James R. Osgood, 1874), Albert Réville's *The Life and Writings of Theodore Parker* (1865), and John Weiss's *Life and Correspondence of Theodore Parker* (New York: D. Appleton, 1864).

The most comprehensive primary source for Parker's speeches and writings is his fourteen-volume *Collected Works* (London: Trübner, 1863–71), edited by Francis Power Cobbe. See also Henry Steele Commager's *An Anthology: Theodore Parker* (Boston: Beacon Press, 1960). Parker's papers can be found in the Andover-Harvard Theological Library at Harvard Divinity School, the Boston Public Library, and the Lexington Historical Society.

### Charles Sumner

The most recent biographies of Sumner are Anne-Marie Taylor's *Young Charles Sumner and the Legacy of the American Enlightenment, 1811–1851* (Amherst: University of Massachusetts Press, 2001) and Frederick J. Blue's *Charles Sumner and the Conscience of the North* (Arlington Heights, Ill: Harlan Davidson, 1994). The most valuable twentieth-century study remains David Donald's two volumes, *Charles Sumner and the Coming of the Civil War* (New York: Knopf, 1960) and *Charles Sumner and the Rights of Man* (New York: Knopf, 1970). Edward L. Pierce's authoritative *Memoir and Letters of Charles Sumner,* 4 vols. (Boston: Roberts Brothers, 1877–93), is the most valuable from the nineteenth century.

Many of Sumner's speeches can be found in *The Works of Charles Sumner,* 15 vols. (Boston: Lee and Shepard, 1870–83). Compiled by Sumner himself, it includes all of his major antiwar addresses. Sumner's correspondence can be found at Harvard University's Houghton Library, and is also available in an eighty-five-reel microfilm collection edited by Beverly Wilson Palmer, *The Papers of Charles Sumner* (Alexandria, Va.: Chadwyck-Healey, 1988). Palmer also edited *The Selected Letters of Charles Sumner,* 2 vols. (Boston: Northeastern University Press, 1990).

### Abraham Lincoln

Secondary resources on Lincoln abound. Particularly useful in writing this book were David Herbert Donald's *Lincoln* (New York: Simon and Schuster, 1995), Mark E. Neely Jr.'s *The Last Best Hope of Earth: Abraham*

*Lincoln and the Promise of America* (Cambridge, Mass.: Harvard University Press, 1993), and James G. Randall's *Lincoln the President,* 4 vols. (New York: Dodd, Mead, 1945–55; vol. 4 by James G. Randall and Richard N. Current). Also useful were Carl Sandburg's *Abraham Lincoln: The Prairie Years,* 2 vols. (New York: Harcourt, Brace, 1926) and William H. Herndon and Jesse W. Weik's *Herndon's Lincoln: The True Story of a Great Life,* 3 vols. (Chicago: Belford, Clarke, 1889).

Donald W. Riddle's *Congressman Abraham Lincoln* (Urbana: University of Illinois Press, 1957; repr., Westport, Conn.: Greenwood Press, 1979) is devoted to Lincoln's years in Congress, which are also surveyed in William C. Harris's *Lincoln's Rise to the Presidency* (Lawrence: University Press of Kansas, 2007). Particularly useful for understanding public reaction to Lincoln's opposition to the Mexican-American war is *Abraham Lincoln, a Press Portrait: His Life and Times from the Original Newspaper Documents of the Union, the Confederacy, and Europe,* ed. Herbert Mitgang (New York: Fordham University Press, 2000; originally published as *Lincoln, as They Saw Him: His Life and Times from the Original Newspaper Documents of the Union, the Confederacy, and Europe,* 1956).

Lois J. Einhorn's *Abraham Lincoln, the Orator: Penetrating the Lincoln Legend* (Westport, Conn.: Greenwood Press, 1992) provides a great deal of rhetorical analysis of Lincoln, and James Engell's *The Committed Word* (University Park: Pennsylvania State University Press, 1999) contains an excellent chapter on Lincoln's rhetorical development and his place as an American literary icon. Garry Wills's *Lincoln at Gettysburg: The Words That Remade America* (New York: Simon and Schuster, 1992), though it focuses solely on the Gettysburg Address, is an indispensable book on Lincoln's oratory. In addition, three excellent recent books have focused specifically on Lincoln's speeches: Douglas Wilson's *Lincoln's Sword: The Presidency and the Power of Words* (New York: Alfred A. Knopf, 2006); John Channing Briggs's *Lincoln's Speeches Reconsidered* (Baltimore: Johns Hopkins University Press, 2005); and Ronald C. White Jr.'s *The Eloquent President: A Portrait of Lincoln Through His Words* (New York: Random House, 2005). Briggs's study is primarily concerned with Lincoln's career before he became president and contains a chapter on Lincoln's Mexican-American War speech.

The most comprehensive collection of Lincoln's letters, speeches, and other compositions is Roy P. Basler's *Collected Works of Abraham Lincoln,* 8 vols. (New Brunswick: Rutgers University Press, 1953–55) and his *Collected Works of Abraham Lincoln: Supplement, 1832–1865* (Westport, Conn.: Greenwood Press, 1974). See also the Abraham Lincoln Papers at the Library of Congress, http://memory.loc.gov/ammem/alhtml/malhome.html. While most of the items in the Lincoln Papers are from the 1850s through Lincoln's presidential years, there are some pre-1850s items as well, including a handwritten draft of his antiwar remarks in Congress on January 12, 1848.


## Civil War

### Clement Vallandigham

Frank L. Klement's *The Limits of Dissent: Clement L. Vallandigham and the Civil War* (Lexington: University Press of Kentucky; repr., New York: Fordham University Press, 1998) gives the most detailed scholarly account of Vallandigham's opposition to the Civil War. Joanna Dunlap Cowden's *Heaven Will Frown on Such a Cause as This: Six Democrats Who Opposed Lincoln's War* (Lanham, Md.: University Press of America, 2001) includes an excellent biographical chapter on Vallandigham. Notable articles on Vallandigham include Ewing E. Beauregard, "The Bingham-Vallandigham Feud," *Biography* 15 (1992): 29–48; Michael Les Benedict, "Vallandigham: Constitutionalist and Copperhead," *Timeline* 3 (1986): 16–25; and Roger Long, "Copperhead: Clement Vallandigham," *Civil War Times Illustrated* 20 (1981): 22–29. American National Biography Online also features a short summary of Vallandigham's life by William G. Andrew.

Primary sources for Vallandigham include *The Record of Hon. C. L. Vallandigham on Abolition, the Union, and the Civil War* (Columbus, Ohio: J. Walter, 1863) and *Speeches, Arguments, Addresses, and Letters of Clement L. Vallandigham* (New York: J. Walter, 1864), both of which were published by Vallandigham himself. After his death, his brother, James L. Vallandigham, published *A Life of Clement L. Vallandigham* (Baltimore: Turnbull Brothers, 1872), which includes biographical material and excerpts from many of Vallandigham's speeches, though it is understandably partisan. One excellent resource regarding Vallandigham's trial, and the evidence against him, is *The Trial of Hon. Clement L. Vallandigham, by a Military Commission: And the Proceedings Under His Application for a Writ of Habeas Corpus in the Circuit Court of the United States for the Southern District of Ohio* (Cincinnati: Rickey and Carroll, 1863). As Andrew notes, no substantial collection of Vallandigham's papers has survived.

*Alexander Long*

Alexander Long has received little scholarly attention. Joanna Dunlap Cowden's *Heaven will Frown on Such a Cause as This: Six Democrats Who Opposed Lincoln's War* (Lanham, Md.: University Press of America, 2001) includes an excellent biographical chapter on Long. "The Autobiography of Alexander Long," ed. Louis R. Harlan, *Bulletin of the Historical and Philosophical Society of Ohio* 19 (April 1961): 99–127, includes a brief scholarly biography. Two unpublished master's theses deserve special note: Edward Spaulding Perzel's "Alexander Long: A Political Study of a Copper-Head Congressman, 1816–1886" (1962) and Louise Schwallie Heidish's "Alexander Long, Ultraconservative Democrat" (1962).

Though some of Long's congressional speeches were published during his lifetime in pamphlet form, the best primary source for them, including his April 8, 1963, address, is the *Congressional Globe*. Long's papers, including over four thousand items, are housed at the Cincinnati Historical Society in Cincinnati, Ohio.

## Spanish-American War and Philippine Insurrection

*Moorfield Storey*

M. A. De Wolfe Howe's *Portrait of an Independent: Moorfield Storey* (Boston: Houghton Mifflin, 1932) was the first full-length biography of Storey. In the second, William B. Hixson's *Moorfield Storey and the Abolitionist Tradition* (New York: Oxford University Press, 1972), Hixson argues that Storey facilitated a shift from the abolitionist tradition to the causes of domestic civil rights and anti-imperialism. Ann Louise Leger's "Moorfield Storey: An Intellectual Biography" (1968) appears to be the only Ph.D. dissertation on Storey, but Storey's grandson, James Moorfield Story, wrote an honor's thesis on his grandfather, "Moorfield Storey: Yankee Moralist" (1953), which can be found in the Harvard University Archives. Richard E. Welch Jr.'s article "The Law, Right Conduct, and Moorfield Storey," *Historian* 41, no. 2 (1979): 225–40, appears to be the most recent scholarly account of Storey's life.

Many of Storey's formal addresses, including "A Civilian's View of the Navy," were published in pamphlet form. Storey also published full-length books, including *Charles Sumner* (New York: Houghton Mifflin, 1900) and, with Marcial P. Lichauco, *The Conquest of the Philippines by the United States, 1898–1925* (New York: G. P. Putnam's Sons, 1926). The Moorfield Storey Papers are housed at the Massachusetts Historical Society in Boston.

*Charles Eliot Norton*

The most recent full-length biographies of Norton are Linda Dowling's *Charles Eliot Norton: The Art of Reform in Nineteenth-Century America* (Durham: University of New Hampshire Press, 2007) and James Turner's *The Liberal Education of Charles Eliot Norton* (Baltimore: Johns Hopkins University Press, 1999). An earlier but valuable account of Norton's life and his opposition to the Spanish-American War is Kermit Vanderbilt's *Charles Eliot Norton: Apostle of Culture in a Democracy* (Cambridge, Mass.: Belknap Press, 1959). Information about Norton's Ashfield Dinners can be found in Betty Gulick's *Charles Eliot Norton and the Ashfield Dinners, 1879–1930* (Ashfield Mass.: Ashfield Historical Society, 1990).

Norton's papers, including his letters, are housed at Harvard University's Houghton Library. Houghton Library contains the most useful primary resource regarding Norton's antiwar stance, Sara Norton's "Records of the hour, wartime" (1898). The two-volume scrapbook contains general clippings about his antiwar stance and the responses in favor of and in opposition to it. Newspaper articles and letters to and from Norton are included in the book. The most important of Norton's letters are compiled in *Letters of Charles Eliot Norton*, ed. Sara Norton and M. A. De Wolfe Howe (Boston: Houghton Mifflin, 1913).

*Carl Schurz*

The most recent biography of Schurz in English is Hans Louis Trefousse's *Carl Schurz: A Biography* (New York: Fordham University Press, 1998). Older biographies are Claude Moore Fuess's *Carl Schurz, Reformer, 1829–1906* (New York: Dodd, Mead, 1932) and Chester V. Easum's *The Americanization of Carl Schurz* (Chicago: University of Chicago Press, 1929). Glenn Reid Harwood's Ph.D. dissertation, "The Movement for Assimilation: A Critical Analysis of the Rhetoric of Carl Schurz," analyzes some aspects of Schurz's rhetoric, and George Cameron Mackenzie's master's thesis, "Carl Schurz and Imperialism" (1947), studies Schurz's anti-imperialist activities. Copies of some political cartoons that took aim at Schurz for his dissenting views are collected by Rüdiger Wersich in *Carl Schurz: Revolutionary and Statesman: His Life in Personal and Official Documents with Illustrations* (Munich: Heinz Moos, 1979).

An excellent primary source for Schurz's antiwar speeches is *Speeches, Correspondence, and Political Papers of Carl Schurz,* 6 vols., ed. Frederic Bancroft (New York: G. P. Putnam's Sons, 1913; repr., New York: Negro Universities Press, 1969). Many of Schurz's anti-imperialist speeches were published in pamphlet form by the American Anti-Imperialist League as well. The Library of Congress houses the main body of Schurz's papers. Other Schurz papers can be found in the State Historical Society of Missouri, the National Archives, the New York Public Library, the Watertown Historical Society in Wisconsin, and the State Historical Society of Wisconsin.

## World War I

### William Jennings Bryan

The standard biographies of Bryan are Paolo E. Coletta's *William Jennings Bryan,* 3 vols. (Lincoln: University of Nebraska Press, 1964–69) and Louis W. Koenig's *Bryan: A Political Biography of William Jennings Bryan* (New York: Putnam, 1971). The most recent Bryan biographies are Gerald Leinwand's *William Jennings Bryan: An Uncertain Trumpet* (Lanham, Md.: Rowman and Littlefield, 2007) and Michael Kazin's *A Godly Hero: The Life of William Jennings Bryan* (New York: Knopf, 2006). Older but still notable biographies include Kendrick A. Clements's *William Jennings Bryan: Missionary Isolationist* (Knoxville: University of Tennessee Press, 1982), Lawrence W. Levine's *Defender of the Faith: William Jennings Bryan, The Last Decade, 1915–1925* (New York: Oxford University Press, 1965), and Merle Eugene Curti's *Bryan and World Peace* (Northampton Mass: Department of History of Smith College, 1931; repr., New York: Octagon Books, 1969). Also useful is Coletta's article "William Jennings Bryan's Plans for World Peace," *Nebraska History* 58 (Summer 1977): 193–217. Donald K. Springens's *William Jennings Bryan: Orator of Small-Town America* (New York: Greenwood Press, 1991) considers Bryan's life through his rhetoric, and Malcolm O. Sillars's "William Jennings Bryan: The Jeffersonian Liberal as Progressive," in *Rhetoric and Reform in the Progressive Era*, ed. J. Michael Hogan, 185–227 (East Lansing: Michigan State University Press, 2003), is useful in this regard as well.

For Bryan's thoughts on imperialism and the Spanish-American War, see *Imperialism: Extracts from Speeches, Interviews, and Articles* (1900; repr. as *Bryan on Imperialism,* New York: Arno Press, 1970). Many of his antiwar speeches in the run-up to World War I were published in pamphlet form. *The Memoirs of William Jennings Bryan* (Philadelphia: John C. Winston, 1925), which his wife, Mary Baird Bryan, completed after his death, include some of his thoughts oratory and about his resignation as secretary of state. Most of Bryan's papers are housed at the Library of Congress. Smaller collections are available at Occidental College in Los Angeles, the Nebraska State Historical Society, and the Illinois State Historical Society.

### George Norris

The definitive biography of Norris is Richard's Lowitt's *George W. Norris,* 3 vols. (Urbana: University of Illinois Press, 1963–78). A one-volume topical analysis of Norris's life is Norman L. Zucker's *George W. Norris: Gentle Knight of American Democracy* (Urbana: University of Illinois Press, 1966). Wayne S. Cole's valuable evaluative summary of Norris's life appears American National Biography Online. John F. Kennedy's *Profiles in Courage* (New York: Harper and Row, 1956) has a chapter on Norris's opposition to President Wilson's war policies. Two full-length biographies appeared in Norris's lifetime: Alfred Lief's *Democracy's Norris: The Biography of a Lonely Crusade* (New York: Stackpole Sons, 1939) and Richard L. Neuberger and Stephen B. Kahn's *Integrity: The Life of George W. Norris* (New York: Vanguard Press, 1937). Norris completed his autobiography, *Fighting Liberal: The Autobiography of George W. Norris* (New York: Macmillan, 1945), during the final months of his life. Arthur M. Schlesinger's foreword, "George Norris and the Liberal Tradition," appears in the 1961 Collier edition and the 1972 University of Nebraska Press edition (reprinted several times). Also of note is John Anthony Oostendorp's Ph.D. dissertation, "A Rhetorical Criticism of Certain Selected Speeches of George W. Norris on the Issue of Public Power" (State University of Iowa, 1965).

Norton's papers are housed at the Library of Congress.

*Robert M. La Follette*

The most recent biography of La Follette is Nancy C. Unger's *Fighting Bob La Follette: The Righteous Reformer* (Chapel Hill: University of North Carolina Press, 2000). An excellent, though inevitably biased, account of La Follette's entire career is the biography compiled by his wife and daughter, Belle Case and Fola: *Robert M. La Follette, June 14, 1855–June 18, 1925,* 2 vols. (New York: Macmillan, 1953). More detached biographies include David P. Thelen's *Robert M. La Follette and the Insurgent Spirit* (Boston: Little, Brown, 1976) and *The Early Life of Robert M. La Follette, 1855–1884* (Chicago: Loyola University Press, 1966) and Bernard A. Weisberger's *The La Follettes of Wisconsin: Love and Politics in Progressive America* (Madison: University of Wisconsin Press, 1994). Carl R. Burgchardt analyzes La Follette's oratory in particular in *Robert M. La Follette, Sr.: The Voice of Conscience* (New York: Greenwood Press, 1992). Arthur J. Amchan analyzes La Follette's opposition to World War I in *The Kaiser's Senator: Robert M. La Follette's Alleged Disloyalty During World War I* (Alexandria, Va.: Amchan, 1994). Michigan State University has a tape of one of La Follette's sons, Philip Fox La Follette, talking in 1939 about his father's persecution as a result of his vote against the declaration of war against Germany in 1917.

Dissertations written on the topic of La Follette's opposition to World War I include Harry Ronald Gianneschi, "An Ideological Analysis of the Senate Wartime Addresses of Robert Marion La Follette" (Bowling Green State University, 1975); Wade Kniseley, "A Study of Woodrow Wilson's and Senator La Follette's Speaking on the World War Issue" (University of Washington, 1945); Samuel Roop Mohler, "Senator Robert Marion LaFollette [*sic*] in the World War Period" (University of Washington, 1936); and Mary Medarda Mazich, "La Follette and American Participation in the World War" (DePaul University, 1935). See also Peggy Anne Kelley, "LaFollette's Legacy: America's Oldest Monthly Opinion Magazine, a Content Analysis of Selected War Coverage in 'The Progressive' Magazine Which Includes World War I, World War II, the Vietnam War and the Persian Gulf War" (M.A. thesis, Michigan State University, 1994) ; and Harold A. Borgh, "Senator Robert M. La Follet[t]e and the World War" (M.S. thesis, Kansas State Teachers College, 1939).

The La Follette Family Papers are housed at the Library of Congress. *La Follette's Autobiography: A Personal Narrative of Political Experiences* (Madison, Wis.: Robert M. La Follette Co., 1913) is useful for, among other things, his early rhetorical education. His Senate speeches appear in the *Congressional Record*. An excerpt from his speech in St. Paul on September 29, 1917, for which La Follette was again eviscerated by the press, was published in *Speech of Senator Robert M. La Follette* (Washington, D.C.: Government Printing Office, 1918). Also notable are the La Follette-Wheeler Joint National Committee's publication of the short pamphlet, La Follette's War Record (Washington, D.C.: The Committee 1924), and La Follette's introduction to Norman Thomas's The Conscientous Objector in America (New York: B. W. Huebsch, 1923).

*Kate Richards O'Hare*

The only full-length biography of O'Hare is Sally M. Miller's *From Prairie to Prison: The Life of Social Activist Kate Richards O'Hare* (Columbia: University of Missouri Press, 1993). There are, however, significant scholarly articles about her: Kathleen Kennedy, "Casting an Evil Eye on the Youth of the Nation: Motherhood and Political Subversion in the Wartime Prosecution of Kate Richards O'Hare, 1917–1924," *American Studies* 39, no. 3 (1998): 105–29; Erling N. Sannes, "'Queen of the Lecture Platform': Kate Richards O'Hare and North Dakota Politics, 1917–1921," *North Dakota History* 58, no. 4 (1991): 2–19; Marla Martin Hanley, "The Children's Crusade of 1922: Kate O'Hare and the Campaign to Free Radical War Dissenters in the Era of America's First Red Scare," *Gateway Heritage* 10 (1989): 34–43; Sally M. Miller, "Kate Richards O'Hare: Progression Towards Feminism," *Kansas History* 7 (Winter 1983): 263–79; Neil K. Basen, "Kate Richards O'Hare: The 'First Lady' of American Socialism, 1901–1917," *Labor History* 21 (Spring 1980): 165–99; and Edward J. Bommel, "Kate Richards O'Hare: A Midwestern Pacifist's Fight for Free Speech," *North Dakota Quarterly* 44 (Winter 1976): 5–19.

Martha Nesselbush Green has written a Ph.D. dissertation on O'Hare: "Outspoken Woman: Gender and Free Speech in the Trial of Kate Richards O'Hare" (Clark University, 2000). Short biographical sketches of O'Hare are David A. Shannon, "Kate Richards O'Hare Cunningham," in *Notable American Women,* ed. Edward T. James, Janet Wilson James, and Paul S. Boyer, 3 vols. (Cambridge, Mass.: Harvard University Press, 1971), 1:417–19; Jacob H. Dorn, "Kate Richards O'Hare, 1876–1948," in *Research Guide to American Historical Biography,* vol. 4, ed. Suzanne Niemeyer (Washington, D.C.: Beacham, 1990); and Philip S. Foner and Sally M. Miller's introduction to O'Hare's *Selected Writings and Speeches* (Baton Rouge: Louisiana State University Press, 1982), which is also the best source for O'Hare's writings.

O'Hare's papers are scattered. Some, consisting mainly of photocopies of official court documents relating to her trial and imprisonment, are located at the University of North Dakota. The originals are held by the National Archives in Kansas City, Missouri. Another collection, primarily covering 1901 to 1930, was produced by Neil Basen while doing research on O'Hare. This collection is owned by Basen and available only on microfilm. The Schlesinger Library at Harvard University houses a collection of O'Hare's papers. O'Hare's husband, Frank O'Hare, published three important pamphlets of his wife's speeches: *Socialism and the World War* (St. Louis: Frank P. O'Hare, 1919), *The Truth About the O'Hare Case* (St. Louis: Frank P. O'Hare, 1919), and *Americanism and Bolshevism* (St. Louis: Frank P. O'Hare, 1919). O'Hare's writings also appeared in the *Appeal to Reason* and *National Rip-Saw* periodicals.

### Eugene V. Debs

The standard Debs biography is Nick Salvatore's *Eugene V. Debs: Citizen and Socialist,* 2nd ed. (Urbana: University of Illinois Press, 2007). Older but still valuable biographies include Bernard J. Brommel's *Eugene V. Debs: Spokesman for Labor and Socialism* (Chicago: Charles H. Kerr, 1978), Ray Ginger's *The Bending Cross: A Biography of Eugene Victor Debs* (New York: Russell and Russell, 1949), and McAlister Coleman's *Eugene V. Debs, a Man Unafraid* (New York: Greenberg, 1930). Debs's rhetoric is considered in a chapter by James Francis Darsey in *The Prophetic Tradition and Radical Rhetoric in America* (New York: New York University Press, 1997). Ernest Freeberg's *Democracy's Prisoner: Eugene V. Debs, the Great War, and the Right to Dissent* (Cambridge, Mass.: Harvard University Press, 2008) examines the legal consequences of Debs's antiwar critique in the broader context of First Amendment rights during wartime.

The Debs Papers are located in the Cunningham Library of Indiana State University at Terre Haute. They are also available on microfilm. Numerous anthologies of Debs's speeches and writings are available. The most recent is *The Eugene V. Debs Reader: Socialism and the Class Struggle,* ed. William A. Pelz with an introduction by Howard Zinn (Chicago: Institute of Working Class History, 2000). *Writings and Speeches of Eugene V. Debs* (New York: Hermitage Press, 1948) includes an introduction by Arthur M. Schlesinger Jr. Debs's correspondence is collected in *Letters of Eugene V. Debs,* 3 vols., ed. J. Robert Constantine (Urbana: University of Illinois Press, 1990).

## World War II

### Norman Thomas

Many full-length biographies of Thomas are available. The most recent is Raymond F. Gregory's *Norman Thomas: The Great Dissenter* (New York: Algora, 2008). Others include W. A. Swanberg's *Norman Thomas: The Last Idealist* (New York: Charles Scribner's Sons, 1976), James C. Duram's *Norman Thomas* (New York: Twayne, 1974), Charles Gorham's *Leader at Large: The Long and Fighting Life of Norman Thomas* (New York: Farrar, Straus and Giroux, 1970), Bernard K. Johnpoll's *Pacifist's Progress: Norman Thomas and the Decline of American Socialism* (Chicago: Quadrangle Books, 1970), Murray B. Seidler's *Norman Thomas: Respectable Rebel* (Syracuse: Syracuse University Press, 1967), and Harry Fleischman's *Norman Thomas: A Biography* (New York: Norton, 1964). Charles William Fleischman's Ph.D. dissertation, "An Analysis and Evaluation of Selected Rhetorical Elements in the Radio Addresses of Norman Thomas on the Issue of Keeping America out of World War II" (New York University, 1975), addresses Thomas's World War II radio addresses in particular.

The Norman Thomas Papers, including an unpublished autobiography, are housed at the New York Public Library. They are available on microfilm, and a finding aid, "The Norman Thomas Papers Guide: 1904–1967," is available as well. In addition, the Columbia Oral History Project includes three interviews with Thomas, a transcript of which is available on microfilm. Thomas was a prolific writer, authoring twenty-one books and numerous articles during his lifetime. His World War II–era books include *War: No Glory, No Profit, No Need* (New York: Frederick A. Stokes, 1935) and *Keep America Out of War: A Program* (New York: Frederick A. Stokes, 1939). For a significant article, see "The Pacifist's Dilemma," *Nation,* January 16, 1937, 66–68. In addition, Thomas gave many antiwar speeches, some of which are available in *Norman Thomas on War: An Anthology,* ed. Bernard K. Johnpoll (New York: Garland, 1974). Many of Thomas's speeches are available in his papers. Audio recordings of some of them are also available. See, for example, *Norman Thomas, Radicalism Audio Cassette Series* (1967).

*Richard Wright*

The most recent biography of Wright is Hazel Roley's *Richard Wright: The Life and Times* (Chicago: University of Chicago Press, 2008). The most comprehensive is Michel Fabre's *The Unfinished Quest of Richard Wright*, 2nd ed. (Urbana: University of Illinois Press, 1993). Others notable biographies include Margaret Walker's *Richard Wright, Daemonic Genius: A Portrait of the Man, a Critical Look at His Work* (New York: Warner Books, 1988), John Alfred Williams's *The Most Native of Sons: A Biography of Richard Wright* (Garden City, N.Y.: Doubleday, 1970), and Constance Webb's *Richard Wright: A Biography* (New York: Putnam, 1968). Addison Gayle's *Richard Wright: Ordeal of a Native Son* (Garden City, N.Y.: Anchor Press / Doubleday, 1980) considers Wright's harassment by American governmental agencies.

A useful starting place for Wright's political nonfiction is *Black Power: Three Books from Exile: Black Power; The Color Curtain; and White Man, Listen!* (New York: Harper Perennial, 2008). *Richard Wright Reader* (New York: Da Capo Press, 1997) includes samples of Wright's nonfiction and journalism, among other things. For a useful guide to primary sources, see Charles T. Davis and Michel Fabre's *Richard Wright: A Primary Bibliography* (Boston: G. K. Hall, 1982). The main body of Wright's papers is housed at the Beinecke Rare Book and Manuscript Library at Yale University. For a useful guide to primary sources, see Charles T. Davis and Michel Fabre's *Richard Wright: A Primary Bibliography* (Boston: G. K. Hall, 1982).

*Charles Lindbergh*

Lindbergh biographies abound. The most recent is Von Hardesty's *Lindbergh: Flight's Enigmatic Hero* (New York: Harcourt, 2002). A. Scott Berg's *Lindbergh* (New York: Putnam, 1998) is a standard Lindbergh resource. Lindbergh's antiwar activities are chronicled in Wayne S. Cole's *Charles A. Lindbergh and the Battle Against American Intervention in World War II* (New York: Harcourt Brace Jovanovich, 1974).

The Charles Lindbergh Papers are housed at the Sterling Memorial Library at Yale University. Lindbergh's autobiographical writing provides some of the best information about his life: *The Spirit of St. Louis* (New York: Scribner, 1953), *The Wartime Journals of Charles A. Lindbergh* (New York: Harcourt Brace Jovanovich, 1970), *Boyhood on the Upper Mississippi: A Reminiscent Letter* (St. Paul: Minnesota Historical Society, 1972), and *Autobiography of Values* (New York: Harcourt Brace Jovanovich, 1978). Pat Ranfranz's excellent website, http://www.charleslindbergh.com, provides the full text and audio recordings of many of Lindbergh's antiwar speeches. Another useful primary resource is the FBI files on Lindbergh, which are now available on microfilm and on FBI's website. Finally, PBS Video's *Lindbergh* (1990) provides a wealth of photographs, films, and interviews with family members regarding Lindbergh's life in general and his Des Moines speech in particular.

# Korean War

*Paul Robeson*

Martin B. Duberman's *Paul Robeson* (New York: Knopf, 1988) is the most detailed biography of Robeson currently available. Other important examinations of his life include the collection of essays *Paul Robeson, the Great Forerunner*, ed. editors of *Freedomways* (New York: Dodd, Mead, 1978), Dorothy Butler Gilliam's *Paul Robeson: All-American* (Washington, D.C.: New Republic, 1976), and Marie Seton's *Paul Robeson* (London: Dennis Dobson, 1958). Colin Chambers's *Here We Stand: Politics, Performers, and Performance: Paul Robeson, Isadora Duncan, and Charlie Chaplin* (London: Nick Hern, 2006) examines how Robeson's artistic work was affected by his critique of racism.

The main body of the Paul Robeson Papers are housed at the Robeson Family Archives in the Moorland-Spingarn Research Center at Howard University in Washington, D.C. Lenwood G. Davis's *A Paul Robeson Research Guide: A Selected, Annotated Bibliography* (Westport, Conn.: Greenwood Press, 1982) is a useful guide to work by and about Robeson. Robeson published his autobiography, *Here I Stand*, in 1958 (London: Dennis Dobson). Philip S. Foner compiled Robeson's most significant works in *Paul Robeson Speaks: Writings, Speeches, Interviews, 1918–1974* (New York: Brunner/Mazel, 1978). Another useful primary resource is the FBI files on Robeson, which are now available on microfilm and on the FBI's website. American National Biography Online features a short but excellent summary of Robeson's life by Larry R. Gerlach.

*W. E. B. Du Bois*

The best account of Du Bois's antiwar views and subsequent trial is Gerald Horne's *Black and Red: W. E. B. Du Bois and the Afro-American Response to the Cold War, 1944–1963* (Albany: State University of New York Press, 1968). Useful general biographies are Manning Marable's *W. E. B. Du Bois: Black Radical Democrat* (Boulder, Colo.: Paradigm, 2005), which focuses on Du Bois's involvement in politics generally, and David L. Lewis's *W. E. B. Du Bois,* 2 vols. (New York: H. Holt, 1993–2000).

The W. E. B. Du Bois Papers are housed at the University of Massachusetts Amherst and are also available on microfilm. In addition, the university has an excellent online finding aid prepared by David Goldberg. Herbert Aptheker has compiled all of Du Bois's published works, including his published speeches, in *The Complete Published Works of W. E. B. Du Bois* (Millwood, N.Y.: Kraus-Thomson, 1982). More recently, Henry Louis Gates has edited *The Oxford W. E. B. Du Bois,* 19 vols. (New York: Oxford University Press, 2007), including *In Battle for Peace: The Story of My 83rd Birthday,* which contains an introduction by Manning Marable. *In Battle for Peace* and chapter 20 of *The Autobiography of W. E. B. Du Bois: A Soliloquy on Viewing My Life from the Last Decade of Its First Century* (New York: International, 1968) recount Du Bois's antiwar activities during the Korean War and the consequences of his dissent.


Vietnam War

*Martin Luther King Jr.*

Biographical works on King abound. David J. Garrow's wide-raging eighteen-volume series Martin Luther King, Jr. and the Civil Rights Movement, particularly the first three volumes, *Martin Luther King, Jr.: Civil Rights Leader, Theologian, Orator* (Brooklyn: Carlson, 1989), contains a great deal of secondary material on King's antiwar activities. Garrow's *The FBI and Martin Luther King, Jr.: From "Solo" to Memphis* (New York: W. W. Norton, 1981) provides a detailed account of King's investigation by the FBI during the Vietnam era. Garrow's *Bearing the Cross: Martin Luther King, Jr., and the Southern Christian Leadership Conference* (New York: W. Morrow, 1986) contains a meticulously detailed account of many aspects of King's life. Other biographies include Stephen B. Oates's *Let the Trumpet Sound: The Life of Martin Luther King, Jr.* (New York: Harper and Row, 1982) and David Levering Lewis's *King: A Biography,* 2nd ed. (Urbana: University of Illinois Press, 1978). Finally, there is Taylor Branch's valuable biographical trilogy: *Parting the Waters: America in the King Years, 1954–63* (New York: Simon and Schuster, 1988), *Pillar of Fire: America in the King Years, 1963–65* (New York: Simon and Schuster, 1998), and *At Canaan's Edge: America in the King Years, 1965–68* (New York: Simon and Schuster, 2006).

Book-length works focusing on King's oratory in particular include Fredrik Sunnemark's *Ring Out Freedom! The Voice of Martin Luther King, Jr., and the Making of the Civil Rights Movement* (Bloomington: Indiana University Press, 2004) and Keith D. Miller's *Voice of Deliverance: The Language of Martin Luther King, Jr., and Its Sources* (Athens: University of Georgia Press, 1998). Carolyn Calloway-Thomas and John Louis Lucaites's *Martin Luther King, Jr., and the Sermonic Power of Public Discourse* (Tuscaloosa: University of Alabama Press, 1993) analyzes King's "Beyond Vietnam" speech, among others. Eric J. Sundquist's *King's Dream* (New Haven: Yale University Press, 2009) examines another of King's famous speeches in its historical, cultural, and rhetorical context.

The Martin Luther King, Jr., Papers are housed at the Martin Luther King, Jr. Center for Nonviolent Social Change in Atlanta. The Martin Luther King, Jr., Research and Education Institute at Stanford University is in the process of making King's most significant correspondence, sermons, speeches, published writings, and unpublished manuscripts available. The first six volumes of *The Papers of Martin Luther King, Jr.* (through 1963) have been published by the University of California Press. A useful one-volume resource for primary texts is James M. Washington's *A Testament of Hope: The Essential Writings of Martin Luther King, Jr.* (San Francisco: HarperSanFrancisco, 1991). Another useful primary resource is the FBI files on King, which are available on microfilm and on the FBI's website.


*Robert F. Kennedy*

The standard biography of Robert F. Kennedy is Arthur M. Schlesinger Jr.'s *Robert Kennedy and His Times* (Boston: Houghton Mifflin, 1978). The most recent biographies are Joseph A. Palermo's *Robert F. Kennedy and the Death of American Idealism* (New York: Pearson Longman, 2007) and *In His Own Right: The Political*

*Odyssey of Senator Robert F. Kennedy* (New York: Columbia University Press, 2001). Older biographies notable for their focus on Kennedy's final years include William Vanden Heuvel and Milton Gwirtzman's *On His Own: RFK, 1964–1968* (Garden City, N.Y.: Doubleday, 1970), Jack Newfield's *Robert Kennedy: A Memoir* (New York: E. P. Dutton, 1969), and David Halberstam's *The Unfinished Odyssey of Robert Kennedy* (New York: Random House, 1968). Thurston Clark's *The Last Campaign: Robert F. Kennedy and 82 Days That Inspired America* (New York: Henry Holt, 2008) examines Kennedy's fateful presidential campaign. It includes some treatment of Kennedy's opposition to the war in Vietnam, as well as the process by which Kennedy (or his aides) composed his speeches. Arnold Norman Weintraub's Ph.D. dissertation, "The Public Statements and Speeches of Robert F. Kennedy on the Vietnam War Issue" (University of Nebraska–Lincoln, 1975), provides analysis and bibliographical references. Relevant to Kennedy's rhetoric during his March 18 speech in Kansas is Jeanine I. Rishel's master's thesis, "A Rhetorical Analysis of Robert F. Kennedy's Speaking on the Issue of Peace in Vietnam, as Revealed in His Kansas Address" (1969). See also Craig Warren Cutbirth's Ph.D. dissertation, "A Strategic Perspective: Robert F. Kennedy's Dissent on the Vietnam War, 1966–1968" (1976), and Frederick C. Sander's Ph.D. thesis "The Rhetorical Strategies of Senator Robert Kennedy and Senator Eugene J. McCarthy in the 1968 Presidential Primaries" (University of Oregon, 1973).

Robert F. Kennedy's papers are housed at the John F. Kennedy Library in Boston. The best collection of his speeches, with accompanying commentary, is Edwin O. Guthman and C. Richard Allen's *RFK: Collected Speeches* (New York: Viking, 1993). Kennedy's speeches were collected and commented upon during his lifetime in Thomas A. Hopkins's *Rights for Americans: The Speeches of Robert Kennedy* (Indianapolis: Bobbs-Merrill, 1964). Guthman and Allen compiled audio recordings of some of Kennedy's speeches in *RFK: Selected Speeches* (St. Paul, Minn.: Penguin HighBridge Audio, 1993). An audio recording of Kennedy's March 18, 1968, speech can now be found on Kansas State University's Landon Lectures Series page. Historic footage of that speech can be found in the NBC News Archives, Tape # VSA0048245. Video of Kennedy's speeches is also available in MPI Home Video's *Speeches of Robert Kennedy* (1990).

Other published primary sources of Kennedy's thoughts relating to Vietnam can be found in the *Congressional Record* and Edwin O. Guthman and Jeffrey Shulman's *Robert Kennedy, in His Own Words: The Unpublished Recollections of the Kennedy Years* (New York: Bantam, 1988).

## John F. Kerry

The best biography of Kerry is Michael Kranish, Brian C. Mooney, and Nina J. Easton's *John F. Kerry: The Complete Biography by the Boston Globe Reporters Who Know Him Best* (New York: PublicAffairs, 2004). Douglas Brinkley considers Kerry's Vietnam-era years in *Tour of Duty: John Kerry and the Vietnam War* (New York: William Morrow, 2004). John E. O'Neill and Jerome R. Corsi's *Unfit for Command: Swift Boat Veterans Speak out Against John Kerry* (Washington, D.C.: Regnery, 2004) is a partisan history of Kerry's Vietnam-era activities written by Kerry's political opponents.

There are many primary sources for Kerry's speeches or writings. Most recently, Kerry has published books that concern, among other things, foreign affairs: *Our Plan for America: Stronger at Home, Respected in the World* (New York: PublicAffairs, 2004); an autobiographical work, *A Call to Service* (New York: Viking, 2003); and *The New War: The Web of Crime That Threatens America's Security* (New York: Simon and Schuster, 1997). For a spirited debate between Kerry and John O'Neill, who would later criticize Kerry during the 2004 election, see their June 30, 1971, appearance on *The Dick Cavett Show* in the ABC News Video Archives. Kerry's class oration on June 12, 1966, also on the subject of American foreign policy, appears in the Yale class of 1966 yearbook.

## Shirley Chisholm

Chisholm authored two autobiographies, *Unbought and Unbossed* (Boston: Houghton Mifflin, 1970) and *The Good Fight* (New York: Harper and Row, 1973). Both address the war in Vietnam. For specimens of her rhetoric generally, see *Can I Get a Witness? Prophetic Religious Voices of African American Women: An Anthology*, ed. Marcia Y. Riggs with biographical sketches and selected bibliography by Barbara Holmes (Maryknoll, N.Y.: Orbis Books, 1997).

There have been many biographies of Chisholm, some for young adults. The most notable are James Haskins's *Fighting Shirley Chisholm* (New York: Dial Press, 1975), Maurine Christopher's *America's Black Congressmen* (New York: Crowell, 1971), and Susan Brownmiller's *Shirley Chisholm: A Biography* (Garden City, N.Y.: Doubleday, 1970). Chisholm's obituary appeared in the *New York Times* on January 3, 2005. For a short summary of her life, see *African American Lives* (New York: Oxford University Press, 2004). Susan

Duffy has compiled a useful bibliography, *Shirley Chisholm: A Bibliography of Writings by and About Her* (Metuchen, N.J.: Scarecrow Press, 1988). On Chisholm's rhetoric, see Susan Duffy's chapter on Chisholm in Bernard K. Duffy and Ryan R. Halford's *American Orators of the Twentieth Century: Critical Studies and Sources* (New York: Greenwood Press, 1987). For a well-researched academic article on Chisholm's political career, see Julie Gallagher, "Waging 'The Good Fight': The Political Career of Shirley Chisholm, 1953–1982," *Journal of African Amerian History* 92, no. 3 (2007): 393–416. Shola Lynch's *Chisholm '72—Unbought and Unbossed* (Beverly Hills: 20th Century Fox Home Entertainment, 2003) is a seventy-six-minute documentary covering Chisholm's campaign for president in 1972.

## Fannie Lou Hamer

Biographical resources for Hamer include her autobiography, *To Praise Our Bridges* (Jackson, Miss.: KIPCO, 1967), Earnest N. Bracey's *Fannie Lou Hamer: The Life of a Civil Rights Icon* (Jefferson N.C.: McFarland, 2011); Chana Kai Lee's *For Freedom's Sake: The Life of Fannie Lou Hamer* (Urbana: University of Illinois Press, 1999), Kay Mills's *This Little Light of Mine: The Life of Fannie Lou Hamer* (Lexington: University Press of Kentucky, 2007), and Christopher Myers Asch's *The Senator and the Sharecropper: The Freedom Struggles of James O. Eastland and Fannie Lou Hamer* (New York: New Press, 2008). Hamer's rhetoric in particular was studied by Adria Battaglia in her master's thesis, "Rhetoric and Heresthetic in the Mississippi Freedom Party Controversy at the 1964 Democratic Convention" (2005). However, Battaglia's study focuses on the Civil Rights Movement, not on the war in Vietnam. American National Biography Online features a short biography and bibliography of Hamer by Mamie E. Locke.

Hamer's papers are housed at the Amistad Research Center at Tulane University, and are also available on microfilm.

## Eugene J. McCarthy

The most recent and best biography of McCarthy is Dominic Sandbrook's *Eugene McCarthy: The Rise and Fall of Postwar American Liberalism* (New York: Alfred A. Knopf, 2004). There are many books that deal with McCarthy's 1968 campaign. See, for example, George Rising's *Clean for Gene: Eugene McCarthy's 1968 Presidential Campaign* (Westport, Conn.: Praeger, 1997), as well as Jeremy Larner's *Nobody Knows: Reflections on the McCarthy Campaign of 1968* (New York: Macmillan, 1970), which was written by one of McCarthy's principal speechwriters.

For a consideration of McCarthy's rhetorical strategy, see Frederick C. Sander's Ph.D. thesis, "The Rhetorical Strategies of Senator Robert Kennedy and Senator Eugene J. McCarthy in the 1968 Presidential Primaries" (University of Oregon, 1973), and Bonnie Ritter Patton's Ph.D. thesis, "The 1968 Political Campaign of Senator Eugene J. McCarthy: A Study of Rhetorical Choice" (University of Kansas, 1969).

The Eugene J. McCarthy Papers are housed at the University of Minnesota. Timothy J. Johnson has authored a finding aid. McCarthy was a prolific writer. In *The Limits of Power: America's Role in the World* (New York: Holt, Rinehart and Winston, 1967) he critiques the Johnson administration's foreign policies, and in *The Year of the People* (Garden City, N.Y.: Doubleday, 1969), republished as *1968: War and Democracy* (Red Wing, Minn.: Loan Oak Press, 2000), he recounts his 1968 presidential campaign. *A Colony of the World: The United States Today: America's Senior Statesman Warns His Countrymen* (New York: Hippocrene Books, 1992) contains some of McCarthy's views regarding the Persian Gulf War. For McCarthy's poetry, see *Selected Poems* (Rochester, Minn.: Loan Oak Press, 1997). McCarthy's final book before his death, *Parting Shots from My Brittle Bow: Reflections on American Politics and Life* (Golden, Colo.: Fulcrum, 2005), contains excerpts from previously published books and articles and purports to be the most comprehensive compilation of McCarthy's writings in print.

There are many video resources on McCarthy. See *Eugene J. McCarthy: Muses and Mementos,* directed by Mick Caouette (2006), a documentary that mixes archival footage of McCarthy with interviews with him in 1996 and 2000; *I'm Sorry I Was Right,* directed by Michael Hazard (St. Paul: Center for International Education, 2001), a documentary that does the same, but also includes interviews with and about him; Emile de Antonio, director *America Is Hard to See* (1970; Oak Forest, Ill., MPI Home Video, 1988), a documentary account of the events surrounding the American presidential campaign of 1968 from McCarthy's entry in the race through the election, and *Sen. Eugene McCarthy* (Minnetonka, Minn.: Hennepin County Library, 1993), a collection of interviews with McCarthy in which McCarthy reads poems and discusses, among other things, the Persian Gulf War. In 1980, McCarthy also conducted a taped "Language and Politics" workshop in which he, among others, examined "what to look for and how to analyze the political language of any candidate in any election" (Park Forest South, Ill.: Instructional Communications Center, Governors State University).

## War on Terror

### Barack Obama

Recent book-length treatments of Obama's life include David Remnick's *The Bridge: The Life and Rise of Barack Obama* (New York: Alfred A. Knopf, 2010) and David Mendell's *Obama: From Promise to Power* (New York: HarperCollins, 2008). Particularly useful resources for this anthology were Edward McClelland's "How Obama Learned to Be a Natural," Salon.com, February 12, 2007, Garrett M. Graff's "The Legend of Barack Obama," Washingtonian.com, November 1, 2006, and Ken Silverstein's "Barack Obama, Inc.," *Harper's Magazine,* November 2006. For a book-length treatment of Obama's 2008 campaign, see Evan Thomas's *"A Long Time Coming": The Inspiring, Combative 2008 Campaign and the Historic Election of Barack Obama* (New York: PublicAffairs, 2009). Shel Leanne's *Say It Like Obama: The Power of Speaking with Purpose and Vision* (New York: McGraw-Hill, 2009) is solely devoted to analyzing Obama's speeches.

Obama's books and speeches provide a rich source on his life and his antiwar activities. Obama's autobiography, *Dreams from My Father: A Story of Race and Inheritance* (New York: Times Books, 1995), was later republished with a new introduction and the text of Obama's July 27, 2004, "Audacity of Hope" speech (New York: Three Rivers Press, 2004). Obama's second book, *The Audacity of Hope: Thoughts on Reclaiming the American Dream* (New York: Crown, 2006), includes information relevant to his antiwar stance. *Power in Words: The Stories Behind Barack Obama's Speeches, from the State House to the White House* (Boston: Beacon Press, 2010) anthologizes a number of Obama's speeches from 2002 to 2008, and offers detailed commentary on each speech. Other collections of Obama's speeches include *An American Story: The Speeches of Barack Obama: A Primer,* by David Olive (Toronto: ECW Press, 2008), which also has a short note on Obama's "oratorical style and its impact," and *Barack Obama: Speeches, 2002–2006,* ed. Maureen Harrison and Steve Gilbert (Carlsbad, Calif.: Excellent Books, 2007). *Barack Obama in His Own Words,* ed. Lisa Rogak (New York: Carroll and Graf, 2007), is a book of quotes and anecdotes. For additional comments on war, in addition to Obama's 2002 speech, see the *Congressional Record*, Remarks on the Iraq War (March 21, 2007); Remarks on the Iraq War De-escalation Act of 2007 (January 30, 2007); Remarks on the President's Decision to Increase Troops in Iraq (January 19, 2007); and Remarks on Iraq Debate (June 21, 2006). See also "A Way Forward in Iraq," Remarks to the Chicago Council on Global Affairs, November 20, Chicago, Illinois (November 20, 2006), and "Moving Forward in Iraq," Remarks to the Chicago Council on Foreign Relations, Chicago, Illinois, November 22, 2005. Obama also published a sharply worded press release, "Escalation Is Not the Answer," on or about December 28, 2006.

### Barbara Lee

There are no book-length secondary resources on Barbara Lee, with the notable exception of her autobiography, *Renegade for Peace and Justice: Congresswoman Barbara Lee Speaks for Me* (Lanham, Md.: Rowman and Littlefield, 2008). Concise summaries of her life written by others appear in various encyclopedias. See, for example, *Notable Black American Women,* vol. 3 (Detroit: Gale Research, 2003) and *Contemporary Black Biography.* The best sources of information regarding Lee's dissent on the war in Iraq are Gary Rivlin, "Looking-Glass Politics," *Los Angeles Times,* June 16, 2002; Mark Z. Barabak, "Uphill Bid to Oust Lone Dissenter," *Los Angeles Times,* December 2, 2001; Susan McHenry, "Barbara Lee: Going Against the Tide," *Essence,* December 2001, 26; John Nichols, "The Lone Dissenter: 'Traitor,' 'Coward,' 'Communist,'" *Progressive,* November 2001, 28; Marianne Costantinov, "Lee, Committed to Ideals, Takes Heat for Vote Against Bush," *San Francisco Chronicle,* September 26, 2001; Marc Cooper, "Rep. Barbara Lee: Rowing Against the Tide," *Los Angeles Times,* September 23, 2001; and Peter Carlson, "The Solitary Vote of Barbara Lee," *Washington Post,* September 19, 2001. See also her interview with John Nichols, "Barbara Lee's Stand," *Nation,* October 8, 2001.

### Noam Chomsky

In addition to his influential academic work as a linguist and philosopher, Chomsky has written prolifically on politics and foreign policy, dating back to *American Power and the New Mandarins* (New York: Pantheon Books, 1969). For a recent survey of his work, see *The Essential Chomsky* (New York: New Press, 2008). For books containing Chomsky's political views in particular, see, for example, *Interventions* (San Francisco: City Lights Books, 2007); *Perilous Power: The Middle East and U.S. Foreign Policy* (Boulder, Colo.: Paradigm, 2007) (coauthored with Gilbert Achcar); *Failed States: The Abuse of Power and the Assault on Democracy* (New

York: Metropolitan Books / Henry Holt, 2006); *Imperial Ambitions: Conversations with Noam Chomsky on the Post–9/11 World* (New York: Metropolitan Books, 2005); *Hegemony or Survival: America's Quest for Global Dominance* (New York: Metropolitan Books, 2003); *Chronicles of Dissent,* new ed. (Vancouver: New Star Books, 2003); *Power and Terror: Post–9–11 Talks and Interviews* (New York: Seven Stories Press, 2003); *Understanding Power: The Indispensable Chomsky* (New York: New Press, 2002); and *9–11* (New York: Seven Stories Press, 2001). In *Language and Politics,* 2nd ed. (Oakland: AK Press, 2004), editor C. P. Otero summarizes Chomsky's political views from 1968 to 1995. In addition to the lecture published here, another Chomsky lecture at Harvard University has been published: *Distorted Morality: A War on Terrorism?* (Oakland: AK Press, 2003).

One of the most valuable collections of Chomsky's work, including essays, interviews and speeches, is Chomsky's official website, http://www.chomsky.info, which features transcriptions of many interviews and links to many video recordings. See also ZNet's Chomsky archive, http://www.zmag.org/chomsky/.

Biographies of Chomsky include Wolfgang B. Sperlich's *Noam Chomsky* (London: Reaktion Books, 2006), Robert Barsky's *Noam Chomsky: A Life of Dissent* (Cambridge, Mass.: MIT Press, 1997), and John Lyons's *Noam Chomsky* (New York: Viking Press, 1970). For a series of essays about his "Values and Politics," see James McGilvray, ed., *The Cambridge Companion to Chomsky* (Cambridge: Cambridge University Press, 2005). On his political thought in particular, see Alison Edgley's *The Social and Political Thought of Noam Chomsky* (London: Routledge, 2000). For opposing views, see Peter Collier and David Horowitz, eds., *The Anti-Chomsky Reader* (San Francisco: Encounter Books, 2004). For a concise summary of his life, see Contemporary Authors Online.

For Chomsky documentaries, see Will Pascoe, director, *Noam Chomsky: Rebel Without a Pause* (New York: Docurama, 2003); John Junkerman, director, *Power and Terror: Noam Chomsky in Our Times* (New York: First Run / Icarus Films, 2002); and Mark Achbar and Peter Wintonick, directors, *Manufacturing Consent: Noam Chomsky and the Media* (Montreal: Necessary Illusions, 1992; reissued, New York: Zeitgeist Video, 2002).

### Robert Byrd

No book-length biography of Byrd is available. The best starting place for research is his autobiography, *Robert C. Byrd: Child of the Appalachian Coalfields* (Morgantown: West Virgiana University Press, 2005). Encyclopedias offer some biographical material; see, for example, Contemporary Authors Online. For a collection of tributes to Byrd when he became longest-serving senator in the history of the United States, see *Tributes Delivered in Congress: Robert C. Byrd, United States Congressman 1953–1958, United States Senator 1959–* (Washington, D.C.: Government Printing Office, 2006). This work also contains a two-page biography.

Byrd published two books dedicated exclusively to criticism of the Iraq War. *We Stand Passively Mute: Senator Robert C. Byrd's Iraq Speeches* (Tualatin, Ore.: Papyngay Press, 2004) contains twenty-seven of Byrd's Senate speeches between October 2002 and April 2004. *Losing America: Confronting a Reckless and Arrogant Presidency* (New York: W. W. Norton, 2004) contains essays on the war in Iraq, as well as eight of Byrd's floor speeches in the Senate. His views on, among other things, the origin of modern-day separation of powers appear in *The Senate of the Roman Republic: Addresses on the History of Roman Constitutionalism* (Washington, D.C.: GPO, 1995). Byrd also authored *The Senate, 1789–1989,* 4 vols. (Washington, D.C.: GPO, 1989–1994), with the assistance of Senate historians. The third volume is an anthology of classic Senate speeches from 1830 to 1993.

## Epilogue: The Globalization of Dissent

### Arundhati Roy

No book-length biography of Roy is currently available. Critical interpretations of her work, however, are readily found. *Globalizing Dissent: Essays on Arundhati Roy,* ed. Ranjan Ghosh and Antonia Navarro-Tejero (New York: Routledge, 2009), anthologizes essays on the intersection of Roy's activism and writing. *Arundhati Roy: Critical Perspectives,* ed. Murari Prasad (Delhi: Pencraft International, 2006), includes criticism and a small amount of biographical detail.

Roy has written a prize-winning novel *The God of Small Things* (New York: Random House, 1997), but most of her published work is nonfiction, ranging in scope from India and globalization to women's rights and the Iraq War. *An Ordinary Person's Guide to Empire* (Cambridge, Mass.: South End Press, 2004) is a collection of critical lectures about the war in Iraq, including "Instant-Mix Imperial Democracy." Roy also published a series of interviews on the same topic with David Barsamian, *The Checkbook and the Cruise Missile: Conversations with Arundhati Roy* (Cambridge, Mass.: South End Press, 2004). Roy's address to the American Sociological Association on August 16, 2004, concerning global politics, presidential elections, war, and resistance movements, was published as *Public Power in the Age of Empire* (New York: Seven Stories Press, 2004). In *War Talk* (Cambridge, Mass.: South End Press, 2003), Roy offers some commentary about the war in Iraq, although her focus is global. In this vein, see also *The Shape of the Beast* (2008), a collection of fourteen interviews conducted between January 2001 and March 2008.

The addresses "Instant-Mix Imperial Democracy" (May 13, 2003) and "Come September" (September 18, 2002), as well as a conversation about the war in Iraq with historian Howard Zinn, are available on video: *Insta-mix Imperial Democracy* (2004). *Public Power in the Age of Empire* (2004) is available in audio as well as in print. In Roy and Zinn's *Arundhati Roy's War Talk*, Roy talks with Zinn about her book *War Talk*, as well as the war in Iraq and the Bush administration.

# INDEX

## CREDITS

Many of the speeches in this volume are in the public domain. For the rest, I would like to thank the following individuals and institutions for their cooperation.

Norman Thomas, "War or Democracy," is reproduced by permission of The New York Public Library, Astor, Lenox and Tilden Foundations.

Paul Robeson, "Address by Paul Robeson," is reproduced by permission of the Moorland-Spingarn Research Center, Howard University.

W. E. B. Du Bois, "The Campaign of 1950," is reproduced by permission of the David Graham Du Bois Trust.

Martin Luther King Jr., "Beyond Vietnam," is reprinted by arrangement with The Heirs to the Estate of Martin Luther King Jr., c/o Writers House as agent for the proprietor, New York, N.Y. Copyright 1967 Dr. Martin Luther King Jr.; copyright renewed 1991 Coretta Scott King.

Fanny Lou Hamer's speech at the Vietnam Moratorium Rally is reproduced by courtesy of Pacifica Radio Archives.

Noam Chomsky, "Why Iraq?," is based on "Why Iraq?," a speech at the Institute of Politics, John F. Kennedy School of Government, Harvard University, Cambridge, Mass., November 4, 2002. Copyright 2002 Noam Chomsky.

Arundhati Roy, "Instant-Mix Imperial Democracy (Buy One, Get One Free)," is based on "Instant-Mix Imperial Democracy (Buy One, Get One Free)," a speech at Riverside Church, New York City, May 13, 2003, published in *An Ordinary Person's Guide to Empire* (Cambridge, Mass.: South End Press, 2004), 41–68. Copyright 2002 Arundhati Roy.